THE VICTORIANS AND THE EIGHTEENTH CENTURY

For Simon Dentith
with admiration

The Victorians and the Eighteenth Century

Century

Reassessing the Tradition

Edited by

FRANCIS O'GORMAN
University of Leeds, UK

KATHERINE TURNER
Exeter College Oxford, UK

ASHGATE

Published by
Ashgate Publishing Limited
Gower House
Croft Road
Aldershot
Hampshire GU11 3HR
England

Ashgate Publishing Company
Suite 420
101 Cherry Street
Burlington, VT 05401-4405
USA

Ashgate website: http://www.ashgate.com

British Library Cataloguing in Publication Data
The Victorians and the eighteenth century : reassessing the tradition
　　1. English literature – 19th century – History and criticism 2. Historiography – Great Britain – History – 19th century 3. Great Britain – Civilization – 18th century 4. Great Britain – Intellectual life – 19th century
　　I. O'Gorman, Francis II. Turner, Katherine, 1966–
　　820'.09358'09034

Library of Congress Cataloging-in-Publication Data
The Victorians and the eighteenth century : reassessing the tradition / edited by Francis O'Gorman and Katherine Turner.
　　　p. cm.
　　Includes bibliographical references (p.).
　　ISBN 0-7546-0718-6
　　1. English literature–19th century–History and criticism. 2. English literature–18th century–History and criticism. 3. Great Britain–Intellectual life–19th century. 4. Great Britain–Intellectual life–18th century. 5. Influence (Literary, artistic, etc.) 6. Eighteenth century. I. O'Gorman, Francis. II. Turner, Katherine, 1966–

PR463.V56 2004
820.9'008–dc22

2003066166

ISBN 0 7546 0718 6

Printed and bound in Great Britain by MPG Books Ltd, Bodmin, Cornwall

Contents

List of Illustrations

Acknowledgements

We are grateful for the help of Erika Gaffney and Ann Donahue at Ashgate. Francis O'Gorman thanks Ben Read, members of the Eighteenth-century Seminar of the University of Leeds, Professor David Fairer, Jane Wright and Dr Helen Small. Our thanks also to Pamela Rhodes for helping out in a last minute crisis, and to Pat FitzGerald for managing the CRC stage of this book. Gratitude also to Trinity College Oxford and the English Faculty Oxford and to the School of English, University of Leeds for financial assistance towards publication costs.

Francis O'Gorman
School of English, University of Leeds

Katherine Turner
Exeter College Oxford

Notes on Contributors

David Amigoni is Senior Lecturer in English at Keele University. He is the author of *Victorian Biography* (1993) and *The English Novel and Prose Narrative* (2000). His monograph *Colonies, Cults and Evolution: The Spread of the Culture Concept in Nineteenth-Century Writing* is forthcoming. He is a member of the editorial board of *Journal of Victorian Culture*.

Dinah Birch is Professor of English at the University of Liverpool. She has edited *Ruskin and the Dawn of the Modern* (1999) and a selection from Ruskin's *Fors Clavigera* (2000), and she is the co-editor, with Francis O'Gorman, of *Ruskin and Gender* (2002). She is currently working on a study of women and education in mid-Victorian fiction.

Simon Dentith is Professor of English at the University of Gloucestershire. His recent books include *Society and Cultural Forms in Nineteenth-century England* (1998), and the volume on *Parody* in the *New Critical Idiom* series (2000).

David Fairer is Professor of Eighteenth-century English Literature at the University of Leeds. His most recent book is *English Poetry of the Eighteenth Century, 1700–1789* (Longman, 2003). He is also the author of *Pope's Imagination* (1984), *The Poetry of Alexander Pope* (1989), and editor of *Pope: New Contexts* (1990) and *The Correspondence of Thomas Warton* (1995). With Christine Gerrard, he has edited *Eighteenth-Century Poetry: An Annotated Anthology* (1999). He is the Consulting Editor for the *English Labouring-Class Poets, 1700–1900*, 6 volumes (Pickering & Chatto, 2003–4).

Hilary Fraser holds the Geoffrey Tillotson Chair in Nineteenth-century Studies at Birkbeck. Her books include *Beauty and Belief: Aesthetics and Religion in Victorian Literature* (1986), *The Victorians and Renaissance Italy* (1992), *English Prose of the Nineteenth Century* (with Daniel Brown, 1997), and *Gender and the Victorian Periodical* (with Judith Johnston and Stephanie Green, forthcoming 2003). She is currently working on an AHRB-funded project 'Gender, History, Visuality: Women Writing Art History in the Nineteenth Century'.

Nick Groom is Reader in English Literature at the University of Bristol. Among his publications are *The Making of Percy's Reliques* (Clarendon, 1999), *Thomas Chatterton and Romantic Culture* (Macmillan, 1999), and *The Forger's Shadow: How Forgery Changed the Course of Literature* (Picador, 2002). He has recently completed a critical edition of Percy's *Reliques* and is currently working on three books, analysing Englishness, noise and the acoustics of poetry, and beer.

Elisabeth Jay is Professor of English and Associate Head of the School of Arts and Humanities, Oxford Brookes University. She has published widely on Victorian women's writing and nineteenth-century religion and literature. Forthcoming publications include editions of Olive Schreiner's *Dreams* and of Elizabeth Gaskell's *North and South*.

Lynda Mugglestone is Fellow in English Language at Pembroke College Oxford and News International Lecturer in Language and Communication at the University of Oxford. Recent publications include *Talking Proper: The Rise of Accent as Social Symbol* (OUP, 1995; 2nd edn 2002), and *Lexicography and the OED: Pioneers in the Untrodden Forest* (OUP, 2000, 2002). She is currently editing *The Oxford History of the English Language* and writing a further book on the history of the *Oxford English Dictionary* for Yale University Press.

Francis O'Gorman is Senior Lecturer in Victorian Literature at the University of Leeds and a Fellow of the Royal Historical Society. His books include *John Ruskin* (1999), *Late Ruskin: New Contexts* (2001), and *Blackwell's Critical Guide to the Victorian Novel* (2002); he has also edited, with Dinah Birch, *Ruskin and Gender* (2002). His *Victorian Poetry: An Annotated Anthology* is due out in 2004 and he is currently writing *Enduring Authorship: Forms of Victorian Literary Survival*.

Helen Small is Fellow and University Lecturer in English Literature at Pembroke College Oxford and a Visiting Scholar at New York University (2002–4). She is the author of *Love's Madness: Medicine, the Novel, and Female Insanity, 1800–1865* (1996), co-editor (with James Raven and Naomi Tadmor) of *The Practice and Representation of Reading in England* (1996), and editor of *The Public Intellectual* (2002).

Katherine Turner is Williams Fellow and Tutor in English at Exeter College Oxford. She has published on eighteenth-century poetry, travelogues, and women's writing, and her most recent publication is *British Travel Writers in Europe 1750–1800: Authorship, Gender and National Identity* (2001).

Carolyn D. Williams is a Lecturer in the School of English and American Literature at the University of Reading. She has published widely on life and literature in the early modern period, and is currently working on a book on literary treatments of Boadicea.

Preface

David Fairer

'Almost everything which my own generation ignorantly called Victorian seems to have been expressed by Addison. It is all there in the *Spectator*... Everything the moderns detest, all that they call *smugness*, *complacency*, and *bourgeois ideology*, is brought together in his work and given its most perfect expression.'[1] With these words C.S. Lewis, born a Victorian (1898) into a generation that embraced Modernism, looks back in 1945 from the 'fidgety' world of 'the cinema and the dance band' to one where he feels at home ('the Addisonian world is ... a good one to fall back into when the day's work is done and a man's feet on the fender and his pipe in his mouth'). As the generations accumulate, one age packages up the one before. But eventually the yellowing labels are re-examined and what was old-fashioned and obsolete finds its place among the ironies of history. Lewis's own smug, bourgeois complacency almost becomes witty as he finds a soul-mate across the centuries. He himself would die in Philip Larkin's 'Annus Mirabilis' of 1963 ('Between the end of the *Chatterley* ban / And the Beatles' first LP'). The writer of one generation is waiting to be absorbed into a later writer's cultural history. The life and work will become part of someone else's pattern.

Fortunately, both the 'smug' Victorian and the 'complacent' Augustan have now become outdated caricatures, and we smile at the way Lewis uses his composite figure of a Victorian Addison to hit back at modernity and its neglect of 'the common ground of daily life', its disdain for 'middle things'. We in turn can see that the complacent Augustan was largely a Victorian creation, part of that age's sense of its own modernity:

> I was exploring some huge house, had gone
> Through room and room complacently, no dearth
> Anywhere of the signs of decent taste,
> Adequate culture: wealth had run to waste
> Nowise, nor penury was proved by stint:
> All showed the Golden Mean without a hint
> Of brave extravagance that breaks the rule.

This is Robert Browning (*Parleyings with Certain People of Importance*, 1887) wandering through the tasteful eighteenth century, just before he opens a door to discover Christopher Smart's *Song to David*. For him, that brilliant poem burst on a scene of decorum and mediocrity in a single inspired flash; but then Smart took off his 'lyric dress' and settled back into his period, 'a drab-clothed decent proseman as before'. The pattern is the familiar one of Matthew Arnold's 'Age of Prose', in which it is Thomas Gray who stands for the uncertain lyric impulse that could not make itself heard ('He never spoke out').[2] Variations on this image of mid-eighteenth-century poetry have been remarkably resilient, and they persisted throughout the twentieth century in the notion of a hesitant sensibility, which lacked the confidence that the next generation of 'Romantics' would bring. To allow that voice to be heard, Francis Palgrave re-shaped the eighteenth century by trimming away all but its 'Lyrical pieces and Songs', so that the third book (1700–1800) of *The Golden Treasury* (1861) could be entitled the 'Book of Gray' in anticipation of the climactic 'Book of Wordsworth'. It was the Victorians who installed Wordsworth as the poet that defined what the eighteenth century failed to be. Ever since, literary history has struggled to tell the story of later eighteenth-century poetry without making Wordsworth its goal. The teleology was firmly in place when Robert Buchanan, in *The Fleshly School of Poetry* (1871/2), characterized English verse as stifled by 'false love, false heroics, false pastoral pictures, false life, false thought', until the publication of Percy's *Reliques* (1765) sowed the 'true seeds of a new life', from which Wordsworth would emerge to 'save' English literature.[3] The Victorians established a narrative of literary history that many twentieth-century Romanticists were happy to reiterate because it made their period its culmination.

But as this collection of essays reveals, some Victorians, most noticeably from the 1870s on, were finding in eighteenth-century culture elements of classical strength and clarity that their own age was perceived to lack. Pope's elegant good sense and Johnson's moral weight commanded increasing respect, and as the 'Romantic Age' in turn began to be historicized, the previous period imprinted its character more positively as a distinctive British achievement. In his lecture on 'The Development of English Literature from Chaucer to Wordsworth' (1852), A.H. Clough argued that eighteenth-century writers had set a classic standard 'wherever the English language is spoken or studied'. Compared with that age, Clough continued, 'our own … is notorious for slovenly or misdirected habits of composition'. Eighteenth-century empiricism ('the spirit of Newton and of Locke') had grounded experience in 'substantial reality', and it was reassuring for Clough to have this eighteenth-century bulwark of sense and responsibility at his back – 'We must not lose it – we must hold fast by it',

> This austere love of truth; this righteous abhorrence of illusion; this rigorous uncompromising rejection of the vague, the untestified, the merely probable; this stern conscientious determination without paltering and prevarication to admit, *if* things are bad, that they are so: this resolute, upright purpose, as of some transcendental man of business, to go thoroughly into the accounts of the world and make out once for all how they stand; such a spirit as this, I may say, I think, claims more than our attention – claims our reverence.[4]

This grounding of principle in human experience was a Johnsonian imperative, and to hear Clough enunciating it with such fervour comes as something of a shock – in the sober, unillusioned tones of *The Rambler* (1750–52), another enduring concept, the 'Age of Johnson' as it would become known, is being enunciated. It is clear that Clough valued the regulated 'adequate culture' which Browning's *Parleyings* found unadventurous and stifling (though for another perspective on Browning and the eighteenth century, see 10–11).

We have only to ask where was vision, imagination, fiction, humour and sensibility in this picture, to realize how selective each writer's focus was, and to see that there were several eighteenth centuries available for the Victorians to use. In both periods tastes were shifting and contested, and what we might take to be a 'Victorian' critical pronouncement could be anticipated by a hundred years. The reaction against Pope, for example, was under way by the 1760s, when some critics were denying his supremacy and seeking 'genuine poetry' elsewhere.[5] By that decade 'wit' was already outdated and a language of 'genius' and 'sensibility' was taking over; idealism and materialism were fighting a running battle; the novel was exploring sentimental responses; and 'nature' was becoming subjectivized. A Victorian attack on one aspect of the eighteenth century should not be taken as dismissing the period as a whole. As this volume will show from a range of perspectives, there was neither a unified eighteenth century, nor a unified Victorian age – the tensions and cross-currents of one period replicated themselves in the other. A Victorian could select what to praise or blame according to his or her own critical agenda.

The age that established the novel and offered models as various as Defoe, Smollett, Richardson, Fielding, Goldsmith, Sterne and Burney, was handing over not a single tradition, but the full gamut of novelistic possibilities. It gave a writer like Thackeray, who had absorbed this eighteenth-century inheritance in all its variety, the confidence to extend himself across different modes – realism, playful invention, satire and sentiment – often in subtle combination. Eighteenth-century sensibility, theorized by men like Shaftesbury, Hutcheson and Adam Smith, and embodied in Richardson's Clarissa, Fielding's Amelia and Parson Adams, or Goldsmith's Dr Primrose, fed directly into Dickens's sentimental vein.[6] But once again, in the later Victorian period a shift is discernible towards the more 'Augustan' aspects of the eighteenth century. The gap is considerable, for example, between Thackeray's lecture on 'Charity and Humour' (1853), with its stress on warm-hearted feeling and the 'laughter of tears and nature',[7] and George Meredith's all-out attack on sentimental humour in *On the Idea of Comedy* (1877), which defines the pure comic spirit in terms of wit and intellect.[8] Sympathy has been replaced by incongruity – Dr Primrose must give way to Swift's Gulliver, and Parson Adams to Molière's Tartuffe. In this, Meredith's taste for a more virile satiric comedy was close to that of his friend Leslie Stephen, the admirer of Swift and Pope; and with Meredith the novel itself moved away from the sentimental towards more hard-edged, ironic, and satiric modes developed in the fiction of Butler and Gissing – and in the plays of Wilde and Shaw. If the eighteenth-century text for the 1850s was Goldsmith's *The Vicar of Wakefield* (1766), for the 1890s it was Pope's *The Rape of the Lock* (1714). Goldsmith's warm-hearted picture of the Primrose family triumphing over malice and misadventure suited the tastes of Dickens's readers at mid-century;[9] whereas the sharp and witty spirit of the *fin de siècle* is distilled into Aubrey Beardsley's illustrations to Pope's mock-heroic poem (1896).[10] Many earlier Victorians distanced themselves from the artificial surface of the Age of Anne – all those fans, powdered wigs and shoe-buckles! – but Beardsley delights in its profusion of playful detail. As in Pope, every line is sharp and finely turned. In terms of a duality of sensibility and wit, then, we might see the tastes of the Victorian age as moving in a contrary direction to those of the eighteenth century, turning away from sentimental modes and becoming increasingly attuned to elements of intellect, satire and artifice that would prove congenial to Modernism.[11] Perhaps this is an over-bold generalization, but literary history is forever weaving ironic strands of aversion and rehabilitation. In the essays collected in this volume these and other patterns are examined from a range of new and distinctive perspectives, and the reader comes to appreciate that, whether prompted by antagonism, ambivalence or admiration, the Victorians' engagement with the previous century was a more varied and intriguing one than literary history has often allowed.

Notes

1   C.S. Lewis, 'Addison', in *Essays on the Eighteenth Century Presented to David Nichol Smith* (Oxford: Clarendon, 1945), 13.

2   Matthew Arnold, 'Thomas Gray', in Thomas Humphry Ward, ed., *The English Poets: Selections with Critical Introductions by Various Writers* (London: Macmillan, 1880), later included in *Essays in Criticism: Second Series* (1888). For a wider view of Gray's Victorian reputation, see Malcolm Hicks, 'Gray Among the Victorians', in W.B. Hutchings and William Ruddick, eds, *Thomas Gray: Contemporary Essays* (Liverpool: Liverpool University Press, 1993), 248–69.

3   *The Fleshly School of Poetry bound together with 'The Stealthy School of Criticism' by D.G. Rossetti* (New York: AMS Press reprint, 1975), 14.

4   *The Poems and Prose Remains of Arthur Hugh Clough ... Edited by His Wife*, 2 vols (London: Macmillan, 1869), I, 351.

5   In *An Essay on the Writings and Genius of Pope* (1756) Joseph Warton argued that Pope's didactic and moral vein cut him off from the highest form of poetry: 'What is there transcendently Sublime or Pathetic in Pope?' ('Dedication'). In 1759 Edward Young attacked imitative, rule-bound poetry as prosaic: 'There is something in Poetry beyond Prose-reason; there are Mysteries in it not to be explained, but admired; which render mere Prose-men Infidels to their Divinity' (*Conjectures on Original Composition*, 28).

6   See Fred Kaplan, *Sacred Tears: Sentimentality in Victorian Literature* (Princeton: Princeton University Press, 1987), 39–70.

7   Thackeray's New York lecture (31 January 1853) was included in the first US edition of *The English Humourists of the Eighteenth Century* (1853).

8   See Robert Bernard Martin, *The Triumph of Wit: A Study of Victorian Comic Theory* (Oxford: Clarendon, 1974), 89–100.

9   According to John Forster, biographer of both Goldsmith and Dickens, 'No book upon record has obtained a wider popularity' (*The Life and Times of Oliver Goldsmith* [1848; 2nd edn, 1854], II, 3). On the novel's influence on Dickens, see Kaplan, 39–40. For more on Dickens and eighteenth-century fiction, see Helen Small, 14–40, below.

10   See Robert Halsband, *The Rape of the Lock and its Illustrations, 1714–1896* (Oxford: Clarendon, 1980), 86–119. Pope's poem was intensely admired by Ernest Dowson, Lionel Johnson, and Edmund Gosse. For more on this edition and Pope's reception during the Victorian period, see Francis O'Gorman, 76–97, below.

11   An imitation of *The Rape of the Lock* originally formed part of 'The Fire Sermon' in T.S. Eliot's *The Waste Land* (1922). Ezra Pound told him: 'Pope has done this so well that you cannot do it better ... you cannot parody Pope unless you can write better verse than Pope – and you can't.' See *The Waste Land: A Facsimile and Transcript of the Original Drafts*, ed. Valerie Eliot (London: Faber, 1971), 22–3, 127n.

Introduction

Francis O'Gorman and Katherine Turner

Literary historians of the past have privileged reaction as a concept essential to comprehending the movement of generation to generation. The notion of the rejection or cauterizing of the past has been a powerful agent in the workings of historical periodization, and in the construction of ideas of literary movements which, as David Perkins has convincingly argued, have persistently dubious intellectual bases but remain indispensable in critical reading.[1] For decades, Modernism was understood – through encouragement from the Modernists themselves – as a reaction against Victorianism, homogenized into a unitary cultural entity. In recent years studies such as Carol Christ's *Victorian and Modern Poetics* (1984), S.P. Rosenbaum's *Victorian Bloomsbury* (1987), David Weir's *Decadence and the Making of Modernism* (1995) and Carolyn Dever's *Death and the Mother from Dickens to Freud* (1998) have helped to develop increasingly subtler models. In the literary-historical assumptions dominant in the first half of the twentieth century, Romanticism, emerging through 'The Pre-Romantic Period' (in the terms of the influential literary historians Legouis and Cazamian), was persistently framed as a reaction to Augustanism, the reassertion of feeling and sincerity after a period of reason and artifice. Robert Griffin's *Wordsworth's Pope: A Study in Literary Historiography* (1996) is only the most recent study comprehensively to query commonplace notions of the boundaries between the Romantics and Augustans.[2] From the literary cartography that saw the writing practices of the Romantics as part of a reaction against Augustanism, it easily followed that the Victorians, inheritors of the Romantics, continued the rejection of the eighteenth century. That rejection – a lingering commonplace today – was and is expressed in numerous oppositional pairings that supposedly clinched the differential between one century and its successor, channelled through the defining event of the Romantic revival: Augustanism and Victorianism; the ages of Pope and of Tennyson; Addison and Ruskin; Sterne and George Eliot; of reason and doubt; mind and spirit; of Classical and Gothic; artifice and sincerity; satire and lyric; of the poetry of public statement and the 'overheard' poetry of personal meditation. Antagonistic pairings of this nature have remained surprisingly dominant in definitions of the Victorians' relationship with the century before them, earning little of the sceptical questioning directed at the Modernists' relation with Victorianism, or Romanticism's relation to the mid and early eighteenth century.[3]

Evidence for the Victorian repudiation of the eighteenth century, of course, has never been hard to find. Thomas Carlyle stood out as the most vocal of the Victorians to have apparently spurned the period, and to have constructed an image of moral and spiritual poverty, defined neither by heroes nor by faith but by '*spiritual paralysis*'. This Carlyean view, as Simon Dentith rightly observes (below, 43), established itself as the *locus classicus* of a tenacious understanding. The eighteenth, Carlyle said, in the lectures *On Heroes, Hero-Worship and the Heroic in History* (1840: published 1841) 'was a *Sceptical* century; in which little word there is a whole Pandora's box of miseries'. The heroic men of letters identified in Carlyle's study – Burns, Johnson, and Rousseau – were great, but only in despite of the age in which they lived. Their greatness resided precisely in their resistance to their historical moment. 'This was not an age of Faith', pronounced Carlyle, and those that deserved the name of the hero had conquered the moral poverty of a century for which the term Enlightenment was only an irony.[4] Alongside Carlyle's resonant disapproval may be placed Matthew Arnold's equally astringent view of the eighteenth-century man of letters. The champion of Classicism, he found the neo-classicism of the Augustans inimicable to poetry: he denied Dryden and Pope even the name of poet. Arnold's 'The Study of Poetry' (1880), one of the most important statements about the poetic canon in the last decades of the Victorian period, with its claim that Dryden and Pope were classics not of poetry but of prose, has seemed almost as talismanic of the Victorian relationship with the previous century as Carlyle's. Francis O'Gorman, 76–97, below, discusses the ironies of Arnold's position.

Articulated through the psychoanalytical metaphors introduced to literary history by Harold Bloom, the conception of a writer's relationship with the past as exclusively hostile has become a powerful assumption.[5] Slaying the father to make room for the child is a potent Oedipal narrative for literary relation, even if one where the son's responsibility for paternal death is seemingly guiltless. Traditional views of the Victorians and the eighteenth century have been crudely Bloomian/Freudian in essence. If the child, as Lacan centrally claimed, gains its individual identity through the working of *méconnaissance*, acts of misconstruction, then it may also seem that the Victorian period's supposedly general lack of sympathy for the eighteenth century was part of a self-defining *méconnaissance*, a strategy for the establishment of self through the misrepresentation of the other. Henry Knight Miller supported this version of the Victorians' reading of the eighteenth century – without invoking Lacan

– when he declared that the Victorians needed the century that preceded them to sharpen their own sense of historical identity: the 'eighteenth century *was* indispensable', Miller said, alluding to Matthew Arnold: 'it was the necessary negative type, or antithesis. Without it, the governing theme of nineteenth-century literary historiography – an inevitable progress through the ages toward the culmination of all values in its own age – was incomplete, made no dramatic sense'.[6] The distinctively negative fashioning of the eighteenth-century played an essential part, Miller declared, in the 'Whig' history of the Victorians: from it they built an enabling antitype of themselves.

The present book resists the application of such rudimentary Freudian/ Lacanian models for understanding the relationship between the nineteenth and the eighteenth century in terms of opposition and the construction of the not-self. In dispensing with paradigms of simple patricide and by complicating models of *méconnaissance*, it searches out subtler conceptions of interrelation, the hidden richness and complexity of the Victorians' settlement with the previous century. Instead of prioritizing the Carlylean procedures of rejection, this collection is dedicated to the exploration of ways in which the Victorians entered more creative relationships with the century before them. It recognizes the persistently ambiguous nature of those relationships, the double-edged regard of many Victorians for the eighteenth century, but always remains engaged with connections in which the positive and productive were vital elements.

Critics have long recognized the central place of history, emerging as a new form of discourse, in the establishment of a specifically Victorian sense of identity. Albertine de Broglie's statement of 1825 that 'we are ... the first who have understood the past'[7] has been extensively tested in its application to Britain in the nineteenth century. Studies such as Peter Allan Dale's *The Victorian Critic and the Idea of History* (1977) and Stephen Bann's *The Clothing of Clio: A Study of the Representation of History in Nineteenth-Century Britain and France* (1984) affirmed authoritatively the significance of the nineteenth-century management and production of history as a distinctive part of its cultural *Gestalt*. But the history with which they were concerned was, aside from the French Revolution, never recent: the uneasy, complicated relationship of the Victorians with the full spread of the eighteenth century was certainly omitted from their cultural topography. Thus, while we are familiar with the Victorians and the ancient classical world, Victorian medievalism, with the Gothic revival, even with Victorian interest in the Civil War era,[8] we have heard almost nothing of Victorian relations with the Hanoverian century. Philippa Levine's claim that paradox lay at the heart of Victorian culture and was nowhere more apparent than in their 'simultaneous adulation of their own age and their reverent fascination for the past' does not allow space, either, for discursive consideration of the intricate relationships which Victorians constructed with the century that preceded them.[9] In dispensing with a temptingly straightforward idea of the eschewal of the high eighteenth century and the 'spirit of its age' (which, as Carolyn Williams suggests, 57–75 below, was perceived in the nineteenth century to include elements that survived into the Regency), the present study aims to provide analysis of a missing element in current thinking about the Victorians and the past and to complicate familiar models of what is meant by the Victorians's understanding and use of their historical inheritance.

Revealingly, some nineteenth-century writers proposed elements of our argument. William James Courthope in 1885 cautioned against denigrating the preceding century. 'Critics of the present day are apt to talk in a superior and patronizing tone of the eighteenth century', he said:

> They say it is 'unpoetical', 'unromantic', sceptical, utilitarian. But surely the wonder is that, after the Revolution through which it had passed, English society was able to construct an ideal life of any kind. The best answer to those who disparage the eighteenth century is the question, 'What should we have done without it?[10]

This sense of connection and continuity between ages may be framed within the structure proposed by Gillian Beer, who recognizes how relationships between literary eras can operate on more than one level. Beer argues that the 'parameters of reading periods are unstable and difficult to descry. Whereas we skein out literary production into controllable periods – the Romantics, the Victorian age, modernism – reading periods are quite otherwise organized, trawling a variety of pasts and varying from person to person, though circumscribed by what is available within the community'.[11] Almost all of the contributions to this volume are methodologically sympathetic to Beer's insight here, excavating an often complicated 'reading history' by which Victorians engaged with eighteenth-century writers.[12]

Sandra Gilbert and Susan Gubar objected in *The Madwoman in the Attic* (1979) to the gender politics of what struck them then as the dominant conceptions of the genealogy of literary relations, the prevalence of models of 'patrilineal literary inheritance'.[13] The present study may seem to take a step backwards and disregard their argument, and the work of their successors, in considering eighteenth-century men largely at the expense of women. But Elizabeth Barrett Browning's memorable complaint in 1845 – 'I look everywhere for grandmothers and see none'[14] – was an authentic challenge for women writers regarding the eighteenth century in the middle of the nineteenth. *The Victorians and the Eighteenth Century* considers how the Victorians imagined the age before them and in doing so it inevitably reproduces the gendered terrain that Barrett Browning perceived. The canonical subjects examined here – Arnold, Dickens, Ruskin, Stephen – looked back to canonical writers, a canon they helped to form, privileging male artistic production and the patterns of male literary relationships. Even George Eliot's intriguing relation to the eighteenth century that Simon Dentith discusses (41–56, below) revolved around the Enlightenment thinking of Jean-Jacques Rousseau. But Barrett Browning's sense of gender dislocation did not pertain across the whole period, nor was it absolute. Margaret Oliphant, as Elisabeth Jay argues, 98–118 below, found in the literary history of the eighteenth century an opportunity to spar with Macaulay and Thackeray. Sustained creative engagement, moreover, between women authors and the writers and aesthetics of the century before them, if not the recognition of grandmothers, developed further at the end of the Victorian period as part of wider shifts in the re-imagining of the eighteenth century (these broader shifts are discussed by David Amigoni, Francis O'Gorman, and Katherine Turner, 182–202, 76–97, and 119–143 respectively). The eighteenth century proved an area particularly attractive to women writers partly because it was less occupied by male scholars than others, certainly than the Classical period or the Renaissance. The consideration of eighteenth-century Italy, for instance, was an important way in which Vernon Lee could contest the cultural authority of male intellectual tradition in the person of John Ruskin, whose textual possession of Italy and focus on the moralized Gothic-Renaissance dynamic was a major force in the English imagination of the newly unified nation-state in the mid to late Victorian period.[15] Lee's writing on eighteenth-century music and theatre and Emilia Dilke's study of eighteenth-century French art and interior design, as Hilary Fraser shows (223–249), were peculiarly enabling, partly in giving expression to their incipient modernism at the end of the nineteenth century. Not unsteadied by the apparent absence of the women who were invisible to Elizabeth Barrett Browning – who herself had imitated Pope in her early *The Battle of Marathon* (1820) – Lee and Dilke, like the young Edith Wharton in *The Valley of Decision* (1902),[16] saw distinctive creative possibilities for the establishment of their own literary identity through investment in the age of Handel, Burney, and Goldoni.

The appropriate metaphorical field for managing the relationship between nineteenth-century creativity and the legacy of the eighteenth is the subject of the first essay in this collection. Helen Small's consideration of the role of debt as a polysemic term in Dickens's negotiations with the work and cultural status of Henry Fielding suggests both Dickens's imaginative obligation to his predecessor, and his efforts to move beyond him, particularly through repudiating many of his attitudes as morally reprehensible. Small employs Nietzsche's argument from *The Genealogy of Morals* (1887) that there is a historical and etymological connection between debts (*Schulden*) and guilt (*Schuld*), in order to map Dickens's double relationship with the 'great historian'[17] from whom Eliot memorably but equivocally distanced herself in chapter 15 of *Middlemarch* (1871–72). Central to the debate is an issue that engaged many Victorian writers who thought carefully about their eighteenth-century inheritance and which is further discussed by David Amigoni (182–202), Elisabeth Jay (98–118), and Francis O'Gorman (76–97): the changing status of the author between the eighteenth and nineteenth centuries, and the emergent cultural category of the professional writer. Although Dickens, Small argues, hoped to professionalize the Victorian writer further than he was able, he acknowledged that they were a more independent and organized body than their eighteenth-century predecessors. Such recognition, however, paradoxically involved a heightened awareness of indebtedness, with all its metaphorical suggestiveness, to the authors of the previous century.

If Eliot detached herself, though not without nostalgia, from the age of Fielding in *Middlemarch*, from the time 'when the days were longer, when summer afternoons were spacious, and the clock ticked slowly in the winter evenings',[18] Simon Dentith locates an overlooked feature of her respect for eighteenth-century philosophical thinking. Although Jean-Jacques Rousseau is often placed in relation to Romanticism, Dentith argues for recognition of Eliot's engagement with him specifically as a figure of the *Aufklärung* in the matter of educational theory. Detailing the complex ways in which Rousseauvian thought came down to Eliot mediated through distinct provincial and metropolitan cultural fractions, Dentith argues that it is possible to recognize the influence of Rousseau the eighteenth-century *philosophe* in the ethical teaching of *The Mill on the Floss* (1860) and *Daniel Deronda* (1876). The discipline of natural consequences is a process of learning from 'natural' events that are nevertheless, in Rousseau's narratives, deliberately engineered by others. This procedure marks the stories of Tom and Maggie, and that of Gwendolen Harleth, and comprises a lucid example of Eliot's sympathetic engagement with Rousseau the eighteenth-century Enlightenment figure, not the proto-Romantic.

The place of the eighteenth century in the fiction of the nineteenth extends well beyond the works of Dickens and Eliot. Carolyn Williams's consideration of a host of popular fictional writers in the next chapter includes examination of the role of the eighteenth-century stereotype in the vibrant historical fiction of the nineteenth century from Thackeray to Mrs Craik, Stevenson, and Conan Doyle. Williams's central contention here concerns the double purchase of these stereotypes, which simultaneously caricature the eighteenth-century past and give shape to the creative energies of popular Victorian novels whose appeal continues into the present. Limited in imaginative sympathy at one level, the novels nonetheless mediated an intriguingly double version of the eighteenth century into the succeeding period that was charged with life.

Matthew Arnold's definition of Alexander Pope as the 'high priest of an age of prose and reason'[19] erected a major impediment to more extensive investigations of Pope's afterlife in the nineteenth century. Francis O'Gorman's chapter assembles a wide range of material that reveals the multiple engagements between Victorian critics and Pope's poetry – encounters occluded by the pronouncements of Arnold's 'The Study of Poetry'. Discussing writers from Thackeray to his son-in-law, Leslie Stephen, O'Gorman proposes that the true history of Pope in the nineteenth century can be summed up neither by Arnold's words nor by easy generalization at all. Connecting with Helen Small's discussion in chapter 1, O'Gorman considers, among other things, the place of the author of the *Dunciad* in Victorian efforts to map the problematic shifts in the status of authorship; he also analyses the admiration for eighteenth-century rationalism by the agnostic intelligentsia in the late nineteenth century who saw Pope as a laudable figure of liberal thinking. O'Gorman's chapter indicates just how misleading are efforts to raise Arnold's declaration as representative of the whole period's historical preferences in poetics.

Dickens looked back to Fielding and assessed how far the profession of authorship had changed. Margaret Oliphant's sense of authorship in Elisabeth Jay's discussion depends not on a textual relationship with Fielding but with two notable literary historians of her own time: Thackeray and Macaulay. For Oliphant, Jay argues, the decision to write historical sketches of the eighteenth century for *Blackwood's Magazine* was calculated to invite comparison with these male rivals and their versions of the relationship of the present age with the past. The sketches were to provide an opportunity for staking out a claim for her own literary identity as a critic of eighteenth-century literary and cultural history. Jay considers how Oliphant's account of the eighteenth century was inflected by John Blackwood's ideological concerns, and she discusses Oliphant's perception of the eighteenth century as the originating site of the Victorian period's gender constructions. Oliphant's work in this period affirms important continua between the present, of the sort Thackeray recognized in the career of Pope (see 98–118, below), and a model of the eighteenth century that, as for Carolyn Williams, extended to the Regency.

Katherine Turner's chapter similarly identifies the eighteenth-century world – embodied in the figure of Samuel Johnson – as an enabling source of quotation, example, and identification. Dismantling the view of Johnson in the nineteenth century as largely the preserve of critics and pedants, Turner excavates Johnson's multivalence to nineteenth-century readers from a range of social and educational backgrounds. She also shows how central Johnson was to a late nineteenth-century re-evaluation of the eighteenth: increasingly attracted by the cultural authority but also by the personal oddities of Johnson, readers and critics came to reappraise the era that produced him. This re-assessment was no matter of nostalgia for a simpler age, but symptomatic of a growing interest in diversity and complexity within and between distinct historical periods.

One of Dr Johnson's specific contributions to eighteenth-century culture is discussed in relation to the Victorians in Lynda Mugglestone's consideration of the connections between Johnson's *Dictionary* and James Murray's *Oxford English Dictionary*. At one level, Mugglestone argues, the nineteenth-century philologists defined themselves against the eccentrically personal achievement of Johnson's work, characterized, as Murray later put it, by its 'whimsicality'.[20] The New Philologists had laid claim to an objective mode of language analysis just as Murray, contemplating the undertaking of the new *Dictionary*, proposed that its method would be one of scientific exactitude. But this division between the eighteenth and nineteenth centuries, Mugglestone argues, is far from watertight; and the conflicted prescriptivism of Johnson's enterprise was also evident in features of the *OED* – Murray sat working on the *OED* with Johnson's dictionary always open before him – blurring the original declared principles of the project and providing one of the suggestive links between the lexicographical endeavours of the two centuries.

Murray had thought – ironically, in the light of Mugglestone's argument – that a Johnsonian dictionary could have been written in the nineteenth century: Carlyle or Ruskin could have done it, he said, with disdain. Ruskin himself is the subject of Dinah Birch's chapter, which seeks to modify the conventional Bloomian reading of Ruskin as a writer whose defining relationship with the past related primarily to his Romantic heritage. Birch's argument supplements this account by drawing attention to the role of the pre-Romantic eighteenth century in Ruskin's life, and its increasing significance for him. Tracing the defining role of Ruskin's parental legacy in his acquaintance with the literature of the eighteenth century, Birch analyses the forces behind the movement of his mind from scepticism about Pope's understanding of landscape in *Modern Painters* III (1856) to his celebration of the moral power of Augustanism in the 1870s. Ruskin's eighteenth century was, as Birch argues, often mediated via Romanticism, but, nonetheless, it came to play a consequential part both in the formation of his literary voice and in the articulation of his moral programme, particularly his critique of the modern.

Ruskin in the 1870s took Pope at his word, and was uninterested in considering the role of artifice or mask-wearing in his poetics. The whole question of sincerity is the subject of David Amigoni's chapter about the cultural forces shaping the representation of the eighteenth century in the *English Men of Letters*. Amigoni accounts for reasons why the eighteenth-century liberal intellectuals appealed to a cadre of largely agnostic liberal thinkers, Leslie Stephen chief among them, at the end of the nineteenth century. His chapter locates the eighteenth century as a site inscribed with the particular anxieties of late Victorian culture, especially concerns about masculinity, Aestheticism, and the relationship between literature, the idea of 'culture', and market forces. Amigoni's argument adds a further dimension to the claims of Small and O'Gorman about the role of the eighteenth-century in Victorian considerations of authorship and the status of the writer.

Authorship and notions of authenticity and writerly sincerity are investigated from a different angle in Nick Groom's chapter that considers the role of eighteenth-century forgers, especially Thomas Chatterton, in Victorian literary culture. Groom argues that eighteenth-century figures were imaginatively amalgamated with nineteenth-century forgers to generate a kind of type around whom a multitude of powerful myths grew. Considering the case of the notorious gentleman forger Thomas Griffiths Wainewright, Groom suggests that consistent subtle allusion to forgery, to Wainewright and Chatterton, inform the imaginative territory of Dickens's fiction, especially *Bleak House* (1852–53), and also play an important role in Oscar Wilde's formulation of the aesthete, the artist without consistent identity and resistant to earlier cultural notions of authenticity. Groom's discussion reveals the shadow of the eighteenth-century forger revitalized in Victorian literary transactions and pertinent for the distinctive shape of *fin de siècle* conceptions of authorship.

Establishing authority as a female writer at the end of the century is the subject of the final essay in this collection. Where David Amigoni was interested in the cultural forces present in the representation of the eighteenth century in the *English Men of Letters* series, Hilary Fraser is concerned with the traces of the Victorian in the fashioning of the eighteenth century in women's art criticism. Fraser's chapter goes beyond England, however, to look at the shaping of eighteenth-century Italy and France by the unconventional and resourceful art historians Vernon Lee and Emilia Dilke, considering, among other things, their pre-modernist sensitivity to the nature of historiography, the gender politics of their representation of the recent past, and their preoccupation with the nature of 'foreignness'. Both Lee and Dilke, Fraser argues, thought of their own identities in terms of the foreign, as in a marginal relation to British society, and their work on eighteenth-century European culture provided subtle ways of exploring and legitimizing their own subject positions. The question of authorial status, of the nature of authorship, which has been variously debated in this collection, receives its final consideration in this chapter as Fraser opens up some of the fruitful opportunities provided by the eighteenth century for ideologically weighted contests about history and gender on the cusp of the modern.

Moving from Dickens to that dawning modern, this collection adopts a broadly chronological organization as the simplest and most obvious. But thematic groups are continually suggesting themselves in this account of the Victorian's multiple inheritance from the eighteenth century, an account that offers, as it must, symptomatic readings rather than a comprehensive overview. Some essays discuss broad questions of historiography, some consider how the Victorian age read one or a small group of eighteenth-century figures, others how one or a small number of Victorians read the eighteenth century. Different groups of essays consider fiction, poetry, or the discourses of non-fictional prose. But while the essays continually speak to each other, we have chosen not to impose what would inevitably be false limits that would create misleading expectations of unity by gathering them in anything other than loosely chronological order. This collection has diversity at the core of its critical investigation and our principle seems to allow that diversity to speak most naturally.

The insular speaker – he has never been out of England – of Browning's 'A Toccata of Galuppi's' (1855) imagines an eighteenth-century world conjured by the music of *maestro* of Venice's Basilica di San Marco. The life which that music recalls – he is listening to a keyboard toccata and imagining the scene it suggests – is shaped primarily by the speaker's own remembered clichés of Venetian culture. He perceives a pleasurable spectacle of carnival and pleasure disconnected from his own provincial nineteenth-century existence of physics, geology, and mathematics. For him, the eighteenth century brought back to life by Galuppi's music is one that ends abruptly and without, it seems, leaving emotional traces: 'Death stepped tacitly and took them where they never see the sun', he remarks with something like indifference to those who lived through the Venetian *settecento*. But the faded eighteenth-century pageant cannot, he finds, be dismissed so easily. The music of Baldassare Galuppi, whom Dr Burney considered one of the four best opera composers of his age, continues its work with Browning's speaker, and its mournful recollection of the end of an eighteenth-century way of living – the death of men and women 'merely born to bloom and drop' – finally touches him. By the conclusion of the poem, the unnamed monologist has found a fragile sympathy for that no longer entirely alienated past, summoned by music; its men and women – 'Dear dead women, with such hair, too – ' cease to be merely figures of an emotionally unengaged imagination. The loss of that aurally-inspired eighteenth-century dream reminds him of his own loss and an imagined *settecento* speaks momentarily to the present.[21]

'A Toccata of Galuppi's' is not about an eighteenth-century English past. But the movement of the speaker's mind towards recognition of a more meaningful connection between himself and an image of the eighteenth century may serve as a final herald for our collection and its investigation of plural filiations between the Victorian period and the preceding century, including, in fact, transactions with eighteenth-century European culture. Browning's Victorian speaker experiences a change of heart: he finds inadequate the clichés that had helped shape his first thoughts about the eighteenth century, and the poem reveals, within his own sensibilities, the possibilities of a deeper relationship. The revisionary efforts of this book to reassess a Carlylean/Arnoldian tradition that has occluded debate for much too long about the whole subject of the Victorians' complex relation with their eighteenth-century inheritance accordingly invite a change of mind. Across a wide domain, this book offers a new view of Victorian literary history by presenting representative instances of the overlooked but exhilaratingly multiple relationship between the Victorians and the Hanoverian age.

Notes

1   See David Perkins, *Is Literary History Possible?* (Baltimore and London: Johns Hopkins University Press, 1992). See also Nicola Trott, 'Framing Romanticism: Keynote Address' in *Wordsworth Circle*, 33 (2002): 90–2, Seamus Perry, 'In Praise of Puny Boundaries', ibid., 119–21.

2   David Fairer's *English Poetry of the Eighteenth Century, 1700–1789* (London and New York: Longman, 2003) is the most recent volume to propose an alternative historical narrative of the 'Romantic' presence in early eighteenth-century verse. The emergence of the category of 'Romanticism' in literary history is discussed in Perkins, *Is Literary History*

The Victorians and the Eighteenth Century

Possible?, 85–119. A recent text to have problematized Romanticism and periodization in a different way is C.C. Barfoot, ed., *Victorian Keats and Romantic Carlyle: The Fusions and Confusions of Literary Periods* (Amsterdam: Rudopi, 2000). Stephen Gill's *Wordsworth and the Victorians* (Oxford: Clarendon, 1998) was an important argument about the way a sense of period changes: it revealed how differently from a twentieth-century perspective one Romantic writer appeared to the Victorians.

3   Studies that explicitly consider Victorian connections with the eighteenth century and their implications for periodization or literary history are few and far between: the most recent monograph to debate relationships as they pertain to the development of the novel is Leah Price, *The Anthology and the Rise of the Novel from Richardson to George Eliot* (Cambridge: Cambridge University Press, 2000). The obvious area in which there has been sustained interest in a creative relationship between the Victorians and the eighteenth century is the Queen Anne Revival in architecture. See Mark Girouard, *Sweetness and Light: The 'Queen Anne' Movement, 1860–1900* (Oxford: Clarendon, 1977).

4   *The Works of Thomas Carlyle*, ed. H.D. Traill, 30 vols (London: Chapman and Hall, 1897–1904), V, 170.

5   The most recent debate with Bloom in relation to Victorian literature is Robert Douglas-Fairhurst, *Victorian Afterlives: The Shaping of Influence in Nineteenth-Century Literature* (Oxford: Oxford University Press, 2002). See also Alison Chapman and Jane Stabler, eds, *Unfolding the South: Nineteenth-Century British Women Writers and Artists in Italy* (Manchester: Manchester University Press, 2003).

6   Henry Knight Miller, 'The "Whig Interpretation" of Literary History', *Eighteenth-Century Studies*, 6 (1972): 63, italic original.

7   Quoted in Stephen Bann, *The Clothing of Clio: A Study of the Representation of History in Nineteenth-century Britain and France* (Cambridge: Cambridge University Press, 1984), 2.

8   See Timothy Lang, *The Victorians and the Stuart Heritage: Interpretations of a Discordant Past* (Cambridge: Cambridge University Press, 1995) and Blair Worden, 'The Victorians and Oliver Cromwell', in Stefan Collini, Richard Whatmore, and Brian Young, eds, *History, Religion and Culture: British Intellectual History 1750–1950* (Cambridge: Cambridge University Press, 2000), 112–35.

9   Philippa Levine, *The Amateur and the Professional: Antiquaries, Historians, and Archaeologists in Victorian England, 1836–1886* (Cambridge: Cambridge University Press, 1986), 1.

10   William James Courthope, *The Liberal Movement in English Literature* (London: Murray, 1885), 115–16. As early as 1845, Henry, Lord Brougham had argued for the crucial role of the eighteenth-century 'philosophers and men of letters' in establishing 'the rights of the people throughout the civilized world' (Henry, Lord Brougham, *Lives of Men of Letters and Science, who Flourished in the Time of George III*, 2 vols (London: Knight, 1845), I. viii.

11   Gillian Beer, *Arguing with the Past: Essays in Narrative from Woolf to Sidney* (London: Routledge, 1989), 3–4.

12   Richard Altick reminds us that, for many nineteenth-century readers, the works of the Romantic poets would have been scarcer and more expensive than eighteenth-century classics that had a dominant presence in private, public, and circulating libraries, in the second-hand book trade, and in the world of affordable reprints. Richard D. Altick, *The English Common Reader: A Social History of the Mass Reading Public, 1800–1900* (1957; repr. Columbus, OH: Ohio State University Press, 1998), 253.

13 Sandra M. Gilbert and Susan Gubar, *The Madwoman in the Attic: The Woman Writer and the Nineteenth-Century Literary Imagination* (New Haven and London: Yale University Press, 1979), 51.

14 *The Letters of Elizabeth Barrett Browning*, ed. Frederic G. Kenyon, 4th edn, 2 vols (London: Smith, Elder, 1898) I, 232.

15 See Francis O'Gorman, 'Ruskin, Vernon Lee, and the Cultural Possession of Italy', *Journal of Anglo-Italian Studies*, 7 (2002), 81–107.

16 See ibid.

17 George Eliot, *Middlemarch* (Oxford: Oxford University Press, 1997), 132.

18 Ibid.

19 *The Study of Poetry*, 41.

20 See 148 below.

21 References to 'A Toccata of Galuppi's' are to *The Poetical Works of Robert Browning*, vol. 5, eds Ian Jack and Robert Inglesfield (Oxford: Clarendon, 1995), 56–61. David Lindley discusses a likely eighteenth-century source for this poem in the work of Charles Burney in 'A Possible Source for Browning's "A Toccata of Galuppi's"', *Browning Society Notes*, 9 (1979), 1–2.

Chapter 1

The Debt to Society: Dickens, Fielding, and the Genealogy of Independence

Helen Small

In a famous passage of *The Genealogy of Morals* (1887), Nietzsche proposes a speculative history of 'resentment'.[1] Positing a historical and etymological connection between debts ('*Schulden*') and guilt ('*Schuld*'), he argues that the concept of guilt grew out of an awareness that the relationship between a given generation and its forebears is structurally equivalent to that between debtor and creditor:

> Within the original tribal association – we are talking about pre-history – the living generation always acknowledged a legal obligation towards the earlier generation, and in particular towards the earliest, which founded the tribe. ... There is a prevailing conviction that the tribe *exists* only because of the sacrifices and deeds of the forefathers, – and that these have to be *paid back* with sacrifices and deeds: people recognize an *indebtedness* [*Schuld*], which continually increases because these ancestors continue to exist as mighty spirits, giving the tribe new advantages and lending it some of their power.[2]

Any strengthening of the tribe is accompanied by an increase in the sense of obligation to the ancestor: a heightened 'dread' and a greater consciousness of the need to pay back. Any lessening of the tribe's power results in a corresponding decrease in respect and fear.[3] Over millennia the 'sacrifices and deeds' through which indebtedness is acknowledged become internalized or 'moralized' into guilt, duty, and religious precept – forms of obligation that inhere in our notion of the self, and that we know can never be discharged.

Nietzsche's metaphors were not, of course, his own. This is, substantially, his point. Since antiquity, the language of debt has pervaded, often sustained, the critical literature on cultural – especially intellectual and artistic – influence: Milton's debt to Shakespeare, Marx's debt to Hegel, but also, more abstractly, modernism's debt to the Victorians, Britain's literary debt to Continental Europe, the novel's debt to the visual arts. Metaphorical 'debt' spreads itself thinly, operating across genres and modes of art, national and linguistic boundaries, generations and centuries. For critical theorists interested in intellectual genealogies, returning to Nietzsche's paradigm has been a means of calling that too easy generalizability to account. So Samuel Weber, reading Derrida's reflections on *The Genealogy of Morals* in *La carte postale*, argues that, in Freud's dealings with Nietzsche, and Derrida's with Heidegger, a debt to an intellectual precursor is pointedly refused only to be readmitted at the level of metaphor and 'motif'. The refusal to pay one's dues here becomes requisite to going beyond the earlier writer's thought, but the status of debtor remains finally inescapable – a negative, as Nietzsche understood, at the heart of subjectivity.[4]

One reason for choosing to acknowledge a debt to Nietzsche and his late twentieth-century descendants at the start of this essay is that, although his model of genealogy has been thoroughly explored in relation to philosophical and intellectual history, it has had surprisingly little impact on writing about literary influence.[5] In what follows I argue that the notion of the debtor's frustrated desire to renege on or (in the old sense of that verb) deny what is owed to his or her predecessors may prove especially productive in relation to the nineteenth-century British novel. This is most obviously so on that familiarly Nietzschean ground where a novelist's indebtedness to an eighteenth-century precursor is expressed through the attitudes and dilemmas of morality. But it is also a pattern observable at a wider level of debate about the conditions of authorship in the mid-nineteenth century. Efforts by certain writers, Charles Dickens most prominent among them, to improve the financial support available to Victorian literary men and women involved a highly polemical representation of the unwelcome persistence of 'eighteenth-century' practices into the nineteenth century. Would-be reformers drew attention to the evils of the preceding century's patronage system and the humiliations it had entailed for so many of that period's authors: heavy obligations to wealthy benefactors; actual financial debts incurred for want of such support. In such contexts debt is not 'just' internalized as morality (though the rhetoric of reformism is intensely moralizing); it persists as a real condition that the reformers wished to see consigned to history. To that extent it complicates the Nietzschean genealogy of morals as a model for how a generation of writers may relate to its ancestors, preserving in the present and very recent past those literal forms of obligation that Nietzsche would identify with pre-history, and making them part of immediate efforts to effect historical change.

Although these issues have a much wider provenance, I pursue them through the example of Charles Dickens's much acknowledged but little discussed indebtedness to Henry Fielding.[6] To be consciously influenced by the earlier novelist's 'profound knowledge of human nature'[7] led to particular literary choices: acts of reaffirmation, but also of firm repudiation on Dickens's part[8] – most obviously when it came to thinking about sex and class. Time and again, echoing Fielding meant putting a clear distance between his social assumptions and Dickens's own. Above all, keeping in view the poverty in which Fielding and so many writers of his era had struggled encouraged Dickens toward a strategic redefinition of the author's relation to his audience, and an explicit reconfiguring of the kind of debtor a writer should be. Dickens was well aware that imaginative debt is unavoidable, just as economic debt is inevitable once we think seriously about the nature of money. (Ruskin gave concise form to a familiar truth when he wrote that 'All money, properly so called, is an acknowledgement of debt'.[9]) In his fiction and in his efforts on behalf of the writing profession, however, Dickens recasts the concept of the writer's indebtedness in such a way as to throw off 'eighteenth-century' constraints and secure a maximum of freedom for the modern author.

Dickens himself was chary of the metaphor of debt in relation to literary influence. In his letters and, especially, his speeches, claims of 'indebtedness' typically involve those arts or professions which abut the literary but do not directly impinge upon it. Almost without exception they involve the collective present-day obligations of the Victorian public, rather than debts, historic or present, that might be thought particular to him. Hence the public's 'great debt' to the theatrical profession, 'the debt which all civilized men ow[e] to Art', even 'how much we, the public, owe to reporters'.[10] When expressing his relation to his literary predecessors, Dickens preferred a more intimate vocabulary, to do less with literary exemplarity and more with registering old affections. The metaphor of debt thus remains Nietzschean rather than Dickensian in its source, here. Dickens's avoidance of it, even as he strove to be seen as Fielding's inheritor, underlines the strength of the desire for writerly self-determination.

The result is a double narrative about literary inheritances: a personal genealogy of writerly style and subject matter, largely 'internalized' into the language and attitudes of moralism, but also a public genealogy of the profession, 'externalized' in efforts to reform the situation of writers. Dickens works hard to repudiate the notion of debt, in the first instance, to reform it in the second; yet debt insistently returns (as Weber would say) at the level of metaphor and motif. In doing so it indicates the extent to which independence was, for Dickens, a historically relative term, its virtue and value derived in no small measure from the intensity and duration of his engagement with the eighteenth century.

*

The wish to be identified with Fielding is unmistakable in Dickens's numerous references to the novels, plays, and other public writings across the course of his career. With some pride he informed the Provost of Eton, Fielding's old school, in 1847 that 'You do me justice in taking it for granted that I am an admirer of Fielding. I knew his books in a child's innocent way, so long ago, that I can almost say I remember nothing before them. And my more mature acquaintance with his extraordinary wit and genius, has been as intimate and close as that first knowledge.'[11] The *Autobiographical Fragment* records that *Tom Jones* was one of the precious collection of books (part of 'a cheap series of novelists then in publication'[12]) that Dickens was forced to pawn, at the age of eleven, to a drunken bookseller in the Hampstead Road as his father's financial affairs approached crisis point.[13] This and at least some of Fielding's other novels were probably among the first books he bought for himself when his own situation permitted, and therefore among the three-volume novels in paper boards which G.H. Lewes saw 'vulgaris[ing]' Dickens's shelves in Doughty Street. A full set of Fielding was certainly part of the 'goodly array of standard works, well-bound' which replaced them in 1 Devonshire Terrace.[14] Both the inventory of the contents of that house in May 1854 and the catalogue taken of Dickens's library at Gad's Hill after his death record that he owned the 10-volume 1806 edition of the *Works*, edited by Alexander Chalmers, and prefaced by Arthur Murray's 1762 'Essay on [Fielding's] Life and Genius'.

Extensive though Dickens's knowledge of Fielding was, his thinking about the nature of that influence hinges on his engagement with *Tom Jones*. Painfully associated with the memory of being a debtor's child, *Tom Jones* was inextricable in Dickens's imagination from anxieties about his own hold on gentility. It was also the work which prompted Dickens's most direct statement of a limit to his admiration for Fielding. In a passage of the *Autobiographical Fragment* absorbed almost verbatim into *David Copperfield*, he recalled the collection of books that went in real life to the pawnbrokers, and echoed the oddly superfluous reference in the Eton letter to the innocence of childhood reading:

> My father had left in a little room up-stairs, to which I had access (for it adjoined my own) a small collection of books which nobody else in our house ever troubled. From that blessed little room, Roderick Random, Peregrine Pickle, Humphrey Clinker, Tom Jones, The Vicar of Wakefield, Don Quixote, Gil Blas, and Robinson Crusoe, came out, a glorious host, to keep me company. They kept alive my fancy, and my hope of something beyond that time and

place ... – and did me no harm; for whatever harm was in some of them was not there for me; *I* knew nothing of it. It is astonishing to me now, how I found time, in the midst of my porings and blunderings over heavier themes, to read those books as I did. It is curious to me how I could ever have consoled myself under small troubles (which were great troubles to me), by impersonating my favourite characters in them – as I did – ... I have been Tom Jones (a child's Tom Jones, a harmless creature) for a week together. I have sustained my own idea of Roderick Random for a month at a stretch ...[15]

More obviously than Smollett, for whom, later in life, Dickens would declare a final preference,[16] Fielding triggers the desire to pre-empt a possible misunderstanding. The narrative focalization insistently prioritizes the child's innocent pleasure in *Tom Jones* over the adult's awareness that there is commonly held to be harm in this writing. '*I* knew nothing of it' is the child's too strenuous protestation of innocence: it 'was not there for me ... a harmless creature'. The child, by implication, can afford to read *Tom Jones* and impersonate its hero with no other thought than 'consolation'; the adult's love of Fielding is necessarily more self-conscious, more defensive.[17]

For Dickens's contemporaries the potential harm in *Tom Jones* was evident, and famously expressed by Thackeray's *The English Humourists of the Eighteenth Century* (1853):

> I cannot offer or hope to make a hero of Harry Fielding. Why hide his faults? Why conceal his weaknesses in a cloud of periphrases? Why not show him, like him as he is, ... with inked ruffles, and claret stains on his tarnished laced coat, and on his manly face the marks of good fellowship, of illness, of kindness, of care and wine? Stained as you see him, and worn by care and dissipation, that man retains some of the most precious and splendid human qualities and endowments. ...
>
> But against Mr. Thomas Jones himself we have a right to put in a protest, and quarrel with the esteem the author evidently has for that character. Charles Lamb finely says of Jones, that a single hearty laugh from him 'clears the air' – but then it is in a certain state of the atmosphere. It might clear the air when such personages as Blifil or Lady Bellaston poison it. But I fear very much that ... when Mr. Jones enters Sophia's drawing-room, the pure air there is rather tainted with the young gentleman's tobacco-pipe and punch. ... a hero with a flawed reputation; a hero spunging for a guinea; a hero who can't pay his landlady, and is obliged to let his honour out to hire, is absurd, and his claim to heroic rank untenable. I protest against Mr. Thomas Jones holding such rank at all.[18]

The two faults, sexual incontinence and financial incompetence, are compounded in Thackeray's arm's-length reference to Tom 'let[ting] out his honour to hire' – selling sexual favours to the older, richer woman in return for rent money. The offence against 'honour' is, clearly, also an offence against 'rank', the inked ruffles, and claret-stained, tarnished laced coat, being the only substantive additions to the Hogarthian portrait of Fielding in Murphy's *Essay*[19] – imagined signs of gentility on its uppers, but still undoubtedly gentility.

One has to assume that, when he offsets the author's freedom with his purse against the character's need to sponge for a guinea and play the gigolo for his rent, Thackeray has conveniently forgotten Fielding's own familiarity with the inside of a sponging house and, very likely, debtor's prison as well.[20] 'All the world knows what was his imprudence', Lady Louisa Stuart observed after Fielding's death:

> if ever he possessed a score of pounds, nothing could keep him from lavishing it idly, or make him think of to-morrow. Sometimes they were living in decent lodgings with tolerable comfort; sometimes in a wretched garret without necessaries; not to speak of the spunging houses and hiding places where he was occasionally to be found. His elastic gaiety of spirit carried him through it all ...[21]

Thackeray's is the indulgent perspective of one gentleman of letters on another, coming to the rescue with a saving distinction between low 'taste' and a low 'mind', the choice exercised and the true quality of the person.

This conflation of sex and class in the moral response to Fielding is equally true of Dickens, though the politics of the class response are, as ever, a long way from Thackeray's confident identification with Fielding's familial and educational background. Where sex is involved, Dickens's acknowledgement of the earlier writer's influence immediately comes into conflict with a strong counter-imperative to lessen or, indeed, deny the harm such an obligation would entail. This is most transparently the case in *Pickwick Papers* where the influence of Fielding is at its most undiluted. In chapter 22, for example, Mr Pickwick, lodging at the Great White Horse in Ipswich for a night, mistakes his bedroom and settles into the curtained bed in his tasselled night-cap only to find that 'a middle-aged lady in yellow curl-papers' is brushing her hair before the dressing glass. The scene directly reprises Book IV, ch. 14 of *Joseph Andrews*, where the incompetently rakish Beau Didapper mistakes Mrs Slipslop's room for Fanny's, attempts to ravish the unexpectedly compliant and malodorous body in the bed, and is valiantly prevented by Parson Adams – who then mistakes his own room and retires to bed beside a soundly sleeping Fanny:

> As the Cat or Lapdog of some lovely Nymph for whom ten thousand Lovers languish, lies quietly by the side of the charming Maid, and ignorant of the Scene of Delight on which they repose meditates the future Capture of a Mouse, or Surprizal of a Plate of Bread and Butter: so *Adams*, lay by the side of *Fanny*, ignorant of the Paradise to which he was so near …[22]

In Fielding the scene is chain farce, the comedy resting largely on the clash between Beau Didapper and Mrs Slipslop's mutually thwarting sexual ambitions but compensatingly loud protestations of innocence, and Parson Adams and Fanny's legitimate virtue but deeply compromising situation. The parson's mistake is only discovered when Fanny wakes and stretches out her hand into his beard.

Mr Pickwick never gets this far, his situation being embarrassing but indubitably chaste:

> Mr Pickwick, it is quite unnecessary to say, was one of the most modest and delicate-minded of mortals. The very idea of exhibiting his night-cap to a lady, overpowered him, but he had tied those confounded strings in a knot, and do what he would, he couldn't get it off. The disclosure must be made. There was only one other way of doing it. He shrunk behind the curtains, and called out very loudly –
> 'Ha – hum.'
> … 'A gentleman!' said the lady with a terrific scream.
> 'It's all over,' thought Mr Pickwick.[23]

Eroticism is all but banished from the *Pickwick* scene, its entire force dwindled into the apology for a symbol that is Mr Pickwick's tasselled night-cap. In the Fielding passage, sex irrepressibly hijacks the language of chastity (the predatory cat and the lap-dog, always a dubious guarantor of innocence, bringing the appetitive back under cover of simile), but in Dickens the narrative voice aligns itself with the unimpugnable Pickwick ('the very idea'). And servants are there to restore order rather than fuel the mayhem. Ejected from the middle-aged lady's room, Mr Pickwick crouches stoically in a corner to await the daylight, but is quickly rescued by Sam Weller: 'You rayther want somebody to look arter you Sir, ven your judgment goes out a wisitin'' (305).

Bowdlerization is one mode of neutralizing the possible 'harm' of a debt to Fielding on the terrain of sex – and at its most startling in *Is She His Wife?*

(1857), Dickens's enfeebled imitation of *The Modern Husband* (1732) and its genre. Disqualifying possible objects of attraction other than the designated heroine is another (think of Fanny Squeers as a latter-day Molly Seagrim); and preventing the designated heroine from plotting for her own sexual happiness yet another (*The Miser*'s Lovegold and worldly-wise Mariana[24] recast as *Nicholas Nickleby*'s Arthur Gride and self-sacrificing Madeleine Bray). But even as Dickens denies a debt to Fielding's diffusive eroticism, he retains strong traces of a social or class logic of sex characteristic of Fielding, whereby the erotic (or, in Dickens, narrative agents who mark the place where the erotic might have been) is, among other things, a decoy from the possibility of downward social mobility. Because sex is 'only' sex, Tom's slips in that regard can always be seen as eluding a more categorical slip in social status. The grotesque spectacle of Fanny Squeers's desire can similarly be seen as debarring any possibility that Nicholas Nickleby will end his life as a Yorkshire boarding-house master.

Lust, or in Dickens its grotesque (or effete) distortions, remains in other words a sufficient cover for what might otherwise be implied by one's persistent association with gamekeepers and rogues and the kinds of people who frequent public inns and lodging houses. Like Fielding's heroes, Dickens's are protected from the threat of the dictum favoured by Partridge, the poor barber surgeon and former schoolmaster who accompanies Tom Jones on his travels in the hope of being able to effect a lucrative reconciliation with Squire Allworthy: '*Noscitur a socio*', 'You may know him by the company he keeps'. It is as dubious a motto for *Oliver Twist* or *Martin Chuzzlewit*, or even a late, less obviously Fielding-influenced novel like *Our Mutual Friend*, as it is for *Tom Jones* or *Joseph Andrews*. One doesn't know, and one certainly doesn't classify, a man by the company he keeps in Fielding or Dickens. The difference is that in Dickens immunity from the taint of association with others is not guaranteed. It has to be preserved by dint of constant discrimination between those who pose a serious threat and those who do not. Women are the most obvious objects of that discrimination, but the rationale behind their disarmed status goes much deeper.

Working against this distinctively Dickensian anxiety about losing one's foothold on the social ladder, there is his celebrated concern to give an accurate rendition of the voices of servants, labourers, the poor – a concern which again involves both debt to Fielding and moralizing resistance to that debt. Consider, for example, Dickens's reworking of Jonathan Wild's love letter to Miss Tishy. This is Fielding's version.

Most Deivine and adwhorable Creture,

I DOUT not but those IIs, briter than the Son, which have kindled such a
Flam in my Hart, have likewise the Faculty of seeing it. It would be the hiest
Preassumption to imagin you eggnorant of my Loav. No, Maddam, I sollemly
purtest, that, of all the Butys in the unaversal Glob, there is none kapable of
hateracting my IIs like you. Corts and Pallaces would be to me Deserts without
your Kumpany, and with it a Wilderness would have more Charms than Haven
itself. For I hop you will beleve me when I sware every Place in the Univarse
is a Haven with you. I am konvinced that you must be sinsibel of my violent
Passion for you, which, if I endevored to hid it, would be as impossible as
for you, or the Son, to hid your Butys. I assure you I have not slept a Wink
since I had the Hapness of seeing you last; therefore hop you will, out of
Kumpassion, let me have the Honour of seeing you this Afternoon; for I am
with the greatest Adwhoration,
                    Most Deivine Creeture,
                    Iour most pessionate Amirer,
                    Adwhorer, and Slave,
                    JONATHAN WYLD. (Bk III, ch. 6)[25]

And this (much condensed) is the equivalent passage from *Pickwick
Papers*:

"'Lovely creetur,'" …
''Tain't in poetry, is it?' interposed the father.
'No, no,' replied Sam.
'Werry glad to hear it,' said Mr Weller. 'Poetry's unnat'ral; no man ever talked
in poetry 'cept a beadle on boxin' day, or Warren's blackin' or Rowland's oil,
or some o' them low fellows; never you let yourself down to talk poetry, my
boy. Begin again, Sammy.'
   Mr Weller resumed his pipe with critical solemnity, and Sam once more
commenced, and read as follows.
"'Lovely creetur i feel myself a dammed" – .'
'That ain't proper,' said Mr Weller, taking his pipe from his mouth.
'No; it ain't dammed,' observed Sam, holding the letter up to the light, 'it's
"shamed," there's a blot there – "I feel myself ashamed,"'
'Wery good,' said Mr Weller. 'Go on.'
… "'Feel myself ashamed and completely circumscribed in a dressin' of you,
for you *are* a nice gal and nothin' but it…. So I take the priviledge of the
day, Mary, my dear – as the gen'lem'n in difficulties did, ven he valked out
of a Sunday, – to tell you that the first and only time I see you your likeness
was took on my hart in much quicker time and brighter colours than ever a

likeness was took by the profeel macheen … Except of me Mary my dear as your walentine and think over what I've said. – My dear Mary I will now conclude." That's all,' said Sam.
'That's rayther a sudden pull up, ain't it, Sammy?' inquired Mr Weller. …
'Ain't you a goin' to sign it?' (435–6)[26]

The Fielding letter is an educated man's joke at the expense of – or rather, by way of – the less literate. Its real target is not Jonathan Wild and his kind at all but the writers of pseudo-aristocratic romances and (that overlapping genre) epistolary manuals for the socially aspirational, Samuel Richardson most famously among them.[27] There are also strong shades here of a *Beggars' Opera*-style social inversion, through which the attribution of gentlemanly sentiments to the criminal Wild exposes the discreditable side of upper-class manners. Fielding offers Wild's literary effort to the reader as 'a much better pattern for that Epistolary kind of Writing, which is generally called LOVE-LETTERS, than any to be found in the *Academy of Compliments*'. The humour lies in the disjunction between ear and eye, with the eye clearly given priority, the overcorrection of the <h> 'hateracting' being almost the only audible sign of Wild's straining after gentility. Read (against its own grain) as speech, the letter is a plausible enough attempt at romantic seduction; read as writing, its mistranscriptions repeatedly betray Wild's true moral and social milieu. Miss Tishy's adorer and admirer would in reality make a whore of her and enmire her.[28] The end of the letter prompts the author/narrator to come clean to the reader and confess that he has throughout this history been 'embellishing' Jonathan Wild's diction 'with some Flourishes of his [the writer's] own eloquence, without which the excellent Speeches recorded in ancient Historians … would have scarce been found in their Writings'.

   Sam Weller's letter, by comparison, is intended principally to be heard, with the result that it conflates Sam's supposed orthographic errors with the phonetic transcriptions used throughout *Pickwick Papers* to register Sam and Tony Weller's speaking voices. ('Walentine' and 'ven' are Sam's pronunciations, but presumably not his spellings.) Broadly speaking the letter lies within the tradition of comic illiteracy that Fielding did much to establish, but Dickens shows no interest in planting a flag over contemporary stylistic disputes. This is not the perspective of the gentleman of letters mocking his fellow writers through an only fitfully attentive ventriloquization of the voice of a London criminal, but a half-journalistic half-theatrical effort to catch the true accents of Cockney English. Perhaps most importantly, the scene in *Pickwick* is a collaborative effort, the son and the father struggling together at the difficult business of putting words onto paper. Viewed from that angle, it says something about Dickens's own aspirations to transform his early circumstances through the profession of writing: circumstances that are codedly present, for readers after Forster, in the reference to Warren's Blacking and (very likely a nod to Fielding's *Amelia*) the statute which prohibited arrests being made on a Sunday, allowing debtors to go unharrassed by bailiffs on that day.

The wish to be identified with Fielding and yet to seal off the risks involved in his too ready flexibility around matters of sex and class thus plays itself out through the moralizing adaptiveness of Dickens's early responses to his predecessor. As it does so it compounds the notion of indebtedness (and restrains the temptation in writing about influence to over-simplify the 'ancestor') by the continuities with Fielding's own contradictions: the assumption of social and educational superiority in so much of his journalism, and yet the fascination with the lower ranks of society. In later career Fielding's familiarity with 'the low' would be made reputable by his work as a magistrate, but for much of his life it seemed to observers largely a matter of preference. 'Where is Fielding?' ran one waggish account of his youthful behaviour, 'he's now at All-fours, / With a parcel of Dam-me Boys, and bob-tailed Whores'.[29] This was famously the man who married his own servant, like his father before him.[30] But also the man who mooted a class theory of comedy inconceivable in Dickens, according to which one of the two general reasons 'why Humour so much abounds in this Nation, seems to me to arise from the great Number of People, who are daily raised by Trade to the Rank of Gentry, without having had any Education at all; or, to use no improper Phrase, Without having served an Apprenticeship to this Calling'.[31] It is not a vision of absolute social exclusivity, but it is an attitude essentially out of sympathy with the labour (including educational labour) necessary to 'burn one's indentures' in the matter of class and therefore essentially out of sympathy with the politics of Dickens's writing.

To take the argument back to the more familiar Fielding territory of sex: Fielding's interest in the lower ranks of society can still be contained within the socially exclusive notion of libertinism and its correlative assumption, voiced by Old Laroon in *The Old Debauchees* (1732), that loving 'a Whore at five and twenty, and a Bottle at Forty' is forgivable under the clause which says that doing 'good in one's generation' will (one trusts) 'make amends'.[32] Dickens's interest in the 'low' is entertained on the understanding that the world and God have higher expectations of one's behaviour, and in the knowledge that seigneurial licence always, in any case, required that one had a credible claim to being seigneurial. It is, in short, founded on a difference

– historically evolving, connected to religious belief, and always classed – in the interpretation of social responsibility.

As Forster suggested, the crucial Dickens text with respect to all these issues is *David Copperfield*. When he comes to account, in the *Life of Charles Dickens*, for the most intimate expression of Dickens's debt to Fielding, the naming of his eighth son Henry Fielding Dickens,[33] Forster describes it as 'a kind of homage' to the novel Dickens was then beginning, in which he would transform his debtor father into the perpetually embarrassed but unfailingly 'elastic' Mr Micawber.[34] This translation of the experience of debt into fiction and thus into the symbolic and actual credit of art had its main novelistic precedent, for Forster, in the work of Fielding: 'as Fielding described himself and his belongings in Captain Booth and Amelia, and protested always that he had writ in his books nothing more than he had seen in life, so it may be said of Dickens in more especial relation to David Copperfield'.[35] Avowedly autobiographical as it is (to Forster), *David Copperfield* marks Dickens's most deliberate effort to articulate a notion of responsibility (social, economic, and professional) by way of his reading of Fielding's *Tom Jones*. A translation, *après* Fielding, of experience into fiction, it is also a more carefully thought-through refusal of Fielding's example than any of the earlier novels (even *Barnaby Rudge*, where he shows a strong historian's interest in Fielding and his brother John[36]). It can, of course, only express that refusal, finally, as another form of indebtedness, but in doing so it serves to make clearer not just the complexities of Dickens's response to Fielding, but the beginnings of a more polemical view of how the economy of literature should be organized.

*

In one of the most telling instances of a Nietzscheanly 'resentful' reading of Fielding, *David Copperfield* reprises the scene in which Tom Jones, evicted from Paradise Hall, discovers that, in his frantic grief at being parted from Sophia, he has lost the pocket book given him by Mr Allworthy containing (though Tom does not know it) 500*l*. Returning to the meadow to hunt for it, he meets his 'old friend' Black George, the game keeper, who heartily condoles with the young gentleman on his misfortune and willingly joins in the search –

> but all to no Purpose, for they found nothing: For indeed, though the Things were then in the Meadow, they omitted to search the only Place where they were deposited; to wit, in the Pockets of the said *George*; for he had just before

found them, and being luckily apprized of their Value, had very carefully put them up for his own Use.[37]

In a structurally equivalent moment at the end of chapter 12 of *David Copperfield*, the much younger and more vulnerable David also prepares to leave his lodging (his third such move away from the protection of family or friends) and, like Tom before him, promptly suffers the loss of almost all his worldly wealth: not 500*l* in his case but a half-guinea (a gift from his former nurse, Peggotty), three halfpennies miraculously saved from his own earnings, and a box containing his few possessions. But the 'long-legged young man with a very little empty donkey-cart' to whom he entrusts the carriage of his box is a true moral descendant of Black George. David has no sooner directed him to go only as far as the King's Bench prison where he will be given further directions, than he 'rattles away' at top speed, leaving David to catch up. Outside the prison, a 'flushed and excited' David pulls the card of directions from his pocket, but in doing so tumbles out the half-guinea:

> I put it in my mouth for safety, and though my hands trembled a good deal, had just tied the card on very much to my satisfaction, when I felt myself violently chucked under the chin by the long-legged young man, and saw my half-guinea fly out of my mouth into his hand.
>   'Wot!' said the young man, seizing me by my jacket-collar, with a frightful grin. 'This is a pollis case, is it? You're a going to bolt, are you? Come to the pollis, you young warmin, come to the pollis!'
>   'You give me my money back, if you please,' said I, very much frightened; 'and leave me alone.'
>   'Come to the pollis!' said the young man. 'You shall prove it yourn to the pollis.' (172–3)

How does one prove money one's own? In Fielding's world, where bank notes were identifiable by their date and their bank of issue, that was still technically possible. Black George's theft is eventually proved against him on just those grounds when Squire Allworthy happens to follow him into a London bank and recognizes the notes he has cashed there.[38] But in David Copperfield's London money is anonymous, issued centrally by the Bank of England. Coins, as Black George knew a century earlier, had in any case long been virtually impossible to trace. Dealing with smaller sums of money than Tom Jones, and in a situation where his ownership of a half-guinea is (in the strict sense of the term) improbable, it is not surprising that the child David should be led to fear that the young man's threats will end in his conviction for criminal insolvency. (The King's Bench – within whose rules Fielding's father had died in 1741 – was the last prison in London to serve as a place of confinement for debtors.[39]) Tom can afford to give up 'almost all Thought concerning' his money, as soon as it is confirmed lost: the novel in any case makes it clear that such a loss is negligible beside the loss of Sophia, and Black George can attract an almost complicit knowingness from the narrative voice. But for David Copperfield a half-guinea is the difference between taking the coach to Dover and walking there, at hazard of his life, in a pair of shoes that will not last the journey. By the time he reaches Dover it will have become the difference between eating and drinking and not eating and drinking – literally what he can or cannot put in his mouth.

Fielding's cheerful elasticity about the state of his hero's purse attracts quiet but persistent criticism in *David Copperfield*. For all the evident desire to pay homage to *Tom Jones*, David is best read as an anti-Tom Jones: an emphatically 'harmless creature' whose re-enactment of scenes and motifs familiar from the earlier novel repeatedly takes the form of a rejection of the social and economic (and sexual) assumptions on which it is based. The most crucial involves the emphasis placed on work – a word which barely comes within the vocabulary of Fielding's heroes (even Joseph Andrews); which is not to say that Fielding himself did not know its value. At the one point in *Tom Jones* when the problem of how to make money arises explicitly, Tom promptly deems himself debarred from all obvious lines of employment by the want of immediate funds:

> the Prospect was all a melancholy Void. Every Profession, and every Trade, required Length of Time, and what was worse, Money; for Matters are so constituted that 'Nothing out of Nothing' is not a truer Maxim in Physics than in Politics …
>
> At last the Ocean, that hospitable Friend to the Wretched, opened her capacious Arms to receive him; and he instantly resolved to accept her kind Invitation. To express myself less figuratively, he determined to go to Sea. (Bk VII, ch. 2) (I, 331)

That characteristic flourish of the figurative at a point of embarrassment marks a point of deep kinship between Fielding and Thackeray, for all their differences of 'taste' and for all Thackeray's articulacy about those who live well on nothing a year. In Fielding, as in Thackeray's account of Fielding, money is separable from honour – if necessary by the time-honoured gentleman's expedient of failing to take it seriously. The price of one's rent may, under pressure of upholding 'rank', be confused with 500*l* (the actual sum Lady Bellaston pays for the letting out of Tom's honour), and the apparent necessity of finding work aboard ship represented as just another welcome embrace by a receptive woman.

At the point where the grown David Copperfield first comes to choose a profession in life, Tom's never-tested solution is imaginatively recapitulated and aggressively parodied. This time the debt is less structurally prominent, more in line with Weber's model of residual metaphors and motifs.

> If I could have been inspired with a knowledge of the science of navigation, taken the command of a fast-sailing expedition, and gone round the world on a triumphant voyage of discovery, I think I might have considered myself completely suited. But, in the absence of any such miraculous provision, my desire was to apply myself to some pursuit that would not lie too heavily upon [my aunt's] purse; and to do my duty in it, whatever it might be. (258)

The narrative perspective registers both David's youthful hint of Tom Jones-like irresponsibility and the adult David's mature distance on it – the pointed absence of any concept of labour in this souped-up version of the Jonesian last-resort unmistakable coming after David's familiarization, at Yarmouth, with how hard it is to make a living from the sea. The fantasy is inflated into gross fantasy, permitted neither the archness nor the lightness of Fielding's play with the figurative.

Unlike Tom Jones, lifted out of his financial embarrassments by the revelation that he is Squire Allworthy's nephew, David must learn, with the news of his aunt's financial failure, to work his way soberly to prosperity through the exercise of what the novel insistently, but not unambivalently, constructs as the labour of writing. Mary Poovey rightly points out that the representation of David's literary work voices a deepset contradiction within mid-nineteenth-century thinking about the writer's profession. Writers were both of the marketplace and outside the marketplace, labourers and not labourers. 'On the one hand, they were touted as superior to the "commercial ideas" that threatened a cultural "decline"; on the other, they felt themselves hostage to the rise and fall of taste and the good will (or business sense) of publishers, advertisers, and booksellers.'[40] If the resulting conflicts within the novel's conception of its hero's agency find expression, as Poovey argues, in David's unwelcome likeness to the predatorily 'humble' Uriah Heep, I want to suggest that the felt strenuousness of its vision of how one achieves solvency and respectability through writing finds a similarly displaced expression in his unconscious identification with two debtors, each of whom has significant links back to Fielding. Even as the novel finally expels them both, it registers the closeness of their kinship with the would-be unindebted David, and the continuing commitment of Dickens to those attitudes that prompted him to such efforts of moral correction when reworking or remembering Fielding.

In the context of thinking about Dickens's debt to Fielding, Mr Micawber stands not for the legacy of any one Fielding character or scene (though he bears strong resemblances to Billy Booth, especially) but for that principle of 'elasticity' that is everywhere to be found in the response of Fielding's heroes (and by all accounts Fielding himself) to economic embarrassment. 'Elasticity' is the quality Dickens most persistently attributes to Micawber – a man for whom it is 'nothing unusual' to be at one instant offering to slit his throat with a razor rather than see his family reduced to beggary, and 'within half an hour afterwards ... polish[ing] his shoes with extraordinary pains, and go[ing] out, humming a tune with a greater air of gentility than ever' (155).

That flexibility is ostensibly alien to David, whose distress and shame at the experience of impoverishment are continually impressed upon the reader. And yet the Micawbers have a signal habit of appearing at points in David's narrative when his gentility is most imperilled, and offering an alternative tenor of response. They make their first appearance in the novel on his first day at the blacking warehouse, they are there immediately after Mr Spenlow has rejected his application for Dora's hand, again on the night when his cramped London lodgings are exposed to the merciless eye of Steerforth's manservant Latimer, and on the night when Uriah Heep manages to inveigle David back to his home and squeeze him for information about Agnes Wickfield and her father. They also have a habit of acting in direct parallel with David. Their conversations about how best to exploit Mr Micawber's talents are comic versions of the debates over what David should do in life, and their peregrinations match his. He leaves London when they do, they take up residence after him in Canterbury, the town where he had most of his schooling. Most importantly, when they emigrate he also leaves England in order to 'discipline his heart' after the death of the child-wife with whom he came perilously close to emulating the Micawbers' domestic incompetence. Away from England he pursues his writing career with new maturity and public acclaim while they 'make good' at last in another country.

At just one point David himself makes the connection a literary/stylistic one. Contemplating his letter to Miss Mills asking for a clandestine meeting to discuss his forlorn hopes of winning Dora, he can't help feeling that it is 'something in the style of Mr Micawber' (513). The comparison is seemingly flippant and certainly self-mocking, but in view of David's subsequent choice of profession it has force – not least given Dickens's mock signing of himself 'Wilkins Micawber' in a contemporaneous letter to John Forster.[41] Words are David's (and Dickens's) means of keeping the threat of debt at bay, just as – or almost just as – Mr Micawber's eloquence is his means of asserting his gentility in the face of the social ignominy that attends his insolvency. The possibility that Mr Micawber himself might become a professional author never seems to occur to David or to Dickens. Its suppression is a necessary consequence of their dedication to a view of writing as the responsible opposite of something which 'turns up'.

Writing is David's means of maturing away from Mr Micawber – and yet, it is Micawber's determined labour to expose Uriah Heep that paves the way for the principal symbolic act of David's adulthood, his marriage to Agnes. It is also Micawber's work and not David's which restores aunt Betsy to prosperity. Representative of a kind of economic irresponsibility which the novel wishes to relocate firmly elsewhere (either in Australia, or in the period of David's youth, or – by means of literary allusion – in Henry Fielding), Mr Micawber also stands, unexpectedly, for the dedicated and mature pursuit of justice. In Australia he becomes, like Henry Fielding before him, an admired magistrate – and, unlike Fielding, a prosperous one. Dickens in fact reread at least part of Fielding's classic recommendations for the reform of the British policing and legislative systems, *An Enquiry into the Causes of the Late Increase of Robbers* (1751), while at work on *David Copperfield*.[42] Writing to the editor of *The Times* in November 1849 to press for the urgent reform of Britain's laws on capital punishment, he included a long quotation from the *Enquiry*, and endorsed the case Fielding had made 100 years earlier for private and immediate execution after sentence of death, in place of the grotesque public spectacles still current. Easily overlooked though it is, the granting of Fielding's second career to Mr Micawber, in the form of a reward, suggests the divided impulse with which Dickens casts out the cheerful elasticity of *Tom Jones* from his narrative of the modern professionalized writer-hero, and yet pays his dues, with the other hand, to a vision of social reform Fielding had bequeathed to Victorian England.[43]

There is another debtor more explicitly connected with Fielding in *David Copperfield*. Returning to London after a long stay in Yarmouth during which he has gone far toward capturing Little Em'ly's affections, James Steerforth goes to present David with a letter from his old nurse, but mistakenly fishes out of his breast pocket a letter bearing the address 'J. Steerforth, Esquire, debtor, to the Willing Mind' (396). More than Fielding or, for that matter,

Micawber, Steerforth possesses what Georg Simmel called 'the blasé attitude' to money: that conviction that money is the key to everything, which results in a loss of the capacity to respond to value.[44] Why he doesn't marry Little Em'ly is never directly explained, but a possible reason is implied by this letter (carelessly shrugged off). 'Such a marriage would', his mother tells Mr Peggotty, 'irretrievably blight my son's career, and ruin his prospects' (434). She may mean only to repeat her earlier protest that a fisherman's daughter is far beneath the Steerforths, but her words also suggest a financial imperative: Steerforth's indebtedness obliges him to marry wealth. His initial choice to remain on the Continent even after Emily deserts him is, among other things, the classic option of Englishmen in financial difficulty.

One of David's acts of schoolboy homage to Steerforth is to tell, at his bidding, stories taken from the little store of books left behind in Suffolk. *Tom Jones* is presumably among them. For David, its hero's captivating qualities are amply reproduced in his friend: the irresistible charm felt by almost everyone he meets (especially women), the physical daring, 'fine face', 'easy manner', not least the generosity with (other people's) money. It is certainly possible to imagine a retelling of *David Copperfield* in which James Steerforth would replace David as a more winningly Jones-like protagonist. But Steerforth is a false hero, as David would know sooner if he could relinquish his desire to make a harmless Tom Jones of him. Tom Jones himself would stoutly reject what Steerforth grows into. He is the boy who doesn't stand up for his oppressed school master but mocks his poverty; the man who refuses to marry the poor girl he has seduced and objects angrily to her telling the children on a beach in France that she was once, like them, a boatman's daughter; above all the man who all but ruins not one but three women's lives.

Steerforth's going to the bad and his death are more obviously necessary for the narrative resolution of *David Copperfield* than Mr Micawber's exile to Australia, and he reveals the less conflicted face of Dickens's wish to exclude Fieldingesque elasticity from David's mature vision. There is no let-out for him of the kind Tom is given when Molly Seagrim is revealed to be not a wronged innocent but a merry wench with more than one man enjoying her favours. Steerforth's is the overt and simplified plot of seduction that puts paid to tolerant affection and makes it possible to clarify the crime of the 'debtor to the willing mind', or the man who refuses to exert his will to the good: namely, that he takes gross advantage of his station in society. His failure to meet his social obligations will inevitably be paid for by those who can least afford to carry his debts: women, symbolically and unarguably, but also, behind them, that whole barely-imagined population of the working poor who find one representative in the unidentified writer of the letter to Steerforth, and another, more vocal but still anonymous, in the dirty-faced man edging up the Micawbers' passageway at seven o'clock of a morning and calling up the stairs 'Come! You ain't out yet, you know. Pay us, will you? Don't hide, you know; that's mean. I wouldn't be mean if I was you' (155).

*

Expelling, or attempting to expel, gentlemanly 'elasticity' from *David Copperfield*'s account of the modern writer was not just a matter of finally refusing to honour an obligation to Fielding. It also involved, more fundamentally, repudiating what Dickens identified as the eighteenth century's failure to support its writers adequately or to protect them from the overt and covert pressures of patronage. In October 1863, 14 years on from *David Copperfield*, *All the Year Round* ran an article entitled 'Literary Adventurers' which drew a self-congratulatory comparison between the previous era's treatment of its writers and the advances made in the first half of the nineteenth century:

> There was one feature of the Eighteenth Century literary world which, it is to be hoped, has gone for ever. The literary vagabond – the Grub-street man-of-all-work – the poor starveling author, dependent for his miserable bread and salt on the patron by whom he was half pitied, half despised – exists no longer in the intellectual republic. ... [Then,] a large proportion of working literary men were little better than outcasts – persons exiled from decent society, partly by their own vices, partly by the fact of their following a profession which had hardly acquired a recognised standing in the world, or found for itself a definite and indisputable sphere of usefulness. The reading public was not sufficiently large to maintain an extensive fraternity of writers; and the writers consequently often starved and broke their hearts in wretched garrets, or earned a despicable living by flattering the great.[45]

The author has not been identified, and judging from the style it is unlikely to be Dickens, but she or he was rehearsing one of Dickens's favourite themes. In a speech to the Southwark Literary and Scientific Institution in 1840, he had earned the cheers of the audience by asserting that 'Had institutions similar to this existed long since, that one disgraceful leaf of dedication which formed the blot upon the literature of past ages, would have been torn from its pages long since'.[46] The theme came back again and again in the course of his speaking career.

There are few better examples of the genre he had in mind than the dedicatory pages to Fielding's novels: addresses such as the one to George Lyttelton at the start of *Tom Jones*. There Fielding insists (ostensibly against Lyttelton's wishes) on craving his lordship's 'Protection of this Work', attributes its origin, completion and final form to Lyttelton's desires, identifies him (and Ralph Allen) as the originals of Squire Allworthy, and declares, *inter alia*, that he will 'always prefer the Indulgence of your Inclinations to the Satisfaction of my own' – before signing himself Lyttelton's 'most Obliged, Obedient Humble Servant, Henry Fielding'. Or, more subtly, the dedication page of *Amelia* in which he rhetorically abjures 'the fulsome Stile of common Dedicators' and intimates that only at Allen's death will it be possible to 'draw a just and true Character' of him 'without Incurring a Suspicion of Flattery in the Bosoms of the Malignant'.

Fielding was a master of flattery, and it is possible to read these dedications as sufficiently formalized to stand as exercises in an established genre rather than in self-abasement. He was also fully capable of dedicating a work to the patronage of a person who was, in fact, an object of satire within it, as he did in invoking Walpole's protection on *The Modern Husband*.[47] But to Dickens these necessary acts, as they then were, reeked of indignity. In his many dealings with official institutions for the promotion of literature and support of writers, the same note of anger makes itself heard against 'That huckstering, peddling, pandering to patronage for the sale of a book, the offspring of intellect and genius'.[48]

But rejecting the concept of debt to a patron did not mean refusing the notion of the writer's reliance on others altogether. At the Farewell Banquet given on his departure from the United States in 1867 Dickens looked back over the course of his professional life in more than usually emotive terms and asked approval for the way in which he had advanced 'the cause of art':

> Never unduly to assert [my calling] on the one hand, and never on any pretence or consideration, to permit it to be patronized in my person on the other, has been the steady endeavour of my life; and I have occasionally been vain enough to hope that I may leave its social position in England something better than I found it. Similarly, and equally, I hope, without presumption, I trust that I may take this general representation of the public here, through so many orders, pursuits, and degrees, as a token that the public believe, that with a host of imperfections and shortcomings upon my head, I have as a writer, in my soul and conscience, tried to be as true to them as they have ever been to me.[49]

Shot through though it is with the sentimentalism of a man who believed, rightly, that he would not see his American public face to face again, the speech is consistent with a career-long effort to reorient the eighteenth-century writer's debt to an individual patron into a much more dispersed obligation to a general 'public', which would preserve the dignity and the credit (financial and moral) of the modern writer.[50] 'To the great compact phalanx of the people', he told a Birmingham audience in 1853, 'Literature has turned happily from individual patrons, sometimes munificent, often sordid, always few, and found there its highest purpose, its natural range of action, and its best reward.'[51]

Hence his decision not to contribute to Eton College's 1847 fundraising campaign to pay for the execution of a bust of Fielding:

> I do not question the propriety of putting Fielding's Bust in Eton College – it appears a most fit and proper proceeding – but I am sorry to add I more than question the reasonableness of my subscribing money to place it there. If it were proposed to set it up in some edifice belonging to the public, and always accessible by them, I should contribute my mite, instantly. But I fear in such a case as this, I must leave the purchase to those who are, or have been, connected with the Institution.[52]

Hence also, perhaps, his choice to affix as a preface to the second volume of *Master Humphrey's Clock* famous lines from the introduction to *Tom Jones*: 'An author ... ought to consider himself, not as a gentleman who gives a private or eleemosynary treat, but rather as one who keeps a public ordinary, at which all persons are welcome for their money.'[53] Thackeray would have picked up immediately on the tacit understanding that if writing is a commercial transaction, a gentleman writer must be engaged in it by choice rather than necessity. But Dickens, characteristically, avoids the reference to the marketplace and translates Fielding's metaphor into something less witty, less urbane, more intimate: 'the host or author ... drinks to his guests in a loving cup, and bids them hearty welcome'.

There are good reasons not to take Dickens's declarations of the demise of eighteenth-century patronage in favour of public patronage at face value. There is an evident partiality and a degree of rhetorical inflation involved in the account of how eighteenth-century writers made their living. Dickens also knew, through his involvement with the Royal Literary Fund committee from 1839, and the numerous begging letters he received directly, the depths of impoverishment in which many Victorian authors were still struggling.[54] His first close involvement with the Fund dated from the year he began *David*

Copperfield, and he was quickly disillusioned enough to moot, with Bulwer-Lytton, an alternative charitable organization for writers, the Guild of Literature and Art.[55] (John Forster was a principal ally, Thackeray one of his chief opponents.) His vigorous efforts to reform the Fund itself were categorically wasted – chiefly because he and Forster were too impatient, and too sure of their success, to exercise the tact necessary to win over a majority of members. In his history of the affair, however, Nigel Cross makes a point of correcting a common misperception among 'some partisan biographers and historians' that the episode amounted to a war of 'professional middle-class writers against upper-class and aristocratic amateurs'. Dickens fully appreciated 'the value of aristocratic support': 'In 1854 the council of the Guild (its management committee) boasted a duke, an earl, a baronet and two knights, compared to the Royal Literary Fund's marquess, two baronets and one knight.'[56]

If further encouragement is needed for scepticism about how far Dickens himself had broken with aristocratic patronage, one could do worse than cite the dedication of Bulwer-Lytton's *Not So Bad as We Seem*, the play Dickens co-directed and acted in at Devonshire House before the Queen, the Duke of Wellington, and a substantial gathering of aristocrats and peers in May 1851 to raise funds for the Guild. Its dedication page to the Duke of Devonshire would be entirely in order at the front of a work by Fielding. 'The debt that we can but feebly acknowledge, may those who come after us seek to repay; and may each loftier Cultivator of Art and Letters, whom the Institution established under your auspices may shelter from care and penury, see on its corner-stone your princely name, – and perpetuate to distant times the affectionate homage it commands from ourselves.'[57] Dickens took the part of the dilettantish Lord Wilmot who matures, in the course of the play's romantic and political intriguing, into an unexpectedly serious protector of literature. Impressed by the refusal of the impoverished poet, David Fallen, to compromise his ethics, though doing so would rescue him and his children from absolute penury, Wilmot declares 'you indeed make me twofold your debtor – in your books, the rich thought; in yourself the heroic example. Accept from my superfluities, in small part of such debt, a yearly sum equal to that which your poverty refused as a bribe' (IV.ii). The lines identify a debt, but bring into being a patron. Spoken by Dickens and penned by the would-be aristocratic Bulwer-Lytton (whose name Dickens gave to the son born after Henry Fielding Dickens), they sum up the persistence of Dickens's immersion in an eighteenth-century vision of his profession, even as they assist him toward imagining a future in which writers will no longer be debtors.

*

This continuing indebtedness where he had so often energetically attempted to repudiate debt should not, however, be read as a critical rebuke to, or final scoring of points against, Dickens. The aristocratic patrons of his Guild of Literature and Art may have been necessary at the outset, but in the longer run they were incidental to rather than definitive of its aims. This was a charitable foundation, not a project that would continue to rely upon acts of patronage from the upper classes. And if Fielding can be used to reveal continuities between Dickens's view of a modern writing profession and the more 'patronizing' system which had obtained in the eighteenth century, Dickens continues to provide a historical and class perspective from which to criticize Fielding's privileged elasticities.

The persistence of Fielding within Dickens's and his contemporaries' vision, even as they registered so many of his attitudes as morally reprehensible and dated, supports Nietzsche's claim that there is a relationship between the strength of the tribe and the felt burden of obligation to the ancestor. Victorian writers were not as fully professionalized as Dickens wished to see them, but in the aggregate they were a more independent and organized social body than their eighteenth-century predecessors. One effect of that organization was a heightened level of awareness about their debt to the previous century's writers. Such tribal self-consciousness could have become merely ritualistic, in effect stalled between the contradictory impulses toward gratitude and resentment. Thinking about how much they owed of their styles, their subject matter and their literary forms to previous generations gave Victorian writers ample cause for both responses – but it also assisted their sense of being part of a process of historical change. If debt 'internalize[d] coercion', as John Vernon claims, after Nietzsche,[58] the combination of acceptance and resistance it brought with it also made possible the articulation of an ideal of autonomy within and in spite of the knowledge of obligation.

Notes

1   '*Ressentiment*' in Nietzsche's original and in Carol Diethe's new translation of the *Genealogy* for the Cambridge Texts in the History of Political Thought series. Friedrich Nietzsche, *Jenseits von Gut und Böse/Zur Genealogie der Moral*, Kritische Studienausgabe Herausgegeben von Giorgio Colli und Mazzino Montinari (Berlin: Deutscher Taschenbuch Verlag de Gruyter, 1999), 309, 373–5. *On The Genealogy of Morality*, ed. Keith Ansell-Pearson, tr. Carol Diethe (Cambridge: Cambridge University

Press, 1994), esp. 52–3. I have opted for the more standard translation of the title in the main body of this essay.

2   Nietzsche, *Genealogy*, 43, 65.

3   From this origin, Nietzsche argues, stems finally our concept of God – to whom we owe everything, whom we never can adequately repay.

4   See Weber, 'The Debts of Deconstruction and Other, Related Assumptions', in Joseph H. Smith and William Kerrigan, eds, *Taking Chances: Derrida, Psychoanalysis, and Literature* (Baltimore: John Hopkins University Press, 1984), 33–65, esp. 41 on debt as the negative condition of selfhood: 'it is both yours and not yours, part of you and that which parts with you, or rather, causes you to take leave from, and of, yourself'. See also 'Responding: A Discussion with Samuel Weber', *Culture Machine*, 1/1 (1998) (http://culturemachine.tees.ac.uk/InterZone/weber.htm) on debt and justice.

5   In the classic 1970s theories of influence, metaphors of debt are prominently employed but not analysed. See, for example, Harold Bloom's central quotation from Freud: 'When a child hears that he owes his life to his parents, that his mother gave him life, the feelings of tenderness in him mingle with the longing to be big and independent himself, so that he forms the wish to repay the parents for this gift and requite it by one of a like value. It is as though the boy said in his defiance: "I want nothing from father; I shall repay him all I have cost him."' Harold Bloom, *The Anxiety of Influence: A Theory of Poetry*, 2nd edn (Oxford: Oxford University Press, 1997), 63–4. Also Walter Jackson Bate, *The Burden of the Past and the English Poet* (Cambridge, MA: Harvard University Press, 1970), 25, quoting Dryden's tribute to Shakespeare and his contemporaries: '"We acknowledge them our fathers," but they have already spent their estates before these "came to their children's hand".'

6   The most detailed assessments of Dickens's relation to Fielding to date are Roger Robinson, 'The Influence of Fielding on *Barnaby Rudge*', *AUMLA: Journal of the Australasian Universities Language and Literature Association*, 40 (1973): 183–97, and a succinct summary discussion of the topic by Andrew Sanders in his *Dickens and the Spirit of the Age* (Oxford: Clarendon, 1999), 174–82.

7   Dickens, Letter to the Editor of *The Times*, 17 November 1849, in *The Letters of Charles Dickens*, eds Madeleine House, Graham Storey, Kathleen Tillotson et al., 12 vols (Oxford: Clarendon, 1965–2002), VI, 652.

8   See Jacques Derrida, *Specters of Marx: The State of the Debt, the Work of Mourning, and the New International*, tr. Peggy Kamuf, intro. by Bernd Magus and Stephen Cullenberg (New York: Routledge, 1994), 16. Derrida's discussion of debt here also lies behind the emphasis in what follows on the debtor/inheritor's 'call to responsibility' (16).

9   John Ruskin, *Unto this Last* (1860), *The Complete Works of John Ruskin*, E.T. Cook and Alexander Wedderburn, eds, 39 vols (London: Allen, 1903–12), XVII, 50 [34n.]. For a general overview of Victorian thinking about debt see Christina Crosby, 'Financial', in Herbert F. Tucker, ed., *A Companion to Victorian Literature and Culture* (Oxford: Blackwell, 1999), 228–34.

10 K.J. Fielding, ed., *The Speeches of Charles Dickens* (Oxford: Clarendon, 1960), 231, 304, 345.

11 Dickens, *Letters*, XII, 607–8.

12 John Forster, *The Life of Charles Dickens* (1872–74), ed. A.J. Happé, 2 vols (London: Dent, 1966), I, 8.

13 Forster, *Life*, I, 17–18; Edgar Johnson, *Charles Dickens: His Tragedy and Triumph*, 2 vols (Boston: Little, Brown, 1952), I, 99; and Peter Ackroyd, *Dickens* (London: Sinclair-Stevenson, 1990), 66.

14   George Henry Lewes, 'Dickens in Relation to Criticism', *Fortnightly Review*, 17 (1872): 141–54. Quoted in Philip Collins, ed., *Dickens: Interviews and Recollections*, 2 vols (Houndmills: Macmillan, 1981), I, 25–6.

15   *David Copperfield* (1849-50), intro. and notes by Jeremy Tambling (Harmondsworth: Penguin, 1996), 59–60; and see Forster, *Life*, I, 7–8.

16   He ranked *Peregrine Pickle* above *Tom Jones*. See J.T. Fields, *Yesterdays and Authors* (1872) and 'Conversations in 1860' (author unknown), both rpt in Collins, ed., *Dickens: Interviews and Recollections*, II, 290, 314.

17   R.H. Hutton, though deprecating the indelicacy of Dickens's higher morality, drew out the comparison Dickens would have wanted with Fielding in an 1869 essay on 'Mr Dickens's Moral Services to Literature': 'His greatest service to English literature will, after all, be … in the complete harmlessness and purity of the immeasurable humour …. Almost all creative humourists tend to the impure – like Swift and Smollett, and even Fielding.' In Collins, ed., *Critical Heritage*, 491.

18   William Makepeace Thackeray, 'Hogarth, Smollett, and Fielding', in *The English Humourists of the Eighteenth Century* (1853), *Thackeray's Works*, 26 vols (London: Smith, Elder, 1911), XI, 300–4. Thackeray took the essentials of his portrait from Murphy, including the term 'manly'. See Murphy, 'Essay', 15.

19   For Murphy on Fielding's dissipation and indebtedness, see *The Works of Henry Fielding, Esq., with an Essay on His Life and Genius*, ed. Alexander Chalmers, 10 vols (London: Johnson et al., 1806), I, 9–12, 44–6, 64, 79–83.

20   See Martin C. Battestin, with Ruthe R. Battestin, *Henry Fielding: A Life* (London: Routledge, 1989), esp. 270, 295–6.

21   'Introductory Anecdotes', in Lord Wharncliffe, ed., *The Letters and Works of Lady Mary Wortley Montagu*, rev. by W. Moy Thomas, 2 vols (London: Bickers, 1861); quoted in Battestin, *Henry Fielding*, 540. Dickens owned the 1837 edition. He would also have known the essentials of Fielding's chronic indebtedness from Arthur Murphy's *Life*. Murphy does not explicitly mention the sponging house, but makes much of Fielding's persistent 'difficulties' and the 'eagerness of creditors'. See Murphy, 'Essay', 15, 19, 30.

22   *Joseph Andrews, with Shamela and Related Writings*, ed. Homer Goldberg (New York: Norton, 1987), 261.

23   *The Posthumous Papers of the Pickwick Club* (1836–37), ed. Mark Wormald (Harmondsworth: Penguin, 1999), 301–3.

24   Fielding's translation and adaptation of Molière's *L'Avare* (1732/3). It is likely that Dickens saw *The Miser* performed at the Strand on 6 February 1850 (see *Letters*, VI, 31n.), and possible that he saw the production at Sadlers Wells in March 1854.

25   *The History of the Life of the late Mr. Jonathan Wild the Great*, in *Miscellanies by Henry Fielding, Esq*, Vol. III, intro. and commentary by Bertrand A. Goldgar, text edited by Hugh Amory (Oxford: Clarendon, 1997), 108.

26   Other direct parallels between this novel and Fielding's work include the mock-heroic opening to *Pickwick Papers*, ch. 2. See John Lucas, *The Melancholy Man: A Study of Dickens's Novels* (Brighton: Harvester, 1980), 16. The incarceration of Pickwick in the Fleet prison recalls Billy Booth's incarceration in *Jonathan Wild*, but is more heavily indebted to Smollett's *Roderick Random*.

27   I am assuming, with Battestin, that though *Jonathan Wild* was probably first drafted in 1737, it was rewritten to a significant degree in 1742. *Pamela* appeared in 1740.

28   See also Lynda Mugglestone's discussion of this letter as a prototype of the novel's representation of the illiterate speaker, with particular attention to 'the inception of those

traditions of <h> usage which were later to become so dominant in fictional form'. *Talking Proper: The Rise of Accent as Social Symbol* (Oxford: Clarendon, 1995), 138–9.

29   *The Dramatick Sessions: or, The Stage Contest* (1734), quoted in Battestin, *Henry Fielding*, 146.

30   See Battestin, *Henry Fielding*, 10–13, 270, 296–301, 628 (nn. 49 and 50).

31   *The Covent-Garden Journal*, 56, 25 July 1752, in Henry Fielding, *The Covent-Garden Journal and A Plan of the Universal Register-Office*, ed. Bertrand A. Goldgar (Oxford: Clarendon, 1988), 306.

32   (III.xiv), quoted in Battestin, *Henry Fielding*, 146.

33   This was the first novelist's name in a long roll call of literary names given to all but the first of the Dickens boys. The others, by 1849, were Walter Landor Dickens, Francis Jeffrey Dickens, Alfred Tennyson Dickens, and Sydney Smith Haldimand Dickens.

34   Forster, *Life*, II, 77.

35   Forster, *Life*, I, 7. See also II, 98.

36   See Robinson, 'Influence of Fielding on *Barnaby Rudge*'.

37   Henry Fielding, *The History of Tom Jones, A Foundling*, 2 vols, with an introduction and commentary by Martin C. Battestin, text edited by Fredson Bowers (Oxford: Oxford University Press, 1975), Bk VI, ch. 12 (I, 314).

38   See John Vernon, *Money and Fiction: Literary Realism in the Nineteenth and Early Twentieth Centuries* (Ithaca: Cornell University Press, 1984), 15.

39   It ceased to perform that function when the law was changed to prevent imprisonment for debt in 1869.

40   *Uneven Developments: The Ideological Work of Gender in Mid-Victorian England* (Chicago: University of Chicago Press, 1988), 103. On Dickens's concern with money, and its relation to his childhood experience of debt, see Ackroyd, *Dickens*, 843, 411. On his financial dealings with publishers and contributors to his periodicals see esp. Lillian Nayder, *Unequal Partners: Charles Dickens, Wilkie Collins, and Victorian Authorship* (Ithaca: Cornell University Press, 2002), ch. 1.

41   The letter notified him that the ninth Dickens child had not yet arrived. See Forster, *Life*, II, 91. (Also *Letters*, VI, 148.)

42   Dickens, Letter to *The Times*, 17 November 1849. He was then in the process of writing chs 22–4. See John Butt, 'The Composition of *David Copperfield*', *Dickensian*, 46 (1950): 90–94, 128–35, 176–80 and 47 (1951): 33–8 [46 (1950): 133].

43   There is another essay to be written on the close parallels between some aspects of Fielding's legal and social-reformist writings and Dickens's fiction and journalism. There are, for example, strong similarities of attitude between the *Treatise on the Office of Constable* (1761) and Dickens's views on the police and detective forces of Victorian London. On the other hand, Dickens would have found much of Fielding's *Proposal for Making an Effectual Provision for the Poor* (1753) repugnant.

44   Georg Simmel, *The Philosophy of Money*, tr. Tom Bottomore and David Frisby from a first draft by Kaethe Mengelberg (Boston: Routledge and Kegan Paul, 1978), 256–7.

45   *All the Year Round*, 10 October 1863, 153–6. Author unidentified.

46   Fielding, ed., *Speeches of Charles Dickens*, 5.

47   Battestin, *Henry Fielding*, 101, 128. He also wrote a number of humorous begging epistles to Walpole from 1730, angling 'however facetiously' for a sinecure. See 79.

48   Fielding, ed., *Speeches of Charles Dickens*, 5. See also p. 213 for the speech to the Royal Literary Fund Annual General Meeting, 12 March 1856.

49   Fielding, ed., *Speeches of Charles Dickens*, 371.

50   See my '"A Pulse of 124": Charles Dickens and a Pathology of the Nineteenth-century Reading Public', in James Raven, Helen Small, and Naomi Tadmor, eds, *The Practice and Representation of Reading in England* (Cambridge: Cambridge University Press, 1996), 263–90.

51   Fielding, ed., *Speeches of Charles Dickens*, 156.

52   Dickens, *Letters*, XII, 608.

53   Rpt. in Charles Dickens, *The Old Curiosity Shop* (1840–41), ed. Norman Page (Harmondsworth: Penguin, 2000), 5. Quoting *Tom Jones*, Bk I, ch. 1 (I, 31).

54   Nigel Cross, *The Common Writer: Life in Nineteenth-Century Grub Street* (Cambridge: Cambridge University Press, 1985), 31. See also K.J. Fielding, 'Dickens and the Royal Literary Fund – 1858', *Review of English Studies*, n.s. 6 (1955): 383–94.

55   See Cross, *The Common Writer*, 32.

56   Cross, *The Common Writer*, 35.

57   *The Dramatic Works by the Right Hon. Lord Lytton*, 2 vols (London: Routledge, 1876), I, 288. And see Daniel Hack, 'Literary Paupers and Professional Authors: The Guild of Literature and Art', *Studies in English Literature*, 39/4 (1999): 691–713, which discusses Dickens's aversion to the financial indebtedness implied by charitable relief for writers and discusses the contradictions inherent in the representation of patronage both in the formation of the Guild and in *Not So Bad as We Seem*.

58   *Money and Fiction*, 116.

Chapter 2

George Eliot, Rousseau, and the Discipline of Natural Consequences

Simon Dentith

In a notorious anecdote recounted in Book 2 of *Émile* (1762), Rousseau takes it upon himself to correct the caprices of a spoilt boy. The child wishes to go for a walk in town irrespective of the wishes of others, among them Rousseau himself, who has taken responsibility for him. He is allowed out by himself, but in the streets he is met by the hostile comments of the passers-by, and is indeed followed by a stranger, who, while not terrifying the child, does at last lead him back 'ashamed and humble' to his father's house. There he meets his father on the stairs who suitably reprimands him. The point of this anecdote is that it demonstrates to the child, without the need of lectures, and without the necessity of direct orders, the consequences and dangers of self-will. The only difficulty, however, is that this is all a massive contrivance; the servants of the household have been warned not to accompany him; the neighbours are primed to be ready with suitable remarks; even the stranger is a friend of Rousseau's who is acting a role – he does so, according to the author, 'to perfection'. In short, in order to demonstrate the 'natural' consequences of capricious, self-willed, or tyrannical behaviour, Rousseau has to arrange a complicated and ingenious fiction, and have it acted out by all who come into contact with the child.[1]

More than 100 years after the publication of *Émile*, one of nineteenth-century England's most fervent admirers of Rousseau, George Eliot, published another account of the moral education of a spoilt child. In *Daniel Deronda* (1876), Gwendolen Harleth is made to realize the consequences of her own actions by a series of fictional contrivances rather more elaborate than those that surround the young tyrant in Rousseau's anecdote. She gets her own way in the matter of her marriage, only to find that she is confronted by a power of egoism very much greater than her own. Most chillingly, she gets to see her murderous wishes with respect to her husband acted out in front of her. It is not surprising that she concludes by saying that 'everything has been a punishment to me – all the things I used to wish for – it is as if they had been made red hot'.[2] Like the child in Rousseau's tale, she has been made tractable by seeing the consequences of her own self-will redound on herself, but these too are consequences that can only be created by the power of fiction.

The resemblance, it may be felt, is too general to be proof of direct 'influence'. However, there is a tradition of educational thought that descends from the eighteenth century in which the paradox of contriving natural consequences repeatedly reappears; Rousseau is at the head of that tradition and George Eliot is at its tail. One way of understanding her relationship to her eighteenth-century forebear – it will be the way of this essay – is by placing it in the context of the many continuities and transformations of Rousseau's educational inheritance over the hundred years that separate the two writers.

There is, nevertheless, more to be said about the direct influence of Rousseau on George Eliot, in addition to the scholarly work that already exists in this area.[3] Her admiration for Rousseau is well known. At the beginning of her intellectual life, the *Confessions*, she revealed, was the first book to have 'wakened her to deep reflection'; as she further wrote to her Coventry friend Sara Hennell, 'Rousseau's genius has sent that electric thrill through my intellectual and moral frame which has awakened me to new perceptions, which has made man and nature a fresh world of thought and feeling to me'.[4]

At the end of her life, on her honeymoon trip with John Cross, she made a pilgrimage to Chambéry (a journey she had already made with Lewes) and there reread, aloud, *Émile* and *La Nouvelle Héloïse*. It is nevertheless hard to describe her as a 'Rousseauvian'; the nature of his influence is rather too nebulous for that. In that same letter to Sara Hennell, she permitted herself an expression that perhaps allows subsequent critics too great a latitude of interpretation: 'it would signify nothing to me if a very wise person were to stun me with proofs that Rousseau's views of life, religion, and government are miserably erroneous – that he was guilty of some of the worse *bassesses* that have degraded civilised man'.[5] It would still remain true that he was the first to send that 'electrifying thrill'. So we should not be looking for specific doctrinal or artistic influence, in the way that characterizes much of the criticism of her writing which places it in the context of nineteenth-century (or earlier) thought.

Where such an effort has been made, however, the result has been to detach George Eliot's Rousseau from the eighteenth century of the Enlightenment and the *philosophes*, and make him over as a proto-Romantic. In this, modern criticism has done no more than follow a powerful impetus of the nineteenth-century inheritors of Romanticism themselves. The *locus classicus* of this kind of argument is to be found in Carlyle's essay on Rousseau (he accompanies Johnson and Burns) in *On Heroes and Hero-Worship* (1841). The 'hero as man of letters' can only achieve heroic status by opposing rather than following the spirit of the age; Rousseau, born into the deeply antipathetic and unheroic eighteenth century, proves his heroism by bitter struggles against the negativity of the period in which he finds himself. In line with this already-existent view of Jean-Jacques, he can appear, for Eliot, as the dreamy proto-Wordsworth who drifts on the lake of Geneva, and can reappear in *Daniel Deronda* as Deronda himself, drifting in his boat on the Thames before the encounter with Mirah rouses him to defining moral and eventually political action. To follow this view is to recognize the influence of an eighteenth-century figure on Eliot only to deny it; he can be allowed to act on her only by denying that he is properly to be thought of as a critical or analytical thinker at all.

This view at least needs to be bolstered, and inevitably complicated, by a consideration of the mediating influence of Comte, whose attitude to the *philosophes* was at least as hostile as Carlyle, but perhaps more dialectical. For Comte, Rousseau was the most extreme of the negative thinkers of the eighteenth century; in the famous progression of phases through which mankind had to pass before reaching the Positive, state now imminent, the eighteenth century was dominated in philosophy by the Negative or Metaphysical state, whose task was to complete the critique of the Theological state which preceded it. In this view, Rousseau's achievement was to give the 'critical' system of government the colouring and warmth of the passions; but his system was fundamentally anarchic, and gave birth to the anarchic utopias of the nineteenth century. In this he was even more extreme than the school of Voltaire, which at least recognized some of the dangers of its own negative critique. But Rousseau's anarchism consists in his denial of society:

> The school of Rousseau ... pushes, in this respect, the backward spirit to its most extravagant delirium, by this wild utopia where a brutal isolation was directly proposed as a model for the social state.[6]

Similarly to Carlyle, then, Comte sees the eighteenth century as a 'negative' period, but Rousseau is not exempted from this criticism; the best that can be said for this whole phase of human history is that it was a necessary clearing of the ground so that the positive social state can be founded on the positive truths of science rather than the illusions of religion.

Comte was still more critical of Rousseau's *Confessions*, the text that had, by her own account, first initiated the young George Eliot into the possibilities of writing:

> No less severe a judgment must certainly be applied to this pernicious work, scandalous parody of an immortal Christian composition, where, in the delirium of an artificial self-regard, Rousseau, revealing, with a cynical willingness, the most ignoble basenesses of his private life, nevertheless dares directly to erect the whole of his conduct as a moral type of humanity ... Rousseau, applying specious arguments to the systematic justification of the most blamably wild behaviour, tended without doubt to pervert, to the highest degree, the simplest moral notions: thus it is particularly thanks to his inspiration, direct or indirect, that can be seen nowadays so many doctoral consecrations, personal or collective, of the most brutal preponderance of the passions over reason.[7]

No wonder that George Eliot felt obliged to concede that she would continue to admire Rousseau *despite* local refutations of his arguments or indeed of his whole attitude to life. Indeed, Comte's use of *bassesses* here ('basenesses') suggests that *he* is the 'very wise person' referred to in her letter to Sara Hennell as convicting Rousseau of miserably erroneous views. At all events, insofar as Eliot was a Positivist, Rousseau came to her stigmatized as the most extreme of the negative thinkers of the eighteenth century, defensible perhaps as a necessary evil, but whose moral influence was wholly pernicious. And if she wished to rescue him from this attack by arguing for its incompleteness, there was Carlyle to hand to propose him as only admirable to the extent that he escaped or combated the influence of the Enlightenment for which Comte condemned him.

Both of these possibilities overestimate the extent to which George Eliot should be thought of as an heir to Romanticism, and discount the continuities between her and that very 'critical' or 'negative' phase of eighteenth-century thought which is the target of Comte's critique. My contention is that these continuities are most visible in the sphere of educational thought; but our notions of intellectual history have surely evolved beyond that notion of the succession of 'stages' which descends to us from both thinkers like Comte and indeed the Enlightenment thinkers from whom he himself drew. We need to qualify (or perhaps even to repudiate) such notions by considering the various groups or cultural fractions by which intellectual positions get transformed and transmitted. Rousseau travelled into the nineteenth century strongly marked by the company he had kept in the eighteenth.

Brian Simon's *Studies in the History of Education* (1960), an archetypal statement of the 'progressive' history of educational thought, still provides a compelling account of one such cultural fraction through which Rousseau passed – the Lunar Society, and the related group around the Manchester 'Literary and Philosophical Society' in the late eighteenth century.[8] The Lunar Society included both Thomas Day, author of the highly Rousseauvian *Sandford and Merton* (1783–89), and Richard Edgeworth, author, with his daughter Maria, of *Practical Education* (1798). The tragi-comedy of Maria's elder brother, Richard, educated on Rousseauvian principles with mixed success, is well known. Here is Edgeworth's own account of the result of the experiment:

> [He possessed] uncommon strength and hardiness of body, great vivacity, and was not a little disposed to think and act for himself ... Whatever regarded the health, strength, and agility of my son, had amply justified the system of my master; but I found myself entangled in difficulties with regard to my child's mind and temper. He was generous, brave, good-natured, and what is commonly called good-tempered; but he was scarcely to be controlled. It was difficult to urge him to anything that did not suit his fancy, and more difficult to restrain him from what he wished to follow. In short, he was self-willed, from a spirit of independence which had been inculcated by his early education, and which he cherished the more from the inexperience of his own powers.[9]

Certainly this was one factor leading to the Edgeworths' retreat from out-and-out Rosseauvism in *Practical Education*, and the chapters in the book on 'Obedience' and moral education more generally represent, if not an outright rejection of the master's principles, at least a very considerable modification of them. The Edgeworths single out for criticism the very anecdote with which I began this essay; it is absurd, they maintain, to seek to deceive children in this way both because children will discover the pretence and because it is better to admit that at times children simply have to obey their elders. So their system of education is 'practical' insofar as it retains many Rousseauvian doctrines especially with respect to learning by practical experiment, but it concedes that children cannot be taught tractability or indeed obedience by relying on the operation of natural causes to demonstrate to them the consequences of their actions. In so many words:

> Rousseau advises, that children should be governed solely by the necessity of circumstances, but there are *one and twenty* excellent objections to this system, the first being that it is impossible: of this Rousseau must have been sensible in the trials which he made as a preceptor.[10]

Both the desirability and the insufficiency of natural consequences to act as moral educators form an inevitable part of reflections on Rousseau's legacy.

Simon is surely right, however, to point to wider influences acting on this group of progressive middle-class intellectuals leading them, in the 1790s, to a retreat from the whole-hearted advocacy of revolutionary principles. Let us simply call these factors 'reaction', and recall the burning down of Joseph Priestley's house and laboratory in Birmingham by a Church and King mob in 1791. At all events, and in however modified a form, Rousseau came to the nineteenth century marked by this association with a powerful and self-confident cultural fraction, engaged in a partial repudiation of its earlier intellectual commitments.

Sharing some connections with this group, but more committed to the Revolution and therefore still more vulnerable in the 1790s, was the intellectual grouping gathered around Mary Wollstonecraft and William Godwin. For Wollstonecraft in particular, Rousseau was both an important and a deeply problematic figure, in view of his rebarbative ideas on the education of women; the larger part of chapter 5 of the *Vindication*, 'Animadversions on Some of the Writers Who Have Rendered Women Objects of Pity, Bordering on Contempt', is devoted to angry quotation from, and expostulation with, *Émile*. Rousseau's principal mistake, in this account, is his abandonment of reason with respect to women's education; inflamed by his own sensibility to their charms, he bases his notions of their upbringing on the idea that they are made by nature to charm and please men. Thus, in attempting to extend the revolutionary principles of 1789 to the liberation of women, Wollstonecraft inevitably confronted Rousseau, and turned him, so to speak, against himself.

In this respect, Wollstonecraft can be compared with Maria Edgeworth, who also found Rousseau's ideas on women's education unsatisfactory. Edgeworth objected to the dishonesty and the coquetry which Rousseau advocated as necessary and indeed natural attributes of women; as the enlightened gentleman in *Letters for Literary Ladies* remarks of his daughter, 'I dread that she should acquire, even from the enchanting eloquence of Rousseau, the fatal idea, that cunning and address are the natural resources of her sex; that coquetry is necessary to attract, and dissimulation to preserve the heart of man'.[11] It is true that Edgeworth and Wollstonecraft draw different conclusions from their disagreements with Rousseau; for the former, education for women will better fit them to be rational companions of their husbands, while for the latter, it will contribute to their moral and social independence (and their ability to educate their children). However, in the light of both their complex responses, and indeed of the whole debate about the rights of women and women's education conducted in these cultural fractions at the end of the eighteenth century, Rousseau came down to George Eliot's generation transformed by these fundamental disagreements on the subject of gender.

What are the 'vectors', to use E.P. Thompson's word, which transmit the ideas of these cultural fractions forward into the nineteenth century?[12] Though it is certainly possible to exaggerate its importance, one such vector must surely be that of Rational Dissent, and above all Unitarianism, which acted as a kind of cultural vanguard for the middle class in many a provincial town in the first half of the nineteenth century. George Eliot's own intellectual formation effectively occurred in one such group, which gathered around the Brays and the Hennells in Coventry in the 1830s and 1840s. It is unnecessary to rehearse here the importance of this group for Eliot; through it she was led both to necessitarian social philosophy and a critique of traditional religion.[13] It was thanks to them that she could make the progression from provincial to metropolitan intellectual; her effective editorship of the *Westminster Review* in the early 1850s, through John Chapman, only happened because the group around Chapman and the *Westminster* was a kind of metropolitan equivalent to the Coventry group, with its roots also in Rational Dissent. For this whole cultural fraction, though of course internally differentiated and with differing intellectual affiliations, the Enlightenment was never eclipsed by Romanticism, for they continued the work of the *philosophes* well into the nineteenth century.

If this was true of these middle-class social and intellectual communities, it was still more true of working-class groups, happily nourished by eighteenth-century rationalism and scepticism throughout the succeeding century.[14] George Eliot's own contact with working-class self-education was small, though one such group does appear in *Daniel Deronda* at the *Hand and Banner*, where Mordecai's brand of idealism is eventually allowed to dominate the discussion. Nevertheless, if we place her in the context of the Bray-Hennell circle in Coventry, and the Chapman-*Westminster* group in London, she begins to appear less as the inheritor of Wordsworth and the Romantics, and more a child of the Enlightenment. She may have been a *religious* atheist, but she was an *atheist* all the same.

And it is through another section of provincial Dissent that George Eliot would have come into contact with explicitly progressive educational thinking in the 1850s, namely through the writings of Herbert Spencer, son of a Baptist Minister and himself now a prominent figure in the *Westminster* group. Spencer's various essays on education were published in several journals (including the *Westminster* itself) in the 1850s, and together in a single volume in the early 1860s. Though, as we shall see, Spencer directly reproduces the Rousseauvian problematic of education by natural consequences, Rousseau does not himself appear by name in the essays; rather, Spencer refers back regularly to Jean-Jacques' Swiss disciple Pestalozzi. So here is another line of descent: Rousseau; Pestalozzi; Spencer. The transformation wrought by this lineage is that Rousseau's method becomes overwhelmingly one for the teaching of Science, and that moral education in turn gets modelled on scientific education.

William Myers describes Spencer's educational theory as governed by a 'fine principle of pedagogic *laissez-faire*', and it is undoubtedly based in part on the operations of consumer demand.[15] However, Rousseau, via Pestalozzi, is also visibly present. So education should begin at birth, and should not be confined to the system of formal schooling. It should be based on the study of things, and not books; and it should start from empirical education and move to general principles. Parents (mothers especially) are remarkably ignorant of how to bring up children:

> She has not the remotest idea that in the nursery, as in the world, that alone is the truly salutary discipline which visits on all conduct, good and bad, the natural consequences – the consequences, pleasurable or painful, which in the nature of things such conduct tends to bring.[16]

This is taken from the essay on 'What Knowledge is Most Worth'; it can be readily seen how an emphasis on 'natural consequences' can become the basis of an argument for the primary importance of scientific education. In this respect, Spencer shows himself to be a fine advocate for learning by discovery, emphasizing not only the practical benefits of such learning, but also the pleasure that accompanies it:

> It has repeatedly occurred that those who have been stupefied by the ordinary school-drill – by its abstract formulas, its wearisome tasks, its cramming – have suddenly had their intellects roused by thus ceasing to make them passive recipients, and inducing them to become active discoverers.[17]

Spencer almost echoes the liberal idealism of John Stuart Mill in his celebration of joyful and pleasurable self-discovery, as when Mill writes in *On Liberty* that 'the mental and moral, like the muscular powers, are improved only by being used. The faculties are called into no exercise by doing a thing merely because others do it, no more than by believing a thing only because others believe it.'[18] Brains, like muscles, get stronger the more they act for themselves.

Of course, the lessons that Nature teaches to Spencer's children are not identical to those taught to Rousseau's. Above all, there is a developmental or evolutionary aspect to Spencer's thought which is absent from Rousseau, so that by allowing the discipline of natural consequences to act on the development of the child, one is contributing to the development of the race. And there is no question of the child being perceived as in any sense naturally good; on the contrary, the moral education of the child must repeat in miniature the development of humanity:

> Do not expect from a child any great amount of moral goodness. During early years every civilised man passes through that phase of character exhibited by the barbarous race from which he is descended. As the child's features – flat nose, forward-opening nostrils, large lips, wide-apart eyes, absent frontal sinus etc. – resemble for a time those of the savage, so, too, do his instincts. Hence the tendencies to cruelty, to thieving, to lying, so general among children – tendencies which, even without the aid of discipline, will become more or less modified just as the features do.[19]

This is a conception of the education of children which is entirely absent from Rousseau. However, this evolutionary discipline is achieved by reproducing the methods of Nature, so that Spencer's seven educational principles are designed to act in 'increasing conformity' to these methods. In addition to such assertions, derived via Pestalozzi from Rousseau, that education should proceed from the simple to the complex, and that the development of the mind is from the indefinite to the definite, Spencer can also assert that 'the education of the child must accord both in mode and arrangement with the education of mankind, considered historically' (60).

How to assure such accordance, however? The paradox, bequeathed by Rousseau, of the arranged accordance with a natural process, reappears in Spencer:

> Is it not manifest that as 'ministers and interpreters of Nature' it is the function of parents to see that their children habitually experience the true consequences of their conduct – the natural reactions: neither warding them off, nor intensifying them, nor putting artificial consequences in place of them? No unprejudiced reader will hesitate in his assent.[20]

Elsewhere, he writes of the necessity of 'systematising' the natural process (67). In short, parental or adult intervention in the education of children should be aimed at ordering what should occur naturally, making these natural

50 *The Victorians and the Eighteenth Century*

consequences apparent, and refraining from substituting artificial consequences for them. Parents have to stage the processes of nature.

In addition, then, to her own direct and extensive reading of Rousseau, George Eliot was the inheritor of a complex and charged process of intellectual descent. As the product of a forward-looking intellectual fraction, both provincial and metropolitan, she would have found Rousseau a deeply ambiguous figure, marked by his transition through her late eighteenth-century Enlightenment forebears, and especially problematic with respect to the question of gender. As a willing Positivist and careful reader of Comte, she found him anathematized as the *ne plus ultra* of the Negative or Metaphysical spirit – a judgement that could readily be aligned with a more general post-Romantic condemnation of the eighteenth century. Rousseau himself, however, was apparently rescuable from this aversion by seeing him as a kind of proto-Wordsworthian lover of Nature. And in the writings of her friend and associate Herbert Spencer, she encountered Rousseau, modified by the intermediate influence of Pestalozzi, in the guise of progressive educational theory: learning by discovery, and moral education by the discipline of natural consequences. The stories of Maggie and Tom Tulliver and of Gwendolen Harleth will be the fruits of this inheritance.

*

One way of understanding the education of Tom and Maggie in *The Mill on the Floss* (1860) is, as William Myers suggests, as a kind of educational *laissez-faire*, in which the children's education is criticized for its failure to allow them to follow their own bents. Thus Tom is clearly a natural engineer or scientist, capable of estimating distances and calculating nicely the physical consequences of his actions. Maggie, meanwhile, has a natural aptitude for books and languages. Both are frustrated in their formal education; Tom is humiliated by being forced to learn Latin, while Maggie is prevented largely because of her sex from pursuing the study for which she is evidently better inclined than Tom. The influence of Spencer is readily visible in these characterizations and their accompanying narratives.

However, behind Spencer can be seen the figures of Rousseau and Pestalozzi, and their influence is most apparent in Tom's educational progress. He is, in effect, an illustration of all those evils against which Rousseau warned – failure to attend to the physical world, inappropriate attention to words rather than things, premature reliance on books before an understanding has been gained of the world to which they refer. These Rousseauvian themes are of course complicated by the success with which George Eliot immerses this narrative in the social world of St Oggs; the Revd Stelling's failure to provide any adequate training in mensuration and accounting, as Mr Tulliver wants, is presented as a particular class-based blindness to the needs of a commercial education. Despite the density of this represented social world, Eliot is aware of the danger of the narrative of Tom's education being perceived as too nakedly illustrative:

> Nevertheless, there was a visible improvement in Tom under this training; perhaps because he was not a boy in the abstract existing solely to illustrate the evils of a mistaken education, but a boy made of flesh and blood, with dispositions not entirely at the mercy of circumstances.[21]

The fabric of the fiction becomes dangerously visible here as the emblematic nature of Tom's education is acknowledged.

Maggie's education, by contrast, can be seen as a critique of Rousseauvian assumptions, across a range of matters. She demonstrates unequivocally the educational value of books – there is no suggestion at all in the novel that her early interest and subsequent immersion in book-learning is at all detrimental to her – indeed, when, in a fit of excessive self-mortification, she refuses to contemplate the wider horizons made visible to her by her reading, Philip is allowed to rebuke her appropriately. Secondly, her unequivocal right to education, of the most demanding kind, directly contradicts Rousseau's views on the education of women; it is tempting to see here the significance of the intervening writing of Mary Wollstonecraft. And finally, her moral education proceeds, in the first instance, from her reading of Thomas à Kempis; the spiritual world of medieval Catholicism is invoked here, in good Positivist fashion, rather than the critical spirit of the eighteenth century.

For all that, it can still be said that the moral education that the novel enacts proceeds by natural consequences, and that in educating Tom and Maggie, the world is effecting an advance in the moral education of the race – or at least, that part of it which inhabits the vicinity of the Floss. In *The Mill on the Floss*, in other words, George Eliot is confident of the connection between the processes of individual education (partly Rousseauvian) and the progressive evolution of society. While the discipline of natural consequences is more visible in the education of Gwendolen Harleth, it is also true that *Daniel Deronda* as a whole is less optimistic than the earlier novel that the moral education of the individual will lead to the elevation of society, insofar as society means the particular social order of mid-nineteenth-century England.

The task that Eliot sets herself in recounting the story of Gwendolen is to demonstrate how a spoilt child can be led to understand the insufficiency of a life based solely on the gratification of personal desires. In this task Deronda takes on the role of Rousseauvian preceptor, making explicit to his pupil what she might not otherwise recognize as the consequences of her own actions. Eliot also has to account for why Gwendolen is spoilt, and in doing so she makes use of a metaphor which has its own history. Gwendolen, we are told, is 'a princess in exile'; later in the same paragraph, she is a 'queen in exile' (32). The metaphor makes visible an important aspect of Rousseauvian education: that it is in effect a kind of democratic training, which demonstrates to all irrespective of their station in life that they are subject to the same physical and moral laws.

This aspect of Rousseau's inheritance is perhaps most visible in yet another intermediary between the eighteenth century and George Eliot; namely the educational thinking of the Utilitarians and especially James Mill. Indeed, the intellectual descent which leads from the *philosophes* through to Bentham and Mill is an especially important and uninterrupted indication of the continuities between the eighteenth and nineteenth centuries. James Mill looked more to Helvetius than to Rousseau; nevertheless, his theory of education, based on the 'laws' of associationism, made him reproduce exactly the paradox of arranged natural circumstances. Trains of ideas must be induced in children which lead them to associate their own happiness with the happiness of others, and their own misery with the misery of others. 'The business of a skilful education is, so to arrange the circumstances by which the child is surrounded, that the impressions made on him shall be in the order most conducive to this happy result.'[22] Failure to do so will result in spoiling:

> The child, while it yet hangs at the breast, is often allowed to find out by experience, that crying, and the annoyance which it gives, is that by which chiefly it can command the services of its nurse, and obtain the pleasure which it desires. There is not one child in fifty, who has not learned to make its cries and wailings an instrument of absolute tyranny. When the evil grows to excess, the vulgar say the child is spoiled. Not only is the child allowed to exert an influence over the wills of others, by means of their pains; it finds, that frequently, sometimes most frequently, its own will is needlessly and unduly commanded by the same means, pain, and the fear of pain. All these sensations concur in establishing a firm association between the idea of the grand object of desire, and the idea of pain and terror, as the means of acquiring it. That those who have been subject to tyranny, are almost always desirous of being tyrants in their turn; that is to say, that a strong association has been

formed in their minds, between the ideas of pleasure and dignity, on the one hand, and those of the exercise of tyranny, on the other, is a matter of old and invariable observation.[23]

This may appear to be the opposite of Rousseau's educational philosophy, which is more famous for encouraging children in their self-will than in discouraging it. But in fact Mill is working within the same problematic, by which the responses which are given to children's demands can be instrumental in their moral training. The use of a political vocabulary here is not therefore accidental; the moral education of all children is necessary to stop them developing into tyrants. A spoilt child makes a spoilt citizen and potentially a tyrant; for all the worrying behaviourist implications of Mill's associationist educational theory, it is still an education designed for the training of democratic citizens.

Gwendolen's story also should be understood in terms of this problematic. The most extensive discussion of the roots of her spoiling occurs at the end of chapter 4 in Book One, 'The Spoiled Child'. Eliot canvasses the idea that her behaviour as a princess in exile is sufficiently accounted for by her beauty and her charm, which win her a sort of pre-eminence. In addition is the behaviour towards her of her mother:

> This potent charm, added to the fact that she was the eldest daughter, towards whom her mamma had always been in an apologetic state of mind for the evils brought on her by a step-father, may seem so full a reason for Gwendolen's domestic empire, that to look for any other would be to ask the reason of daylight when the sun is shining (32).

However, these explanations are clearly insufficient, though they are allowed to stand in part by being suggested so forcefully. Eliot particularly wishes to make it clear that it is not because she is a young woman that Gwendolen has come to be spoiled. Domestic tyrants are more characteristically male:

> I remember having seen the same assiduous, apologetic attention awarded to persons who were not at all beautiful or unusual, whose firmness showed itself in no very graceful or euphonious way, and who were not eldest daughters with a tender, timid mother, compunctious at having subjected them to inconveniences. Some of them were a very common sort of men. And the only point of resemblance among them all was a strong determination to have what was pleasant, with a total fearlessness in making themselves disagreeable or dangerous when they did not get it. Who is so much cajoled and served with trembling fear by weak females of a household as the unscrupulous

male – capable, if he has not free way at home, of going and doing worse
elsewhere? (32–3)

Eliot is naturally leaving her possibilities open at this early stage of the book;
while providing a plausible account of the specificity of Gwendolen's spoiling,
she nevertheless advances a more general explanation which grounds it in a
more general egoism. However, she *has* been spoiled, and that leads Eliot to
describe her in a vocabulary reminiscent of Mill's – she is a 'queen in exile',
who is exercising her 'domestic empire' over those who surround her. Rather
later in life than either Rousseau or Mill would have liked, her imperiousness
will have to be cured by arranging for her to be subjected to the discipline of
natural consequences.

And this indeed is what the narrative of the novel achieves. Gwendolen is
taught to recognize that to act in a way in which one's own gain is another's
loss brings its own consequences of misery. It is important that this should
occur as a result of plot alone; Deronda's role is to make these consequences
explicit, and not to intervene directly in the sequence of events other than in
the opening incident of the novel when he rescues her from the consequences
of her gambling by redeeming the necklace she has been forced to pawn.
Thus in one of the many colloquies between the two about the nature of
moral action, he tells her that 'Lives are enlarged in different ways. I dare
say some would never get their eyes opened if it were not for a violent shock
from the consequences of their own actions' (377). If this is part of the truth
of Gwendolen's story, Deronda is doing no more than rendering explicit what
should anyway be a visible conclusion.

There are, however, a couple of points in the narrative when the
Rousseauvian paradox of contrived natural consequences becomes visible
also. The first concerns Mrs Davilow's loss of fortune, which is the immediate
cause for Gwendolen's acceptance of Grandcourt after her decision to refuse
him following the revelation of the existence of his mistress and their children.
This is a moment when the strict verisimilitude of the narrative is interrupted
by a more obviously fictional event; its purpose is to make the story take on
the nature of an object lesson. More strikingly, Grandcourt's death in front
of Gwendolen also has the role of visible demonstration of the undesirability
of murderous wishes – though it should be said that Rousseau never went to
the extreme of having someone murdered in order to demonstrate an ethical
point. This event, convenient for the narrative and thus driven by the logic of
fiction rather than of the reality to which the novel aspires, is what provokes
Gwendolen's remark that 'everything has been a punishment to me – all the

things I used to wish for – it is as if they had been made red-hot' (593). There could be no clearer statement of the consequentialist educational position, with perhaps a submerged reference to the classic instance of that view in the presumed unwillingness of children to place their hands twice in the fire.

These fictional instances can be seen, therefore, as the equivalents in the novel of the carefully contrived demonstrations of natural consequences that are characteristic of *Émile*, and which mark the various traditions of educational thought which descend from its author. Doubtless the comparison between the two writers points to different difficulties or weaknesses in their positions. For Rousseau, the necessity of contriving explicit demonstrations of natural consequences indicates the difficulty of passing from physical to moral education – a difficulty that will haunt all the educational thinkers that derive directly or indirectly from him. For George Eliot, the necessity of inventing object lessons which rely on too-visible fictional contrivance suggests a more fundamental act of faith on her part – that the world is indeed arranged to provide those object lessons, and thus to guarantee that moral education of the race which relies on the moral awakening of its individual members.

More widely however, and in conclusion, there is a fundamental ground of continuity between the two authors, which is their common assumption of consequentialist and associationist moral and psychological theories. What I have sought to trace in this chapter is the working-out, by various routes and in differing contexts, of the implications of these theories. This wider narrative runs directly from the eighteenth into the nineteenth century; whatever the apparent repudiations made of the critical spirit of the Enlightenment, some of its fundamental intellectual dispositions nevertheless persisted to provide the problematics of those that succeeded it. George Eliot's complex transformation of Rousseauvian intellectual themes testifies to the persistence into the nineteenth century of eighteenth-century ideas, not only as anticipations of Romanticism, but as notions that retain their primary, critical, edge.

Notes

1   Jean-Jacques Rousseau, *Émile*, tr. Barbara Foxley (London: Everyman, 1993), 103–5.
2   George Eliot, *Daniel Deronda*, ed. Graham Handley (Oxford: Oxford University Press, 1988), 593. All subsequent references are to this edition and follow the quotation in brackets in the body of the text.
3   See, in particular, Hugh Witemeyer, 'George Eliot and Jean-Jacques Rousseau', *Comparative Literature Studies*, 16 (1979): 121–30; and Judith Still, 'Rousseau in *Daniel Deronda*', *Revue de littérature comparée*, 56 (1982): 62–77.

4 *The George Eliot Letters*, ed. Gordon S. Haight, 7 vols (New Haven: Yale University Press, 1954), I, 271n; I, 277.

5 Ibid., I, 277.

6 Auguste Comte, *Cours de philosophie positive*, *Oeuvres d'Auguste Comte* (Paris: La Société Positiviste, 1894), V, 614. My translation.

7 Ibid., 620.

8 Brian Simon, *Studies in the History of Education 1780–1870* (London: Lawrence and Wishart, 1960).

9 Richard Edgeworth, *Memoirs*, I, 268–9. Quoted in Simon, *Studies in the History of Education*, 39–40.

10 Maria Edgeworth and Richard Lovell Edgeworth, *Practical Education* (London: Johnson, 1798), 178.

11 Maria Edgeworth, *Letters for Literary Ladies*, ed. Claire Connolly (London: Everyman, 1993).

12 E.P. Thompson uses the term to consider the transmission of antinomian ideas from the mid-seventeenth century to the late eighteenth century in *Witness Against the Beast: William Blake and the Moral Law* (Cambridge: Cambridge University Press, 1993).

13 For a brief indication of the importance of this cultural fraction to George Eliot, see my *George Eliot* (Brighton: Harvester, 1986).

14 See Edward Royle, *Victorian Infidels: The Origins of the British Secularist Movement 1791–1866* (Manchester: Manchester University Press, 1974), for an account of one section at least of this tradition.

15 William Myers, *The Teaching of George Eliot* (Leicester: Leicester University Press, 1984), 50.

16 Herbert Spencer, *Essays on Education and Kindred Subjects* (London: Dent, 1911), 23.

17 Ibid., 77.

18 John Stuart Mill, *On Liberty*, in *Utilitarianism, Liberty and Representative Government* (London: Dent, 1968), 116–17.

19 Spencer, *Essays on Education*, 108.

20 Ibid., 93.

21 George Eliot, *The Mill on the Floss*, ed. A.S. Byatt (Harmondsworth: Penguin, 1979), 244.

22 W.H. Burston, ed., *James Mill on Education* (Cambridge: Cambridge University Press, 1969), 99. The quotation comes from Mill's *Encyclopedia Britannica* article on 'Education' (1815).

23 Ibid., 101–2.

Chapter 3

'The Dreams of thy Youth': Bucks, Belles and Half-way Men in Victorian Fiction

Carolyn D. Williams

Victorian historical novelists achieved impressive feats of temporal colonialism. Their zest for the unique and distinctive, both in characters and the societies in which they lived, reacted with a growing taste for realism to inspire unprecedented combinations of creative energy with authentic detail. Six years before Victoria's accession, 'The Spirit of the Age' (1831) by John Stuart Mill (1806–73) already records an increasing awareness of period: 'The idea of comparing one's own age with former ages, or with our notion of those which are yet to come, had occurred to philosophers; but it never before was the dominant idea of any age.'[1] The previous century received special attention: John Ashton (1834–1911), a specialist in eighteenth-century social history, exemplifies the application of the Victorian work ethic to eighteenth-century documents. His *Eighteenth Century Waifs* (1887) is based on the British Museum's Musgrave Tracts, comprising 'more than 1760 volumes', plus 'over 200 other books and newspapers used for reference, &c'.[2] Abundantly equipped with background information, authors produced accessible yet challenging fiction, depicting worlds sufficiently familiar to be set initially against Victorian frames of reference, but which, on closer inspection, proved an awkward fit. A range of ambiguous attitudes appears in passing references to the period, and in the depiction of elderly eighteenth-century survivors in fiction with nineteenth-century settings, as well as in novels dealing directly with the previous century. Generation, gender and class distinctions complicate the pattern and are in turn destabilized by the ensuing temporal and moral flux. The eighteenth century emerges as an era of doubleness and self-contradiction, where vice and virtue separate out into dastardly villains and idealized heroes or mingle perplexingly in the same personality, while 'ordinary' characters can be the most enigmatic and complex of all.

Many apparent contradictions can be resolved by the recognition that, in the eighteenth century, forces engendering aspects of the Victorian age were set in motion. The period's cultural diversity generated a wide variety of views on issues which were aired in Victorian novels. This also accounts for some apparent anachronisms, which may arise from a biased selection of source material, rather than the application of Victorian standards. Authors who see themselves and their contemporaries as the beneficiaries of previous reforms often design double mirror effects, creating characters whose idealistic dreams of the future reflect their creators' present. These historical go-betweens are sometimes drawn in a manner which suggests they would be fully at home in neither age, but the possibility that they have authentic eighteenth-century roots should not be too hastily dismissed.

The eighteenth century, when measured by the generous standards of many present-day academic publications and syllabuses, is also long enough to accommodate great changes: it tends to begin with the conflict and controversy accompanying the restoration of Charles II to the throne in 1660 and culminating in the accession of William III and Mary II in 1688, and to end with the Regency (1810–20), a period distinguished by upper-class decadence, cynicism and debauchery, and British victory in the Napoleonic Wars. The Victorian age, too, covers a generous span, reflected by the overlapping generations of novelists mentioned in this chapter: William Makepeace Thackeray (1811–68), Charles Dickens (1812–70), Dinah Maria Craik (née Mulock) (1826–87), Robert Louis Stevenson (1850–94), and Sir Arthur Conan Doyle (1859–1930). All the works selected for discussion in this chapter enjoyed substantial critical and popular success, and reflected conscientious attempts to depict eighteenth-century life. They also demonstrate manifold manipulations of narrative time. Author, narrator and reader are involved in unsettling negotiations between different stages of the eighteenth and nineteenth centuries. *Waverley: or, 'Tis Sixty Years Since* (1814), by Walter Scott (1771–1832), is a useful pre-Victorian comparator: at the date of its first publication, it was already dealing with events that occurred not 60, but 70 years previously. Conan Doyle's *Rodney Stone* (1896) offers his *fin de siècle* readership a similarly multi-levelled timescape, with a narrator whose reminiscences concern the exploits of bucks, naval heroes and pugilists, factual and fictitious, from 1790 to 1803, but whose aggressively modern present is already receding into another historical past:

> On this, the first of January of the year 1851, the nineteenth century has reached its midway term, and many of us who shared its youth have already warnings

which tell us that it has outworn us. We put our grizzled heads together, we older ones, and we talk of the great days that we have known; but we find that when it is with our children that we talk it is a hard matter to make them understand. We and our fathers before us lived much the same life, but they with their railway trains and their steamboats belong to a different age.[3]

What, exactly, made an age different? One of the most important questions historical novelists had to address was whether each age had a distinctive 'spirit', and, if so, whether the differences were more important than the similarities to the writer's own time. Belief in historical constants, like the unchanging and universal laws of human nature current among eighteenth-century supporters of the 'Ancients', discouraged obsession with differences and discontinuities.[4] Sherlock Holmes sets his arch enemy in a temporal cycle which includes a notorious eighteenth-century criminal: 'Everything comes in circles, even Professor Moriarty. Jonathan Wild was the hidden force of the London criminals, to whom he sold his brains and his organization on a fifteen per cent. commission. The old wheel turns and the same spoke comes up. It's all been done before and will be again.'[5] The importance, yet shiftiness, of the notion of 'period' appears in Dickens's *A Tale of Two Cities* (1859), whose first chapter is reassuringly entitled 'The Period'. It announces with portentous vagueness that 'It was the best of times, it was the worst of times, it was the age of wisdom, it was the age of foolishness'. Contradictory claims accumulate, offering conflicting views of an eighteenth-century present that is, so far as the readers are concerned, safely over. Then Dickens springs his trap: 'in short, the period was so far like the present period, that some of its noisiest authorities insisted on its being received, for good or for evil, in the superlative degree of comparison only'. By the time we learn that 'It was the year of Our Lord one thousand seven hundred and seventy-five', we know that there are important respects in which it might as well be 1859 – or any other year.[6] The novel's ending gives readers grounds to believe that great improvements have taken place since then. Nevertheless, many of the most unwholesome features in Dickens's version of the eighteenth century survive into his own era. For example, he raises contemporary concerns in his description of the squalid setting where Doctor Manette first appears:

Such a staircase, with its accessories, in the older and more crowded parts of Paris, would be bad enough now; but, at that time, it was vile indeed to unaccustomed and unhardened senses ... The uncontrollable and hopeless mass of decomposition so engendered, would have polluted the air even if poverty and deprivation had not loaded it with their intangible impurities.[7]

The scene also bears uncomfortably strong resemblances to the slums of Victorian London, like Tom-all-Alone's, as described in chapter 16 of *Bleak House* (1852–53). Readers are implicated in history as a continuous process.

If the eighteenth century does have distinctive characteristics, they can be hard to define. Doyle is typical of those Victorians who express a double vision. In 'The Adventure of the Second Stain' (1904), Dr Watson describes an eighteenth-century house as 'high, dingy, narrow-chested …, prim, formal, and solid, like the century which gave it birth'.[8] Yet there is nothing formal about Sir Robert Norberton in 'The Adventure of Shoscombe Old Place' (1927), a modern man who would be more at home among the Corinthians of *Rodney Stone*:

> He should have been a buck in the days of the Regency – a boxer, an athlete, a plunger on the Turf, a lover of fair ladies, and, by all account [*sic*], so far down Queer Street that he may never find his way back again.[9]

Could this contradiction be resolved by regarding the period as a century of two halves? People who today use 'Victorian' to express everything prim and proper are doing just what our Victorian predecessors did when evoking the early eighteenth century. For example, in the libretto of *Patience* (1881) by W.S. Gilbert (1836–1911), Bunthorne advises aspiring *poseurs* to

> Be eloquent in praise of the very dull old days which long since passed away,
> And convince 'em, if you can, that the reign of good Queen Anne was culture's palmiest day. (I, i, 'If you're anxious for to shine', ll. 9–10)[10]

After Queen Anne's death, the eighteenth century supposedly degenerated into an era of moral apathy, sensuality and greed, culminating in the Regency: this degeneration is embodied in Sir Pitt Crawley, the 'reeling old Silenus' of Thackeray's *Vanity Fair* (1847–48).[11]

Yet novels focusing on any part of the eighteenth century present a more complex state of affairs. Thackeray's *Henry Esmond* (1852) portrays Queen Anne's reign as an era sufficiently rich in vice and skulduggery to throw his virtuous characters into sharp relief, while the good Queen herself is seen 'tearing down the park slopes after her staghounds, and driving her one-horse chaise – a hot, red-faced woman'.[12] Mrs Craik's *John Halifax, Gentleman* (1856) depicts the end of the century as an era of even greater polarization, contrasting good and evil characters with a verve uninhibited by Thackerayan subtleties. As Joseph Shaylor admits, it may not be classed as 'one of our choicest specimens of literature', but it deserves attention as a cultural phenomenon in its own right, being a long-enduring best-seller, 'a welcome guest in almost every English household'.[13] John Halifax is an earnest Christian whose energetic involvement in domesticity, steam power, religious toleration and political reform have laid the foundations of the Victorian age as Craik and her grateful readers know it. Born on '*June 18th*, 1780', he represents an age with a bright future.[14] Its murky past appears in the corrupt Earl of Luxmore, who, like Dickens's Marquis de St Evrémonde, seems incapable of getting from point A to point B without running over a child.

Novelists write interestingly about the eighteenth century when they admit that its inhabitants, like the age itself, can be double-natured. Rodney Stone declares:

> In an age when the Premier was a heavy drinker, the Leader of the Opposition a libertine, and the Prince of Wales a combination of the two, it was hard to know where to look for a man whose private and public characters were equally lofty.[15]

The gifted but dissolute politician Charles James Fox (1749–1806) displays a particularly impressive contrast:

> I have never seen a countenance in which the angel and the devil were more obviously wedded. Above, was the high, broad forehead of the philosopher, with the keen, humorous eyes looking out from under thick, strong brows. Below, was the heavy jowl of the sensualist curving in a broad crease over his cravat.[16]

In Doyle's 'The Adventure of the Speckled Band' (1892), the eighteenth century itself becomes the dividing line between good and evil. The sinister Grimesby Roylott is the last survivor of one of the oldest and richest families in England; according to his stepdaughter, who is justifiably terrified of him, 'In the last century, however, four successive heirs were of a dissolute and wasteful disposition, and the family ruin was eventually completed by a gambler, in the days of the Regency'.[17] Doyle makes it hard to imagine a more appropriate time.

The eighteenth century offers opportunities for doubleness of every kind. The most complex and subtly drawn case is a tale of two brothers, James and Henry Durie, in Stevenson's *The Master of Ballantrae* (1889):

there is continual confusion as to which brother is good and which bad, not to mention which is really 'Master'. James, whose exploits drive the plot, combines courage, intelligence, and charm with ruthlessness and duplicity. He loses his inheritance through rivalry between the houses of Stuart and Hanover: a historical duality that shaped many eighteenth-century destinies. At the novel's climax he confuses another set of categories: as the subject of an almost successful resuscitation attempt, he obscures the boundaries of life and death just long enough to give his brother a fatal heart attack. Other Victorian authors exploited different types of ambiguity: Dickens, for example, created Sydney Carton and Charles Darnay, two men with one face. The most celebrated embodiment of eighteenth-century duality did not appear until the Edwardian era: the Scarlet Pimpernel, a man with two identities created by Baroness Orczy (1865–1947), took the stage in 1903.

The most convincing characters are seldom exponents of exceptional moral, mental or physical endowments, or masters of disguise masquerading as nonentities. Their doubleness lies in their status as fictional links between eighteenth-century and Victorian standards, which in turn derives from their ability to strike a social or moral average at a meeting point between high and low, or good and evil. The necessary calculations are not always simple. The pattern is set in Scott's *Waverley*, whose well-meaning but unheroic protagonist eventually embodies the triumph of common sense. He marries a nice girl and lives happily ever after, while the line of the glamorous Jacobites, Flora and Fergus MacIvor, is doomed to tragic extinction. Claire Lamont, in her 'Introduction' to *Waverley*, objects on aesthetic grounds to Scott's provision of a happy ending for characters 'ordinary enough to be allowed it'.[18] Definitions of 'ordinary' depend on the observer's viewpoint: the educated gentry who first read Scott's novel had much in common with Edward Waverley; that is probably the case with most of Scott's readers today. But the Jacobite clansmen who modelled for the most picturesque and exotic inhabitants of Scott's novel would have found Edward's sensibilities impenetrably complex and modern. It is easy to forget the innovative and dynamic qualities of this kind of ordinariness.

In conformity with the taste for the ordinary, virtuous and amiable characters may appear initially unremarkable. Rodney Stone introduces himself with typical lack of style:

> For my own part, if I were only assured that I was as clever and brave as the average man about me, I should be well satisfied. Men of their hands have thought well of my brains, and men of brains of my hands, and that is the best

that I can say of myself. ... In all things I have been a half-way man, for I am of middle height, my eyes are neither blue nor grey, and my hair, before Nature dusted it with her powder, was betwixt flaxen and brown.[19]

Craik, in *John Halifax, Gentleman*, uses a different strategy. Her hero radiates charisma, while Phineas Fletcher, the narrator, is a lifelong invalid: neither can lay claim to Stone's blend of mental and physical ordinariness. But she stresses John's role as a half-way man in temporal and social terms. He turns twenty in 1800, when 'between the upper and lower classes there was a great gulf fixed; the rich ground the faces of the poor, the poor hated, yet meanly succumbed to, the rich'.[20] John, 'with a few more, stood as it were midway in the gulf, now slowly beginning to narrow, between the commonalty and the aristocracy'.[21] This is no default position, but a demanding social role, vital to the nation's future, which he has deliberately chosen. To remove any doubt as to his rank, Craik allows his wife's aristocratic cousin to name it: he belongs to 'the bourgeoisie'.[22]

Stevenson excels at the creation of characters with hidden depths. In *The Master of Ballantrae*, the most rewarding psychological studies are Henry, James Durie's unattractive younger brother, and the perpetually terrified yet doggedly devoted steward, MacKellar. Sometimes Stevenson creates commonplace, fatherless cubs who make mistakes, but eventually redeem their courage and integrity, despite harrowing dangers and temptations. These lads might look like representatives of Victorian bourgeois ethics evolving spontaneously from primal moral turpitude, but they have not been left entirely to their own devices. They have caring, virtuous mentors who provide a solid grounding in eighteenth-century morality: in *Treasure Island* (1883), Jim Hawkins has Dr Livesey to guide him, while David Balfour, narrator of *Kidnapped* (1886) and *Catriona* (1893), is tutored by Dr Campbell. The influence of less exemplary characters shades black-and-white moral distinctions into more interesting greys. The affective core of *Treasure Island* (1883) is the relationship between Hawkins and Long John Silver, who has been 'unweariedly kind' to him.[23] When Hawkins, hiding in the apple barrel, overhears Silver persuading 'the youngest hand on board' to join his piratical enterprise, his immediate reaction looks like jealousy.[24] He declares, 'You may imagine how I felt when I heard this abominable old rogue addressing another in the very same words of flattery as he had used to myself. I think, if I had been able, that I would have killed him through the barrel.'[25] Pirate and cabin-boy deploy similar survival strategies. Hawkins knows his life, and those of the law-abiding members of the crew, depend on his acting normally in Silver's presence: 'I had ... taken such a horror of his cruelty, duplicity, and power, that I could scarce conceal a shudder when he laid his hand upon my arm.'[26] Since the shudder was concealed, it appears that Hawkins's own duplicity is in perfect condition. But although he is capable of adopting Silver's methods, Hawkins feels no sympathy with the older man's ethos. Matters are different with the self-confessed 'plain man' who narrates *Kidnapped* and *Catriona*.[27] Stevenson acknowledges that his most powerful sources of inspiration were mysteriously unlocked while he was wrestling with the ethical and emotional complexities presented by the Jacobite agent, Alan Breck, and his dealings with the whiggish David Balfour. The magic moment came when, in *Kidnapped*, David learned to respect values different from his own: 'Alan's morals were all tail-first; but he was ready to give his life for them, such as they were.'[28] Stevenson writes, 'from that time, my task was stenographic – it was they who spoke, it was they who wrote the remainder of the story'.[29] This raises an important question: if authors can imagine characters learning to abandon local prejudices, can they persuade readers to relax their temporal preconceptions?

The belief that our elders are necessarily our betters, which underlies most moral teaching instilled in childhood, is frequently undermined by historical novels. Generational differences become an incessantly shifting feature of the psychological landscape. Henry Esmond is too temporally aware to nag his wastrel cousin: 'For ages past, I know how old men preach, and young men practise; and that the patriarchs have had their weak moments, too, long since Father Noah toppled over after discovering the vine.'[30] David Balfour invites his younger children to cast a sceptical eye on their parents and elder siblings: 'It is true we were not so wise as we might have been, and made a great deal of sorrow out of nothing; but you will see as you grow up that even the artful Miss Barbara, and even the valiant Mr. Alan, will be not so very much wiser than their parents.'[31] An eighteenth-century precedent is provided by Samuel Johnson (1709–84) in *The Rambler*. He adopts the persona of Myrtilla, who has been 'sixteen these ten weeks', and finds her aunt's restraints unreasonable:

> both she, and all the antique part of the world, talk of the unreserved obedience which they paid to the commands of their parents, and the undoubting confidence with which they listened to their precepts; of the terrors which they felt at a frown, and the humility with which they supplicated forgiveness whenever they had offended. I cannot but fancy that this boast is too general to be true, and that the young and old were always at variance. (No. 84, 5 January 1751)[32]

The impact of such passages changes over time: Victorian readers might be shocked, and post-industrial readers delighted, to think that their own foremothers might have been uppity teenagers.

Some historical novelists imply that gender boundaries depend on changing custom rather than eternal biology. They even cast doubt on the traditional assumption that men of former generations were more masculine than those of later times.[33] A satirical essay, garnered from the 1733 issue of *The Gentleman's Magazine* (a precursor of *The Reader's Digest*), illustrates this belief by contrasting a violently antisocial, but impeccably macho, seventeenth-century rake with an effeminate eighteenth-century wimp. The former spent his time in the following reprehensible fashion: 'he tripp'd to the playhouse; and thence return'd to the Bottle, by which having regain'd his Vivacity, about Midnight scour'd the Streets, broke a Woman of the Town's Windows, beat a Bully, ran a Watchman thro', and then reel'd off, either to the *Round-House* [prison] or his Lodgings'. The contemporary beau, however, 'lives at Home with his *Mamma*, and recreates himself with raising *Paste, Candying* and making *Jellies*'.[34] Present-day readers, while being duly disgusted by the former, might find the latter a charming vignette of a vanished past rather than a threat of future emasculation. For this, we have to thank a sense of detachment and cultural relativity developed by Victorian historians and novelists.

Victorian masculine self-confidence was bolstered by a trend towards plainer men's fashions. The change is indicated by editorial reaction to Samuel Johnson's remark that 'Greek ... is like lace; every man gets as much of it as he can'. In 1799 Edmund Malone (1741–1812) annotates as follows: 'It should be remembered, that this was said twenty-five or thirty years ago, when lace was very generally worn.'[35] Malone realizes that lace and other trimmings might be perceived as a marker of effeminacy, unless period is taken into account. Not all historical novelists make such concessions. Walter Scott apparently distrusts his readers' willingness to abandon their own standards. Consequently, even when he apologizes for the old-fashioned dowdiness of 'the court dress of George the Second's reign, with its no collar, large sleeves, and low pocket-holes', he glosses over the lace and long, powdered hair that accompanied it.[36] Later, he takes advantage of Highland dress conventions to give Fergus MacIvor a silhouette and hairstyle like his readers:

> He wore the trews, or close trowsers, made of tartan, checked scarlet and white ... The martial air of the bonnet, with a single eagle's feather as a distinction, added much to the manly appearance of his head, which was besides ornamented with a far more natural and graceful cluster of close black curls than ever were exposed to sale in Bond-Street.[37]

Dickens, on the other hand, far from seeking acceptable compromises, deliberately enlists Victorian attitudes to transform French courtiers' costumes into indications of effete inefficiency:

> The exquisite gentlemen of the finest breeding wore little pendant trinkets that chinked as they languidly moved; these golden fetters rang like precious little bells; and what with that ringing, and with the rustle of silk and brocade and fine linen, there was a flutter in the air that fanned Saint Antoine and his devouring hunger far away.[38]

Thackeray, more interested in celebrating difference, tries to get under the skin of men for whom choice of ornament indicates temperament or class, rather than fluctuating masculinity. In *Henry Esmond*, he defies Victorian conventions by using the elaborate costume of Richard Steele (1672–1729) to make him more appealing to the reader than Joseph Addison (1672–1719), who was 'very sober, and almost shabby in appearance – at least when compared to Captain Steele, who loved to adorn his jolly round person with the finest of clothes, and shone in scarlet and gold lace'.[39] Effeminacy, while contemptible in Esmond's eyes, appears in conduct, not in dress. This is evident in his condemnation of Henry St John, Viscount Bolingbroke (1678–1751): 'When he should have struck for King James, he faltered and coquetted with the Whigs', so that James's court 'despised him, as the manly and resolute men who established the Elector in England before had done.'[40] The narrator of *Barry Lyndon* (1844), who is far too busy killing men and seducing women to be considered effeminate, regrets the passing of an age when finery was an index of rank: 'There was a difference between a gentleman and a common fellow in those times. We wore silk and embroidery then. Now every man has the same coachman-like look in his belcher and caped coat, and there is no outward difference between my lord and his groom.'[41]

Viewed from a different standpoint, that very belcher (a coloured handkerchief knotted about the neck) evokes vanished splendours. Rodney Stone describes James Belcher (1781–1822), the pugilist who originally set the fashion:

> his superb figure thrown back in his chair, a flush upon his handsome face, and a loose red handkerchief knotted carelessly round his throat in the picturesque fashion which was long known by his name. Half a century has passed since then, and I have seen my share of fine men ... Yet during all that time I have never seen a finer man than Jem Belcher.[42]

Doyle associates lace with effeminacy in an account of a conversation between Buck Tregellis and Beau Brummell, which was 'filled out with many little bows, and opening and shutting of snuff-boxes, and flickings of laced handkerchiefs'.[43] Stone claims that such exquisites were 'often men of strong character and robust personality', but it is significant that they appear to need defence.[44] Strength is explicitly attributed to the period in general: 'with all its faults it was a *strong* age, and you will be fortunate if in our time the country produces five such names as Pitt, Fox, Scott, Nelson and Wellington'.[45] But even Nelson has a case to answer: 'iron-hard as he was as seaman and a fighter, there ran through his complex nature a sweet and un-English power of affectionate emotion, showing itself in tears if he were moved, and in such tender impulses as led him afterwards to ask his flag-captain to kiss him as he lay dying in the cockpit of the *Victory*.[46] When forced to admit that a famously virile hero indulged in behaviour considered unmanly by Victorian standards, Doyle does not allow his narrator to claim that this was acceptable in 1805. Instead of a temporal warp, he uses spatial distance: Nelson's emotional displays, once defined as 'un-English', can be excised from British history.

Eighteenth-century women are generally allowed less latitude than men in Victorian historical fiction. The patriarchal view that tends to divide women into two categories – angel or whore – is inimical to social, moral or historical relativity. The presentation of costume is again a helpful indicator of Victorian attitudes. The dress code that protected women's modesty was perceived as an unchanging, universal law: details might vary, but some parts of the female anatomy should never be on view – including those that became regrettably visible in the 1790s. Craik ventriloquizes a proper male response to this outrage:

> it was very horrible to see gentle English girls clad, or rather un-clad, after the fashion of our enemies across the Channel ... where high-bred ladies went about dressed as heathen goddesses, with bare arms and bare sandalled feet, gaining none of the pure simplicity of the ancient world, and losing all the decorous dignity of our modern times.[47]

Where conduct is concerned, a definite pattern emerges: aristocratic ladies of fashion are condemned for selfishness, frivolity, gambling, coarseness, and indifference to family values; women who meet high middle-class standards of bourgeois domesticity are held up for admiration. Dickens duly idealizes Lucie Darnay, who impeccably combines the duties of daughter, wife, and mother, and condemns the aristocratic French ladies: it was 'hard to discover among the angels of that sphere one solitary wife, who, in her manners and appearance, owned to being a Mother'.[48]

Both these Victorian stereotypes have eighteenth-century ancestry, through different lines of descent. Ashton's uncritical use, in *Eighteenth Century Waifs*, of allegedly factual materials illustrates this process. He reprints Jonathan Swift's poem, 'The Journal of a Modern Lady, in a Letter to a Person of Quality' (1728) – a satirical, generalized, and two-dimensional verse portrait of a vapid, spiteful, obsessive gambler that, in Ashton's opinion, is 'not at all exaggerated'.[49] Yet the only evidence he adduces consists of news reports on a particularly scandalous gambling case at the other end of the century, and a collection of misogynistic satires. If the satirical accusations were rather less similar to those made by Swift, the case for his accuracy would be stronger, since there would be less likelihood of formulaic repetition. But pamphlets and other published works by and about the middle-class reformer, Jonas Hanway (1712–96), yield a very different picture of an individual woman: Mrs Hanway, who, between 1712 and 1729 (when Swift's 'Lady of Quality' would have been in full swing), 'brought up her children by her own exertions, and with such care and affection that Jonas never spoke, or wrote, of his mother but in terms of the highest reverence and gratitude'.[50]

Thackeray emphasizes similar contrasts in *Henry Esmond*, where the lovely but wayward Beatrix mocks the narrator, while assigning herself and her mother, Lady Castlewood, to separate categories of womanhood:

> I intend to live to be a hundred, and to go to ten thousand routs and balls, and to play cards every night of my life till the year eighteen hundred ... I like a coach-and-six or a coach-and-eight; and I like diamonds, and a new gown every week. ... And as for you, you want a woman to bring your slippers and cap, and to sit at your feet, and cry, 'O caro! O bravo!' whilst you read your Shakespeares, and Miltons, and stuff. Mamma would have been the wife for you, had you been a little older ... You might have sat, like Darby and Joan, and flattered each other; and billed and cooed like a pair of old pigeons on a perch.[51]

Beatrix's penchant for self-description provides the reader with broad hints as to the material from which she has been created:

> I can dance the last dance, I can hunt the stag, and I think I can shoot flying. I can talk as wicked as any woman of my years, and I know enough stories to amuse a sulky husband for at least a thousand and one nights. I have a pretty taste for dress, diamonds, gambling, and old china.[52]

Thackeray would expect any reader to pick up Beatrix's passing allusion to the precarious marriage of Scheherezade in *The Arabian Nights*. More esoteric, but more fundamentally constitutive of Beatrix's character, are her allusions to specifically eighteenth-century tastes and practices. The reference to 'old china' alone evokes, in the specialist's mind, many satiric attacks on fine ladies as consumers of commodities as expensive, frail and useless as themselves.[53]

Beatrix's undomestic tastes prepare the ground for her sexual fall. The narrative voice must convince readers that such a fall was possible in the days of good Queen Anne. But it would be inconsistent with Esmond's character, as the fastidious husband of the virtuous Lady Castlewood, to permit any inference that all women of the period behaved improperly. Thackeray consequently allows Esmond to explain that Beatrix was typical of her specialized milieu, and to give authority for his assertions:

> If the English country ladies at this time were the most pure and modest of any ladies in the world – the English town and Court ladies permitted themselves words and behaviour that were neither modest nor pure; and claimed, some of them, a freedom which those who love that sex most would never wish to grant them. The gentlemen of my family that follow after me (for I don't encourage the ladies to pursue any such studies), may read in the works of Mr. Congreve, and Dr. Swift, and others, what was the conversation and what the habits of our time.[54]

Congreve's comedies and Swift's satires were originally calculated for a sophisticated, upper-class audience; Esmond's words add gender bias to social exclusivity by implying that they should be inaccessible to women of any rank.

Esmond is not just speaking in character, but expressing a common Victorian attitude. Thackeray elsewhere depicts indiscriminate indulgence in eighteenth-century literature as a deplorable habit for women. In *Vanity Fair*, he pours irony into his account of Rebecca Sharp's choice of reading matter for herself and her young pupil:

> She and Miss Rose thus read together many delightful French and English works, among which may be mentioned those of the learned Dr. Smollett, of the ingenious Mr. Henry Fielding, of the graceful and fantastic Monsieur Crébillon the younger, whom our immortal poet Gray so much admired, and of the universal Monsieur de Voltaire.[55]

This is meant to be a comprehensive catalogue of licentiousness, pornography, and atheism, demonstrating, at the very least, Rebecca's unfitness to be a governess. That some men, at least, are immune to this moral contamination is implied by Charles Dickens in *David Copperfield* (1849–50), whose hero finds boyhood solace in novels by Smollett and Fielding: 'They kept alive my fancy, and my hope of something beyond that place and time, ... and did me no harm: for whatever harm was in some of them was not there for me; *I* knew nothing of it.'[56] Nothing in his story suggests that he has subsequently been corrupted by realizing what a potentially harmful passage must have meant.

Since the thought of women roaming free among eighteenth-century literature engendered moral panic, it is not surprising that Victorian observers took a dim view of the ladies about whom, or by whom, these books were originally written and read. William Forsyth (1812–99) argues that, even if they remained technically innocent, the girls who read them, and especially those who admitted to doing so, compromised their modesty to a degree that his own contemporaries found unacceptable:

> Such scenes as they described, and such language as they put into the mouths of their heroes, would now make a book unsaleable – whereas, then, *Clarissa Harlowe* was thought to teach lessons of virtue, and young ladies were not ashamed to avow their familiarity with *Tom Jones*. We are not therefore to conclude that they were rakes and ready to throw themselves into the arms of the first adventurer they met; but we must infer that their delicacy was less susceptible and their modesty less sensitive than now.[57]

The moral flaws of old ladies who fulfilled Beatrix's threat of surviving into the nineteenth century were closely associated with their reading habits. Miss Crawley, in *Vanity Fair*, 'read Voltaire, and had Rousseau by heart; talked very lightly about divorce, and most energetically of the rights of women'.[58] The genteelly cynical Miss Marrable in *The Vicar of Bullhampton* (1869–70) by Anthony Trollope (1815–82) is more discreet, but her antipathy to such sentimental nonsense as romantic love, which almost drives the heroine into a soul-destroying marriage of convenience, is consistent with her general approach to life and literature.

> Fielding, she said, described life as it was; whereas Dickens had manufactured a kind of life that never had existed, and never could exist. The pathos of Esmond was very well, but Lady Castlemaine [*sic*] was nothing to Clarissa Harlowe ... I think she liked her literature rather strong. It is certain that she

had Smollett's novels in a cupboard up-stairs, and it was said that she had been found reading one of Wycherley's plays.[59]

Although Miss Marrable's favourite reading is obscene by Victorian standards, Trollope implies that it has considerable aesthetic merit, enabling her to judge the fiction of his immediate predecessors with a disconcertingly critical eye: however deep their disapproval, the zest with which he and Thackeray draw their naughty ladies suggests a hankering after the frankness of the bad old days.

Female historical novelists were at an obvious disadvantage: even if they dared to consult eighteenth-century literature in their research, how could they deploy the information thus acquired? It is easy to imagine that this restriction might have hampered the respectable Mrs Craik, whose memory was destined to be perpetuated by a 'chaste and beautiful' memorial in Tewkesbury Abbey, 'in recognition of her blameless life, and the deserved popularity of her works'.[60] In fact, she draws on different traditions, more bourgeois and whiggish (with a very small 'w'), akin to the sources from which Ashton drew his portraits of Jonas Hanway and his exemplary mother. An autodidact, learning from borrowed books, John Halifax emulates that prodigy of self-help, the heroine of *Little Goody Two-Shoes* (1765), probably by Oliver Goldsmith (1728–74) or John Newbery (1713–67): she 'used to meet the little Boys and Girls as they came from School, borrow their Books and sit down and read till they returned; By this Means she soon got more Learning than any of her Playmates.'[61] John's early career closely resembles 'The History of Mr *Lovewell*' in the same volume, who hired himself 'as a common Servant', 'spent his leisure improving his Mind', and became 'a complete Master of Accompts. His Sobriety, Honesty, and the Regard he paid to his Master's Interest, greatly recommended him in the whole Family.'[62] John's thrift and industry enable him to set up in business for himself and, like Mr Lovewell, marry an upper-class heiress.

A different set of bourgeois values come into play when John is involved in a *fracas* with the boorish squire, Richard Brithwood, whose insults culminate in a blow – which, in the eighteenth century, would normally elicit a challenge from any man with pretensions to gentility. Setting human and divine law above the code of honour, John adopts the principles enacted in Steele's didactic sentimental comedy, *The Conscious Lovers*, IV, ii (1722). A model he follows even more closely is the exemplary hero of Samuel Richardson's *History of Sir Charles Grandison* (1753–54), an exceptionally respectable example of its genre: it is the only novel recommended by the heroine's mother in

Jane Austen's *Northanger Abbey* (1818). Charles, after refusing a challenge, declares, 'I am passionate: I have pride: And am often afraid of myself; and the more, because I am not naturally, I will presume to say, a timid man.'[63] These words could serve as a running commentary to John's antics:

> John staggered. For a moment he seemed as if he would have sprung on his adversary and felled him to the ground – but – he did not. He returned not blow for blow.
> Some one whispered, 'He won't fight. He's a Quaker.'
> 'No!' he said, and stood erect; though he was ghastly pale, and his voice sounded hoarse and strange – 'I am a Christian.' [64]

He wins the unqualified admiration of his future wife, who hammers home the message: 'You have but showed me what I shall remember all my life – that a Christian only can be a true gentleman.'[65] Although John appears inappropriately Victorian in his refusal to follow eighteenth-century example, he is at least following genuinely eighteenth-century precepts. Craik is coping as best she can with an awkward predicament which frequently faced Victorian historical novelists when they tried to show how the present developed from the past.

It was easy to invent characters who imagined, or even helped to bring about, the material, moral and intellectual conditions within which, as Victorian artifacts, they were being created. The difficulty lay in making their aspirations and conduct comprehensible and convincing in terms of their own historical period: there was a danger that these 'half-way' characters might become temporally displaced outsiders. Doyle, at the conclusion of *Micah Clarke* (1889), is blatantly, though perhaps unconsciously, anachronistic. His hero, narrating his adventures in the Monmouth Rebellion of 1685, employs Victorian ideals and terminology in his vision of future harmony between Anglicans and Protestant Dissenters: 'let the strife be which shall lead the higher life, which shall take the broader view, which shall boast the happiest and best cared-for poor'.[66] Dickens's Sydney Carton becomes an intermediary between past and future, but only when his eighteenth-century existence is about to be terminated. Our knowledge of subsequent history confirms his prophetic power when he muses, 'I see the evil of this time and of the previous time of which this is the natural birth, gradually making expiation for itself and wearing out'.[67] This lends credence to his more personal vision of Lucie's son, whose birth will be the consequence of Carton's self-sacrifice: he will grow up to be 'foremost of just judges and honourable men', eventually bringing his own son 'to this place – then fair to look upon, with not a trace of this day's disfigurement – and I hear him tell the child my story, with a tender and a faltering voice'.[68] By now, they must be well on the way to Victoria's reign. But Carton cannot perform his mediation for long: the narrative thread that suspends his consciousness between time zones is both spun and severed by Madame Guillotine.

On the day John Halifax dies, Craik forges more plausible, and durable, links between past, present, and future, by performing a deft intertextual negotiation with an eighteenth-century tragedy that is deeply concerned with projecting present aspirations into the past. In *Don Karlos* (1787), the German poet, Friedrich Schiller (1759–1805), draws a heavily romanticized portrait of Don Carlos of Spain (1545–68), improbably depicted as an idealist who develops a zeal for reforms, including freedom of thought and worship, that strongly resemble an agenda from the eighteenth-century Enlightenment.[69] His friend, the Marquis von Posa, facing his own imminent death, boasts that he has built a paradise for millions in the prince's soul, and sends him a final message: he must remain faithful to his youthful dreams.[70] The moment is heavily ironized by the audience's knowledge that Carlos will not live to enact his reforms. But John Halifax quotes Schiller in a statement which combines Romantic aspiration with a sense of achievement in keeping with the novel's Victorian perspective: '"Keep true to the dreams of thy youth," saith the old German; "I have not been false to mine".'[71] Like many other liberals across Europe, he has endeavoured to turn Schiller's imaginary past paradise into a future reality.

Victorian historical novels can appear like exceptionally vivid dreams of the past, inhabited by characters whose faults are judged by Victorian standards, and whose virtues spring from aspirations to become Victorians before their time. Readers will miss the authors' own sense of continuity if they fail to realize that these aspirations are presented as eighteenth-century dreams, while the faults are often condemned by eighteenth-century moralists. Academics now seek to demolish such simplistic categories as gloomy Tory satirists, optimistic bourgeois Whigs, cynical aristocrats and idealistic early Romantics. Yet those of us whose interest in the eighteenth century was triggered by Victorian depictions of the period have particular reason to acknowledge the creative potential of the grand old clichés which inspired such splendid stories.

Notes

1   *Collected Works of John Stuart Mill*, ed. J.M. Robson et al., 33 vols (London: Routledge and Kegan Paul, 1965–91), XXII, 228.
2   John Ashton, *Eighteenth Century Waifs* (London: Hurst and Blackett, 1887), iv.
3   Sir Arthur Conan Doyle, *Rodney Stone*, in *The Conan Doyle Historical Romances*, 2 vols (London: Murray, 1931–32), II, 3. Hereafter cited as *Historical Romances*.
4   See Joseph Levine, *The Battle of the Books: History and Literature in the Augustan Age* (Ithaca, NY: Cornell University Press, 1991).
5   Sir Arthur Conan Doyle, *The Valley of Fear* (1914), in *The Annotated Sherlock Holmes*, 2 vols in 1, ed. William S. Baring-Gold (New Jersey: Wings, 1992), I, 479–80. Hereafter cited as *Sherlock Holmes*.
6   Charles Dickens, *A Tale of Two Cities* (London: Dent, 1923), 5.
7   Ibid., 37.
8   Doyle, *Sherlock Holmes*, Vol. I, 313.
9   Ibid., Vol. II, 631.
10 W.S. Gilbert, *The Savoy Operas* (London: Macmillan, 1926), 164.
11 William Makepeace Thackeray, *Vanity Fair*, ed. M.R. Ridley (London: Dent, 1963), 76.
12 William Makepeace Thackeray, *The History of Henry Esmond, Esq.*, ed. Donald Hawes (Oxford: Oxford University Press, 1991), 14.
13 Mrs Craik, *John Halifax, Gentleman* (London: Dent, 1928), 'Introduction', x, vii.
14 Ibid., 10.
15 Doyle, *Rodney Stone*, II, 103.
16 Ibid., II, 83.
17 'The Adventure of the Speckled Band' (1892), I, 245.
18 Sir Walter Scott, *Waverley: or, 'Tis Sixty Years Since*, ed. Claire Lamont (Oxford: Oxford University Press, 1986), xiv.
19 Doyle, *Historical Romances*, II, 4.
20 Craik, *John Halifax, Gentleman*, 63.
21 Ibid., 214.
22 Ibid., 184.
23 Robert Louis Stevenson, *Treasure Island* (London: Cassell, 1911), 95.
24 Ibid., 100.
25 Ibid., 101–2.
26 Ibid., 112.
27 Robert Louis Stevenson, *Kidnapped* and *Catriona* (Oxford: Oxford University Press, 1929), 238.
28 Ibid., 109.
29 'Some Gentlemen in Fiction' (1888), in *R.L. Stevenson on Fiction: An Anthology of Literary and Critical Essays*, ed. Glenda Norquay (Edinburgh: Edinburgh University Press, 1999), 152. See Graham Balfour, *The Life of Robert Louis Stevenson*, 2 vols (London: Methuen, 1901), II, 16.
30 Thackeray, *Henry Esmond*, 231.
31 Stevenson, *Kidnapped* and *Catriona*, 458.
32 Samuel Johnson, *The Rambler* (London: Jones, 1824), 145.
33 See Carolyn D. Williams, *Pope, Homer, and Manliness: Some Aspects of Eighteenth-century Classical Learning* (London: Routledge, 1993), 33–43.
34 *The Universal Spectator*, No. 262, in *The Gentleman's Magazine*, 2 (1733), 529.

35 James Boswell, *Life of Johnson*, ed. George Birkbeck Hill, 6 vols (Oxford: Clarendon, 1887), VI, 23, text and note 1.
36 Scott, *Waverley*, 4.
37 Ibid., 89.
38 Dickens, *A Tale of Two Cities*, 107.
39 Thackeray, *Henry Esmond*, 251.
40 Ibid., 446.
41 William Makepeace Thackeray, *The Memoirs of Barry Lyndon, Esq.*, ed. Andrew Sanders (Oxford: Oxford University Press, 1984), 248.
42 Doyle, *Historical Romances*, II, 181.
43 Ibid., II, 107.
44 Ibid., II, 256.
45 Ibid., II, 103.
46 Ibid., II, 164.
47 Craik, *John Halifax, Gentleman*, 58.
48 Dickens, *A Tale of Two Cities*, 106.
49 Ashton, *Eighteenth Century Waifs*, 17.
50 Ibid., 255.
51 Thackeray, *Henry Esmond*, 363–4.
52 Ibid., 342.
53 See, for example, William Wycherley (c. 1640–1716), *The Country Wife* (1675), IV, iii; Alexander Pope (1688–1744), *The Rape of the Lock* (1717), II, 105–6 and III, 157–60; John Gay (1685–1732), 'To a Lady on her Passion for Old China' (1725).
54 Thackeray, *Henry Esmond*, 351.
55 Thackeray, *Vanity Fair*, 85.
56 Charles Dickens, *David Copperfield*, ed. Nina Burgis (Oxford: Oxford University Press, 1983), 44.
57 William Forsyth, *The Novels and Novelists of the Eighteenth Century, in Illustration of the Manners and Morals of the Age* [1871] (London: Kennicat Press, 1970), 51–2.
58 Thackeray, *Vanity Fair*, 88.
59 Anthony Trollope, *The Vicar of Bullhampton*, ed. David Skilton (Oxford: Oxford University Press, 1988), 62.
60 Craik, *John Halifax, Gentleman*, ix.
61 Anon., *Goody Two-Shoes: A Facsimile Reproduction of the Edition of 1766*, intro. by Charles Welsh (London: Griffith and Farran, 1881), 24–5.
62 Ibid., 82.
63 Samuel Richardson (1689–1761), *The History of Sir Charles Grandison*, ed. Jocelyn Harris (Oxford: Oxford University Press, 1986) Part I, Vol. II, Letter 4, 265–6.
64 Craik, *John Halifax*, 162.
65 Ibid., 163.
66 *Conan Doyle Historical Romances*, I, (1931), 1267.
67 Dickens, *A Tale of Two Cities*, 373.
68 Ibid., 374.
69 See Geoffrey Parker, *Philip II* (London: Hutchinson, 1979), 87–93.
70 See Friedrich Schiller (1759–1805), *Don Karlo*), IV, xxiv, ll. 5038–9; 5070–2, Paul Böckmann and Gerhard Kluge, eds, in *Schillers Werke: Nationalausgabe, Sechster Band* (Weimar: Hermann Böhlaus Nachfolger, 1973), 268-9.
71 Craik, *John Halifax, Gentleman*, 417.

Chapter 4

The 'High Priest of an Age of Prose and Reason'? Alexander Pope and the Victorians

Francis O'Gorman

In November 1882, the Secretary to The Leeds Library recorded in his *Stock Book* the purchase of the fourth volume of *The Works of Alexander Pope*, published that year in a projected ten-volume series edited by Whitwell Elwin and, in due course, John Courthope, based in part on the collection of John Wilson Croker.[1] As that of a subscription organization, the acquisition policy of The Leeds Library, founded in 1768 and now England's oldest subscription library, was responsive to its readers' current interests, more so than those organizations publicly or institutionally funded. It was neither building up a research archive, nor supporting a hospital or theological college, but directly serving the needs of its diverse membership of fee-paying customers. The habitual model of the relationship between the Victorians and Alexander Pope is one of disapproval: Victorians, admiring lyric poetry over other forms, could supposedly find little room for the satirist and bravura exponent of the heroic couplet. So why did The Leeds Library buy that volume? What might be additionally deduced from the fact that this was no one-off purchase? The Library had been collecting its Pope edition dutifully as it was published from 1871, and would continue to do so until it was complete in 1889.[2] These were not its only Pope investments. Amid the various Pope biographies and letter collections it acquired, the committee also purchased Edwin Abbott's *Concordance to the Works of Alexander Pope* new in 1875,[3] a volume not for casual admirers. Pope's poetry has never been remembered as a favourite of the age of Arnold, Swinburne, and Tennyson. Matthew Arnold, indeed, is best recalled as declaring in 1880 in the General Introduction to Ward's *The English Poets*, that Pope was not to be classed as a poet at all, but was rather the 'high priest of an age of prose and reason', and, with Dryden, a classic not of poetry but 'of our prose'.[4] Pat Rogers exemplifies the persistence into the late twentieth century of the assumption that Arnold's disgruntlement was a measure of the period's. Where Donald Greene in 1988 thought that Pope was still not fully recovered 'from Victorian detraction',[5] Rogers plainly noted in his Oxford edition in 1994 that the 'Victorians disliked Pope',[6] chiefly on account of his malice. The 'official manuals', Rogers went on, choosing terms to suggest the dullness of the period such as Pope might have zestily denounced in the *Dunciad* (1728–43), 'portrayed him as less lofty in his aims and less delightful in his effects than any number of nineteenth-century versifiers'.[7]

The Leeds Library acquisition policy provides a tiny clue to a narrative that disputes the paradigm of which Rogers is an instance, and challenges the supposition of Edith Sitwell's *Alexander Pope* (1930) that Lytton Strachey's Leslie Stephen Lecture on *Pope* (1925) was the first text to restore the status of the poet after his 'eclipse' in the nineteenth century.[8] The subscribers at The Leeds Library were not alone in their taste, and the force that left its mark on their shelves and manifested itself in Elwin and Courthope's important, though problematic, edition was one that exhibited itself across the century. It was there in Tennyson's remark, that 'Dryden has the grander sweep, but Pope has done some perfect things';[9] in the familiar exchange of Pope quotations in Elizabeth Barrrett's letters to Robert Browning in the 1840s; in George Howard, Lord Carlisle's lively lecture in 1850 – coincidentally also in Leeds – that endeavoured to recommend 'that orderly and graceful muse'[10] of Alexander Pope as greater in genius than any English poet save Shakespeare, Milton, and Dryden; in William Michael Rossetti's opinion that Pope would always occupy 'the position of that one among the Understanding Intellects who has most clearly appreciated his own true province in Poetic Art';[11] in Mark Pattison's statement that the author of *The Rape of the Lock* (1712/14) and the *Epistles* 'lives, and must continue to live as long as the English language, by the perfection of his form';[12] in John Ruskin's declaration in the third of the *Lectures on Art* at Oxford in 1870 that 'I hold Pope to be the most perfect representation we have, since Chaucer, of the true English mind; and I think the *Dunciad* is the most absolutely chiselled and monumental work "exacted" in our country';[13] and in Leslie Stephen's admiration in 1880 'for [Pope's] extraordinary literary talents, respect for the energy which … turned these talents to the best account; [and] love of the real tender-heartedness which formed the basis of the man's character'.[14]

Pope was, *pace* the familiar story, read and admired during the Victorian period. By 1888, a few years before the publication of Aubrey Beardsley's illustrations to *The Rape of the Lock* (1896) brought Pope elegantly, and salaciously, into the visual culture of the *fin de siècle*, the Pope Commemoration Committee for the bicentenary included some of the most significant men of letters of the day: Sir Mountstuart E. Grant Duff, W.J. Courthope, Austin Dobson, Henry Morley, Alfred Austin, A. Stopford Brooke, Edmund Gosse, J. Russell Lowell, John Murray, Frederick Pollock, Leslie Stephen, and A.W. Ward. But assembling the narrative of Pope's survival in the nineteenth century must not involve the construction of a simple binary as problematic as the views of Greene and Rogers. It is to caricature the Victorian reaction to him if the assertion of his neglect is countered merely with the documentation of facts, however ample, which demonstrate the widespread approval he enjoyed despite his almost complete omission from Palgrave's lyric-based *Golden Treasury* (1861).[15] Pope's place in the nineteenth century was a multifarious one. Many critics resisted him, certainly, but their resistance was often a productive one, and sometimes it had the unexpected consequence of making the poet acceptable to other readers with different priorities. Elsewhere, Pope played a role in Victorian poetic and moral discourse that was more extensive than Arnold's doubts about his contribution to culture suggest. The views of Ruskin, Pattison, and Leslie Stephen on Pope, to name only the most prominent, were in variously ironic relationships with Arnold's critique and the shape of these easily forgotten ironies forms the subject of the second half of this essay. The full account of Pope's tangled presence in Victorian literary culture fits no easy pattern, and much of significance lies beyond my scope here. No comprehensive effort is made, for instance, to discuss the presence of Pope in the textures of Victorian poetry itself. But, concentrating on critical discourses, this essay recounts the varied roles Pope played in the nineteenth century, focusing on how he was understood to have contributed to Victorian commercial culture, the ways in which he provoked analysis of the assumptions of post-Romantic poetics, and his construction as a peculiarly lucid voice of order in a culture uncertain of its authorities.

Becky Sharp may have thrown her copy of 'Johnson's Dixonary'[16] out of her coach window at the end of chapter 1 of *Vanity Fair* (1847–48), but Thackeray's own debts to the eighteenth-century literary tradition were, like Dickens's, extensive.[17] Most evident in the satirical energies of his fiction, Thackeray's concern with the position of Pope, and Pope's relation to the nineteenth century, revealed his sense that the Victorians were the successors of a preceding generation and that there was no logic in speaking of the writers of his own age simply as reacting against their grandparents. Thackeray's historiographical model privileged inheritance and was predicated on the assumption that the eighteenth century imparted terms that its successor continued to inhabit and without which it could not understand its own complex, fractured identity. Central to Thackeray's interest in *English*

Humourists of the Eighteenth Century (written 1851, published 1853) were questions of authorship that reflected debates explored in *The History of Pendennis* (1848–50) and the fashioning of Pope as the architect of modern conceptions of the literary man. Pope was, Thackeray said, the 'highest among the poets and humourists with whom we have to rank him', and a man of 'brilliant genius'.[18] This exceptional public profile was consequential for the century that followed with its own increasingly prominent debates about publicity, fame, and the costs of fame. Imagining Pope 'in a fever of victory, and genius, and hope, and anger … struggling through the crowd of shouting friends and furious detractors to his temple of Fame',[19] the poet appeared in *English Humourists*, the most popular of the early Victorian accounts of eighteenth-century literature, shaped by Thackeray's engagement with forms of modern celebrity.[20] Pope, serenaded as a genius in his own day, and the first poet to secure an independent income through the success of his art, silently emerged in *English Humourists* as a mythic origin of the modern commercially successful writer, the man of letters lionized – and to some degree jeopardized – by an enthusiastic and riotous public.

Thackeray's historiographical paradigm fashioned the eighteenth century as setting terms by which the nineteenth could understand the nature of authorship that characterized its own literary life, and Pope's biography provided a template for the inscription of a new and increasingly troubled form of cultural identity. But as Thackeray continued to explain, Pope's contribution was more than this. Genius he may have been, Pope was also a 'ruthless little tyrant'[21] – Thackeray's vicious change of perspective could have come from the fiction – and, while courting fame, he 'contributed, more than any man who ever lived, to depreciate the literary calling'.[22] The *Dunciad* lambasted the impoverished hack, making the public associate penmanship with poverty, and thereafter, Thackeray said, the 'condition of authorship began to fall'.[23] Pope, in the double mapping of *English Humourists*, was a defining exemplum of the lionized poet, but also the writer who stood in the way, ever after, of the elevation of the literary profession to moral decency and social acceptability. George Gissing's *New Grub Street* (1891) recorded a predicament, in the terms *English Humourists* announced, that was brought into being by the flower of eighteenth-century Augustanism. Understanding Pope like this, Thackeray's lecture proposed, was to comprehend a central aspect of the mythical genesis of a new, fraught cultural category, and to realize the full implications of Pope's triumphant personal success was to perceive his two-sided bequest to the nineteenth century in the form of his endowment to the problematic modern identity of the creative artist.

Pinpointing Pope's double role in the shifts in status of the author, Thackeray further complicated his response by finding in Pope's history a form of personal legitimation. The depreciation of the figure of the author had followed Pope's late satire, and yet this poetry, Thackeray said, the bitter wit of the *Dunciad*, was appealingly vigorous: it was 'so pleasant to read!'[24] The author of *The Book of Snobs* (1852), whose work extended practices of eighteenth-century satire, discerned in Pope a validating authority. By locating in him a respected forefather, a fellow opponent of shams and facades, Thackeray enhanced the cultural visibility of his own literary practice. Pope's *Dunciad* was 'heroic courage speaking', he said: 'It is the gage flung down, and the silver trumpet ringing defiance to falsehood and tyranny, deceit, dullness, superstition.'[25] In part he was speaking of his own aspirations. Harold Bloom's emphasis on the anxiety of influence and the forefather as oppressor, or W. Jackson Bate's equal concentration on the burden of the past[26] are inappropriate models for this aspect of Thackeray's inscription of a literary tradition. At the level of their shared satirical enterprise, Pope was imagined in *English Humourists* neither as an overwhelming predecessor nor castrating power, but as an enabling writer through whom Thackeray obliquely celebrated his own literary identity. Thackeray's Pope was at once the architect of the popular notion of Grub Street and a founding figure of modern literary fame, the man responsible for the decline of the profession of the writer and the genius whose personally enabling satire was 'wonderful and victorious single combat'.[27] The mid-nineteenth century, as Thackeray scripted it, was the legatee – as the author of *Vanity Fair* was in particular – of a plural Pope whose influence on the modern was only half to be celebrated. Understanding his life was, nevertheless, essential for comprehending the genealogy of modern literary culture.

English Humourists found in eighteenth-century literary history the forms of knowledge that contributed to the cultural diagnosis of the middle of the nineteenth: Pope did not belong to an alien past. But Augustanism could be made to speak more pragmatically to the present and its local and colonial needs in a prominent area of Pope's cultural circulation at the end of the period after Thackeray's and Lord Carlisle's buoyant lectures. Looking at the school editions in print in 1887, the ten most favoured authors for 'classroom dissection',[28] as Richard Altick remarks, included Pope. The reason was obvious. Pope's technical mastery recommended him as a model for incisive writing, and focusing on this alone did not of necessity involve discussing the question that challenged many other readers in the mid period: the issue of Pope and sincerity. Ruskin observed in 1870 that Pope was one of 'the two most accomplished *Artists*, merely as such, whom I know in literature'.[29] He was speaking at the beginning of a decade, which, after the Education Act of 1870, would see Pope assimilated into the educational institution precisely on the grounds of his verbal virtuosity through a range of editions destined for the schoolroom. There were a great many of these, but they were bound by a common logic that privileged Pope's language over his intellectual statement. The editors were typically explicit about the status of the art with which they were dealing. John Hunter, in his 1879 edition of the *Essay on Man* designed for competitive examinations, remarked that Pope's work could not be classed as poetry and was, rather, 'prose elegantly versified',[30] while Mark Pattison, editing the *Satires and Epistles* for the Clarendon Press in 1872, was more aggressive, providing a long criticism both of Pope and his age that obliged him to ask at the end: 'How comes he to be a classic at all, and his poetry to be put forward still as a study?'[31] The resounding answer to this question, and the reply to all doubts about Pope's worthiness as a writer for the editors of these educational texts, was always his unparalleled grasp of language and form. It was 'on account of [his] literary excellence',[32] as Hunter put it, that he deserved study, or, as Pattison said in his 1869 school edition of the *Essay on Man*, it was all to do with the fact that 'In the art of metrical composition, Pope was a master'.[33] Pope's exacting competence, his 'polished style, and ... rare harmony of versification',[34] in the words of an anonymous 1860 edition of the *Essay on Man*, helped reveal the felicities of the language itself. Pope, to the mind of Edwin A. Abbott, could even be successfully transported to the colonies for the educational advantage of their peoples and the increased status of England and the English language: through the international circulation of Pope's chiselled words, something peculiarly effective could be done 'to spread the knowledge of our noble Mother-tongue'.[35]

Matthew Arnold was not thinking of proselytizing for the mother tongue overseas in the 1853 'Preface' to his *Poems*, but he was considering what language was appropriate as a model for modern poets at home. Shakespeare, he thought, certainly was not. Many editors of pedagogic texts in the 1860s and 1870s implicitly agreed. But where Arnold in 1880 had denied Pope even the name of poet, it was specifically the great Augustan who seemed to the cadre of educational writers the best model for the composition of effective English. As far as Mark Pattison was concerned, however, in his intervention into the state of modern poetics, Pope's work prompted a more complicated relationship with Arnold's views. Arnold in 1853 had turned against the introspective musing of 'Empedocles on Etna' in which there was 'everything to be endured, nothing to be done',[36] in favour of the classicism and epic temper of 'Sohrab and Rustum' and the poetry of great human actions that addressed itself to 'the domain of our permanent passions'.[37] Mark Pattison thought that Pope, properly read, would help poets effect a similar turn against their own past, and point the way to an escape from a now debased post-Romantic inheritance and to the embrace of a stricter classicism, a clarity of thought, and more assured handling of the proper language of verse. Using Pope to plot a history of Romanticism as reaction, Pattison urged a new form of retrospective gaze that recuperated aesthetic principles of the early eighteenth century to refresh the modern:

> In the latter half of the eighteenth century, when the reaction against the poetry of good sense set in, it was not thought enough to depart from the style of Pope, unless his metre was rejected also. The return to nature, in the poetical as in the political revolution, was attempted by throwing off the law. The aspiration to reach a 'higher melody' by means of lawless rhythms, has led us back to the barbarous versification of the seventeenth century, and much is written as poetry which can only deserve to be so called because it is not prose.[38]

Against the barbarities of the contemporary, the 'licentious taste' of the present, the best 'preservative' was, for the Rector of Lincoln, 'the diligent study of Pope'.[39] The redemptive turn to the classicism of Pope was intended, like Arnold's encouragement in 1853 of the return to the classical virtues of the epics of antiquity, to set modern poetics aright and to deal effectively with the post-Romantic legacy of the Victorian muse. T.E. Hulme, likewise fretful about the directions of contemporary writing at the beginning of the twentieth century, would recommend a similar investment in the poetics of a renewed classicism at the cusp of Modernism, making an effort to escape from the 'Romanticism' of the Victorian, in a defining text for the emergence of the Eliotian generation.[40] In Mark Pattison's literary history, the poetry of Alexander Pope and the revival of classicism in poetic discourse he would sponsor had served a cognate curative purpose more than forty years earlier, ironically, not wholly dissimilar from Arnold's classicist aspirations a decade and a half before that.

If Pattison's approach to poetry had been less influenced by class, he would have thought differently about the continuation of Pope in the mid-Victorian period. In declaring that contemporary poetry was too much characterized by lawlessness, he was not considering the fact that much working-class writing, especially in the first half of the Victorian period, had found in Augustan practices more satisfactory models for poetic form and diction than the introspective modes of the Lake Poets. This was partly because eighteenth-century literature remained more cheaply accessible than the Romantics.

Hugh Miller, the Scottish stone mason and popular geological writer, grew up with books from family libraries comprising 'a broad selection of English essayists and poets – of the Queen Anne period',[41] and this was a typical case of working-class access to literature at the beginning of the century. But the endurance of the eighteenth century in working-class culture was not only a matter of textual availability. For some working-class poets, Augustan poetics facilitated a form of cultural and political authority, a discourse with public resonance, and a practice of social critique and outrage not so readily available from the self-reflexive voices of Keats or earlier Wordsworth. Brian Maidment usefully brought some of these poets, such as John Critchley Prince and George Richardson, into print in *The Poorhouse Fugitives* (1987), using for them the appropriately classical name of Parnassians. But his claim that their eighteenth-century roots made for 'backward-looking, even anachronistic'[42] poetics does not read so convincingly when set against Mark Pattison's hopes for the recovery of Pope as a way of rejuvenating high poetic culture in 1869. For Pattison, *contra* Maidment, Pope was the way forward, and high culture might have learned protifably from the working-class Parnassians, as from Pope himself.

Pattison's conviction that Pope would breathe new life into modern poetry was not a statement that would be welcomed by Harold Bloom's Freudian readings of the emasculating power of the forefather.[43] Rather than wrestling with the mighty dead – to borrow Robert Douglas-Fairhurst's distinction – Pattison recommended conversing with them, or at least with one of them.[44] But Pope's role in Victorian debates about poetics, and the nature not only of authorship but poetic evaluation and taste, was more ample than this in the second half of the nineteenth century. In conversing *about* him and his place amid the forms of eighteenth-century literary practice, Victorian critical discourse located a space in which discussions of the nature of poetry became bound up, sometimes anxiously, with the notion of cultural difference, the pastness of the past, and the troubling or inevitable conception of the mutability of taste.

Pope made Victorian critics think carefully about what poetry was. Matthew Arnold had ruled Pope out as a poet because he lacked the 'high seriousness' or even the 'poetic largeness, freedom, insight, benignity'[45] that distinguished the authentically poetic, but he could by no means cast him out of the literary altogether and recatalogued him as a master of a different genre. Others were differently sceptical of Pope's identity as a poet because he lacked a desideratum of their own preference, usually a quality of passion or abstractness of thinking. George Gilfillan, even in his 1856 edition of

Pope's poetry, remarked, somewhat perversely, that 'The object of poetry is, we think, to show the infinite through the finite – to receive the ideal in the real',[46] and Pope, on such terms, could not be judged as possessing the poetical faculty. Mark Pattison, in his introduction to the Pope selection in Ward's *The English Poets,* found that, alongside the pre-eminent virtues of his perfectly handled language, Pope lacked a whole catalogue of qualities both personal and poetic so that the judgement of this 'Introduction' fell both on Pope the writer and the man. He did not have 'inspiration, lofty sentiment, the heroic soul, chivalrous devotion, the inner eye of faith', and, 'above all', he was deficient in 'love and sympathy'.[47] These were certainly not elements of his art from which the nineteenth century could profit. Unsurprisingly, those who believed Pope lacked soul and could not feel deeply found 'Eloisa to Abelard' (1717) the most appealing of his works: many Victorian women poets found refreshing its dramatic form that allowed for ventriloquization without the dialectic of sympathy and judgement that characterized the Browningesque dramatic monologue.[48] 'Eloisa to Abelard' came from a poet writing from the heart rather than weaving the elaborate artifices of 'wit divorced from truth'.[49] The remark reprinted in the 1863 *Poetical Works of Alexander Pope* would have found a receptive audience: 'Pope elevated [Eliosa's Latin Letters] into poetry!', the editor wrote, to produce the 'deep pathos, the glowing eloquence, the picturesque imagery, the dramatic effect of that enchanting monologue'[50] which was a real work of art.

Approaching Pope in the mid-nineteenth century with an expectation of poetry's sincerity, its capacity to speak to and from the heart, was to bring a Romantic criterion to bear. Pope suffered from this. But sometimes, Romantic criteria were themselves to come under scrutiny, to Pope's advantage. Pope, hailed by one century as the greatest of its poets, but incompatible for some critics a hundred years later with the aesthetic priorities of the next, helped make visible expectations about the nature of what was poetry in the mid-nineteenth century visible. He also caused others at the end of the century to be nervous about those expectations. A revealing case was the 'Introduction' to John Hogben's selected edition of Pope in 'The Canterbury Poets' series of 1887. Following his many predecessors, Hogben announced that Pope was deficient in the highest poetic senses, privileging familiar Romantic expectations in the process: 'there is not that inner companionship with the Ideal', he said, 'through which alone comes the Diviner Voice'.[51] He did not find Pope original – his 'message was in no sense new'[52] – and he did not possess that quality of 'intensified life'[53] that marked the poet of greatness in a tradition of Wordsworth and Shelley. But this left Pope awkwardly placed. If his writing did not fit with the definitions of poetry Hogben had been taught to accept, but yet Pope remained, as he felt he did, a poet of distinction, what could this mean? Perhaps those post-Wordsworthian criteria themselves were awry? Musing on the way Pope's greatness chafed against mid-Victorian post-Romantic taxonomies, Hogben was on the verge of formulating a notion of the historical relativity of taste. Such an idea, affirming the culturally contingent aspects of poetics, would have challenged the apparent certainties of Gilfillan, Pattison, and Ruskin, whose assumption in 1870 of Pope's sincerity as a moral teacher was the reverse product of the same post-Romantic expectation of poetry.

But Hogben, in the end, could not commit himself to historical relativity. His discussion of Pope's location in the topography of taste at the end of the 'Introduction' metamorphosed into a statement, rather than a resolution, of the difficulty. 'There are many definitions of poetry' was the generalization to which he resorted:

> but few of them all are [*sic*] made with due allowance for growth. The 'impassioned expression' in the countenance of science, which Wordsworth regards as poetry, kindles upon and spreads with the enlarging features of all knowledge. The wider the definition, perhaps, the better; provided, of course, it be based on that wise division without which no definition can be true, or serviceable. It is, at any rate, certain, that a definition which excludes Pope's writings, leaves us with the enormous difficulty of finding a place, somewhere, for one whose work is as far above that of many whose claims have never been questioned as it is below that of the veritable kings of song.[54]

Unwilling to embrace the consequences of identifying the intersection of aesthetics with history, Hogben's discomfort, his transparent dissatisfaction with the evaluations he had applied to one who was 'far above' many of the accepted great men of English letters yet below the usual mid-nineteenth-century definitions of what poetry was, hinted at a fault-line in the Victorian apprehension of the Augustan in post-Romantic terms.

Edmund Gosse, an enthusiastic reader of Pope and eighteenth-century literature generally, opened up that fault-line in his combative engagement with Hogben's dilemma in *A History of Eighteenth Century Literature (1660–1780)* (1889). Gosse was not without hostility to Pope or his age, finding 'a certain hardness and want of sympathy'[55] characteristic of both, but he took the step Hogben could not when insisting on the context in which Pope could be rightfully celebrated. Considering Pope's *Messiah* (1712), Gosse declared it 'Technically ... one of the most faultless of [his] writings', but registered Wordsworth's criticism[56] that had destroyed its reputation in the early nineteenth century. Quoting some of the 'splendour and fullness' of the verse, Gosse made a telling announcement that located reading Wordsworth as a culturally distinct activity from reading Pope. 'If we persist', he said, 'in applying to classical and rhetorical poetry the tests framed to measure romantic and naturalistic poetry, the result will simply be to exclude ourselves from all possibility of just appreciation of the former.'[57] Marking a link between poetics and history, Gosse momentarily destabilized the Thackerayan model which, through the figure of the celebrity Pope, saw the nineteenth century in a form of cultural continuum with the eighteenth; he replied to the recurrent mid-Victorian discourse that could not understand or sympathize with large sections of Pope's *oeuvre* because they were at odds with the principles of its own poetics; and he inscribed a concept of historical difference in the patterns of literary history that meant not loss but gain. Roger Sale has discussed those moments in literary history – Dr Johnson's incomprehension of 'Lycidas' as 'easy, vulgar, and therefore disgusting',[58] for instance – in which tradition becomes discontinuous, misunderstanding takes priority, and a form of cultural bereavement occurs that leaves a later generation only to muse on the blindness of a past moment to a point in its own past. Edmund Gosse's incisive intervention in the afterlife of Pope in 1889, amid a poetics that sought to incorporate his work into itself but found it wanting, was, however, to insist on discontinuity in literary history, the recognition of the distance of the past from the present and what Gillian Beer has called its 'suggestions not on our terms',[59] precisely to avoid cultural bereavement. Insisting on a form of historicized reading that was redemptory, Gosse used discontinuity to preserve Pope as a writer of stature.

Those critics who, without the unease of Hogben, doubted Pope's claims to Parnassus (continuing a Romantic suspicion that John Whale began to document in 1990),[60] unexpectedly enabled another turn in Pope's ghostly life in Victorian poetics at the end of the century. Donald Greene thought the Victorians deeply inconsistent in their disapproval of the preceding age. They 'denounce[d] the eighteenth century', he said, '– definitely including Pope – as being, at the same time, aridly restrained and decorous, and shockingly libertine'.[61] The nature of the Victorian management of its eighteenth-century legacy that is the subject of our book challenges Greene's broadest assumption as it challenges all such commonplaces, but his more local summary judgement of Pope and the Victorians is also provocatively inadequate. One of the twists in the winding narrative it misses, and ironically invokes, is that it was exactly that tranche of mid-nineteenth century writers who doubted Pope's sincerity but admired his 'decorous' language who helped facilitate Pope's emergence in the supposedly 'shockingly libertine' *fin de siècle* as an engagingly erotic poet. The educational editions of Pope that grew in number beyond 1870 had pressed on their readers the qualities of Pope's diction and syntax while urging them to set to one side his morals, political critique, acid wit, and irregular theological doctrines. Form mattered; content and tone were better overlooked. Readers in the last years of the century, those who had found Pope first in the school text books of the 1860s and 1870s, had been encouraged to appreciate his work from the first as textures of language. Ironically, such an aesthetic preference was precisely that which facilitated Pope's acceptance in the culture of the *fin de siècle*, with its accent on exteriority and form, and investment in language as self-referential.[62]

Pope certainly found enthusiasts in the last years of the century. Oscar Wilde was surprisingly dismissive,[63] but Austin Dobson, author of the popular series of *Eighteenth Century Vignettes* (1892–96), sat on the Centenary Committee to celebrate the memory of 'the great Mr. Pope',[64] while Lionel Johnson responded to Pattison's belief in the necessity of a return to Pope in the classical elegance of his own poetic discourse. Edmund Gosse, moreover, declared him 'the greatest artist in verse'[65] of the eighteenth century, and said of *The Rape of the Lock*, the text most celebrated in Aesthetic and Decadent culture, that 'Poetic wit was never brighter, verse never more brilliantly polished, the limited field of burlesque never more picturesquely filled, than by this little masterpiece in Dresden china'.[66] Yet in the final years of the nineteenth century, the arresting celebration of Pope's art, intimately bound up with the erotic and linguistic preoccupations of the Decadence specifically, was to appear not in writing but photo engraving. The opinion of the author of *A History of Eighteenth Century Literature* on the accomplishment of *The Rape of the Lock* had consequences for Aubrey Beardsley in the 1890s as Gosse suggested to him that he consider illustrations to the 'brilliantly polished … burlesque' he so much admired. The resulting volume of *The Rape*, 'Embroidered by Aubrey Beardsley', issued by Leonard Smithers's publishing house, appeared in 1896, and was dedicated to Gosse. It comprised an exotic/erotic exploration of the episodes of the poem as elegant Rococo fantasy, 'spiced', as Robert Halsband puts it, 'with bits of symbolist decoration and art nouveau'.[67] Gosse had spoken of the original's brilliance of polish. Beardsley, in choosing to 'embroider' Pope, was acting out the notion of illustration as surface ornamentation, as highly-worked and highly-visible exteriority that developed the terms of Gosse's metaphor and the central feature of Decadent linguistics and aesthetics it articulated. Prioritizing the artificial, valorizing appearance, and even making what first appears to be a garden in the illustrations of 'The Toilet' and 'The Baron's

Prayer' really decorated *trompe-l'œil* scenes (see Illustrations 4.1 and 4.2),[68] Beardsley revelled in the possibilities of Pope's poem as it could be read in terms of the enclosed autonomy of the visual/verbal. His edition brought into the visual culture of the 1890s an 'embroidered' version of *The Rape*, from the poet whose work pedagogic texts in the 1870s had affirmed valuable, as a paradoxical result of their privileging of sincerity in literary discourse, as well-crafted verbal artefacts. Beardsley translated their suspicion of Pope's insincerity into a celebration of an art that was, to his mind, one of pleasing surfaces, helping manage the emergence of Decadence from terms set in critical debates about art's integrity in the preceding generation.

Pope's appeal to Beardsley had its roots, ironically, in the dislike of Pope's insincerity earlier in the period. But there were other ironies in the intricate patterns of Pope's continuation through posterity in the second half of the nineteenth century. The sharpest instances concerned Arnold's 1880 criticism and its totemic significance for later readings for the Victorians' perception of Augustanism. Arnold saw Pope as lacking in the 'high seriousness' and the quality of moral criticism that distinguished those who formed a part of the great tradition *avant la lettre*. Pope had appealed to Ruskin ten years previously, however, on contrary grounds. For the newly appointed Slade Professor of Fine Art at Oxford, Pope possessed a clear moral vision and his criticism of life – the *sine qua non* of Arnoldian poetry – was exceptionally valuable. Pope's theology, Ruskin said, was 'two centuries in advance of his time', and enabled him 'to sum the law of noble life in two lines which, so far as I know, are the most complete, the most concise, and the most lofty expression of moral temper existing in English words: – '*Never elated, while one man's oppress'd; / Never dejected, while another's bless'd*'.[69] Ruskin's inaugural lectures in 1870 – from where this statement comes – were focused on the values of English artistic and literary culture, on what could be learned from a native tradition that, at the beginning of his Slade Professorship, he saw it Oxford's task to introduce to the upper classes and the future national leaders under its tutelage. Pope, whom Ruskin had read since his childhood, contributed to these national purposes, and his (Ruskin's) declaration of respect was part of his broader revaluation of an eighteenth-century inheritance that reached him partly through his father.[70] But, placed on the broader cultural stage, Ruskin's words proved ironic, for, though Arnold's statement against Pope has endured as representative of the postures of the period, it was published only ten years after another major cultural critic, as authoritatively concerned with the dynamics of culture and its moral substance as Arnold, had declared more or less the opposite.

Illustration 4.1   'The Toilet' photoengraving from Aubrey Beardsley, illustrations for *The Rape of the Lock* (1896)

Illustration 4.2   'The Baron's Prayer' photoengraving from Aubrey
Beardsley, illustrations for *The Rape of the Lock*
(1896)

Leslie Stephen's reading of Pope in 1877 would set up further ironies with Matthew Arnold's opinions in 1880. His views in *Hours in a Library* on 'Pope as a Moralist' tried a fall – to borrow Stephen's wrestling metaphor – with what he understood to be Ruskin's conviction that great art was consistently the product of great soul. Stephen doubted Pope's personality, seeing him – with a link between physical and moral nature that was not unique in the period – as a 'little cripple, diseased in mind and body, spiteful and occasionally brutal'.[71] Acknowledging this, he had to dissent from Ruskin's seductively organic model, which, indeed, Ruskin himself, particularly after working on the Turner Bequest, had come to doubt. But Stephen found in Pope's temper more of value than many, and he was sufficiently sympathetic to acknowledge that his art proceeded ultimately from a good heart. He was a writer who, despite it all, 'had in him the spirit of a man. The monarch of the literary world was far from immaculate; but he was not without a dignity of his own.'[72] Forming an explicit textual settlement with Ruskin on the matter of the personality of the artist, the more oblique implication of 'Pope as a Moralist' was to set up terms that would complicate Arnold's reading in the 'Preface' to Ward's influential *English Poets* and further problematize its future status as representative of the Victorian perception of Pope. Where Arnold lamented Pope's failure to provide poetry that offered an adequate 'criticism of life', Stephen, like Pattison and Ruskin, thought Pope spoke to the contemporary condition, this time offering poetry possessed of a rare virtue lacking in late nineteenth-century discourse: 'good sense'.[73] Stephen's terms mimicked as much as they subverted Arnold's: the sense articulated by Pope was scarcely likely to impress amid the intellectual muddle of today, he said, for 'it is the guide of a time of equilibrium, stirred by no vehement gales of passion'. Pope's clarity was admirable but inaccessible to a culture where men's minds were ill-fitted to thinking, where judgement was persistently clouded, and where 'we are permanently in a passion'.[74] Pope's classical poise, the aptness of his critique and intelligence, provided, if only he could be heard, wise words for the modern auditor not altogether unlike the idealized Arnoldian voice of culture amid the threat of anarchy.

If Stephen, whose 1880 biography of Pope is considered by David Amigoni later (182–202), proposed the poet as an Arnoldian voice of sense, he also entered an intriguing relationship with the author of *Culture and Anarchy* (1869) in his salutation of Pope – specifically the Pope of the *Essay on Man* – as theologian. George Gilfillan's eccentric general edition of the poetry informed its audience that the poet was, as a thinker, 'dim and uncertain'. No Whig but 'no very ardent Tory either', he was equally obscure in his religion and 'neither an infidel nor a Christian'.[75] But where Gilfillan objected to this apparent indecision as part of the general inadequacy of Pope's intellect, it was exactly because of the permeable borders of his theology that Leslie Stephen, former clergyman and now agnostic, valued him as a teacher for a culture struggling free of the cramping certainties of Christian orthodoxy. To be sure, he accepted inconsistencies in Pope's thought (to a reader expecting sincerity) but he insisted that what lay behind these was broad-mindedness, a 'width of sympathy'[76] that was a mark of the man. Writing the encomium on Pope's mind that formed the high point in the fortunes of Augustanism (understood as the poetry of statement) in the later Victorian period, Stephen declared that:

> Tolerance of all forms of faith, from that of the poor Indian upwards, is so characteristic of Pope as to have offended some modern critics who might have known better. We may pick holes in the celebrated antithesis
>
> For forms of government let fools contest:
>   Whate'er is best administered is best;
> For forms of faith let graceless zealots fight,
> He can't be wrong whose life is in the right.
>
> Certainly, they are not mathematically accurate formulæ; but they are generous, if imperfect, statements of great truths, and not unbecoming in the mouth of the man who, as the member of an unpopular sect, learnt to be cosmopolitan rather than bitter, and expressed his convictions in the well-known words addressed to Swift: 'I am of the religion of Erasmus, a Catholic; so I live, so I shall die; and hope one day to meet you, Bishop Atterbury, the younger Craggs, Dr. Garth, Dean Berkeley, and Mr. Hutchinson in heaven.'[77]

The liberal Stephen inscribed Pope as an avatar of a generous if imperfectly expressed liberalism, a broadmindedness that exceeded the normally well-policed bounds of sectarian interest. In *Hours in a Library*, Pope emerged as a man who had not, in theological terms, 'developed one side of [his] humanity at the expense of all others',[78] – provocatively to borrow Arnold's language from *Culture and Anarchy* – for his work was the product of a 'tolerant, reverent, and kindly heart'.[79] The Pope Stephen read in the 1870s was a persuasive voice from the previous century who revealed a breadth of mind, munificence of feeling, and a theological toleration, however encumbered with 'weeds'[80] and bitternesses, which even Arnold, had he read him with Stephen's sympathy, might have found appealing.

Austin Dobson wrote a brief poetic drama, 'A Dialogue to the Memory of Mr. Alexander Pope', for the Pope Centenary Commemoration in 1888. Not the most important, but certainly the most exuberant statement of the ceremonies, it concluded with a series of triumphant couplets:

> So We, that love the old Augustan Days
> Of formal Courtesies and formal Phrase;
> That like along the finish'd Line to feel
> The Ruffle's Flutter and the Flash of Steel;
> That like our Couplet as compact as clear;
> That like our Satire sparkling tho' severe,
> Unmix'd with Bathos, and unmarr'd by Trope,
> We fling our Caps for Polish – and for POPE![81]

Such a public statement of enthusiasm in the late nineteenth century, such enjoyment of the artifice celebrated in Augustan poetic discourse and approval of its classical principles, has not been remembered enough. The assumption of early twentieth-century literary historians of the Victorians' dislike of the eighteenth has proved tenacious. Henry Knight Miller, in a broadside against the nineteenth century's apparently uniform objections, thought such historians merely processing an authentically Victorian view anyway. That view, he declared, saw the 'essential element' of the 'nineteenth[-]century vision [as] the polarization between itself and the eighteenth century'. Without that polarization, he went on, 'half the drama, half the meaning, of the Victorian self-image was gone'.[82] The intriguingly involved patterns of Pope's presence in the age of Thackeray, Ruskin, Gosse, and Stephen dispute such a view. That plural presence resists Miller's too simple model, as it challenges the historiographical paradigm that perceives the Victorians' self-image – the Modernists are often imagined in a similar relation to the Victorians[83] – as necessarily involving self-inscription *against* the recent past. Pope's continuance in the century that followed him suggests a model that was much less tidy, and the debates his poetry provoked, the values with which his work was invested, the aspirations that freighted his legacy, are not so swiftly assimilable into sonorous generalization. Miller, 30 years ago, thought that the eighteenth century as a whole continued to suffer in the academy from views he believed inherited from the Victorians. But we, in a different academy, should not be tempted to misread the complexities of the Victorians' view of the poetry of their grandparents' and great-grandparents' age because of the lingering persistence of a historical paradigm of rejection that on first glance seems to find its most authoritative source in the words of Matthew Arnold.

The true nature of the Victorian's engagement with Pope and the 'old *Augustan Days*', at the very least, was more convincingly creative and various.

Notes

1   See Leeds Library, Leeds, *Acquisition Stock Book* (1882); stock number 578.

2   See *The Works of Alexander Pope*, collected in part by J.W. Croker, with an introduction and notes by W. Elwin and W.J. Courthope, 10 vols (London: Murray, 1871–89).

3   See Edwin Abbott, with Introduction by Edwin Abbott Abbott, *A Concordance to the Works of Alexander Pope* (London: Chapman and Hall, 1875).

4   *The Complete Prose Works of Matthew Arnold*, ed. R.H. Super, 11 vols (Ann Arbor: University of Michigan Press, 1960–77), IX, 181.

5   Donald Greene, 'An Anatomy of Pope-Bashing', in G.S. Rousseau and Pat Rogers, eds, *The Enduring Legacy: Alexander Pope Tercentenary Essays* (Cambridge: Cambridge University Press, 1988), 241.

6   *Alexander Pope: Selected Poetry*, ed. Pat Rogers (Oxford: Oxford University Press, 1994), [ix].

7   Ibid.

8   See Lytton Strachey, *Pope: The Leslie Stephen Lecture for 1925* (Cambridge: Cambridge University Press, 1925) and Edith Sitwell, *Alexander Pope* (London: Faber, 1930).

9   *The Letters of Alfred Lord Tennyson* ed. Cecil Y. Lang and Edgar F. Shannon, Jr., 3 vols (Oxford: Clarendon, 1982–90), III, 393; on Tennyson's allusions to Pope in his poetry, see Archie Burnett, 'Tennyson's "Mariana": Two Parallels', *Notes and Queries*, 225 (1980): 207–8.

10   [George William Frederick Howard], *The Viceregal Speeches and Addresses, Lectures and Poems, of the Late Earl of Carlisle, K.G*, ed. J.J. Gaskin (Dublin: McGlashan and Gill, 1865), 389.

11   *The Poetical Works of Alexander Pope*, edited, with a critical memoir, by W.M. Rossetti (London: Moxon, 1873), xxxix.

12   *Pope: Epistles and Satires*, ed. Mark Pattison (Oxford: Clarendon, 1872), 18.

13   *The Library Edition of the Works of John Ruskin*, ed. E.T. Cook and Alexander Wedderburn, 39 vols (London: Allen, 1903–12), XX.77.

14   Leslie Stephen, *Alexander Pope, English Men of Letters Series* (London: Macmillan, 1880, 1909 edition), 210. For more on this text, see David Amigoni, 182–202, below.

15   Only one item by Pope was included which Palgrave called 'The Quiet Life' ('Solitude: An Ode'): see Francis Turner Palgrave, *The Golden Treasury of the Best Songs and Lyrical Poems in the English Language* (London: Macmillan, 1861), 108–9.

16   William Makepeace Thackeray, *Vanity Fair: A Novel without a Hero* (Harmondsworth: Penguin, 1968), 45.

17   For more on Johnson and the Victorians, see Katherine Turner, 119–43 below; for more on Dickens and the eighteenth century, see Helen Small, 14–40 above.

18   William Makepeace Thackeray, *The English Humourists of the Eighteenth Century: A Series of Lectures, delivered in England, Scotland, and the United States of America*, 2nd edn (London: Smith, Elder, 1853), 181.

19   Ibid., 208–9.

20 See Nicholas Dames, 'Brushes with Fame: Thackeray and the Work of Celebrity', *Nineteenth-Century Literature*, 56 (2001): 23–51 and Richard Salmon, 'Authorship and Celebrity' in Francis O'Gorman, ed., *Concise Companion to Victorian Fiction* (Oxford: Blackwell, forthcoming).

21 Thackeray, *The English Humourists*, 214.

22 Ibid., 215.

23 Ibid.

24 Ibid., 216.

25 Ibid., 217.

26 See Harold Bloom *The Anxiety of Influence* (1975) and *A Map of Misreading* (1975); W. Jackson Bate, *The Burden of the Past and the English Poet* (Cambridge, MA: Belknap, 1970).

27 Thackeray, *The English Humourists*, 217.

28 Richard D. Altick, *The English Common Reader: A Social History of the Mass Reading Public 1800–1900* (Chicago: University of Chicago Press, 1957), 161n.

29 *The Library Edition of the Works of John Ruskin*, XX.77. The other artist to whom Ruskin referred was Virgil.

30 Pope, *Essay on Man*, ed. John Hunter (London: Longmans, Green, 1879), v.

31 Pope, *Epistles and Satires*, ed. Mark Pattison, 18.

32 Pope, *Essay on Man*, ed. John Hunter, viii.

33 Pope, *Essay on Man*, ed. Mark Pattison (Oxford: Clarendon, 1869), 17.

34 *Essay on Man and The Universal Prayer* (London: Whittaker, 1860), anonymous prefatory note (unpaginated).

35 Abbott, *A Concordance to the Works of Alexander Pope*, xvi.

36 *The Poems of Matthew Arnold*, eds Kenneth Allott and Miriam Allott (London: Longman, 1979), 656.

37 Ibid., 657.

38 Pope, *Essay on Man*, ed. Mark Pattison, 22.

39 Ibid.

40 See *The Collected Writings of T.E. Hulme*, ed. Karen Csengeri (Oxford: Clarendon, 1994), 59–73.

41 Jonathan Rose, *The Intellectual Life of the British Working Classes* (New Haven and London: Yale University Press, 2001), 119. For more on Miller's work as a geological writer, see Michael Shortland, ed., *Hugh Miller and the Controversies of Victorian Science* (Oxford: Clarendon, 1996).

42 Brian Maidment, ed., *The Poorhouse Fugitives: Self-Taught Poets and Poetry in Victorian Britain* (Manchester: Carcanet, 1987), 97.

43 Catherine Maxwell has recently revived discussion of Bloomian patterns of influence in Victorian poetry in *The Female Sublime from Milton to Swinburne: Bearing Blindness* (Manchester: Manchester University Press, 2001).

44 Robert Douglas-Fairhurst, *Victorian Afterlives: The Shaping of Influence in Nineteenth-Century Literature* (Oxford: Oxford University Press, 2002), 51: Douglas-Fairhurst is in turn taking his terms from Bloom and Hazlitt.

45 *The Complete Prose Works of Matthew Arnold*, IX, 180.

46 George Gilfillan, ed., *The Poetical Works of Alexander Pope*, I, viii.

47 Mark Pattison's 'Introduction' to 'Pope' in Thomas Humphry Ward, ed., *The English Poets: Selections with Critical Introductions by Various Writers and a General Introduction by Matthew Arnold*, 4 vols (London: Macmillan, 1880), III, 58.

48 For a recent perspective on this, see Cynthia Scheinberg, 'Recasting "Sympathy and Judgement": Amy Levy, Women Poets, and the Victorian Dramatic Monologue', *Victorian Poetry*, 35 (1997): 173–92.

49 Ibid., 59.

50 *The Poetical Works of Alexander Pope, with a Life by Rev. Alexander Dyce*, 3 vols (Boston: Little, Brown, 1863, first published London, 1831), I.cxxxix.

51 John Hogben, ed., *The Poetical Works of Alexander Pope (Selected)* (London: Scott, 1887), xxviii.

52 Ibid., xxxi.

53 Ibid., xxx.

54 Ibid., xxxii–iii.

55 Edmund Gosse, *A History of Eighteenth Century Literature (1660–1780)* (London: Macmillan, 1889), 113.

56 For Wordsworth's criticism of the 'poetic diction' of *Messiah,* see W.J.B. Owen and J.W. Smyser, eds, *The Prose Works of William Wordsworth*, 3 vols (Oxford: Clarendon, 1974), I, 162.

57 Gosse, *A History of Eighteenth Century Literature*, 115.

58 Quoted in Roger Sale, *Literary Inheritance* (Amherst: University of Massachusetts Press, 1984), 2.

59 Gillian Beer, *Arguing with the Past: Essays in Narrative from Woolf to Sidney* (London: Routledge, 1989), 6.

60 John Whale, 'Romantic Attacks: Pope and the Spirit of Language' in David Fairer, ed., *Pope: New Contexts* (Hemel Hempstead: Harvester Wheatsheaf, 1990), 153–68. See also Upali Amarasinghe, *Dryden and Pope in the Early Nineteenth Century: A Study of Changing Literary Taste 1800–1830* (Cambridge: Cambridge University Press, 1962).

61 Greene, 'An Anatomy of Pope-Bashing', 241.

62 For more on this, see Linda Dowling, *Language and Decadence in the Victorian* fin de siècle (Princeton: Princeton University Press, 1986).

63 To Wilde is attributed the remark: 'There are two ways of disliking poetry, one way is to dislike it, the other is to read Pope'; cf. Rupert Hart-Davis, ed., *The Letters of Oscar Wilde* (London: Hart-Davis, 1962), 482.

64 Austin Dobson, *Eighteenth Century Vignettes*, 2nd series, new edn (London: Chatto & Windus, 1907), II, 31.

65 Gosse, *A History of Eighteenth Century Literature*, 108.

66 Ibid., 113.

67 Robert Halsband, *'The Rape of the Lock' and its Illustrations 1714–1896* (Oxford: Clarendon, 1980), 96.

68 Cf. Halsband, ibid. There is a real garden visible in the illustration capturing the very moment of 'The Rape of the Lock', but it is a severely ordered one: even the birds are well regulated.

69 *The Library Edition of the Works of John Ruskin*, XX.77.

70 For more on Ruskin and the Eighteenth Century, see Dinah Birch, 163–81, below.

71 Leslie Stephen, *Hours in a Library*, new edn, 3 vols (London: Smith, Elder, 1892), I, 1259.

72 Ibid.

73 Ibid., 119.

74 Ibid.

75 Gilfillan, ed., *The Poetical Works of Alexander Pope*, I, xiv.

76　Stephen, *Hours in a Library*, 131.
77　Ibid., 132.
78　Matthew Arnold, *Culture and Anarchy* (Cambridge: Cambridge University Press, 1960), 11.
79　Stephen, *Hours in a Library*, 135.
80　Ibid., 138.
81　*The Pope Commemoration*, 10.
82　Henry Knight Miller, 'The "Whig Interpretation" of Literary History', *Eighteenth-Century Studies*, 6 (1972): 61.
83　For more on Modernism and Victorianism, see the Introduction to the present volume, 1–13 above.

Chapter 5

The Cultural Politics of Eighteenth-century Representation in Victorian Literary Histories

Elisabeth Jay

> Pacing up and down the Athenæum club together, Macaulay and Thackeray came to talk of Richardson's masterpiece. The great novelist asked the great historian whether he had ever read it. 'Not read *Clarissa*!' cried out Macaulay …[1]

In 1868 E.S. Dallas, anxious to reintroduce *Clarissa* to the British reading public, hit on this anecdote as advertising copy from the two best-known writers on eighteenth-century history. In recounting the story, originally told by that most 'clubbable' of men, Thackeray,[2] Dallas also carefully skewed the tale so that it seemed to offer belated proxy membership of a London gentleman's club to hypochondriacal Samuel Richardson, a tradesman, renowned for preferring women's company and country life. For, in *The English Humourists* (written in 1851, published in 1853), Thackeray had set up 'the manly, the English Harry Fielding' against Richardson 'the puny cockney bookseller … whose goddess was attended by old maids and dowagers, and fed on muffins and bohea'.[3] The touchy professional rivalry and personal acrimony surrounding Thackeray's relations with his own contemporary Dickens can all too readily make the binary opposition he constructs here appear entirely personal in origin. Rather, as this essay will show, Thackeray found no trouble in shaping these two predecessors to suit his private agenda, because he was entering into a discourse of eighteenth-century representation that was already heavily politicized. Those who commissioned, wrote, or published literary histories of the eighteenth century in the Victorian period were well aware that these books and articles would be read as much for their attitude to contemporary issues as for any information they might yield about their literary forebears.

Richardson and Fielding were likely to be positioned for Victorian readers as raising issues of class and gender. The potentially subversive message of Richardson's *Pamela*, in which the virtuous poor are shown capable of disrupting and contaminating the power structures of the oppressive rich, may have been a contributory factor to Richardson's virtual eclipse for a period of almost fifty years. Whereas Fielding's *The History of Tom Jones, a Foundling* (1749) resurfaced in two 1857 editions, having last been published in 1820, Richardson's *Clarissa* (1747–48), also reprinted in 1820, had to wait until 1868 for two abridged editions to appear.[4] Where Dallas had endeavoured to reposition Richardson in the male space of the library, Mrs Harriet Ward, editor of the alternative 1868 edition, built on Richardson's known appeal to female readers, while simultaneously distancing her intended readership from any contamination by the élitist sybaritism of the eighteenth century:

> The redundancy of Richardson's style had a charm for the readers of his day, when time hung heavy on the hands of fine ladies shut up in country houses, or dawdling over fancywork and pug-dogs, with small interest in passing events, and dead to the delights of that earnest work for good which all may find who seek it.[5]

Leslie Stephen, repeatedly returning to study the writers of a century whose rational caste of mind he found congenial, was equally alive to the party political agenda at work both in shaping the literature of any given period, and in his own generation's readings of their predecessors' output. Stephen explained that Addison had remained more popular than some of his contemporaries because he was able, at one and the same time, to cultivate a Wit which reflected 'the opinions of the upper social stratum', and encoded 'the Tory view in a form fitted for the intelligent' in a series of squibs, burlesques and fables; and to write with a 'gentleness' theoretically at odds with that culture. Stephen's more radical contemporaries had not been slow to align the 'anti-democratic' tendencies of the eighteenth-century Wits with those manifested by contemporary clubmen.

> Enthusiastical politicians of recent days have been much given to denouncing modern clubs, where everybody is a cynic and unable to appreciate the great ideas which stir the masses. It may be so; my own acquaintance with club life, though not very extensive, does not convince me that every member of a London club is a Mephistopheles; but I will admit that a certain excess of hard worldly wisdom may be generated in such resorts; and we find many conspicuous traces of that tendency in the clubs of Queen Anne's reign.

In Stephen's view, Addison's periodical essays, by engaging the emotions in the pursuit of morality, had succeeded in anticipating 'the method of later novelists, who incarnate their ideals in flesh and blood', and so discovered a 'mode by which the most cultivated writer could be brought into effective relation with the genuine interests of the largest audience'.[6]

Stephen's turn at the helm of the *Cornhill Magazine* helps to explain why he singled out the periodical essay as the most successful of eighteenth-century innovations. The *Cornhill* had been founded in 1860 with the mission to make a high-quality magazine accessible to a wider audience. The first editor of the *Cornhill*, Thackeray, Leslie Stephen's father-in-law, was an established essayist and novelist, and had a political reputation known to be at variance with that of the Tory publishing house of Blackwoods, and their periodical, the *Blackwood's Edinburgh Magazine* (1817–1890), or *Maga* as it was often known. John Blackwood and Thackeray became personal friends, but Thackeray, having staked his colours early in life to the mast of the London-based rival, *Fraser's Magazine* (1830–82), was not offered work in *Maga,* even when he promised to avoid politics,[7] since Blackwood, as an astute publisher, knew perfectly well that the political could not be kept out of texts by the simple expedient of avoiding contemporary issues.

Thackeray's writings on the eighteenth century, which included *The Four Georges*, *The English Humourists*, and the novel of the same decade, *The History of Henry Esmond, Esq., A Colonel in the Service of her Majesty Queen Anne, Written by Himself* (3 vols, 1852) were to offer a handsome demonstration of the use of history to set out a cultural and philosophical agenda. Twentieth-century critics have, on the whole, been unkind to Thackeray's historical lectures, seeing them as symptomatic of the later, inferior writer who prostituted his talent to entertain rich patrons.[8] In particular they have cited the disapproval of Macaulay and Carlyle, both in the audience for the 1851 series of lectures, *The English Humourists*; yet these two men were bound to feel short-changed since Thackeray was challenging the philosophical assumptions upon which their histories had been constructed.[9]

Macaulay's famous celebration of the glorious material progress wrought by the systematic application of Protestant Whig principles between the reign of the Stuarts and 1848[10] was implicitly challenged by Thackeray's account of German Protestant princes made rich by the spoils achieved at the expense of the lives of common soldiers, while 'hunger is stalking about the bare villages' of Europe. More topically, Thackeray's attack on the house of Hanover also invited comparison with a German Prince Consort who had recently promoted the Great Exhibition of 1851 at the end of 'the hungry forties',[11] and his strictures on the casual waste of battalions, headed by commanders with more idea of courtly chivalry than soldiering, also cast a satirical glance at the maladministration of the Crimean campaign.[12]

Stylistically, Thackeray's historical narrative owed much to Carlyle's cumulative building of particularized pictures and dramatization of selected episodes, but Carlyle must have been well aware, before attending his lectures, that Thackeray had no truck with his contention that 'Universal History, the history of what man has accomplished in this world, is at bottom the History of the Great Men who have worked here ... One comfort is that great Men, taken up in any way, are profitable company.'[13] If the subtitle of Thackeray's most famous novel, *Vanity Fair: A Novel without a Hero* (1848) had not struck home, the opening paragraphs of Thackeray's essay on Richard Steele would have done:

> What do we look for in studying the history of a past age? Is it to learn the political transactions and characters of the leading public men? ... You bid me listen to a general's oration to his soldiers: Nonsense! he no more made it than Turpin made his dying speech at Newgate. You pronounce a panegyric of a hero: I doubt it, and say you flatter outrageously.[14]

Thackeray's objection to history as biography stemmed mainly from his awareness of the extent to which any one person's apprehension of their own or previous times was largely class-determined. It was Thackeray's consequent intellectual commitment to undermining his audience's desire for emotional engagement with particular characters or positions that resulted in his finding less favour with a Victorian readership than Carlyle as a historian, or Dickens as a novelist.

Carlyle believed it was the duty of the historian to detect the 'Truth', first discerned by the Prophets, Priests, and Kings who were history's true agents. Carlyle knew what he thought about the eighteenth century because he knew what he felt about it:

> The Eighteenth was a *Sceptical* Century; in which little word there is a whole Pandora's Box of miseries. Scepticism means not intellectual Doubt alone, but moral Doubt; all sorts of *in*fidelity, insincerity, spiritual paralysis ... It would take many Discourses, not a small fraction of one Discourse, to state what one feels about that Eighteenth century and its ways.[15]

These opinions would appear to make Carlyle's subsequent decision to spend 12 years writing a six-volume *History of Frederick the Great* all the stranger. He devoted his opening pages to precisely this conundrum:

> One of the grand difficulties in a History of Friedrich is, all along, the same, That he lived in a century which has no History and can have little or none … How show the man, who is a Reality worthy of being seen, and yet keep his Century, as a Hypocrisy worthy of being hidden and forgotten, in the due abeyance?
> … What to do with it, and its forgotten fooleries and 'Histories,' worthy only of forgetting? – Well so much of it as by nature *adheres;* what of it cannot be disengaged from our Hero and his operations: approximately so much, and no more! Let that be our bargain in regard to it.[16]

In 1868, therefore, when a spate of eighteenth-century novels started to be reissued, readers in search of general histories of the period could turn to Macaulay's and Thackeray's elegant, politically-engaged accounts, or to Carlyle for a rather different perspective on the period. Macaulay had died in 1859, Thackeray in 1863, and Jane Carlyle's death in 1866 seemed to have stemmed the flow from her husband's pen.

Margaret Oliphant's usual shrewd sense of literary fashion was once again demonstrated when, in August 1867, spotting a gap in the market, she decided to offer John Blackwood a series of articles on the eighteenth century.

> I have been … thinking over my biographical scheme, and I think George the Second's would be a good period – fresh ground; and there is Queen Caroline, Duke John of Argyle, Prince Charlie, and quantities of interesting people, – an age that has not been touched by any recent historian, except, by the way, Carlyle in his Frederick, but only very slightly there.[17]

The inclusion of Duke John of Argyle (who did not make it into her series) and Prince Charlie (who did), formed a blatant appeal to Blackwood's Scottish romanticism. Oliphant could afford to be sanguine about the likelihood of Carlyle revisiting his least favourite epoch, but she worked on this series with the shadow of Macaulay and Thackeray always before her. Even with the articles successfully completed, she found her way barred when she came to write the introductory essay to their publication in book form:

> I don't find that I get on well with my essay on the period of George the Second. I fear I should only repeat myself, and that my attempt to give a general view would but come into weak comparison with Macaulay's famous description of the state of affairs in the end of the previous century, which indeed in many respects might stand for any period. As I don't see my way of doing it well, perhaps I had better not attempt to do it at all.[18]

Three important points emerge from Oliphant's discussions of the project with John Blackwood. First, she conceived of it as a coherent scheme and thus distinct from her regular 'hack' reviewing work for *Maga*.[19] Second, she had a sense of it as sufficiently sustained and ideologically consistent in its treatment of 'fresh ground' to provoke comparisons with other historical accounts of the period. Third, she saw the project not in terms of summarizing earlier historical accounts of the eighteenth century, but as potentially affording her a voice in the nineteenth-century debate on the use of history.

What better date than August 1867, a week before the passing of the much-debated Second Reform Bill, to start designing a series of articles that would indulge Blackwood's readers in one of their favourite pastimes: contemplating history with a view to estimating whether the nineteenth-century 'march of progress' had improved on the past, or cut their society adrift from its finest traditions? The part played by John Blackwood and *Maga* in the political revisionism of Oliphant's representation of the eighteenth century is crucial. Blackwood's firm editorial control of the house journal kept his Tory middle-class readership loyal in the 1860s, during which a welter of new periodicals appeared and editors came and went. His staunch conservatism, indeed, was a subject of banter with favoured contributors. After reading the manuscript of George Eliot's *Felix Holt* he added a postscript to his fulsome letter of praise: 'I had nearly forgot to say how good your politics are. As far as I see yet, I suspect I am a radical of the Felix Holt breed, and so was my father before me.'[20] That Blackwood saw *Maga*, renowned primarily for its literary coverage, as also exercising a political force, is clear from the extraordinary step he took next of commissioning George Eliot to use her fictional hero as a mouthpiece for radical Tory views. Eliot was writing 'Address to Working Men, by Felix Holt' at the same time as Oliphant was penning her historical sketches, and the two appeared in adjacent issues.[21]

A degree of creative tension existed in the political banter between Blackwood and his 'general utility woman',[22] Margaret Oliphant. An adolescence spent, as Oliphant's had been, in the lower middle-class, expatriate, Scottish environs of Liverpool, in the troubled economic climate of the 1840s, was likely to produce a different mind-set from that shaped by the comparative stability of Blackwood's Scottish upbringing or by Eliot's childhood spent in the mixed economy of the Midlands. Oliphant had been raised in a family that was 'tremendously political and Radical'; as a young girl she had participated in collecting signatures for a women's petition to Parliament at the time of the Anti-Corn Law agitation.[23] She had been 'brought up with a high idea of the honour and virtue of working men', but the experience of observing the 'selfish and cruel' behaviour of the artisans employed by her husband in the London of the late 1850s had given her a more jaundiced view of the likelihood of newly-enfranchised working men heeding the appeal to use their votes to preserve the 'treasure of knowledge, science, poetry, refinement of thought, feeling, and manners'.[24] By 1867, Oliphant had finally settled on sending her boys to Eton and living in the upper-class milieu of the Royal Borough of Windsor, after a number of years spent among social groups as diverse in their political allegiances as London's artistic world, Italy's expatriate bohemia, Liverpool's merchants, and the families of the Scottish clergy. This breadth of experience had developed both an ability to take on as much of the colouring of her different surroundings as was necessary for social engagement, and a sturdily independent private judgement.

In 1876, when Oliphant had been working with John Blackwood for over 20 years, the teasing tone of the letter which accompanied her review of Trevelyan's *Life of Macaulay* depends on their mutual recognition of certain non-negotiable differences: 'I hope we shall not come to blows over it, though it is ticklish ground ... I do not mind if you throw in a bit of Toryism on your own account, though I think I am gloriously Tory now and then.'[25] Oliphant knew that Blackwood would wish to exact full and ceremonial retribution on this biography of the leading proponent of Whig history and chief contributor to *Maga*'s ancient rival, the *Edinburgh Review*. She herself felt that one, brief, dignified reference to Trevelyan's rehearsal of past feuds would suffice, and that it was 'highly expedient that the book should be reviewed in a loftier and more generous spirit'.[26] The review she had written, however, had its sights trained elsewhere: on the making of the historian. She traced the grand simplicity and certainty of direction in Macaulay's work to the loneliness and cultural isolation of the human being, seeing neither dishonesty nor political folly in his partisan enthusiasms, but an energy undeflected by other commitments. The biography explained for her the flaws she had detected, in his historical approach 20 years before when, reviewing his *History of England*, she had admired his captivating style but questioned whether it was fair to make such partial and selective use of sources, or so simplify and blacken real characters.[27] This earlier piece on Macaulay had formed part of a series of articles she wrote for *Maga* on 'Modern Light Literature': in them she had mulled over current available models and developed her own generic criteria. She noted, for instance, the inauguration of a distinct school of minor historical fiction, spawned by Agnes Strickland's tales of longsuffering queens and princesses whose afflictions and adversities were magnified and whose domestic virtues enhanced to provide the stuff of historical romance. At the same time she observed the growing sophistication of a reading audience increasingly able to detect any element of charade in historical novels. She took her own message to heart: in her early experimental phase she had written two historical novels, the last, *Magdalen Hepburn: A Tale of the Scottish Reformation*, published only a year before this review. After 1854 she never again essayed a novel set in a remoter period than 70 years previously. Nevertheless, her reading had also shown her that history was a subject at which women writers might now excel. 'The Muse of History' had ceased to be 'a solemn matron' on a pedestal acting as the silent inspiration for famous men and had become a professional middle-class woman:

> There she is – behold her! – in the library of the British Museum, with her poke bonnet, her umbrella, her india-rubber overshoes; perhaps – most likely – some sandwiches in that pocket where weighty tablets and bits of antiquity alone were wont to be. There she sits all the dull November day, the London fog peering in at her through the big windows; nobody blowing a trumpet to clear the way as she goes home through the dingy streets of Bloomsbury, – instead of her triumphal car, putting up with an omnibus, and possibly carrying her notes in her little bag or basket, like any ordinary womankind who has been buying buttons or hooks-and-eyes.[28]

The Gibbons and Macaulays were good in their masculine way, but 'your true domestic chronicler, your real historian of homes and manners – let nobody deny it – is a woman'.[29] It took time for Oliphant to realize the full implications of this discovery for her own writing: meanwhile, she developed her *aperçu* in three different ways: chronicling the 'homes and manners' of contemporary society in the Carlingford series of novels; familiarizing herself with the habits and duties of a researcher in compiling *The Life of Edward Irving* (1862); and reviewing serious historical studies.[30] By 1867 she had gauged the possibilities and limitations imposed by working with John Blackwood and developed her own thinking on history. Choosing the eighteenth century as her field of engagement was not accidental. She had never confined herself to intellectual territory disowned or little visited by male writers, and in electing this period for her first major historical excursion she knew she was inviting comparison with Macaulay, Carlyle, and Thackeray. Underlying her selection of figures and her approach to them are two debates: the one with her predecessors, and the other with an editor keenly in touch with the politics of his Scottish and English readership.

Her *Historical Sketches of the Reign of George II* comprised a dozen biographical essays on Queen Caroline, Sir Robert Walpole, Lord Chesterfield,

Lady Mary Wortley Montagu, Alexander Pope, Bonnie Prince Charlie, John Wesley, Admiral Anson, Bishop Berkeley, Samuel Richardson, David Hume, and William Hogarth. The first thing to observe is that these were not the titles she gave to her essays: rather her headings suggested an examination of eighteenth-century social roles: 'The Queen', 'The Minister', 'The Man of the World', 'The Woman of Fashion', 'The Poet', 'The Young Chevalier', 'The Reformer', 'The Sailor', 'The Philosopher', 'The Novelist', 'The Sceptic', and 'The Painter'. These topics do more than conflate Thackeray's coverage of court life in *The Four Georges* and his treatment of the cultural scene in *English Humourists of the Eighteenth Century*. In Thackeray's account it is notable that women, when they do appear, walk on only as bit parts, 'to swell a scene or two', whereas Oliphant lays down a marker by starting her series with the same Queen Caroline whose fidelity to her charmless, unfaithful husband was the only feature that made her worthy of remark to Thackeray. His Mary Wortley enters and exits in one sentence designed to illustrate the 'splendid, embroidered, beruffled, snuff-boxed, red-heeled, impertinent society of Bath: 'Mary Wortley was there, young and beautiful; and Mary Wortley old, hideous and snuffy.'[31] From the start of her reviewing career Oliphant had deplored Thackeray's inability to characterize women: 'Mr Thackeray does not seem acquainted with anything feminine between a nursery-maid and a fine lady – an indiscriminate idolater of little children, and an angler for a rich husband ....' Of *Vanity Fair*, she complained, 'Amelia is a greater libel upon womankind than Becky herself', and expressed the wish that Thackeray would 'add a little commonsense to his feminine goodness'. Instead, she noted Thackeray's gift for depicting 'good, simple-minded honest English gentlemen' like Rawdon Crawley and Harry Foker, and added, 'Some scores of Harry Fokers, doing with simple straightforwardness what their commander ordered, have ridden with open eyes, and without a moment's faltering, right into the open-mouthed destruction and made heroes of themselves upon the wintry heights of Sebastopol'. 'Manliness, truthfulness, honour, and courage', she concluded, were the qualities Thackeray cherished.[32] It will come as no surprise, then, that the novelist Oliphant chose to study in *Historical Sketches* was Samuel Richardson.

By starting with the sketches of Queen Caroline and Robert Walpole, it might appear that Oliphant was following the tradition, deplored by both Macaulay and Carlyle, of regarding history as the chronicle of Court life and political wrangling. In execution, however, these two essays apply Carlyle's dictum that true 'History' is 'the essence of innumerable Biographies'.[33] What interests her in Walpole is not the ups and downs of his political career, but the kind of person he was: Oliphant's ruminations hit a Trollopian vein as she ponders this man who, had he not been the great Walpole, could easily have been another 'rude country squire' of his day and whose genius, such as it was, lay in his capacity for work, in which 'he was more honest, true, and worthy than he meant to be'.[34] Oliphant's biographical sketches permitted her to dispense with the panoramic view of society that Thackeray, with his respect for 'the great social canvases of the eighteenth century',[35] felt compelled to attempt. Although Thackeray repeatedly claimed to be sketching the manners and life' of eighteenth-century society, his angle of vision focused firmly on court life: the common people and the infantrymen become visible only in generic form as mistreated servants or cannon-fodder. In her treatment, as well as her selection, Oliphant was responding to Carlyle's vision of a time 'when History will be attempted on quite other principles; when the Court, the Senate and the Battlefield, receding more and more into the background, the Temple, the Workshop and Social Hearth will advance more and more into the foreground'.[36]

The opening of her essay on 'The Reformer', John Wesley, would also have resonated with those who had read Macaulay's appalled disclosure in his essay on 'History' [1828]: 'We have read books called Histories of England, under the reign of George the Second, in which the rise of Methodism is not even mentioned.'[37] The essay as a whole, moreover, responded to Macaulay's clarion call to historians to discover the 'spirit of the age' by abandoning their aristocratic contempt for the writers of memoirs:

> A history in which every particular incident may be true may on the whole be false. The circumstances which have most influence on the happiness of humankind, the changes of manners and morals, the transition of communities from poverty to wealth, from knowledge to ignorance, from ferocity to humanity – these are, for the most part, noiseless revolutions. Their progress is rarely indicated by what historians are pleased to call important events. They are not achieved by armies, or enacted by senates. They are sanctioned by no treaties, and recorded in no archives. They are carried on in every school, in every church, behind ten thousand counters, at ten thousand firesides.

The student of history, Macaulay continues, 'must obtain admittance to the convivial table and the domestic hearth'. Oliphant, with her popular domestic saga, *The Chronicles of Carlingford*, behind her, was quick to recognize how her talent could best respond to this recipe for History: she unabashedly domesticized her gallery of fame, never neglecting an opportunity to show her characters' off-duty behaviour, or comment on their relations with family and friends. Perhaps it was precisely because she shared something of

Thackeray's self-reflexive tendency to question his own narrative procedures that she identified this deficiency in Thackeray's analysis: 'Human nature in its company dress, and with all its foibles on, is the subject he delights to treat of; but Mr Thackeray is not great in home scenes, where the conventional dress is off, and the good that is in a man expands under the cheerful glow of the domestic fire.'[38] Oliphant's own method was to work out from the particular to the general observation. Viewed through the perspective of Georg Lukács' Marxist critique, Oliphant had sold out entirely to the 'freely roaming subjectivity' and trivial anecdotalism that characterized the post-1848 generation of writers who concerned themselves with 'historical figures ... separated from the real driving forces of their epoch'.[39] Thackeray's writing interested Lukács because he illustrated the fissure Lukács wished to argue between two phases of historical writing: despite the fact that Thackeray had lost sight of history's deeper 'plot', he still wanted to emulate the style and structure of the great eighteenth-century classical realist novels, whose characters had been plausible because of their writers' interest in historical-social types. The criticism Lukács levelled against Thackeray's fictional depiction of Swift in *The History of Henry Esmond*, as a psychologized figure wholly divorced from the professional achievement that made him an important representative of his epoch, could equally have been raised against the Swift of Thackeray's lecture series. Even Carlyle, seen by Lukács as in the vanguard of the Romantic reactionary movement that mystified history and marked out heroes for their very superiority to the historical process, could see that Thackeray had overdone the subjectivity of his judgements – especially when these preferences happened not to coincide with Carlyle's own: 'I wish I could persuade Thackeray that the test of greatness in a man is not whether he (Thackeray) would like to meet him at a tea-party.'[40]

The clue to Oliphant's approach is given in her essay on 'The Sceptic', David Hume, whose greatness, she averred, had been limited by a failure of human sympathy. 'He knew human nature so little, even while knowing it so much, that the signs of the times were a sealed book to him.' This deficiency, she argued, had led to his inability to read from the evidence of the peasant oppression that must have been visible around him during his sojourn in France, and conclude, as that 'much inferior thinker' Chesterfield had done, 'that everything was darkening towards some great catastrophe'. It was precisely because Hume's honest and good-natured scepticism served as a metaphor for his age's 'immense and astonishing indifference to everything spiritual and unseen' that she felt his case justified attention, despite Blackwood's known antipathy to the genus 'sceptic'.[41]

The political position adopted by John Blackwood was the final element influencing Oliphant's choice of biographical subjects. Thackeray had followed Macaulay's Whiggish lead in celebrating history's winners: the Protestant Dutch William and the Hanoverian dynasty over against the Roman Catholic and despotic Stuarts.[42] Indeed, in Thackeray's history the Stuarts, in the persons of Mary and James II, are summoned merely as pawns to be deployed in evaluating others' political astuteness. Oliphant, who had been born into Lowland Protestantism,[43] privately concurred with Thackeray's verdict on Mary Queen of Scots as a schemer,[44] but when she had presented her to *Maga*'s editor and readers, only a few months before starting the *Historical Sketches,* she had been well aware of the passionate Scottish, Tory, and monarchist loyalties with which she had to contend. The manuscript of her article on the two queens, Elizabeth of England and Mary Queen of Scots, had been accompanied by this note to John Blackwood:

> (15 March 1867) I hope you will like it – it has given me no end of trouble: in short, I have felt that I would gladly strangle both the ladies in question with my own hands, simply to get rid of them. I wonder how history-writers survive it. I trust the admiration which Mary has extorted from me will reconcile me sufficiently with 'Maga's' chivalrous creed in respect to her. All the same, I think you are all doing that wonderful woman the greatest injury by setting her up as innocent. Mary innocent! You might as well say at once that she was a fool, which comes to much about the same thing.[45]

Admitting, in her portrait of the Young Chevalier, Bonnie Prince Charlie, that 'no hereditary enthusiasm for the house of Stuart moves the mind of the present writer', she adopted perhaps the only framework within which she could present him attractively. Rather than championing his cause, she presented an inverse version of the Whig historical narrative, lamenting him as the symbolic figurehead of one of history's lost causes. Charles's heroism, such as it is, is seen in his alliance with the romantic and the marginal, 'the wild pibroch' and the Highland heather, in an age which would be dominated by an 'artificial', London-focused court.[46]

However, on some political issues she was not prepared to accommodate. Blackwood particularly admired her portrait of the philosopher, Berkeley, but he was unhappy with her critical remarks about the liberal-minded Bishop's inability to recognize 'the simplest rules of natural justice' as applied to the disabling penal laws against Roman Catholics, which Berkeley saw 'as a matter of course, unalterable, and founded on everlasting justice' and to 'the righteousness of the arrangement, about the slaves in the plantations'.[47]

Blackwood, whose sympathy with Carlyle's ultra-conservativism on this matter is reflected in his vocabulary, wrote to her:

> On the second last slip I have marked a passage which I should wish either to be modified or deleted. It was not in the least surprising that Berkeley in those days did not think of negro emancipation or the removal of R. C. disabilities. There are many tolerably sensible people who think that the way in which our West Indian negroes were emancipated was a cruel piece of humbug. As to the removal of Roman Catholic disabilities, I think Berkeley could ask you now to show what good it has done; they will always ask for more and more, and I do not blame them for it. You will observe that the Pope is so pleased with Scotland's support of Gladstone that he has given us a whole hierarchy.[48]

Unfortunately Oliphant's manuscript for the original *Maga* article does not survive, but it seems likely that the following remark constituted the only modification she was prepared to make: 'We are far from taking up the extreme side of those great questions, or of going wild, for instance, with rapture over that most doubtful and insoluble problem of negro emancipation, the practical difficulties of which are immense.' However, a concession whose oblique phrasing makes it at the very least ambiguous in its sympathies is promptly undercut by her subsequent, uncancelled remarks about a man who could accept these injustices so calmly, 'And yet he could not take for granted the existence of a stool or a table!'[49]

John Blackwood's desire to control every detail of his monthly publication can seem a formidable drag on his contributors' freedom, but, as this incident reveals, the sense enjoyed by his favourite authors of writing for an intelligent, interventionist audience, imparted a distinctive flavour to the magazine, and ultimately served to make the wider readership feel that they were somehow involved in a discussion. This sustained debate seems to have worked particularly well with women contributors, who must have felt that in the cut and thrust with Blackwood they were engaging with the patriarchy itself, even if in its most benign and thoughtful guise. Blackwood's daughter, Geraldine Porter, claimed that her father 'always steadily held out a helping hand to feminine literary talent', arguing that, 'The woman ... when she has attained distinction in any line, did so, in his opinion, *quand même* [in spite of this], and admiration was undoubtedly heightened in his eyes by the fact that she was a woman, and working under disabilities which made her achievements the more creditable'.[50] Writing to another female contributor, Ann Mozley, he praised Oliphant's essay on Queen Caroline, and another she had just completed on Queen Victoria's *Highland Journal*, before remarking, 'I always find that it is really accomplished women like yourself and those above mentioned [George Eliot and Oliphant] who are least distressed by the Rights of Women'.[51]

I have written elsewhere of Oliphant's appropriation of the supposedly male voice of the anonymous Victorian essayist to educate male readers into the understanding of a woman's point of view, using her essay from *Historical Sketches* on Samuel Richardson as my prime example.[52] For my current purpose I do not so much wish to draw attention to her awareness of the way in which gender inflected Victorian preferences for either Richardson or Fielding – 'one of the differences between men and women', she wrote to Blackwood, 'which even Ladies' Colleges will not set to rights'[53] – but her sense that the eighteenth century was crucially important to her as the originating site of the gendered construction of Victorian society.

> And then, his knowledge of the world! Richardson's knowledge was only of a good sort of people, and secondary *litterateurs*, and – women, who are not of the world, as everybody knows. This curious distinction of what life is and is not, which has prevailed so widely since then, probably originated in the eighteenth century.[54]

From the opening paragraph of the first sketch on Queen Caroline, cited as a remarkable example of 'how kindly the feminine mind takes to the trade of ruling whenever the opportunity occurs to it', these essays serve to challenge 'every ordinary theory men frame about women'. The essentialist position, that Oliphant's analysis of Queen Caroline is used to explode, states that there are 'two fundamental principles of a woman's nature' – that the 'model woman … is a jealous wife', and that 'maternity destroys all power of discrimination in a mother' – which 'lie beyond or above all argument. They are proved, and over again proved, every day'. Queen Caroline's tolerance of her husband's infidelities and her dislike of her son, and heir to the throne, are summoned as evidence of 'the one great advantage which fact has over fiction, and the historic over every other Muse', in that they allow a picture of a woman which 'if a woman in fiction had been created with such failings, even had she been the highest heroine of tragedy, she would have been flouted as an impossible creature'.[55] Oliphant's Caroline is, as fits her counter-essentialist thesis, woman as construct, forming her own agenda in response to her peculiar position as puppeteer of her little 'strutting' monarch and husband, and reconstituted by Oliphant as a particular case of a general thesis:

> It would be vain to say that the means by which Caroline procured her will were of the most dignified kind. They were such means as we see continually

employed in private life, when a clever woman is linked (unfortunately, not a very uncommon circumstance) to an ill-tempered, headstrong, and shallow man.[56]

Just as the first paragraphs of this essay leave open the question as to whether we are reading a particular history of Queen Caroline, or being led to contemplate a Victorian estimate of females as sovereigns, public or domestic,[57] so the entire series of sketches approaches the past with the present always in mind. Lady Mary Wortley Montagu is used as a further case history to challenge contemporary ideology:

> The unobtrusive domestic creature which is held up to us as the great model and type of the sex, could never be guessed at as its representative, did we form our ideas according to experience and evidence, instead of under the happy guidance of the conventional and imaginary.

Lady Mary's advocacy of inoculation, for which she gained the 'princely Caroline's' support, is held up as an instance of enlightened altruism that challenges contemporary theories of women's ill-educated small-mindedness; not that it is to be expected, Oliphant concludes, that actual historical evidence 'should for a moment stand before the force of theory'. Oliphant even managed to reclaim Lady Mary's 23 years of self-imposed exile from the denunciations of 'the unsympathetic, respectable critic': Lady Mary may have 'transgressed many of the chief articles in the code of respectability, which ordains that a woman, when lonely and abandoned, shall make up her mind to it, and die or sink into apathy without showing any frivolous inclinations towards a life which the world has pronounced over for her', but, Oliphant assured her readers, 'we believe it would be better for humanity, better for our common chances of happiness, if the wounded, the lonely and the deserted shared her instinctive wisdom, and asserted their forlorn right to such existence as suited their constitutions, instead of sinking into the tedium of uniformity, as so may shipwrecked people do'.[58]

By such means Oliphant sought to make these eighteenth-century figures, popularly supposed to be repugnant to the Victorians because they existed in a brittle world of artificial display and open immorality, accessible, intelligible, and even instructive to a Victorian readership.[59] Even the 'nauseous details as explicit as the frankest of French novels', into which Richardson goes when describing the attempts on the virtue of Pamela, which at first sight seem to confirm a taste and morality wholly at odds with those of Oliphant's implied readership, provide fruit for salutary reflection: 'Perhaps we are not so much better in reality as we think ourselves – for is not the sensation novel a resurrection of nastiness?'[60] Behind this comparative, reflective approach to the past lies a literary-political inheritance, established in a line of historical fiction that extends from Sir Walter Scott to George Eliot, where human nature is assumed as a constant bedrock, manifesting itself differently according to prevailing tastes, customs, circumstances, and opportunities. The mind-set nurtured and fostered by John Blackwood's *Maga* can be glimpsed by setting Oliphant's remarks on the reformer, John Wesley, alongside the 'Prelude' to Eliot's *Middlemarch.*

> Had Wesley ... been a Roman Catholic, from his hermitage he would have come forth like Benedict to form a great community. His country, his race, and birth were, however, too many for him. There are few notable lives in which one can trace so clearly the modifying influence of circumstances.[61]

> Many Theresas have been born who found for themselves no epic life wherein there was a constant unfolding of far-resonant action; perhaps only a life of mistakes, the offspring of a certain spiritual grandeur ill-matched with the meanness of opportunity ... for these later-born Theresas were helped by no coherent social faith and order ...[62]

Reading John Blackwood's two most famous women authors alongside each other, as readers so often did in the pages of *Maga*, illuminates the relations with their mutual editor that prompted such dissimilar authors to adopt a similar stance in their considered evaluations of the past and of women's historical lot. 'The only publisher in the world in whom the rebellious subject has such perfect confidence', wrote Oliphant just before she started the *Historical Sketches*; a man, Eliot wrote of him after his death, 'who has been bound up with what I most cared for in my life for more than twenty years'.[63] Revisiting Eliot's much-quoted reference to the great, self-styled novelist-historian, Henry Fielding, in the light of this essay's discussion of the nineteenth-century cultural politics of eighteenth-century representation, suggests that 'Looking Backward' was often a more complex and contested process for Victorian writers than twentieth-century critics always appreciated:

> A great historian, as he insisted on calling himself, who had the happiness to be dead a hundred and twenty years ago, and so to take his place among the colossi whose huge legs our living pettiness is observed to walk under, glories in his copious remarks and digressions as the least imitable part of his work,

and especially in those initial chapters to the successive books of his history, where he seems to bring his arm-chair to the proscenium and chat with us in all the lusty ease of his fine English. But Fielding lived when the days were longer (for time, like money, is measured by our needs), when summer afternoons were spacious, and the clock ticked slowly in the winter evening. We belated historians must not linger after his example; and if we did so, it is probable that our chat would be thin and eager, as if delivered from a camp-stool in the parrot-house. I at least have so much to do ...[64]

The narrator's shifting pronouns gesture, as they often do in this novel, to a protean gender position, and the need for the reader to tread warily. The great male progenitor of the realist tradition in fiction is summoned, only to have his claim to greatness undermined by the suggestion that it is either self-generated, or an effect created by a historical perspective that delights in magnifying past achievement, especially when embodied in 'lusty' masculine form. Reminding Blackwood of Fielding's more leisurely, less straightened circumstances, and drawing attention to the feminized characteristics of the current writer's 'living pettiness' and 'thin and eager' chat, seems curiously like the kind of 'insider' joke of which Eliot's late essays, *Impressions of Theophrastus Such* (1879), would make such a speciality. It was, after all, only two years before Eliot penned chapter 15 of *Middlemarch* that Oliphant had faced Blackwood with the complicated cultural politics that were at stake when women agreed to discuss eighteenth-century literature in the pages of Tory *Maga*:

> I suppose I ought to be ashamed to confess that, tedious as [Richardson] often is, I feel less difficulty in getting through him than in reading Fielding, and that as a matter of taste I actually prefer Lovelace to Tom Jones! I suppose that is one of the differences between men and women which even Ladies' Colleges will not set to rights. Pray don't tell of me; if I betray my sentiments in public they shall be laid upon the heavily burdened shoulders of what Clarissa would call 'my sex', and your contributor shall sneer at them as in duty bound.[65]

Notes

1   E.S. Dallas, 'Introduction', *Clarissa: A Novel* by Samuel Richardson, 3 vols (London: Tinsley, 1868), I, i–lvi.

2   Thackeray had told the story of Macaulay's introducing *Clarissa* to the expatriate community of an Indian hill station to illustrate the historian's prodigious memory. W.M. Thackeray, 'Nil Nisi Bonum', *Roundabout Papers; The Four Georges; The English Humourists*: in *The Works of William Makepeace Thackeray*, 12 vols (London: Smith, Elder

1880), X, 175. Leslie Stephen was probably truer to his father-in-law's view of Richardson when he glossed the anecdote, in his dismissive *Dictionary of National Biography* article on Richardson: 'Probably Indian society was then rather at a loss for light literature.'

3   *English Humourists*, 3 vols (London: Tinsley, 1868), 555, 548.

4   Fierce competition for the market in cheap reprints probably explains the sudden appearance of two such editions in one year.

5   *Clarissa Harlowe by Samuel Richardson*, ed. Mrs. Harriet Ward (London: Routledge, 1868).

6   *Leslie Stephen: Selected Writings in British Intellectual History*, ed. Noel Annan (Chicago: University of Chicago Press, 1979). The quotations from Stephen's last publication, *English Literature and Society in the Eighteenth Century* (1904), are taken from the excerpted chapters in Annan's edition, 141–3.

7   Thackeray had pursued a sustained satirical campaign against Bulwer-Lytton, one of *Blackwood's* most treasured authors, in the pages of *Fraser's Magazine*: Michael Sadleir, *Bulwer: A Panorama* (Boston: Little, Brown, 1931), 255–66. By 1857, they were good enough friends for Blackwood to put Thackeray up when he delivered *The Four Georges* to an Edinburgh audience. See Margaret Oliphant, *Annals of a Publishing House: William Blackwood and his Sons: Their Magazine and Friends*, 2 vols (Edinburgh: Blackwood, 1897), 240–41. The third volume (1898), by Mrs Gerald Porter, John Blackwood's daughter, offers further details of Thackeray's relations with her father, 35, 99.

8   The lectures on the English Humourists are represented as meretricious pandering to fashionable audiences in John Carey, *Thackeray: Prodigal Genius* (London: Faber, 1977), 22, 157; and Catherine Peters, *Thackeray's Universe: Shifting Worlds of Imagination and Reality* (London: Faber, 1987), 196–7. Edgar F. Harden, *Thackeray's English Humourists and Four Georges* (Newark: University of Delaware Press; London: Associated University Presses, 1985) attempts a recuperation of the two lecture series.

9   In a letter of 27 January 1857 to his sister Frances, Macaulay deplored the fact that Thackeray, 'a man of real genius', was again indulging in 'mountebank' lecturing to improve his finances, *The Letters of Thomas Babington Macaulay*, ed. Thomas Pinney, 6 vols (Cambridge: Cambridge University Press, 1981), VI, 76.

10   Thomas Babington Macaulay, *History of England*, 2 vols (London: Longmans, 1848), ch. 3.

11   'George the First', *Four Georges*, 288–93.

12   See Gordon N. Ray, *Thackeray: The Age of Wisdom* (London: Oxford University Press, 1958), 253–6.

13   Thomas Carlyle, 'Lecture I: The Hero as Divinity', *Heroes, Hero-Worship and the Heroic in History* (1841. London: Dent, 1959), 239.

14   *English Humourists*, 450–51.

15   Lecture V, 'The Hero as Man of Letters', *Heroes*, 398–9.

16   *History of Frederick II of Prussia, called Frederick the Great*, 6 vols (London: Chapman and Hall, 1886), 8–10.

17   Letter dated 8 August 1867, quoted in *Autobiography and Letters of Mrs Margaret Oliphant*, ed. Mrs Harry Coghill (Edinburgh and London: 1899; reprinted with an introduction by Q.D. Leavis, Leicester, 1974), 217.

18   Undated letter [1869], *Autobiography and Letters of Oliphant*, 223.

19   Before preparing the collected edition of the series, she had told Blackwood, 'I am extremely glad you like the historical papers. With modesty so do I'. Ibid., 219.

20 *The George Eliot Letters*, ed. G.S. Haight, 9 vols (New Haven: Yale University Press, 1954–78), IV, 246.

21 'Address to Working Men', *Blackwood's Edinburgh Magazine*, 103 (January 1868): 1–11. Eliot was careful, on 7 December 1867, to give John Blackwood *carte blanche* to write 'a preliminary note washing your hands of any over-trenchant statements on the part of a well-meaning Radical'. On 11 December 1867 Blackwood replied, 'I am quite ready to accept All that Felix Holt says, and I think the Address comes more dramatically without any introductory words from me' (*George Eliot Letters*, IV, 404, 406). Oliphant's series of sketches began in February and continued in April, May, July, August, September, October, December 1868; January March, June, and August 1869. The sympathy in outlook (rather than party affiliation) between Eliot and Blackwood was one of the binding ties that restored their partnership after her brief flirtation with George Smith, who had published *Romola* in 1863.

22 *Annals*, II, 475.

23 *The Autobiography of Margaret Oliphant: The Complete Text*, ed. Elisabeth Jay (Oxford: Oxford University Press, 1990), 25.

24 *Autobiography of Oliphant*, ed. Jay, 65. G. Eliot, 'Address to Working Men', *Blackwood's*, 103 (January 1868): 1–11.

25 Letter dated 15 April 1876, *Autobiography and Letters of Oliphant*, 257.

26 Letter dated 11 April 1876, *Autobiography and Letters of Oliphant*, 257.

27 'Macaulay', *Blackwood's*, 80 (August and September 1856): 127–41; 365–78.

28 'Modern Light Literature – History', *Blackwood's*, 80 (October 1855): 437–51. Agnes Strickland is recorded as holding a British Museum Library reading ticket in the 1828–37 swathe of readers, and by 1848 extra facilities for women were being demanded. P.R. Harris, *A History of the British Museum Library, 1753–1973* (London: British Library, 1998), 228, 767.

29 'Family History', *Blackwood's*, 80 (October 1856): 456–71.

30 The experience of translating Montalembert's *Monks of the West* also played its part in enabling her to recognize, by contrast, the new air of impartial scepticism abroad among the historians. 'The History of Scotland', *Blackwood's*, 101 (March 1867): 317–38.

31 *Four Georges*, 321. In her review of John Burton Hill's *History of Scotland,* she had criticized Hill's obliteration of the first visible women in Scottish history: 'It is not a point without importance that St Margaret did for Scotland what "every female saint does to somebody"', *Blackwood's*, 101 (March 1867): 324.

32 'Mr Thackeray and his Novels', *Blackwood's*, 77 (January 1855): 86–96.

33 Carlyle, 'Boswell's Life of Johnson', *English and other Critical Essays* (London: Dent, 1950), 19.

34 Margaret Oliphant, *Historical Sketches*, 3rd edn. (Edinburgh: Blackwood, 1875), 47–9.

35 George Lukács, *The Historical Novel*, trans. Hannah and Stanley Mitchell (London: Merlin, 1962), 201.

36 T. Carlyle, *English and other Critical Essays*, 19.

37 'History' (contributed to the *Edinburgh Review*, May 1828), *The Miscellaneous Writings of Lord Macaulay*, 2 vols (London: Longman, Green, Longman, and Roberts, 1860), I, 232–81.

38 *Blackwood's*, 77 (January 1855): 96.

39 Lukács, *Historical Novel*, 177–8, 182.

40 Quoted in G.N. Ray, *Thackeray: Age of Wisdom*, 144–5.

41 *Historical Sketches,* 455–6. Blackwood had not been enthusiastic about Oliphant's review of her friend JohnTulloch's book on Renan's *La Vie de Jésus* (*Blackwood's*, 96 [October 1864]: 417–31). 'My feeling is always to let the heathens rage and say nothing about them. I look upon the "good" sceptics with profound contempt as the most uncalled-for destroyers of paper going' (*Annals*, iii, 166–7).

42 Thackeray, 'George the First', *Four Georges*, 298, 302–3.

43 Carlyle, a fellow Lowland Scot of Protestant origins, complained that the History of Scotland had been reduced to a 'most dainty little Scandalous Chronicle ... of two persons: Mary Stuart, a Beauty, but over lightheaded; and Henry Darnley, a Booby who had fine legs', *English and other Critical Essays*, 19.

44 She would, however, have been annoyed by Thackeray's view that the verdict was usually arrived at along gendered lines: 'How devotedly Miss Strickland has stood by Mary's innocence! Are there not scores of ladies in this audience who persist in it too?'. (*Four Georges*, 298).

45 *Autobiography and Letters of Oliphant,* 213–4. Blackwood's daughter recollected how the Blackwood family had warmed to a woman writer, whose visit they were rather dreading on account of her fearsome reputation for classical learning, because on a tour of Edinburgh she had demonstrated 'a thoroughly feminine interest in Queen Mary, no foolish masculine wish to saddle her with political intrigues or even baser designs' (*Annals*, III, 161).

46 *Historical Sketches*, 210–11.

47 Ibid., 371.

48 *Annals*, III, 342–3.

49 *Historical Sketches*, 371–2.

50 *Annals*, III, 159.

51 Ibid., III., 164.

52 Elisabeth Jay, *Mrs Oliphant: 'A Fiction to Herself'. A Literary Life* (Oxford: Clarendon, 1995), 76ff.

53 Letter dated 3 February 1869. *Autobiography and Letters of Oliphant*, 221.

54 *Historical Sketches*, 379.

55 *Historical Sketches*, 2–3. Oliphant is frank in her acknowledgement of George's adulterous relation with Lady Suffolk, the Queen's 'bed-chamber woman', where Thackeray had been evasive. Thackeray's infamous 'reticence' in openly alluding to such matters and Oliphant's candour lie either side of the 1857 Matrimonial Causes Act which Barbara Leckie has argued as the pivotal cultural event of the nineteenth century: *Culture and Adultery: The Novel, the Newspaper, and the Law, 1857–1914* (Philadelphia: University of Pennsylvania Press, 2000).

56 *Historical Sketches*, 14.

57 The signs of Oliphant's most recent engagement, in *Miss Marjoribanks* (1866), with the women's sphere debate, brought into renewed prominence by Ruskin's lecture 'Of Queens' Gardens' (published, 21 June 1865) are everywhere evident.

58 *Historical Sketches*, 128, 150, 155, 160–61.

59 Only Alexander Pope, probably included because he was known to be John Blackwood's favourite poet (*Annals*, III, 160), seems to have proved resistant to such treatment. For more on Pope and the Victorians, see Francis O'Gorman, 76–97, above.

60 *Historical Sketches*, 388.

61 *Historical Sketches*, 263.

62 *Middlemarch: A Study of Provincial Life*, ed. Rosemary Ashton (Harmondsworth: Penguin, 1994), 3.

63 Blackwood MS 4213, 20 March 1866, *George Eliot Letters*, VII, 217.
64 *Middlemarch*, 141.
65 Letter dated 3 February 1869, *Autobiography and Letters of Oliphant*, 221.

Chapter 6

The 'Link of Transition': Samuel Johnson and the Victorians

Katherine Turner

The purpose of this chapter is to recuperate the many and various functions of Samuel Johnson and his works in the nineteenth century, and to shed light on changing Victorian notions of literary history, especially that of the eighteenth century.

Johnson's nineteenth-century reputation has not been neglected by literary historians, but it has been oversimplified. Bertrand H. Bronson in 1951 first diagnosed the essential 'problem' for scholars of Johnson's critical history, identifying a 'double tradition' established during the nineteenth century by which the cult of Johnson's personality gained popular appeal while interest in Johnson the author became increasingly the preserve of the 'learned' academy.[1] In 1971, Steven Phillips offered a tripartite developmental model of nineteenth-century interest in Johnson's *Lives of the Poets*: an early 'post-Romantic' interest in personality (embodied in the essays of Macaulay and Carlyle), and a generally hostile view of Johnson's actual works, gives way to a more pragmatic mid-Victorian interest in the *Lives*, which in turn modulates into a late-Victorian and early twentieth-century reappraisal of Johnson's work within its historical context.[2] More recently, Kevin Hart has outlined the way in which nineteenth-century critical discussions of Johnson reflected changing notions of the relationship between the individual and the historical epoch, yet served more statically to enshrine Johnson, by the end of the century, as a nostalgic embodiment of the English character.[3]

The versions of Johnson's Victorian afterlife provided by Bronson, Phillips and Hart are focused mainly on the realm of high intellectual history (Bronson's interest in the 'popular' tradition is not extensive), and are centrally concerned with Johnson, rather than with the Victorians. Nevertheless, they draw our attention to several issues which have not only been crucial to Johnson's critical history, but which also ramify far beyond their specific reference to the eighteenth-century man of letters: the relationship between popular and academic tastes; the practice and value of periodization; and the function of literature within the cultural life of the nation. The following essay will address these issues while also paying attention to some of the finer detail of what Andrew Elfenbein has described as 'the range of discourses through which earlier writers become accessible to later ones' (or indeed to later readers).[4] Victorian readers engaged with Johnson in a variety of ways: although it is difficult, in any period, to piece together a history of reading (as opposed to writing), the information that can be gleaned about how Victorians read Johnson presents some surprising findings. This is more emphatically the case with textual responses to Johnson. The complex significance of Johnson and his works to the Victorian age presents, in microcosm, the issues at stake within the evolving canon of literature which was being constructed by Victorian critics, educators, and men of letters.

The following chapter falls into two halves. The first argues for recognition of the continuing presence of Johnson in Victorian reading culture, but suggests that this fact did not necessarily imply a great interest in his age. The second explores the renewal of enthusiasm for Johnson in critical and educational contexts towards the end of the nineteenth century, a shift in reading habits that both prompts and is part of a reappraisal of the eighteenth century in general. This more complex consideration of Johnson's cultural significance is related to growing interests in periodization, and is bound up with revisionist approaches to English history and literature.

When Thackeray's Becky Sharp hurls Johnson's 'Dixonary' out of the coach window in *Vanity Fair* (1847–48), she is violating an icon of cultural authority whose relevance is already being questioned.[5] Although Robert Armitage, author of the pious *Doctor Johnson: His Religious Life and his Death*, can assert in 1850 that 'All men [sic] that are in any degree acquainted with English literature, have heard the name of Dr Johnson, and have perused his works',[6] Thomas Carlyle had already complained in his influential 1840 lecture on Johnson (published a year later in *On Heroes, Hero Worship, and the Heroic in History*) that his writings are 'now as it were disowned by the younger generation'.[7] Similarly, Thomas Macaulay's 1856 entry on Johnson in the *Encyclopaedia Britannica* observes that,

> Since his death, the popularity of his works – the *Lives of the Poets*, and perhaps, the *Vanity of Human Wishes*, excepted – has greatly diminished. His Dictionary has been altered by editors till it can scarcely be called his. An allusion to his *Rambler* or his *Idler* is not readily apprehended in literary circles. The fame even of *Rasselas* has grown somewhat dim.[8]

Still more emphatically, in 1884 James Hay, compiler of *Johnson: His Characteristics and Aphorisms*, is confident that 'Johnson's works are now almost forgotten'.[9] The truth must lie somewhere between these extremes of oblivion and intimate familiarity: but to judge from the number of editions of Johnson's works published during the Victorian period, his popularity and influence continued to be extensive. The *Dictionary* was reissued in 1835–37, 1843, 1845, 1852, 1853, 1856 (illustrated, 'for the use of schools and general students'), 1860, 1866 (expanded by Robert Gordon Latham), 1868 ('modernised'), 1876 ('pocket'), and 1883 ('pocket' again): and this despite the fact that critics frequently pronounced it 'now worthless to the student of language, being very poor and incorrect in etymology'.[10] *Rasselas* saw over twenty editions between 1837 and 1900, some with introductory essays (by Macaulay, Henry Morley, Birkbeck Hill), some with notes. The *Lives of the Poets* saw at least a dozen editions during the Victorian era, and many of the individual biographies were separately printed as introductions to volumes of poetry by, for example, Milton, Dryden, Congreve, Pope, Swift, Gay, Thomson, and Gray. Essays from the *Rambler*, *Idler*, and *Adventurer* were reprinted in 1848, 1876, 1878, 1888, and 1889. The poems, notably *London* and *The Vanity of Human Wishes*, were frequently anthologized, and Johnson's poetic *oeuvre* was printed in 1853, 1855 (by Gilfillan) and 1878 (in Cassell's Library Edition of British Poets). His letters were edited by Birkbeck Hill in 1892, but long before that the letter to Lord Chesterfield had entered national mythology as the original assertion of authorial independence of aristocratic patronage. The *Comic English Grammar* in 1863 punningly asserts that 'Dr Johnson's letter to Lord Chesterfield is a capital letter',[11] and numerous literary histories of the eighteenth century cite it as a paradigm shift in the world of English letters.[12]

The reading public, then, had ample opportunity to encounter new editions of Johnson's works. And we should not forget the unguessable numbers of old copies which must have been knocking about in people's houses, circulating libraries, and second-hand bookstalls. Richard Altick cites Henry Mayhew's account of the second-hand book trade in nineteenth-century London, in which one street seller informs Mayhew that 'nothing sold better than eighteenth-century prose classics, from Addison to Goldsmith', whereas 'the poems of such nineteenth-century writers as Hood, Shelley, Coleridge, Wordsworth, and Moore, however, seldom turned up on the stalls'.[13] (A report into the holdings of ten Westminster libraries in 1838 discovers with alarm, however, that 'Works of a Good Character, Dr Johnson, Goldsmith, etc' are outnumbered fiftyfold by 'Novels of the lowest character'.[14]) Peter Cunningham, who published his edition of Johnson's *Lives of the Poets* in 1854, recalls in his 'Preface' how as a young man in Edinburgh his own father, a 'common stone-mason', spent all available spare funds on bargain books:

> When his labours of the day were over ... he would repair to a sale-room kept by old Blackwood ... where books were sold at night by cheaper advances in price than those now in use. For three shillings and eleven pence he bought Johnson's 'Lives of the Poets' in four volumes, then comparatively a dear book. ... From this acquisition (gained by the sweat of the brow, in later years honoured with a better binding) my father learned much, and I have learned something. ... To my father's cheap but highly prized acquisition the public is mainly indebted for a good work (the Lives of the British Painters, Sculptors, and Architects), and in that edition I first read Johnson, and determined twenty years ago to become his editor.[15]

When Matthew Arnold felt in need of 'get[ting] money to retire',[16] it was to Johnson's *Lives* that he turned as a reliable generator of cash, producing an edited selection of *Six Chief Lives*, prefaced with a substantial essay originally published in *Macmillan's Magazine*, and including also Macaulay's 1856 *Encyclopaedia Britannica* biography of Johnson.

W.J. Linton's Chartist anthology of stirring and edifying quotations, *The National: A Library for the People* (1839) included a sprinkling of Johnson's more liberal observations, and implicitly placed him within a pantheon of radical literary tradition which included Milton, Voltaire, Paine, Rousseau, Wordsworth, Leigh Hunt (and Socrates). Johnson would doubtless have turned in his grave. An irregular serial publication called *Materials for Thinking*, compiled by John Taylor, brought writers like Addison, Sterne, Pope, and Johnson to a working-class audience:[17] unlike many other periodicals devoted to self-consciously working-class literature, Taylor's deliberately colonized works 'already canonical to the middle class'.[18] *Materials for Thinking* has as its title-page epigraph Johnson's observation that 'He that recalls the attention of mankind to any part of learning which time has left behind it, may be truly said to advance the literature of his own age'.[19]

So, we find that Armitage's assertion – 'All men that are in any degree acquainted with English literature, have heard the name of Dr Johnson, and have perused his works' – probably reflects the reading reality of Victorian society with some accuracy. As J.F. Waller argues in 1881, in a whimsical account of *Boswell and Johnson: Their Companions and Contemporaries* (Cassell's Monthly Shilling Library):

It is often said, Who reads Johnson's books now? – none but scholars and bookworms. To this we answer, They are not indeed read, as the 'Pilgrim's Progress,' or 'The Vicar of Wakefield,' or 'Robinson Crusoe;' but they are read as much, and more, than works which, as well as they, were in their day in the hands of every reader – the novels of Richardson and Fielding and Smollett.[20]

There is a moral dimension to such claims: the novelists cited here had, long before Waller's remark in 1881, become by-words for yobbish sauciness. William Spalding's influential *History of English Literature* (1853: in its eleventh edition by 1870) observes that 'When we pass from Johnson to the Novelists of his time, we seem as if leaving the aisles of an august cathedral, to descend into the galleries of a productive but ill-ventilated mine. Around us clings a foul and heavy air, which youthful travellers in the realm of literature cannot safely breathe' (336). In similar vein, the *Quarterly Review* in 1885 attributes the denigration of Johnson's works as much to the 'carelessness which finds its intellectual food in the freshest productions of the circulating library, as to a deliberate distaste for Johnson's works'.[21]

On the reading habits and opinions of *literary* Victorians, as opposed to the common reader, we have much more information. The correspondence of Robert and Elizabeth Barrett Browning, for example, reveals an easy familiarity with the *Lives of the Poets* and the *Dictionary*, which Macaulay also recommends as a source of literary 'pleasure',[22] and Ruskin cites frequently and with enthusiasm. Charlotte Brontë recommends the *Lives of the Poets* to Ellen Nussey as exemplary biographical writing,[23] and later in the century Gissing lists the *Lives* (as well as Boswell's *Life*) as one of his favourite books.[24] Several of George Eliot's letters describe re-readings of favourite Johnsonian texts. In 1872 she observes in a letter to Mrs Richard Congreve, who is currently reading Milton, that she and Lewes

> also are rather old-fashioned in our light reading just now; for I have rejected Heyse's German stories, brand new, in favour of dear old Johnson's 'Lives of the Poets', which I read aloud in my old age with a delicious revival of girlish impressions ...[25]

and in 1875 she writes to Blackwood that 'it is a long time since I read a story newer than Rasselas, which I re-read two years ago with a desire to renew my childish delight in it, when it was one of my best-loved companions'.[26]

John Ruskin, who frankly despised the 'sententious pentametre' of Johnson's verse and opined that he had 'neither ear nor imagination', nevertheless acknowledges that Johnson's prose had been an important stylistic model and personal moral influence.[27] He recalls how

> On our foreign journeys, it being of course desirable to keep the luggage as light as possible, my father had judged that four little volumes of Johnson – the *Idler* and the *Rambler* – did, under names wholly appropriate to the circumstances, contain more substantial literary nourishment than could be, from any other author, packed into so portable compass. And accordingly, in spare hours, and on wet days, the turns and returns of reiterated *Rambler* and iterated *Idler* fastened themselves in my ears and mind ... I never for an instant compared Johnson to Scott, Pope, Byron, or any of the really great writers whom I loved. But I at once and for ever recognized in him a man entirely sincere, and infallibly wise in the view and estimate he gave of the common questions, business, and ways of the world. ...
>
>   I hold it more than happy that, during those continental journeys, in which the vivid excitement of the greater part of the day left me glad to give spare half-hours to the study of a thoughtful book, Johnson was the one author accessible to me. No other writer could have secured me, as he did, against all chance of being misled by my own sanguine and metaphysical temperament. He taught me carefully to measure life, and distrust fortune; and he secured me, by his adamantine common-sense, for ever, from being caught in the cobwebs of German metaphysics, or sloughed in the English drainage of them.[28]

The epithet 'adamantine' here nicely recalls the 'adamant' to which Johnson had likened Shakespeare in his 1756 'Preface'.[29]

Admittedly, the bracing properties of Johnson's moral essays were not thus appreciated by all Victorian readers. Leslie Stephen, for example, although he does much to popularize Johnson in the closing decades of the century, condemns the *Rambler* as the 'culminating period of Johnson's worst qualities of style', and pronounces it 'as heavy reading as the heavy class of lay-sermonising to which it belongs'.[30] Negative though such observations may be, they do nevertheless assume that readers will know what they are talking about. Similarly, within literary texts of the Victorian era, Johnson's works not infrequently function as touchstones in a manner which assumes their popular familiarity (Becky Sharp and the *Dictionary* is a case in point). Jane Eyre's first conversation with the saintly Helen Burns uses a Johnsonian text to delineate the fundamental differences between the two girls:

> I saw a girl sitting on a stone bench near; she was bent over a book, on the perusal of which she seemed intent: from where I stood I could see the title – it was 'Rasselas;' a name that struck me as strange, and consequently attractive.

In turning a leaf she happened to look up, and I said to her directly:–

'Is your book interesting?' I had already formed the intention of asking her to lend it to me some day.

'I like it,' she answered, after a pause of a second or two, during which she examined me.

'What is it about?' ...

'You may look at it,' replied the girl, offering me the book.

I did so; a brief examination convinced me that the contents were less taking than the title: 'Rasselas' looked dull to my trifling taste; I saw nothing about fairies, nothing about genii; no bright variety seemed spread over the closely printed pages. I returned it to her ...[31]

The dual narrative perspective here acknowledges both the superficial dullness of Johnson's tale; and the superficiality of this judgement, since Jane's youthful taste is described as 'trifling'. Arguably, much of the impact of Brontë's novel derives from its bold challenge to the defeatist moral of *Rasselas* (according to which happiness is perpetually out of reach).

Rasselas also has a surprisingly energetic afterlife on the Victorian stage. The second half of the nineteenth century witnessed several theatrical versions and parodies of the story, ranging from the Christmas pantomime at Bradford in 1854 (*Rasselas, Prince of Abyssinia; Or, Harlequin and the Happy Valley*), to a Haymarket production by William Brough in 1862 of *Rasselas, Prince of Abyssinia; Or, The Happy Valley. An Extravaganza, Founded on Dr Johnson's well-known Tale, but at times getting very wide of its foundation*, to W.S. Gilbert's satiric rendering, initially (in 1872) as *Happy Arcadia*, whose inhabitants' pastoral happiness disintegrates as money, crime and dissipation lead them astray, and finally as *Utopia Limited*, in which the Happy Valley proves elusive not because mankind ought not to desire its unnatural ease, but because it would be extremely boring.[32] These snapshots of Victorian light entertainment suggest that Johnson's tale retained a powerful hold over the popular imagination, which nevertheless took a particular delight in overturning its solemn philosophy.

None of this evidence of the continuing vitality of Johnson's works in the Victorian period can however gainsay the increasingly powerful appeal of his biography to readers, students, and critics as the century progressed. Just as the continuing interest in the works was fuelled by ongoing republication in a variety of formats, many of them inexpensive, the growing fascination with Johnson's life was encouraged by a series of publishing landmarks. J.W. Croker's edition of Boswell's *Life of Johnson* had appeared in 1831, to the famous derision of Macaulay, who lambasted Croker's reckless interpolations of material from other sources (contemporary memoirs and personal correspondence).[33] By mid-century, the essays of Carlyle and Macaulay on Johnson had also done much not only to elevate him to the status of literary hero ('one of our great English souls'),[34] but also to privilege the biography over the works, since it offered more scope for humour, curiosity (as in Macaulay's memorable description of the man who 'dressed like a scarecrow, and ate like a cormorant'),[35] and sentiment (Johnson's acts of charity and his household menagerie of lost souls was especially congenial in this respect).

Despite Macaulay's vitriol, Croker's was the most substantial version of Johnson's life available during the first half of the Victorian era, and an additional volume of *Johnsoniana: Or, Supplement to Boswell* was issued by Croker in 1836, printing recollections of Johnson from almost 50 hands, collected from 'nearly a hundred different publications'. In 1842 were published the *Diary and Letters* of Mrs d'Arblay (formerly Fanny Burney), offering yet another biographical perspective on Johnson, which Elizabeth Barrett Browning for one found more congenial than the Boswellian 'great lumbering bookcase of a man': she urges Mary Russell Mitford 'do read the book – I mean, at once – read it at once. Dr. Johnson is softer in it than he is to be seen elsewhere – more as Tetty beheld him than as Boswell did!'[36] In *Middlemarch* (1871–72), Eliot has a vignette of Mary Garth 'in her usual corner, laughing over Mrs Piozzi's recollections of Johnson':[37] during the 1830s (the period at which *Middlemarch* is set), there would have been numerous editions of Piozzi's affectionate memoirs of Johnson available, and the *Anecdotes* (first published in 1786) had also been recently republished for the benefit of Eliot's own contemporaries.[38]

In 1874, Percy Fitzgerald sought to replace Croker's edition of Boswell's *Life* with an unadorned version, on the grounds that annotation and interpolation destroyed the integrity of Boswell's vision. A few years later, George Birkbeck Hill began to publish a range of Johnsoniana, beginning with anecdotal essays and selections, and culminating in Boswell's *Life of Johnson* in six heavily annotated volumes for Oxford University Press in 1887. Although it was attacked by Fitzgerald as a 'catalogue of mistakes, misapprehensions, wild flounderings, and speculations',[39] Birkbeck Hill's biographer in the *Dictionary of National Biography* (Thomas Seccombe) pronounces that the *Life* was 'accepted as a masterpiece of spacious editing', and Leslie Stephen likewise defended it.[40] With Birkbeck Hill's project, the shift in emphasis from Johnson's works to his life has been institutionalized, and assertions such as that made in the 'Introduction' to *Wit and Wisdom of Samuel Johnson* are becoming commonplace later in the nineteenth century:

'his written wisdom was indeed great, but it is in his spoken wisdom that he lives'.[41] By 1909, Lord Rosebery can observe, only slightly facetiously, that Boswell's *Life of Johnson* is now 'annotated and commentated as if it were Holy Writ'.[42]

Such was the interest in Johnson's 'spoken wisdom' that numerous abbreviations of Boswell or portable anthologies of Johnsoniana began to appear. The Rev. J.F. Russell in 1847 provided an abridgement of Boswell intended 'chiefly for such readers as may not have leisure or inclination for the perusal of Boswell's celebrated but voluminous biography' ('Advertisement'), published in Burns' *Select Library* in the 'New and Cheap Series of Entertaining and Instructive Publications, suited especially for Youth'. In 1881 J.F. Waller offered an affordable 'abridgment [*sic*] of what is in Boswell and, in addition, somewhat that is not to be found there – in relation to the literature of Johnson's day' (iii), published in Cassell's *Monthly Shilling Library* series; and in 1892 Robina Napier edited a compact collection of *Anecdotes of the Late Samuel Johnson, LLD, by Mrs Piozzi, Richard Cumberland, Bishop Percy and Others, together with the Diary of Dr Campbell and Extracts from that of Madame d'Arblay*, venturing to hope that readers will enjoy the opportunity of reading 'a different, not a better or a fuller representation than Boswell's' (v). By this time, Birkbeck Hill himself has entered the abridgement market: indeed, his earliest published Johnsoniana were in a more popular vein than the later Oxford editions of the *Life*. In 1878 he published a collection of anecdotal essays, *Dr Johnson: His Friends and his Critics*, and in 1888 a small handbook of quotations entitled *Wit and Wisdom of Samuel Johnson*, usefully arranged under subject headings (from 'Accounting for Everything Systematically' and 'Acquaintances' to 'Youth' and 'Zeal in Religion'). Macaulay's and Carlyle's essays were likewise reprinted many times in affordable formats, often as introductions to selections of Johnson's own works.

In 1874 George Eliot's admirer, Alexander Main, leapt on the Johnson bandwagon, publishing the *Life and Conversations of Dr Samuel Johnson (founded chiefly upon Boswell)*, with a 'Preface' supplied by George Henry Lewes, observing how necessary such an abridgement is, since so many 'cultivated men and women' appear 'satisfied with vague second-hand knowledge' of Boswell (viii). Main's reworking of Boswell is mawkish and exclamatory, and was derided by the press: 'A Hash of Boswell's Johnson' was the *Saturday Review*'s headline, which marvelled that Lewes could have put his name to such a work.[43] As a literary event, however, it is not without significance. Main was already the successful compiler of *Wise, Witty, and Tender Sayings in Prose and Verse Selected from the Works of George Eliot*

(1872) – derided as 'unendurable Johnsonese' by one reviewer[44] – and the *George Eliot Birthday Book* (1874). Leah Price has recently speculated that Lewes may have hoped to distract Main from his rather embarrassing hero-worship of Eliot by suggesting the Boswell project: if so, however, the strategy backfired, since Eliot's name and literary status became enmeshed in Main's Johnson, not only through the perceived similarity of the *Conversations* to the Eliot anthologies (the second edition of the *Sayings* appeared within weeks of Main's Boswell), but also through the placing of an epigraph from *The Spanish Gypsy* at the beginning of *Conversations*.[45] Clearly, Main (like Boswell, a persistent and adulatory young Scot) perceives striking similarities between Eliot and Johnson, particularly in their status as literary sages. The project of the *Sayings* is implicitly to elevate Eliot's moral status above that of a mere (female) novelist, and the parallel with Johnson (who never wrote a novel, though confessing to a saucy enjoyment of romances) serves further to enhance the nigh-Biblical wisdom of her work. Although Main (like Boswell again) is in many ways a ridiculous figure, his account of the value of Johnson's biography is arresting:

> [T]he life of Johnson ... helps to correct the vicious idealism of novelists and biographers, – an idealism which does not proceed by the selection and purification of typical truths, but by the suppression of the lasting facts of human nature and human life: an idealism which is afraid to paint goodness and greatness blended with evil and weakness, but will only paint in black and white ... the distinct recognition of serious defects in a character otherwise dear and venerable to us, will help us to feel charitably towards the defects of others. (xi–xii)

Ironically, this philosophy is exactly the reverse of Johnson's own: he had argued in *Rambler* 4 against the use of 'mixed' characters in fiction, lest impressionable readers be morally confused.[46] But Main's perspective testifies to the influence of Eliot's notion that 'the greatest benefit we owe to the artist ... is the extension of our sympathies',[47] and suggests that (perhaps in part educated into moral subtlety by Eliot's work), late nineteenth-century readers were increasingly interested in complexity and contrariness – qualities abundantly embodied in Johnson.

Lewes and Eliot seem to have been unimpressed by Main's Boswell: Lewes writes to him that

> I can't promise to read your book for some time yet ... nor do I think Mrs. Lewes will be able to do so. But if we thought it a masterpiece *that* wouldn't

alter the fact – and if we thought it rubbish hundreds of others might think it a masterpiece – and *they* are its real public.[48]

This superior attitude towards the reading 'public' who stoop to anecdotal anthologies embodies a growing separation between recreational reading on the one hand, and on the other the 'serious' study of authors in the evolving canon of English literature.

The growth in educational literary study in the nineteenth century is associated with the general culture of self-help and self-improvement, but more specifically with the increasing pressures to meet the changing educational needs of the nation and its empire through the institutionalization of English literature (far more accessible than the linguistically challenging Classics as a humanizing discipline).[49] Chris Baldick identifies three main factors which worked to gain English literature a place in higher education:

> first, the specific needs of the British empire expressed in the regulations for admission to the India Civil Service [following the 1853 India Act]; second, the various movements for adult education including Mechanics' Institutes, Working Men's Colleges, and extension lecturing; third, within this general movement, the specific provisions made for women's education.[50]

Johnson, a writer whose chief works fell into the category of criticism rather than creative literature, became an important figure in the Victorian history of criticism as a cultural enterprise. In 'The Bishop and the Philosopher', an essay in *Macmillan's Magazine* for January 1863, Matthew Arnold argued that the 'chief sources of intellectual influence' in England during the previous 150 years had been 'its chief organs of criticism – Addison, Johnson, the first Edinburgh Reviewers'.[51] In 1881, J.F. Waller claims that 'it is to Johnson that we owe the elevation of the magazine, from little better than a contribution of gossiping to an organ of literary and political power'.[52]

Pedagogically, the morally impeccable works of Johnson provided eminently suitable material. And his prose style was generally considered a good model for students: as Arnold observes in 1878, although in Johnson's prose 'the words are often pompous and long ... the structure is always plain and modern'.[53] The steady flow of editions of Johnsonian texts described earlier in this essay is to some extent attributable to the need for pedagogical material, a need met also by a deluge of literary surveys, 'Standard Poet' volumes, and enterprises such as the *English Men of Letters*.[54] Such works catered simultaneously for educational establishments and 'private students', whose needs were acknowledged, for instance, in William Spalding's *The History of*

English Literature ... Illustrated by Extracts (1853), which the author offers as 'an Elementary Text-Book, to those who are interested in the instruction of young persons' (1). James Hannay's *A Course of English Literature* (1866) was 'intended for the use, not of schools only, but of the large and increasing class of young men in our great cities, who desire to be guided to the acquirement of a respectable knowledge of our national literature',[55] and presupposes no more than interest, and 'access to a tolerable library, such as is now happily to be obtained in all our chief towns' (1). Similar surveys were offered by, for example, Henry Morley's *A First Sketch of English Literature* (1873) and Austin Dobson's *The Civil Service Handbook of English Literature* (1874), whose 'primary object is to assist those whose time and opportunities are restricted' (1).[56]

Within this climate of interest in the functional value of literature, Johnson's works (especially the moral essays and *Rasselas*) proved particularly congenial, and appeared in several editions designed for schools and colleges. *Rasselas* fell victim to a series of earnest and Gradgrindian editors, chief among them the formidable Rev. John Hunter, MA, 'Instructor of Candidates for the Military and Civil Service Examinations, &c.; and formerly Vice-Principal of the National Society's Training Institution, Battersea'. In 1860, he issued a massively-annotated version of Johnson's tale, in an educational series published by Longman which also included *Paradise Lost, Henry VIII* and *The Deserted Village*. The title page announces Hunter's educational ambitions:

> With Introductory Remarks; Explanatory and Grammatical Annotations; Specimens of Interrogative Lessons; Answers to Questions Set at the Oxford Middle-Class Examination, etc; and a Life of Dr. Johnson. Adapted as a Reading-Book for Schools, and specially designed to prepare Young Persons for the University Middle-Class Examinations.

The 'Preface' to the volume asserts that 'Johnson's Rasselas, on account of its peculiar rhythm, may, as a reading-book in schools, prove an excellent means of promoting the deliberate and expressive elocution which teachers often find it so difficult to make their pupils acquire' (v), and ventures to hope that the structure and contents of the annotations will enable 'an understanding of the subject-matter of Rasselas' to be 'as it were *questioned into* the mind of the pupil' (vi). Appendix 1 provides 'Specimens of Interrogative Lessons', such as 'Repeat the first paragraph of this chapter'; 'State what you know geographically about Abyssinia' (139); and, dauntingly, the following barrage:

What was the state of vegetation in this valley? Give some zoological account of the place. What zoological name have we to denote animals that bite the grass? And what for beasts of prey? What is suggested by the epithet *solemn* as applied to the elephant? (140)

Appendix 2 supplies 400 explicatory notes, and Appendix 3 a sample Oxford University Middle-Class Examination paper on *Rasselas*, which requires considerable contextual knowledge of Johnson, his other works, and his age. Lord Rosebery probably speaks for many who were educated during the Victorian period when he recalls that '"Rasselas" I read not voluntarily, but assiduously at school, and, probably for that reason, never wish to read again'.[57] Becky Sharp's treatment of the *Dictionary* bespeaks a similar attitude: but we should beware of assuming that Johnson functioned universally as a tiresome embodiment of establishment authority. Working men and women, including those of a radical persuasion, took inspiration from his example. An essay in the *Chartist Circular* for 16 May 1840, 135–6, 'The Genius of Working Men', argues that not only Shakespeare but also Homer, Aesop, Socrates, Milton, Johnson, Defoe and others 'sprang from humble origins', thus proving that 'genius is almost exclusive to working men'.[58]

Johnson's poetry (*London* and *The Vanity of Human Wishes*) is absent from the predominantly lyrical collection of Palgrave's *Golden Treasury*, and also from most anthologies aimed at schoolchildren.[59] However, it features in many anthologies and surveys aimed at older readers (Civil Service examinees, for example), and as the century draws to a close it begins to resurface in more general collections, such as Macmillan's *The English Poets: Selections with Critical Introductions* (5 vols, 1880–1918), and Morley's five-volume *Cassell's Library of English Literature* (1876–81).

With the institutionalizing of English literature came a need not only for student editions of primary literary texts, but also for secondary material by way of critical guidance. Here, Johnson's *Lives of the Poets* came into their own. Between 1800 and 1900 there were 25 reprints or new editions of the *Lives*. As early as 1844, the Rev. James Pycroft had recommended them as the definitive 'handbook or guide to the poets' in *A Course of English Reading* (304). In his 1856 *Encyclopaedia Britannica* biography of Johnson, Macaulay recommends the *Lives* for their 'often excellent' critical insights, and praises them as Johnson's best works.[60] Still more influentially, Matthew Arnold in his prefatory essay to the 1878 selected edition of the *Lives* insists that

I know of no such first-rate piece of literature, for supplying in this way the wants of the literary student, existing at all in any other language; or existing in our own language for any period except the period which Johnson's six lives cover. ...

I should like to think that a number of young people might be brought to know an important period of our literary and intellectual history, through means of the lives of six of its leading and representative authors, told by a great man. I should like to think that they would go on, under the stimulus of the lives, to acquaint themselves with some leading and representative work of each author. In the six lives they would at least have secured, I think, a most valuable *point de repère* in the history of our English life and literature, a point from which afterwards to find their way; whether they might desire to ascend upwards to our anterior literature, or to come downwards to the literature of yesterday and of the present.[61]

Naturally, Arnold (keen, as we have seen, to generate cash for his retirement) here has a vested interest in trumpeting the virtues of Johnson's *Lives*, which Edmund Gosse in 1891 is to disparage as 'one of the worst of guides'.[62] But the combined cultural influence of Johnson and Arnold was significant, and Arnold's little volume was very successful, seeing new editions in 1879 and 1881, as well as modified versions for schools in 1886 and 1889, which were 'compressed by the elimination of matter unsuited to the juvenile & feminine mind and moderately *annotated*'. They were still in use as school textbooks until the middle of the twentieth century.[63] The *Lives* also functioned as a model for other literary biographies: in 1884 James Hay recalls how Byron had pronounced the *Lives* 'the finest critical work extant', and observes that it has 'led the way to several subsequent editions on an improved and extended scale'.[64] Johnson's mode of literary biography was the template for almost all Victorian exercises in the genre, culminating in the *English Men of Letters* project and the *Dictionary of National Biography*, which William Hoste in 1900 sees as deeply indebted to the model of Johnson's biographies as well as Boswell's, and a matter of 'the highest public interest and importance'.[65]

As Johnson's life and works (particularly the *Lives*) became better known and increasingly influential, the number of publications *about* Johnson increased. Victorian scholars and amateurs alike responded to Johnson's growing cultural status, often harnessing them to a favoured cause or hobby-horse. As with his works, the varied texture of Johnson's life offered scope for writers and readers from a variety of social and educational backgrounds. An anonymous author in 1840 produces an account of *The Last Days of Dr Johnson* as a case study in the inadequacy of good works as opposed to the conviction of salvation, and the 'insufficiency of the unaided human intellect, though of the very highest order, ... to conduct the mind to the perception and enjoyment of vital religion' (6–7). More Anglican in emphasis is the Rev. Robert Armitage's *Doctor Johnson: His Religious Life and his Death* (1850), where Johnson is celebrated (echoing Carlyle) as 'one of our great English souls', a 'prophet to our people', and 'the unflinching friend of the poor, the humble, and the weak'.[66] Henry, Lord Brougham, the abolitionist and educationalist, who published a two-volume *Lives of Men of Letters and Science, who flourished in the Time of George III* (1845), only really engages with Johnson once he can discern that Johnson 'always was an enemy of Negro Slavery', and therefore clearly an 'independent thinker' whose understanding was of a 'masculine strength'.[67] Dawson Burns in 1884 recruits Johnson to the temperance cause in his pamphlet discussion of *Dr Samuel Johnson as a Temperance Witness and Moralist*. Regretting the fact that few readers are 'probably cognizant of the extent and value of his opinions and experience in regard to the Temperance Question' (iii), Burns sets out to correct this ignorance, and establish (on some fairly selective evidence, such as the fact that Boswell once recommended 'Dr Cheyne's "Essay on Health", a thoroughly anti-wine book') that 'if now living, his masterly pen and voice would be cheerfully enlisted on the side of those who teach, that neither to drink strong liquors nor to license their sale is the wisdom of Christian men and of a Christian state' (51). Conspicuously absent from Burns' account is Johnson's observation that 'there is nothing which has yet been contrived by man, by which so much happiness is produced as by a good tavern or inn'.[68]

The abundant biographical evidence of Johnson's philanthropy and compassion increasingly endeared him to the humanitarian sensibilities of Victorian readers, as did his relative freedom from political controversy. On this latter point, Lieut.-Col. F. Grant representatively observes in 1887 that although Johnson was 'in principle a strong Tory, and his worst form of abuse was to call his adversary a vile Whig', almost all of his 'personal friends' were Whigs, and he appears, 'in fact, to have taken little interest in practical politics'.[69] By 1900, James Hoste can more floridly declare that Birkbeck Hill's characterization of Johnson as a 'Radical' will 'surprise those only who imagine Conservative principles to exclude zeal for equal liberty and justice to every class, and a warm desire for the comfort and progress of all races and conditions of men'.[70]

Johnson's personal independence as a writer was another point of attraction for Victorian commentators. I have already remarked on the proverbial status in the nineteenth century of the letter to Lord Chesterfield. More generally, many writers praise Johnson for being 'the first who made literature stand upon its own merits, without patronage'.[71] Paradoxically, even while some

Victorian readers and critics are beginning to locate Johnson as a pivotal point in English literary culture – a point at which the culture of patronage gave way to the professional literary marketplace within which it was, to an extent, every man (or woman) for themselves – others were also beginning to display nostalgia for that moment in eighteenth-century literary life when the culture of a nation was, so the myth would have it, embodied in and overseen by a single figure of authority: Samuel Johnson. In his landmark account of Johnson, in the very first of the *English Men of Letters* series, Leslie Stephen in 1878 describes him, following the publication of the *Dictionary*, 'sitting in the chair previously occupied by his namesake Ben, by Dryden, and by Pope; but which has since that time been vacant. The world of literature has become too large for such authority.'[72] In 1892, Stephen echoes his own earlier words, regretting that a 'literary dictator' has 'ceased to be a possibility', because 'the art of conversation is disappearing', and 'society has become too large and diffuse'.[73] Birkbeck Hill in 1898 confirms that Johnson was 'the great Cham of Literature, who ruled the world of letters as no man has ever ruled it since his time'.[74] Although not mentioning Johnson by name, Robert Buchanan seems to have his image in mind when he calls for a 'Sultan of Literature' to cleanse the polluted literary landscape of London, currently corrupted by the 'Fleshly School' of poetry (itself corrupted by filthy French influence) in the early 1870s.[75] In 1900, James William Hoste opens his survey of Johnsoniana old and new with a paragraph in which Johnson is cast triumphantly in the roles of 'Monarch of Literature' and unshaken 'Colossus'.[76] For the *Quarterly Review* in 1885, Johnson's authoritative status makes him peculiarly appealing to the present era:

> It would almost seem as if, in an age like our own, which can boast of little independent judgment, and is so easily swayed by the caprices of superficial fashion in thought as well as in literature, we were attracted by the very sense of our own weakness to the manly and vigorous independence which, even in his prejudices, never deserted Johnson.[77]

The epithet 'manly' here applied to Johnson's independence reflects a growing trend in Johnson criticism during the 1880s and 1890s, such that by 1898 the young scholar Caroline Spurgeon can dutifully observe in her prize essay at University College London that Johnson is 'the most manly of Englishmen'.[78] In 1895 W.H. Craig published *Dr Johnson and the Fair Sex: A Study of Contrasts*, which presents a detailed account of Johnson's personal and social relationships with the opposite sex and of his views on women (such as the observation that 'Wise married women don't trouble themselves about infidelity in their husbands', which must have resonated reassuringly in a decade plagued by controversial divorce cases in high society).[79] Johnson's 'masterfulness' is located as the source of his attraction for women – 'Every woman, every child, likes that which it can look up to, and which expects to be obeyed' (14) – and his authority over the females in his world offers an attractive contrast to the state of affairs in the Britain of 1895:

> And here we may point to the distinction between the 'New Woman' of the eighteenth century and her successor of our own times. However 'advanced' the former might be, she never sought to divest herself of her femininity. The notion of the divided skirt had not dawned upon her; the problem of sexuality troubled her not. … She might dabble in republicanism, denounce the injustice of the laws affecting her sex, protest against the excessive domination of men, and assert her right to education, representation, and all the rest; but she was content to remain, a woman, in a sphere absolutely distinct from that of man. (77–8)

As with the life, the works too could be invoked as a healthy antidote to contemporary ills. As early as 1866, James Hannay had observed that

> there is something in Johnsonian literature, which, by its vigour, decisiveness, and humour, has a tendency to counteract some of the more morbid symptoms of the literature of our own day. A youthful student, foaming under the influence of the 'spasmodic' school, could not be more wholesomely treated than to a dose of Johnson's poetry …[80]

The accumulation of Johnsonian publications which this chapter has outlined elevated Johnson to a unique position in the canon of English literature, itself being formalized by many of the writers and critics whose work on Johnson we have here encountered. 1885, the centenary of Johnson's death, was celebrated somewhat modestly in comparison to the lavish tercentenary celebrations of Cromwell's birth in 1899. There was a simple memorial service at St Clement Danes, and 'many articles alluding to the subject' in 'newspapers and periodicals'.[81] Nevertheless, the *Quarterly Review* in 1885 observes that 'Johnson's influence is not only an enduring one, but is probably stronger now than it has ever been since his death'.[82] This development presented an interesting conundrum, given a tendency in certain quarters to denigrate the eighteenth century as an age of superficiality, dullness, or impiety. Carlyle early in our period ('The Hero as Man of Letters' was delivered in 1840) got round the problem by seeing Johnson's struggle for eminence (like that of Burns and Rousseau) in the mire of the eighteenth century – 'a time of scepticism, simulacra and universal decadence' – as part of his heroism: he 'lived under galling conditions; struggling as under mountains of impediment'. Johnson is heroic because he is absolutely atypical of his age: indeed, Carlyle insists, 'in few centuries that one could specify since the world began, was a life of Heroism more difficult for a man'.[83] Henry Francis Cary in 1843 comes at the question from a rather more downbeat perspective, suggesting that

> It was the chance of Johnson to fall upon an age that rated his great abilities at their full value. His laboriousness had the appearance of something stupendous, when there were many literary but few very learned men. ... He would have been of less consequence in the days of Elizabeth or of Cromwell.[84]

What one begins to see later in the century, however, is a reversal of emphasis, by which the steadily more impressive status of Johnson and his works forces a reconsideration of eighteenth-century history in general. Increasingly exercised by the problem of precisely how such a dreadful age could possibly have produced such a phenomenon, readers come increasingly to conclude that it was not such a dreadful age after all.

On the contrary, if the eighteenth century could produce a Johnson, it must be worthy of serious consideration: several studies of the period appear in the 1890s.[85] This movement towards revisionism goes hand in hand with a growing interest in national literary history as a story not of reaction and revolution, but of evolution. Where Macaulay had described the eighteenth century as 'the most dreary part of the dreary interval which separated two ages of prosperity'; where Grant had observed that 'Johnson lived between two brilliant epochs of literature'; and where Buchanan had exclaimed with teleological moral rapture that 'at last, however, Wordsworth came, and English literature was saved':[86] in 1884 James Hay could observe that 'the life of Johnson is the link of transition by which the literature of the last century has developed into that of our own',[87] and William John Courthope, in his influential study *The Liberal Movement in English Literature* (1885) could state that the eighteenth century, 'far from being a time of destruction and revolution, was a necessary link in a long chain of historic national development', and its role 'consisted in providing a safe transition from the manners of the mediaeval to those of modern society' (40–41).

The paradigm shift engineered by nineteenth-century science may also have exerted an influence on models of literary history, fostering an interest in gradual evolution, transition, and development. Employing a metaphor of organic change, Edmund Gosse in his 1891 *History of Eighteenth-Century Literature* traces a slow but direct line of evolution from Congreve, Gay, Thomson and Winchelsea, through Gray, Gilpin, and Gilbert White: 'we perceive that a slow and slender, but ever-broadening stream of natural observation has been meandering down the whole length of the very century which is supposed to be so characteristically devoid of it' (379). Trends in political thought may likewise have extended into the literary. Just as the later nineteenth century witnesses a radical reappraisal of Oliver Cromwell and his era,[88] Johnson's England likewise earns new respect as an age which oversaw 'the passage of our nation to prose and reason',[89] and established the stable, tolerant, humane, and predominantly middle-class culture which had shaped the Victorian age, notwithstanding the turbulent years of Revolution and Romanticism. Although many Victorians, including Macaulay, blamed the alleged coarseness and superficiality of the eighteenth century on the cultural dominance of the Hanoverian court and the dissolute aristocracy, later nineteenth-century historians came to place greater emphasis on the growing cultural force of the middle classes, whose increasing centrality in national life is attributed to the rational tranquillity of Britain's socio-political landscape, post 1688. Within this framework, Johnson increasingly became typical of an entire class. Leslie Stephen writes in *Hours in a Library* that 'To the fact that Johnson was the typical representative of a large class of Englishmen, we owe it that the Society of Rights did not develop into a Jacobin Club' (i. 24), echoing the view of Isaac Disraeli in 1795 (reprinted by his more famous son in 1881) that 'Johnson was of the order of men whose individual genius becomes that of a people',[90] which in turn is reiterated in 1907 by Walter Raleigh, who claims that Johnson 'has almost become the tutelary genius of the English people'.[91]

Gradually, then, with Johnson at the centre of the debate, the contours of literary history are redescribed such that steady development rather than reversal becomes the preferred model. Even in 1866, James Hannay's *Course of English Literature* had presented the Romantic era as almost an aberration, and constructed an affinity between the Victorian age and the eighteenth century: 'the spirit of our present literature is historical and critical rather than original and inventive. It is not so poetical as that of the last generation' (305). By 1900, Thomas Seccombe can affirm (in a volume of literary history entitled *The Age of Johnson*) that, 'In a word, the literary landscape in Johnson's day was slowly but surely assuming the general outlines to which we are all accustomed' (xxxiv). As affinities are (re)constructed between the Victorian age and that of Johnson, Bloom's model of Freudian rejection of one generation by the next gives way to a more extensive model, a desire to recuperate a longer family history which may be the more potent for its slowness and steadiness of evolution. Johnson's venerable and eccentric demeanour makes him peculiarly congenial to those in search of a literary ancestor or grandfather, a figure who provokes mingled amusement, fondness and respect. Curiously, his lack of biological progeny perhaps makes him more universally available as a literary forebear.

Nor should these representations of Johnson and his age be read simply as expressions of nostalgia for a safer epoch. Although Birkbeck Hill for one can lapse into such behaviour ('there are persons who, weary of endless talk on reforms and improvements, like at times to drop out of the stream of this uneasy age to seek for quiet thought among men who never so much as heard that there was a social science'),[92] others emphasize the period's dynamism and variety. Seccombe pronounces it 'one of the greatest creative periods in our national annals', characterized by energetic 'contradictions' and by the breeding of men such as 'Howard and Wilberforce, Bentham and Romilly', who have worked to 'elevat[e] the national conscience since the death of Dr Johnson'.[93] We are reminded of Alexander Main's interest in Johnson as an Eliot-like case study in moral complexity. Similarly, the *Quarterly Review* in 1885 celebrated the 'discursive intellectual habit of his age' (164), and observed that 'Johnson is interesting chiefly because he unites in himself so much that was great, but yet diverse, in his own age' (168). Birkbeck Hill himself in racier mood can wax lyrical over Johnson's love of innovation, speculating for instance that he would have been 'gratified' and 'excited' by the Great Exhibition.[94] Such imaginings reach a marvellous culmination (albeit – in 1907 – slightly beyond the horizons of our period) in Walter Raleigh's query: 'Who would not wish to be the first to travel with Johnson in a motor-car?'[95]

Somewhat self-consciously summing up the changing critical fortunes of the eighteenth century during the nineteenth, Leslie Stephen's 1903 Ford Lectures at Oxford on *English Literature and Society in the Eighteenth Century* argue for a historically sensitive form of literary criticism which recognizes that the 'material' upon which the writer works 'is the whole complex of conceptions, religious, imaginative and ethical, which forms his mental atmosphere'.[96] Stephen firmly redefines the eighteenth century:

> the century, as its enemies used to say, of coarse utilitarian aims, of religious indifference and political corruption; or, as I prefer to say, the century of sound common sense and growing toleration, and of steady social and industrial development. (97)

Stephen's own reading relationship with Johnson – the man and the works – had played no small part in this influential reorientation. He had written extensively on Johnson, producing three separate biographical essays (in *Cornhill Magazine*, later reprinted in *Hours in a Library* (1876); in the inaugural volume of the *English Men of Letters* (1878); and in the 1886 *Dictionary of National Biography* entry), each of which bear witness to a deep engagement with his subject. Stephen was probably reading Boswell's *Life of Johnson* on his deathbed, if his friend and later biographer Frederick William Maitland can be believed.[97] And his daughter, Virginia, inherited Stephen's heavily-annotated 12-volume *Works of Samuel Johnson* (edited by Alexander Chalmers in 1806) which had been bequeathed to him by his own grandfather. Woolf's choice of that thoroughly Johnsonian title, *The Common Reader*, for her own early volumes of criticism, is eloquent testimony to the successful recuperation of Johnson and his age which had been achieved by the end of the nineteenth century.[98]

Notes

1   Bertrand H. Bronson, 'The Double Tradition of Dr Johnson', *Journal of English Literary History*, 28 (1951): 90–106.

2   Steven R. Phillips, 'Johnson's *Lives of the English Poets* in the Nineteenth Century', *Research Studies*, 39 (1971): 175–90.

3   Kevin Hart, *Samuel Johnson and the Culture of Property* (Cambridge: Cambridge University Press, 1999), 39–100.

4   Andrew Elfenbein, *Byron and the Victorians* (Cambridge: Cambridge University Press, 1995), 8.

5   William Makepeace Thackeray, *Vanity Fair: A Novel without a Hero* (London: Bradbury & Evans, 1848), 7. For discussion of Johnson's *Dictionary* in the nineteenth century, see Lynda Mugglestone, 144–62 below.

6   Robert Armitage, *Doctor Johnson: His Religious Life and his Death* (London: Bentley, 1850), 501.

7   Thomas Carlyle, 'The Hero as Man of Letters: Johnson, Rousseau, Burns', in *On Heroes, Hero-Worship and the Heroic in History*, in *The Works of Thomas Carlyle*, 30 vols (London: Chapman & Hall, 1897), V, 154–95, 182.

8   Thomas Babington Macaulay, *Life of Johnson* (1856), ed. John Downie (London: Blackie, 1918), 45.

9   James Hay, *Johnson: His Characteristics and Aphorisms* (London: Gardner, 1884), vi.

10   This observation is from William Spalding's oft-reprinted *The History of English Literature; with an Outline of the Origin and Growth of the English Language: Illustrated by Extracts. For the Use of Schools and of Private Students* (1853: Edinburgh, Oliver & Boyd, 11th edn 1870), and similar judgements can be found in literary histories and in reviews of the *Dictionary*'s reissues, for example *North British Review*, December 1864 (repr. in George

Webbe Dasent, *Jest and Earnest: A Collection of Essays and Reviews*, 2 vols [London: Chapman & Hall, 1873], II, 1–109).

11 *The Comic English Grammar: A New and Facetious Introduction to the English Tongue* (London: Ward & Lock, 1863), 13.

12 For full bibliographical details of Johnson's works during the nineteenth century, see David Fleeman and James McClaverty, *A Bibliography of the Works of Samuel Johnson, treating his published works from the beginnings to 1984*, 2 vols (Oxford: Clarendon, 2000).

13 Richard D. Altick, *The English Common Reader: A Social History of the Mass Reading Public, 1800–1900* (1957; repr. 1998, Columbus, OH: Ohio State University Press), 253.

14 Ibid., 217–18.

15 Samuel Johnson, *Lives of the most Eminent English Poets ... with Notes corrective and explanatory by Peter Cunningham*, 3 vols (London: Murray, 1854), I, xxvi–xxvii.

16 Park Honan, *Matthew Arnold: A Life* (London: Weidenfeld & Nicolson, 1981), 388.

17 *Materials for Thinking: Extracted from the Works of the Learned of all Ages* (London: Chidley, 1846), titlepage. Earlier printings of *Materials for Thinking* (edited by John Taylor and Richard Reynolds) had appeared from 1801 onwards.

18 Paul Thomas Murphy, *Toward a Working-Class Canon: Literary Criticism in British Working-Class Periodicals, 1816–1858* (Columbus, OH: Ohio State University Press, 1994), 50.

19 *The Yale Edition of the Works of Samuel Johnson*, 16 vols (Newhaven: Yale University Press, 1958–90), II, 265 (*Idler*, 85, 1 December 1759).

20 J.F. Waller, *Boswell and Johnson: Their Companions and Contemporaries* (London: Cassells, 1881), 117–18.

21 *Quarterly Review*, 159 (1885): 149.

22 Macaulay, *Life of Johnson*, 22. On Ruskin and the eighteenth century, see Dinah Birch, 163–81, below.

23 *The Brontës: Their Lives, Friendships and Correspondence*, 4 vols (Oxford: Blackwell, 1932), I, 122.

24 David Grylls, 'The Annual Return to Old Grub Street: What Samuel Johnson meant to Gissing', *The Gissing Newsletter*, 20 (1984): 1–27.

25 Gordon S. Haight, ed., *The George Eliot Letters*, 9 vols (Oxford and Newhaven: Yale University Press, 1954–78), V, 238.

26 Ibid., VI, 123.

27 *The Complete Works of John Ruskin*, ed. E.T. Cook and Alexander Wedderburn, 39 vols (London: Allen, 1903–12), *Elements of English Prosody*, 31.372.

28 Ibid., *Praeterita*, 35. 225–6.

29 Johnson, *Works*, VII, 70.

30 Leslie Stephen, *Samuel Johnson, English Men of Letters* series (London: Macmillan, 1878), 40.

31 Charlotte Brontë, *Jane Eyre* (1847), ed. Margaret Smith and Sally Shuttleworth (Oxford: Oxford University Press, 2000), 49–50.

32 See Jane W. Stedman, 'The Victorian After-Image of Samuel Johnson', *Nineteenth-Century Theatre Research*, 11 (1983): 13–27.

33 *Edinburgh Review*, 54 (Sept 1831): 1–38.

34 Carlyle, 'The Hero as Man of Letters', 178.

35 Macaulay, *Life of Johnson*, 215.

36 *The Brownings' Correspondence*, ed. Philip Kelley and Scott Lewis, 14 vols (Kansas: Wedgestone, 1993), V, 231; 239. Elizabeth is referring to Charlotte Frances Barrett, ed., *Diary and Letters of Madame d'Arblay, edited by her Niece*, 5 vols (London: Colburn, 1842–6).

37 George Eliot, *Middlemarch* (1871–72), ed. David Carroll (Oxford: Clarendon, 1986), 247 (Book III, Chapter xxv).

38 Abraham Hayward, ed., *Autobiography, Letters and Literary Remains of Mrs Piozzi (Thrale)*, 2 vols (London: Longman, 1861).

39 Percy Fitzgerald, *A Critical Examination of Dr G. Birkbeck Hill's 'Johnsonian' Editions, issued by the Clarendon Press, Oxford* (London: Bliss, Sands, 1898), 'Preface', no page number.

40 Thomas Seccombe, 'George Birkbeck Hill', *Dictionary of National Biography* supplement, January 1901–December 1911 (Oxford: Oxford University Press, 1912; repr. 1939), 263–5.

41 George Birkbeck Hill, *Wit and Wisdom of Samuel Johnson* (Oxford: Clarendon, 1888), [v].

42 Lord Rosebery, *Dr Johnson: An Address delivered at the Johnson Bicentenary Celebration, at Lichfield, September 15, 1909* (London: Humphreys, 1909), 12.

43 *Saturday Review*, 17 January 1874, 83–4.

44 Cited in a shortened version of the *Sayings*, published as *The Wit and Wisdom of George Eliot* (Boston: Roberts, 1873), 44.

45 Leah Price, *The Anthology and the Rise of the Novel* (Cambridge: Cambridge University Press, 2000), 111–12.

46 *Works of Samuel Johnson*, iii. 19–25 (*Rambler*, 4, 31 March 1750).

47 Eliot, 'The Natural History of German Life', first published in the *Westminster Review*, lxvi (July 1856), 51–79; repr. in George Eliot, *Selected Critical Writings* ed. Rosemary Ashton (Oxford: Oxford University Press, 1992; repr. 1999), 260–95, 263.

48 *The George Eliot Letters*, ed. Gordon S. Haight, 9 vols (Oxford and Newhaven: Oxford and Yale University Presses, 1954–78), V, 13.

49 See Chris Baldick, *The Social Mission of English Criticism 1848–1932* (Oxford: Clarendon, 1983).

50 Baldick, *The Social Mission*, 61.

51 *The Complete Prose Works of Matthew Arnold*, ed. R.H. Super, 11 vols (Ann Arbor: Michigan University Press, 1960–77), III, 41.

52 Waller, *Boswell and Johnson*, 109.

53 Arnold, *Complete Prose Works*, VIII, 314. A similar disjunction between form and content in the afterlife of Pope is described by Francis O'Gorman, 76–97, above.

54 On the *English Men of Letters* series, see David Amigoni, 182–202, below.

55 James Hannay, *A Course of English Literature* (London: Tinsley, 1866), 'Preface' (no page number).

56 See Ian Michael, *The Teaching of English: From the Sixteenth Century to 1870* (Cambridge: Cambridge University Press, 1987).

57 Rosebery, *Samuel Johnson*, 3.

58 Murphy, *Toward a Working-Class Canon*, 147.

59 Michael, *The Teaching of English*, 223 ff.

60 Macaulay, *Life of Johnson*, 40.

61 Arnold, *Complete Prose Works*, VIII, 310, 312.

62   Edmund Gosse, *A History of Eighteenth-Century Literature* (London: Macmillan, 1891), 294.

63   Arnold, *Complete Prose Works*, VIII, 460.

64   Hay, *Johnson: His Characteristics and Aphorisms*, xli.

65   James William Hoste, *Johnson and his Circle: With some Notices of Recent Johnsonian Literature* (London: Jarrold, 1900), 55.

66   Armitage, *Doctor Johnson*, title-page; 508.

67   Henry, Lord Brougham, 'Johnson', in *Lives of Men of Letters and Science, who Flourished in the Time of George III*, 2 vols (London: Knight, 1845), II, 1–85, 60.

68   George Birkbeck Hill and L.F. Powell, eds, *Boswell's Life of Johnson*, 6 vols (Oxford: Clarendon, 1934–50), II, 452 (21 March 1776).

69   F. Grant, *Life of Samuel Johnson* (London: Scott, 1887), 74.

70   Hoste, *Johnson and his Circle*, 5.

71   Hay, *Johnson: his Characteristics and Aphorisms*, xcv–xcvi.

72   Stephen, *Samuel Johnson*, 47. This view is echoed by many as the century draws to a close: for example, F. Grant in 1887 observes that 'of the small circle, which then composed the literary world, he was the undoubted chief, and his authority was never questioned' (*Life of Samuel Johnson*, 163).

73   Leslie Stephen, *Hours in a Library*, 3 vols (1876; London: Smith, Elder, 1892), I, 30–31.

74   George Birkbeck Hill, 'Preface' to R. Brimley Johnson, ed., *Eighteenth-Century Letters*, 2 vols (London: Innes, 1898), II, xviii.

75   [Robert Buchanan], *The Fleshly School of Poetry and other Phenomena of the Day* (London: Strahan, 1872: previously published in the *Contemporary Review*, 1871), 90.

76   Hoste, *Johnson and his Circle*, 5.

77   *Quarterly Review*, 159 (1885): 148–9.

78   Caroline Spurgeon, *The Works of Dr Samuel Johnson* (London: University College, 1898), 47.

79   W.H. Craig, *Dr Johnson and the Fair Sex: A Study of Contrasts* (London: Low, 1895), 211.

80   Hannay, *A Course of English Literature*, 161–2.

81   Grant, *Life of Samuel Johnson*, 168.

82   *Quarterly Review*, 159 (1885): 148.

83   Carlyle, 'The Hero as Man of Letters', 175, 158, 170. See also Simon Dentith, 43, above, and Introduction, 2, above.

84   Henry Francis Cary, *Lives of English Poets from Johnson to Kirke White: Designed as a Continuation of Johnson's Lives* (London: Bohn, 1843).

85   For example, Edmund Gosse, *A History of Eighteenth-Century Literature (1660–1780)* (London: Macmillan, 1891); William Minto, *The Literature of the Georgian Era* (Edinburgh: Blackwood, 1894); Thomas Seccombe, *The Age of Johnson (1748–1798)* (London: Bell, 1900).

86   Macaulay, *Life of Johnson*, 8; Grant, *Life of Samuel Johnson*, 161; Buchanan, *The Fleshly School*, 14.

87   Hay, *Johnson: His Characteristics and Aphorisms*, clxix.

88   See Blair Worden, 'The Victorians and Oliver Cromwell', in Stefan Collini, Richard Whatmore and Brian Young, eds, *History, Religion, and Culture: British Intellectual History 1750–1950* (Cambridge: Cambridge University Press, 2000), 112–35.

89   Arnold, 'Preface' to *Six Lives: Complete Prose Works*, VIII, 311.
90   Isaac Disraeli, *Literary Character of Men of Genius, Drawn from their own Feelings and Confessions* (London: Warne, 1881), 12.
91   Walter Raleigh, 'Samuel Johnson', the Leslie Stephen Lecture at Cambridge (1907), repr. in Walter Raleigh, *Six Essays on Johnson* (Oxford: Clarendon, 1910), 32.
92   Birkbeck Hill, *Dr Johnson: His Friends and his Critics*, 328.
93   Seccombe, *Age of Johnson*, xiii, xx, xxi.
94   Birkbeck Hill, *Wit and Wisdom*, xxi–xxii.
95   Raleigh, 'Samuel Johnson', 38–9.
96   Leslie Stephen, *English Literature and Society in the Eighteenth Century* (London: Duckworth, 1904), 8.
97   See Philip Mahone Griffith, 'Boswell's Johnson and the Stephens (Leslie Stephen and Virginia Woolf)', *The Age of Johnson*, 6 (1994): 151–64, 155.
98   The allusion is to Johnson's account, in his 'Life of Gray', of the 'Elegy Written in a Country Churchyard', in which he states that 'I rejoice to concur with the common reader; for by the common sense of readers ... must be finally decided all claim to poetical honours' (*Lives of the English Poets*, 2 vols [London: Dent, 1964], II, 392).

Chapter 7

Departures and Returns: Writing the English Dictionary in the Eighteenth and Nineteenth Centuries

Lynda Mugglestone

'Becky Sharp, here's a book for you ... – Johnson's Dixonary, you know; you mustn't leave us without that ....' But, lo! and just as the coach drove off, Miss Sharp put her pale face out of the window, and actually flung the book back into the garden.[1] (W.M. Thackeray, *Vanity Fair: A Novel Without A Hero* [1848])

The departure of Becky Sharp from Miss Pinkerton's academy for young ladies is marked by the memorable image of Johnson's *Dictionary* – 'the interesting work which [Miss Pinkerton] invariably presented to her scholars' – being determinedly jettisoned through the carriage window. Lying thus discarded on the paving, Johnson's *Dictionary*, first published in 1755, becomes an effective symbol of irrelevance. If Miss Pinkerton (the 'friend of Dr Johnson') continued to adhere to the standards of linguistic propriety that the *Dictionary* endorsed (censuring, for example, her sister Jemima's fallible use of language in the latter's selection of *bow-pot* rather than the 'more genteel' *bouquet*), then Becky instead signifies a new iconoclasm in this respect. 'So much for the Dixonary; and, thank God, I'm out of Chiswick',[2] as she declared in her emphatic leave-taking. Miss Pinkerton's veneration of the 'Great Lexicographer' was to have no place in Becky's future life.

As the nineteenth century advanced, Becky Sharp was by no means to be alone in her rejection of Johnson's perceived validity. *Johnsonianism*, for instance, came to be possessed of markedly negative associations: 'In England, the Johnsonianism is a prevalent disease', as Christian Goede had commented already in 1807;[3] 'Pompous, meaningless, and empty Johnsonianisms', James Murdoch later noted in similar condemnatory fashion in 1892.[4] Johnson's abilities in terms of language could receive still greater censure. Alexander Ellis, President of the London Philological Society in 1872–74 (and again in 1882), quoted Johnson's statement that 'Shakspere had enough Latin to grammaticise his English' with evident disdain. 'We know now what to conclude of Johnson's own knowledge of English grammar', as Ellis added.[5] Victorian estimations of the *Dictionary* could adopt similarly critical perspectives. As James Murray stressed in 1883, four years after becoming editor of the *New English Dictionary* (later known as the *Oxford English Dictionary*),[6] Johnson's work in this context was almost inevitably outmoded, not least because he had been denied 'the new methods of knowledge which were to grow up over the nineteenth century'. Johnson's *Dictionary* was therefore necessarily 'uncritical' and 'imperfect', the product of an era when 'philology was in the pre-scientific age, when real analogies were overlooked, and superficial resemblances too easily seized'.[7]

Philology, and its nineteenth-century reorientation, is in many ways the key to the dismissiveness which could so often inform Victorian accounts of Johnson's lexicographical endeavours. Included in Johnson's *Dictionary* of 1755 in the sense 'criticism; grammatical learning' (and provided with a citation from Walker in which readers were advised to 'temper all discourse of philology with interspersions of morality'),[8] *philology* was to undergo a process of semantic transformation over the ensuing years, its dominant sense in nineteenth-century usage instead coming to signify 'the science of language' with all the claims to empiricism, objectivity, and scientific rigour which this involved. Evident in the diverse agendas which prompted the founding of the London Philological Society in 1842 (under whose auspices the idea of the *OED* was first discussed),[9] the emergence of philology as a prominent Victorian science was to have significant implications for the role, and the realization, of lexicographical research. The work of Emile Littré in France on the *Dictionnaire de la langue française* and of the Grimm brothers in Germany on their *Deutsches Wörterbuch* set Continental precedents for its necessary integration, informing new conceptions of historicism, etymology, and the flux of meaning through time.[10] As Murray would inform his audience at the Philological Society in 1884, the fact that philology, especially in England and France, 'had been positively *made* during the last fifteen years' meant that even if it had been possible to begin the new dictionary at any earlier date 'it was certain that by this time they would all have been ashamed of it, and agitating to do it all over again'.[11]

Johnson's image in 1755 of the 'dusty desarts of barren philology'[12] was in this respect to prove significantly out of line with later thinking in which, as for Murray and the *OED*, philology was to be seen as a highly fertile terrain, in need of none of the 'verdure and flowers' by which Johnson had proposed to enliven it. With its investigations of the relationships between past and present, it was, for instance, rapidly assimilated into other scientific discourses, forming a pertinent aspect of evolutionary discussion between Darwin and his cousin Hensleigh Wedgewood (another prominent member of the Philological Society)[13] or discoursed upon by G.H. Lewes in 1860 with reference to the 'remarkable affinity between philology and zoology'.[14] Lexicography also naturally shared these preoccupations; it was in terms of evolution that Murray would present the history of the English dictionary in his Romanes lecture of 1900,[15] and in terms of science that he chose to define his own role as dictionary-maker. 'I am a man of science', he proclaimed; 'I am interested in that branch of Anthropology which deals with the history of human speech.'[16] As in the 'General Explanations' of the *OED*, the lexicographer, rather than claiming affinities with Johnson's 'harmless drudge',[17] would instead be figured as an astronomer, a botanist, or a naturalist engaged in the classification of phenomena which here explicitly embraced language too.[18] Johnson's self-fashioning as 'a poet doomed at last to wake a lexicographer'[19] was therefore to seem distinctly anachronistic. After all, as Murray argued in 1889 while searching for a suitable assistant to work on the dictionary, 'literary attainments give no special preparation'; what was wanted was a man who 'has studied *language*, and knows something of Germanic & Romantic philology'.[20]

Science, and specifically philological science, hence regularly provided the basis for the Victorian dialectic between past and present in terms of the dictionary, setting up a context in which earlier dictionaries were necessarily found wanting, marred by their subjectivity, their lack of rigour, their inconsistency, and their absence of systematic investigation.[21] The *OED* was in these terms deliberately conceived as a departure, a redefinition of what a dictionary could and should be. The seminal lectures given by Richard Chenevix Trench to the Philological Society in November 1857 illustrate this with particular acuity, setting the 'deficiencies' of existing English dictionaries against an inspirational vision of what the dictionary might henceforth become. Johnson, perhaps predictably, occupies a prominent place in this critique. His policy of admitting obsolete words 'when they are found in authours [*sic*] not obsolete, or when they have any force or beauty that may deserve revival'[22] elicited, for example, marked disfavour. Categorically dismissing Johnson's evident belief that lexicographers should play a part in 'the question of whether a word deserves revival or not', Trench further highlighted Johnson's inconsistency, calling 'attention to the fact that Johnson does not even observe his own rule of comprehension, imperfect and inadequate as that is'.[23] As it was, 'the words omitted can be counted by hundreds, I suppose by thousands', as Trench continued. Johnson's weaknesses in terms of the history of words attracted similarly stringent condemnation. Whereas establishing a word's first use in the language was, for Trench, 'in every case desirable', Johnson's fallibilities were again transparent. 'I doubt whether Johnson even so much as set this before him as an object to be obtained', as Trench declared. The treatment of historical sense-development was, if anything, still worse. 'Johnson is very faulty here; perhaps in nothing more so', the Philological Society was informed: 'Nothing is commoner with [Johnson] than to take the latest meaning at which a word has arrived ... and to put this first and foremost, either quite over-passing, or placing last, the earlier uses which alone render the latter intelligible.'[24] The new English dictionary which Trench proposed was in these terms to be Johnson's polar opposite, systematic where Johnson was inconsistent, and accurate where he was flawed.

The maker of dictionaries was redefined in parallel. If Johnson's conception of critical lexicography allowed individual predilections to intervene in the presentation of what should be purely linguistic facts, then the Victorian dictionary-maker was to be of a different order entirely. He was 'a historian, and not a critic', Trench observed, a scholar engaged in providing an inventory of the English language in which personal preferences (or antipathies) were irrelevant.[25] Johnson's celebrated definition of *oats* ('A grain, which in England is generally given to horses, but in Scotland supports the people') would in this sense find no counterpart in the *OED*, and not only because of the Scottish heritage of Murray as its editor-in-chief.[26] Johnson's overt censorship of scores of other words was still more problematic, especially in the wanton disregard for linguistic evidence that such judgements often implied. The *OED* would, for instance, trace the history of adjectival uses of *roundabout* back into the seventeenth century, analysing subsequent usage with scholarly precision; Johnson instead chose to proscribe the word in his own *Dictionary* as 'a colloquial licence of language, which ought not to have been admitted into books'. The accompanying citation from Locke's *Essay on Human Understanding* ('Those sincerely follow reason, but for want of having large, sound, roundabout sense, have not a full view of all that relates to the question') was clearly deemed inadequate to confer the requisite legitimization on its use. Such normative views, and lexicographical dictates, were fundamentally at odds with Trench's linguistic ideal in which the neutrality of the lexicographer was paramount. 'The business which [the maker of dictionaries] has undertaken is to collect and arrange all the words, whether good or bad, whether they do or do not commend themselves to his judgment', Trench insisted. Even if 'he may think of this article, which he inserts in his catalogue, that it had better be consigned to the lumber-room with all speed', no suspicion of this must enter the dictionary.[27] The notion of the dictionary as 'inventory', with its deliberately objective overtones, was the only critical element to be considered.

Johnson's dictionary was therefore inevitably seen as deficient, marred by what Murray came to see as its 'whimsicality' when seen from the intentionally impartial standpoint adopted by the *OED* ('We should probably have had something of the kind even in the C19 c. [*sic*], if say, Mr Ruskin, or better still Mr Carlyle had undertaken to make a dictionary', as Murray remarked),[28] and deeply flawed in the cavalier attitude towards data which its entries so often revealed. Many of the quotations inserted by Johnson in supposed illustration of a word's history and use proved, for instance, to be 'merely an echo of the original'. As a result, though initially seen 'as being as true as Gospel' and hence 'accepted with implicit trust', further research on Johnson's citations often served to produce marked scepticism. 'It was', Murray admitted, 'only very slowly, and with reluctance, that we realized that the caution "Verify your references" was just as needful in the case of Johnson as any man who ever lived.'[29] Many quotations disturbingly failed even to 'contain the word which they were supposed to illustrate'. As Murray instead resolved for the *OED*, though it was inevitable that 'we shall introduce some errors of our own ... they will be our own errors, and not a perpetuation of those of others'.[30] The 'new dictionary' would thus be an emphatic return to first principles. New in more than name, it would pursue independent research and enquiry with scientific exactitude. 'It is because of the novelty of its aims, the originality of its method, the fresh start it makes from materials never before collected, that it claims in a distinctive sense the title of the NEW ENGLISH DICTIONARY', Murray stressed as he drafted the 'Notice of Publication' which would herald publication of its first part. Lexicography, and the advances promised by this entirely 'new' dictionary', thereby came to participate fundamentally in the scientific confidence of Victorian England, and the improvements envisaged as being necessarily attendant upon this. 'I firmly believe in the advent of an English epoch in science and art, which will lick the Augustan ... into fits', the scientist Thomas Henry Huxley proclaimed in 1858, one year after Trench's own lectures to the Philological Society.[31] Lexicography too would come to participate in a variety of ways in this process of transcendence and advance.

'Those who have attentively considered the history of mankind, know that every age has its peculiar character', observed Johnson in the *Adventurer*.[32] Over a century separates Johnson's *Dictionary* from the inception of the *OED* in the 1850s, over 130 years if one takes into consideration the date at which its first part, *A-Ant*, appeared in 1884, still more if one considers the entirety of the *OED*, the first edition of which was not to reach completion until 1928. In the diachronic gap which results, this difference in character is particularly marked. If Johnson was found wanting from the vantage point often adopted in nineteenth-century scholarship, then to see him in his own time is to enforce a radically different perspective, one in which the fallibilities of regarding 'the dictionary' as a single unitary (and unilinear) model are forcefully brought home. Against Trench's insistence on the dictionary as an objective inventory of all words used in English, eighteenth-century discussions of lexicography instead often actively prioritized the normative as part of the proper remit of the maker of dictionaries, stressing the interventionist stance which must be taken in the interests of linguistic control. *The Many Advantages of a Good Language to any Nation*, a text published anonymously (by Thomas Wilson) in 1724, is, for instance, explicit on the necessary 'polishing' of English, a task to be accomplished in part by the provision of dictionaries 'to fill up what is wanting, streighten [*sic*] what is crooked'.[33] 'We have no good *Dictionary* to bring it into Method', Wilson laments, setting out a detailed agenda for the subsequent improvement of the national tongue. The legacies of the prescriptive ethos earlier articulated by writers such as Swift, Addison, and Dryden were marked: 'to observe errors is a great step to the correcting of them', as Dryden had said,[34] placing usage within a framework in which it was not merely to be recorded (as in the later descriptive stance of the *OED*) but to be regulated and reformed. Dictionaries in this light were to be seen as the domain of 'proper' against 'improper' meaning as Johnson's contemporary, Nathaniel Bailey, directed in his own *Universal Etymological Dictionary* ('in order to form our Judgments right, [words] must be understood in their proper Meaning, used in their true Sense').[35] Popular linguistic rhetoric likewise embraced the validity of linguistic discrimination. 'Due Correction of our Language' was needed in order to bring it 'to a competent Standard of Purity', as well as to prevent 'any farther Decay of our Tongue', as Thomas Stackhouse opined, deploying a vocabulary in which reason, analogy, and ascertainment all emerge as prominent linguistic ideals.[36] Johnson's *Dictionary* must then be seen in the context of this particular linguistic climate, one in which an ideological commitment to fixing the language, as well as to refining its constituent parts, regularly underpinned work on language. 'It is hoped that our language will be more fixed and better established when the public is favoured with a new dictionary, undertaken with that view', as William Strahan proclaimed in the *Gentleman's Magazine* in 1749, whetting the public appetite for the appearance of Johnson's own work.[37]

The lexicographical principles employed by Johnson were in many ways to reveal a marked consonance with such contemporary ideals. The terms of eighteenth-century prescriptive discourse are transparent in both his *Plan* for the dictionary of 1747 and in the discussions of language that preface the dictionary proper. 'The chief intent of [the dictionary] is to preserve the purity and ascertain the meaning of the English idiom', Johnson stressed in the *Plan*, not least since 'one great end of this undertaking is to fix the English language'.[38] 'Adulterations were to be detected, without a settled test of purity', as the *Preface* confirmed of Johnson's linguistic methodology, further detailing the expressed need to recall English from the '*Gallick* structure and phraseology' towards which it had been 'deviating'.[39] Whereas the *OED* would embrace a formally democratic rubric with reference to the politics of inclusion ('All, all … must enter', Frederick Furnivall declared to the Philological Society),[40] the image of language in Johnson's dictionary often instead suggests a strictly hierarchical model with recommended usage being founded only on the 'best writers', on a system which gives preference to those of 'the first reputation' above 'those of an inferior rank'.[41] 'Low' conversely appears as a pervasive epithet of linguistic demerit: 'a low word', Johnson decrees of *nonsense*, supplying a similar verdict on *ignoramus*. Hierarchical relationships likewise inform the negative images of colloquial discourse against the literate proprieties of 'good' written texts, evident in Johnson's disdain for 'colloquial licentiousness' and his active proscription of 'colloquial corruption' in, for example, *light* used as an adverb or *extraordinary*, adjudged a 'colloquial barbarism used for the ease of pronunciation'. 'Language was at its beginning merely oral', he states,[42] according clear cultural (and linguistic) priority to the learned minority against those restricted to the primacy of speech. 'This word I should not have expected to find authorized by a polite author', Johnson notes, for example, of *spick and span*, though since it had been used (as by Swift), he duly saw fit to include it in his dictionary too.

Such images clearly run counter to the impartiality which Trench and others saw as essential for the nineteenth-century lexicographer. Where Trench stressed that if the dictionary-maker 'begins to pick and choose, to leave this and to take that, he will at once go astray',[43] Johnson instead actively engages in the politics of selection, noting in his *Preface* that 'when I took the first survey of my undertaking, I found our speech copious without order, and energetick without rules … choice was to be made out of boundless variety … and modes of expression to be rejected or received'.[44] In line with such precepts, the *Dictionary* regularly betrays a clear commitment towards regulating the 'boundless chaos of a living speech', censuring perceived redundancy (*slippy* against *slippery*, *cheery* against *cheerful*)[45] as well as castigating the laxity with which phrasal verbs could be deployed.[46] Usage, central to nineteenth-century descriptive ideologies, is not ignored (authoritative citations accompany, for example, the entries for both *slippy* and *cheery*). Instead, such evidence is often filtered through distinctly eighteenth-century preconceptions, leading to what might be termed dichotomous entries where empirical evidence of a given word's existence is tempered by the authoritarian edict of the lexicographer as, for example, in the entry for *nowadays*, judged both 'common and used by the best writers' as well as 'barbarous'. Though Johnson might therefore acknowledge that custom 'has long possessed, whether by right or usurpation, the sovereignty of words', this was by no means to prevent the lexicographer's 'vicarious jurisdiction' usurping such sovereignty where deemed necessary. Ordinary usage could thereby be declared flawed, as in Pope's use of *desperate* in his 'Essay on Criticism' ('Concluding all mere desp'rate sots and fools / That durst depart from Aristotle's rules'). 'It is sometimes used in a sense nearly ludicrous, and only marks any bad quality predominating in a high degree', as Johnson remarked, plainly opposed to this form of semantic extension. Such evaluative considerations accord precisely with his account of his own method. 'We must', he wrote, 'remark how the writers of former ages have used the ... word' and, by so doing, consider whether the writer in individual instances 'can be acquitted of impropriety'.[47]

Usage is thereby framed by the 'scholar's reverence for antiquity'[48] rather than the linguist's insistence on the quantitative validity of consensus norms, a position which frequently leads to the censorship of on-going change. Johnson's entry for *precarious*, for instance, mentions current usage with marked disfavour, censuring what to his mind clearly constituted a departure from its 'proper' (and Latinate) meaning. 'No word is more unskilfully used than this with its derivatives. It is used for uncertain in all its senses; but it only means uncertain, as dependent on others', he declared. *Abominable* (deriving from Latin *abominabilis*) was similar, likewise partaking in that 'exuberance of signification' on which Johnson comments in his *Preface*. In consequence, while the sense 'hateful, detestable; to be loathed' is given without comment, the use of *abominable* as a wide-ranging term of popular disapprobation is expressly confined to 'low and ludicrous language'. Discourses of this order inform the definition of countless words and senses, providing a marked contrast to the Victorian lexicographers of the *OED* who strenuously sought to distance themselves from their own subjectivities when it came to writing the dictionary. 'If a word gains currency, the lexicographer, whether he likes it or not, has to take it', as Murray, for instance, would stress, enforcing another intended departure from the past.[49]

As Johnson indicates in his *Plan*, 'that part of lexicography which is strictly critical' was nevertheless a salient aspect of the eighteenth-century dictionary-maker's role, evident in his adherence to contemporary ideals of rationality above the authority of language *per se*. *Irresistless*, for instance, conspicuously fails the test of reason, being, as Johnson declared, 'A barbarous ungrammatical conjunction of two negatives'. *Disannul* was similar; 'formed contrary to analogy' by its 'needless use of the negative particle', it could not be recommended as a constituent part of 'good' usage. The entry for *disannul* in the relevant fascicle of the *OED* conversely acts as a paradigm of descriptive objectivity, precisely as Trench had wished: 'To cancel and do away with; to make null and void, bring to nothing, abolish, annul'. Both dictionaries in this respect conspicuously reveal an element of 'psychological fit' with their respective eras,[50] the *OED* influenced by the demands of an empiricist and scientific age, Johnson's *Dictionary* fostering the images of selectivity and control which are prominent at various points in his *Preface*, as well as in much discussion of language from the late seventeenth century onwards. 'Every language has ... its absurdities and improprieties, which it is the duty of the lexicographer to correct or proscribe', Johnson declared.[51]

Of course, in other entries, Johnson displays the scholar's regard for the evidence at his disposal, carefully separating sense from sense, and deploying a skill in definition which would see many of his formulations repeated word for word even within the *OED*. 'The quality of being affected, or of making false appearances', Johnson wrote in defining *affectedness* in 1755. While scrupulously identifying Johnson as the source, this was later incorporated as the *OED*'s definition of the same word. *Abscond* is similar. 'To hide one's self; to retire from the public view: generally used of persons in debt, or criminals eluding the law', states Johnson's careful phrasing in a definition later transferred in its entirety to the *OED* where, in an element of textual symbiosis, it was accompanied (under *abscond*, sense 3) by a further gloss courtesy of Murray himself: 'to go away hurriedly and secretly'. Johnson's citational evidence, in spite of the reservations which Murray voiced, often also finds a new home; relevant quotations from the poems of Elijah Fenton and James Thomson, both of which had been used by Johnson in illustration of *bright*, reappear in the corresponding *OED* entry for the sense 'clear, translucent'; Johnson's selection of Dryden under *broadness* ('I have used the cleanest metaphor I could find, to palliate the broadness of the meaning') is likewise employed in the *OED* to provide evidence of its first use in the language. Such elements of lexicographic recycling can be paralleled on countless occasions. Murray, as his grand-daughter records, worked in his

Scriptorium with an open copy of Johnson always before him, just as Johnson is said to have worked with his own most significant predecessor, Bailey's *Dictionarium Britannicum*, open on his own desk.[52]

Johnson's literal presence in the definitions and quotations of the *OED* to some degree undermines the categoric images of distance and departure within which discussions of this 'new dictionary' of the Philological Society were so often framed. Even though the *OED* was therefore emphatically 'new', it is clear that its achievements still in part depend on previous dictionaries, and earlier lexicography. 'The English Dictionary, like the English Constitution, is the creation of no one man, and of no one age', as Murray himself admitted; instead 'it is a growth that has slowly developed itself adown the ages'.[53] The history of lexicography is, in reality, less a sequence of discrete stages than a record of cumulative achievement, incremental and additive in its development. Even while Trench censured the deficiencies of the past, he was still compelled to acknowledge the contributions of those who had toiled to produce the word-books which had gone before. As he admitted, if nineteenth-century scholarship rendered it 'comparatively easy to pick a hole here, or to detect a flaw there', it nevertheless remained true that 'such edifices as our English Dictionaries could only have been reared by enormous labour, patience, and skill'.[54] Just as in the closely analysed entry for *departure* in the *OED*, it is clear that every departure implies a pre-existing state or condition from which severance or movement must be made.

If historical continuities thus in part enforce an enduring connection between the work of Johnson and the later editors of the *OED*, then it is unsurprising that other continuities can also be detected, fracturing the easy rhetoric by which Trench had initially proclaimed the advent of 'an entirely new Dictionary; no patch upon old garments, but a new garment throughout',[55] as well as complicating the neat separation of prescriptive past from the descriptive ideologies of the later nineteenth century. The binary contrast of historian and critic in terms of the dictionary-maker proves a case in point. While the etymologies of the *OED* revealed the new rigour of a scientific age ('One does not look in Johnson for Etymology, any more than in 18th c. writers for biology or electricity', as Murray had dismissively averred),[56] attitudes to on-going change can, for instance, reveal distinct parallels with earlier lexicographical subjectivities. *Allude*, for example, a word included in the very first fascicle of the *OED*, is provided with a number of senses in which its use is evidently unexceptionable. Murray's account of its use with the meaning 'to refer (directly)' is, however, somewhat different, sharing a metalanguage which has marked affinities with Johnson's own preferred terms of proscription. Just as Johnson censured those who deviated from the spelling *vail* ('Modern writers have ignorantly written veil'), so too is ignorance given as the underlying cause of the semantic degeneration which was, in Murray's eyes, also affecting nineteenth-century uses of *allude*. 'Often used ignorantly as = *refer* in its general sense', opined Murray, distancing the dictionary from any implied legitimization of this sense. The tensions thereby generated between usage (signified by 'often') and correctness were evidently to be disregarded. *Hideously* is similar, the meaning 'in a hideous manner' being sanctioned without further comment while a distinctly negative perspective informs the presentation of *hideously* as an intensifier ('It is sometimes misused as an intensive, intended to be stronger than "awfully, terribly, dreadfully"'). *Misuse* in this respect ('to use or employ wrongly or improperly', as the relevant definition in the *OED* specifies) is clearly at odds with the oft-stated purpose of the dictionary with regard to the materials on which it was founded. 'We entirely repudiate the theory, which converts the lexicographer into an arbiter of style', as the original *Proposal* for the publication of the *OED* had stressed.[57] Yet such arbitration is, in reality, pervasive in a wide range of entries, informing Murray's censure of semantic change in *allude* and embedded in Henry Bradley's resistance to the changing meanings and use of words such as *littler*, and *enthuse*.[58] 'An ignorant back-formation from ENTHUSIASM', Bradley would, for instance, declare of the latter while he flatly refused to countenance forms such as *littler* or *littlest* at all. 'Some writers have ventured to employ the unrecognized forms *littler*, *littlest*, which are otherwise confined to dialect or imitations of childish or illiterate speech', he wrote (under *little*), in a form of words which expressly withholds lexicographical approval even in the face of available evidence, as indeed in Thackeray's use of an 'unrecognised form' of precisely this kind in *Pendennis*: 'She was called tall and gawky by some … of her own sex, who prefer littler women.'[59]

Rather than Murray's preferred image of scientific impartiality, such entries return us to the subjectivities apparent in Johnson's own selected role as dictionary-maker in which his empiricism in gathering citational evidence is tempered by the desire to 'retard what we cannot repel, … palliate what we cannot cure'.[60] Alongside the iterated salience of descriptive precepts, the metalanguage of prescriptivism and individual lexicographical preference can at times be detected in the *OED*, influencing the presentation of usage in constructions such as 'I should have liked to have seen'. 'Certainly faulty', the *OED* declares, equally rejecting the validity of Lawrence Oliphant's 'I should much preferred to have seen you there', in his *Altiora Peto* of 1883. In such ways the later dictionary develops an uneasy relationship not only with the ostensibly transcended past, but also with the popular prescriptive texts of the nineteenth century. The edicts which works such as *Don't: A Manual of Mistakes and Improprieties More or Less Prevalent in Conduct and Speech* offered for the guidance of the linguistically insecure can at times hence find disturbingly close parallels within the *OED*. 'Don't say "I *expect*" for "I *suppose*"', *Don't* dictates, for example,[61] foreshadowing in this respect Henry Bradley's evident antipathies in terms of this particular usage: 'The misuse of the word as a synonym of *suppose*, without any notion of "anticipating" or "looking for", is often cited as an Americanism, but is very common in dialectal, vulgar or carelessly colloquial speech in England', Bradley averred in the intentionally objective *OED*. *Person* is similar; 'Don't say *party* for *person*. This is abominable and yet very common', *Don't* advised, again finding an unexpected echo in the *OED*. 'Shoppy, vulgar, or jocular, the proper word being *person*', as the entry categorically declares, revealing a class-based ideology which is markedly at odds with the democratic ideals with which work on the dictionary had begun. As Béjoint has perceptively observed, the real difficulty for lexicographers is 'to disentangle themselves from generally accepted prejudices'.[62] For the *OED*, the legacies of such incomplete 'disentangling' can be seen to recur intermittently throughout its pages, linking past and present in ways which disturb the rhetoric of descriptivism formally adopted, yet which ultimately serve to confirm the enduring reality of the dictionary as a consummately human product. 'Such is design, while it is yet at a distance from execution', as Johnson had written in his *Preface*; dictionaries, like language, are 'the work of man, of a being from whom permanence and stability cannot be derived'.[63] As a result, if innumerable entries do indeed reveal the surpassing achievement of the objectivity at which the editors of the *OED* aimed, others nevertheless offer glimpses of an all-too-human engagement with the flux of speech, revealing a resistance to the facts of change which bears affinities with Johnson's own reluctance to sanction, for instance, newer uses of, say, *skilful at* (condemned as 'ludicrous') against *skilful in* (adjudged the 'proper' use).

The conditions of reception likewise confirm the salience of such continuities, once more making plain the fact that if prescriptive sensibilities could prove difficult to shed entirely in the dictionary, they could be strikingly pervasive in the world outside its confines. It is perhaps here in particular where the intended divide between Victorian and Augustan breaks down most fully. Johnson for many remained the prototypical dictionary, his dictates on usage continuing to inform popular nineteenth-century notions of 'good' and 'bad' in language, 'right' and 'wrong'. As for Lord Macaulay (whose copy of Johnson's *Dictionary* required rebinding four times over the course of the nineteenth century in consequence of the frequency with which he referred to it), Johnson was seen to have a continuing role in 'keeping up to the classical standard'. He 'made particular use of it', Macaulay added, 'to prevent himself from slipping into spurious modernisms'.[64] The image of the dictionary – especially perhaps Johnson's *Dictionary* – as a force (and agent) of standardization remained a powerful one. Even if Trench had been adamant that a dictionary 'is nothing of the kind',[65] it is clear that such perceptions lingered on, informing countless letters to Murray in which ordinary writers and speakers sought clarification and advice, seeking the normative dictates which had been so easy to locate in Johnson's earlier work. 'I have come to regard the function of a Dictionary to be not merely to record popular usage in its greatest license but to correct abuses by insisting on well-defined and recognised principles of language', Jasper Davidson thus informed Murray in 1888, censuring popular usages such as *relation* for *relative*, and *verbal* for *oral*.[66] A dictionary was, he stressed, required to intervene in such matters, a subject on which he offered his own prescription for the *OED*: 'Instead of giving and thereby authorizing the blunders of ignorant and irresponsible writers, the great Dictionary should give only inherently correct definitions.'[67] Davidson was by no means alone in such preconceptions. Irrespective of his own fundamental linguistic beliefs, Murray was thereby regularly constructed as linguistic arbiter and required to pronounce on the varied legitimacy of, for example, *whiskey* against *whisky*, *license* against *licence*, or the propriety of recent coinages such as *advertismental*.[68] His replies without exception insist on the descriptive imperative of usage in ways which, at least popularly, were often seen as an abdication of that authority which the lexicographer should properly wield. 'For *whisky* or *whiskey*, there is no etymological or historical preference, both forms are current and equally correct or incorrect', Murray stated, insisting that usage in this sense has its own validity 'so, when in a hurry you may save a fraction of time by writing *whisky*, and when lingering over it you may prolong it to *whiskey* . . . in matters of taste there is no "correct" or "incorrect"; there is the liberty of the subject'.[69]

Reviewers too could partake in this ideological ambivalence, formally appreciating the advances being made in nineteenth-century lexicography ('The value of recording contemporary usage is obvious', as an 1884 review of the first fascicle in *The Times* states, for example) while also clearly harking back to the days before the advent of such descriptive imperatives. As *The Times* review continues therefore, 'Though a scientific dictionary should be by no means Della Cruscan in its selection of words, it should surely maintain as far as possible a classical standard in its selection of authors'.[70] Similarly in the *Athenaeum*, a celebration of the 'new start in English lexicography on scientific principles and by scientific methods' exists alongside the application of evidently popular sympathies (and dislikes). Scientific words are, for instance, deemed to 'belong to a cosmopolitan jargon' rather than the English language and their inclusion in the dictionary was regrettable. 'How can [Murray] excuse the fourteen lines expended on *amphiarthrosis* and the nine lines on *æcidium*?', it demanded.[71] Ironically, it could at times be the presence rather than the absence of prescriptive antipathies for which the dictionary was praised. 'We observe with some regret that the Dictionary recognises the hideous Americanism "enthuse", though it very properly stigmatises it as "an ignorant back-formation"', the *Manchester Guardian* declared.[72] Bradley's censure of *expect* received similar commendation: 'the common misuse of words is not overlooked ... "expect" is rightly said to be "very common in dialectal, vulgar, or carelessly colloquial speech" as a synonym for suspect, suppose'.[73] If the Philological Society repeatedly endorsed productive images of departure by means of the 'new' dictionary, it is clear that, at times, this seemed to have left the mass of the populace behind. As such comments reveal, notions of the needful 'vicarious jurisdiction' of the lexicographer identified by Johnson so many years before could not be neatly confined to the past. Johnson's legacy as prototypical dictionary-maker lingered on, informing common images of the 'proper' role of lexicographical activity and the evocative ideals of 'correctness'.

To posit an absolute divide between Victorian and Augustan in terms of lexicography is, in many ways, therefore, misjudged. Trench's rhetoric of difference collapses in the light of enduring continuities. Dictionary-makers would remain speakers of their language, and would therefore also remain susceptible to the prejudices of ordinary speakers in their adherence (or otherwise) to the politics of change. Prescriptivism would inevitably infuse descriptive practices, blurring the relationship between what were often erroneously envisaged as two mutually exclusive domains. Ideologies of scientific objectivity could slip, revealing an individual engagement with language which returns us to Johnson's spirited interaction with the perceived fallibilities of common usage. Murray in turn would fail to countenance newer meanings, such as that of *avocation* ('Ordinary employment, usual occupation, vocation, calling', which he regarded as being 'improperly foisted upon the word'), even though it was readily employed by other writers. Spellings such as *rhyme* and *axe*, well-established in contemporary texts, would likewise be rejected in favour of other variants (*rime, ax*) which he declared were 'intrinsically the best'.[74] Conversely, in the eighteenth century a commitment to linguistic reality (and the validity this may be seen to have) could and did exist alongside normative ideals, a principle which informs Adam Smith's criticism of Johnson for being, as he felt, unduly descriptive: 'We cannot help wishing, that the author had trusted less to the judgement of those who may consult him, and had oftener passed his own censure upon those words which are not of approved use, tho' sometimes to be met with in authors of no mean fame.'[75] Johnson's refusal to attempt to fix the language by means of the dictionary serves in other ways to indicate his own departure from the prescriptive models of lexicography insisted on by his contemporaries (and affirmed in his original plans for the dictionary). Instead, as he came to realize, 'when we see men grow old and die at a certain time one after another, from century to century, we laugh at the elixir that promises to prolong life to a thousand years; with equal justice may the lexicographer be derided, who being able to produce no example of a nation that has preserved their words and phrases from mutability, shall imagine that his dictionary can embalm his language, and secure it from corruption and decay'.[76] Even the historicist ideologies on which Trench (and others) based the 'new philology' of the nineteenth century could be parallelled in earlier lexicographical discourse. By means of the dictionary, as Johnson had himself declared, 'every word will have its history, and the reader will be informed of the gradual changes of the language, and will have before his eyes the rise of some words and the fall of others'.[77] Even if imperfectly realized in Johnson's own *Dictionary*, his words hence offer a precedent for the renowned philologist Franz Passow's canonical statement of 1812 ('every word should be made to tell its own story') which lay at the heart of much nineteenth-century scholarship in this field.[78] What is promoted as a departure may, in the end, constitute merely a return, a restatement and development of what has gone before.

Johnson in his clear-sighted engagement with the fallibility of human wishes should, in this, have the last word. As in the poem he wrote while drafting the *Dictionary*, the 'vanity of human wishes' was, he realized, a recurrent image in human history. Against the inevitability in which 'Year chases Year, Decay pursues Decay / ... New Forms arise, and diff'rent Views engage', was the eloquence (and fragility) of human aspiration, destined to fragment in the face of wider realities.[79] A similar dialectic between hope and experience frames Johnson's engagement with the concerns of lexicography. Recognizing that he had 'indulged expectation which neither reason nor experience can justify' in the normative ideals of ascertainment with which he had originally set out, it is clear that his underlying hopes of linguistic perfectability nevertheless remained, even while he also recognized their futility. 'I wish', he confessed, 'that [language] might be less apt to decay, and that signs might be permanent like the things they denote.'[80] In such matters, he observed, it is indeed 'unavoidable to wish, as it is natural to hope'. Translated to a different era and framed with different aspirations, the tension between hope and reality endures. Trench's hopes for the completeness of the dictionary would be frustrated by a variety of concerns; usage labels such as 'vulgar' and 'shoppy' would in turn compromise the scientific rigour at which he had aimed; the Delegates of Oxford University Press (by whom the dictionary would eventually be published) would censor the use of non-canonical authors, and what they perceived as the over-liberal introduction of new words.[81] Even the *OED* would prove fallible in the wider realization of its aims. In this respect, as another eighteenth-century writer on language, Archibald Campbell, had pertinently proclaimed, the 'perfect Dictionary' would necessarily remain 'like the Philosopher's Stone'. While 'a great Desideratum among some people', it was therefore, as Campbell concluded, 'impossible to obtain'.[82]

Notes

1   W.M. Thackeray, *Vanity Fair: A Novel Without a Hero* (London: Bradbury & Evans, 1848), 7.
2   Ibid., 8.
3   C.A. Goede, *The Stranger in England; or, Travels in Great Britain*, trans. T. Horne (London: Barnard, 1807), II, 142 .
4   J. Murdoch, *From Australia and Japan* (London: Scott, 1892), 78.
5   A.J. Ellis, 'First Annual Address of the President to the Philological Society, delivered at the Anniversary Meeting, Fri 17th May 1872', *Transactions of the Philological Society*, 1873–74: 12.
6   The first edition of the *OED* began publication in parts in 1884 (–1928) under the title of *A New English Dictionary (NED)*. This designation continued to hold pride of place on the title pages of the individual parts throughout the first edition, although *Oxford English Dictionary* as an alternative title was established from 1895. For a full account of the publishing history of the *OED* (and its title), see L.C. Mugglestone, ed., *Lexicography and the OED: Pioneers in the Untrodden Forest* (Oxford: Oxford University Press, 2002), 1. The present chapter will employ *OED* throughout.
7   Bodleian Library, MP/17/9/1883. Proof of *Notice of Publication of a New English Dictionary on a Historical Basis.* Part 1. *A-Ant.*
8   S. Johnson, *A Dictionary of the English Language*, 2 vols (London: Strahan, 1755).
9   See H. Aarsleff, *The Study of Language in England, 1780–1860* (Princeton: Princeton University Press, 1967), 211ff.
10   See N. Osselton, 'Murray and his European Counterparts', in Mugglestone, *Lexicography and the OED*, 59–76.

11 [Philological Society] Monthly Abstract of Proceedings: 'Annual Dictionary Evening', *Proceedings of the Philological Society* (1884): vi.

12 Johnson, 'Preface', B2v.

13 See A. Desmond and J. Moore, *Darwin* (London: Joseph, 1991), 218, 283. Wedgewood was a key member of the Etymological Committee of the *OED* instituted in 1860.

14 G.H. Lewes, *Studies in Animal Life* (New York: Smith, Elder, 1860), 102.

15 J.A.H. Murray, *The Evolution of English Lexicography* (Oxford: Clarendon, 1900).

16 J.A.H. Murray, ms of 'Lecture to the Ashmolean Natural History Society' [n.d.], Murray Papers, Bodleian Library.

17 See Johnson's definition of *lexicographer*: 'A writer of dictionaries; a harmless drudge, that busies himself in tracing the original, and detailing the signification of words.'

18 'In its constitution [the English vocabulary] may be compared to one of those natural groups of the zoologist or botanist, wherein typical species forming the characteristic nucleus of the order, are linked on every side to other species, in which the typical character is less and less distinctly apparent ... For the convenience of classification, the naturalist may draw the line, which bounds a class or order, outside or inside of a particular form; but Nature has drawn it nowhere – the lexicographer must, like the naturalist, "draw the line somewhere"', J.A.H. Murray, 'General Explanations', *A New English Dictionary on Historical Principles*, Vol.1, A–B, edited by J.A.H. Murray (Oxford: Clarendon, 1888), xvii.

19 Johnson, 'Preface', C1v.

20 MP/30/10/1889. J.A.H. Murray to P.L. Gell, 30 October 1889.

21 Though this chapter will principally focus on Johnson's *Dictionary* of 1755, the same weaknesses can be detected in other eighteenth-century dictionaries such as Bailey's *Universal Etymological English Dictionary* (1721) or John Wesley's *Complete English Dictionary* (1753). Even dictionaries that followed Johnson revealed similar problems; many, such as Thomas Sheridan's *A General Dictionary of the English Language* (1780) or John Walker's *Critical Pronouncing Dictionary* (1791), simply adopted Johnson's entries and definitions, while incorporating elements such as individualized transcription systems to indicate pronunciation. This habit of systematic plagiarism continued through the nineteenth century, though even dictionaries which soundly rejected Johnson ('No man can possibly succeed in compiling a truly valuable Dictionary of the English Language, unless he entirely deserts the steps of Johnson', as Charles Richardson argued in his own *New Dictionary of the English Language* [1836–37]) tended to reveal other (fundamentally unscientific) weaknesses of their own. See P. Silva, 'Time and Meaning: Sense and Definition in the *OED*', in Mugglestone, *Lexicography and the OED*, 77–8.

22 Johnson, 'Preface' B1v.

23 R.C. Trench, *On Some Deficiencies in Our English Dictionaries* (London: Parker, 1860), 10.

24 Ibid., 44.

25 Ibid., 4.

26 *Oat*, in line with Trench's ideals, is defined with impeccable objectivity in the *OED*: 'The grains of a hardy cereal (see sense 2) forming an important article of food in many countries for men and also a chief food of horses; usually collectively, as a species of grain.'

27 Trench, 5–6.

28 MP/9/11/1910. J.A.H. Murray, ms of lecture on 'Dictionaries' delivered to the London Institute, 9 November 1910, 12.

29 Ibid.

30 J.A.H. Murray, 'Ninth Annual Address of the President to the Philological Society', *TPS,* 1880–81, 128.

31 T.H. Huxley to J. Hooker, 5 September 1858, in L. Huxley, *Life and Letters of Thomas Henry Huxley* (London: Macmillan, 1900), I, 160.

32 S. Johnson, *Adventurer* No.115, Tuesday 11 December 1753, *The Yale Edition of the Works of Samuel Johnson,* Vol. II, *The Idler* and *The Adventurer,* ed. W.J. Bate, J.M. Bullitt, and L.F. Powell (New Haven: Yale University Press, 1963), 456.

33 [T. Wilson], *The Many Advantages of a Good Language to Any Nation* (London: Knapton, 1724), 5.

34 J. Dryden, 'Defence of the Epilogue' (1672), *Essays of John Dryden,* ed. W.P. Ker, 2 vols (New York: Russell, 1961), I, 165.

35 N. Bailey, *An Universal Etymological Dictionary,* 7th edn (London: Knapton, 1735), A3r.

36 T. Stackhouse, *Reflections on the Nature and Property of Languages in General, and on the Advantages, Defects, and Manner of Improving the English Tongue in Particular* (London: Batley, 1731), 192–3.

37 Cited in J.L. Clifford, *Dictionary Johnson. Samuel Johnson's Middle Years* (London: Heinemann, 1979), 54. Strahan, as one of the consortium of booksellers who paid Johnson £1,575 in instalments (beginning in 1746) for the making of the dictionary, had a vested interest in keeping the ongoing work in the public mind. See A. Reddick, *The Making of Johnson's Dictionary 1746–1773* (Cambridge: Cambridge University Press, 1990) for a full account of the history of the dictionary.

38 S. Johnson, *The Plan of a Dictionary of the English Language* (London: Knapton, 1747), 4, 11.

39 Johnson, 'Preface' to the *Dictionary,* A2r, C1r. Such interventionist positions exist, with evident inconsistency, alongside other statements which, at least formally, assert the validity of usage (see, e.g., Johnson's intention not to 'form, but register the language ... not teach men how they should think, but relate how they have hitherto expressed their thoughts' ('Preface', C1v).

40 F.J. Furnivall, 'Circular to the Philological Society', cited in K.M.E. Murray, *Caught in the Web of Words: James Murray and the* Oxford English Dictionary (New Haven: Yale University Press, 1977), 137. Furnivall, a prominent member of the Philological Society, as well as founder of the Early English Text Society, the Chaucer Society, and the New Shakspere Society (among others), took over the editing of the *OED* in 1861, handing over the assembled materials to Murray when the latter became editor in 1879.

41 Johnson, *Plan,* 31.

42 Johnson, 'Preface', A2r.

43 Trench, 4–5.

44 Johnson, 'Preface', A2r.

45 *Slippy* is, for instance, condemned as 'A barbarous provincial word' against *slippery* which, covering the same semantic territory, is entirely unmarked. The entries for *cheery/ cheerful* reveal a similar dichotomy, Johnson declaring the former 'a ludicrous word' in the 4th edition of his *Dictionary* (1773).

46 *Dispense with* is declared to be 'ungrammatical' while *ponder on* ('To think, to muse') is condemned as an 'improper use of the word'.

47 Johnson, *Plan,* 19.

48 Johnson, 'Preface', A2v.

49 J.A.H. Murray, '"Couvade" – the Genesis of a Modern Myth', *The Academy* (1892): 458.

50 See T. McArthur, 'Culture-Bound and Trapped by Technology: Centuries of Bias in the Making of Wordbooks', in B.B. Kachru and H. Kahane, eds, *Cultures, Ideologies, and the Dictionary: Studies in Honor of Ladislav Zgusta* (Tübingen: Niemeyer, 1995), 382.

51 Johnson, 'Preface', A2r.

52 See K. Murray, 298.

53 Murray, *English Lexicography*, 6–7.

54 Trench, 4.

55 Ibid., 1.

56 MP/20/12/1906. J.A.H. Murray to Mr Jenkinson, 20 December 1906.

57 [Philological Society], *Proposal for the Publication of a New English Dictionary* (London: Trubner, 1859), 3.

58 Bradley was appointed co-editor of the *OED* in 1886, followed by W. Craigie in 1901, and C. Onions in 1914.

59 Cited in *OED* under 'Little', sense 1a.

60 Johnson, 'Preface', C2v.

61 [O. Bunce], *Don't: A Manual of Mistakes and Improprieties More or Less Prevalent in Conduct and Speech* (London: Griffith & Farran, 1884), 58.

62 H. Béjoint, *Modern Lexicography. An Introduction* (Oxford: Oxford University Press, 2000), 136.

63 Johnson, *Preface*, B2v, *Plan*, 18.

64 D. Coleridge, 'Observations on the Plan of the Society's Proposed New English Dictionary', *TPS*, 1860–61: 155.

65 Trench, 4.

66 MP24/10/1888. J.W. Davidson to J.A.H. Murray, 24 October 1888.

67 Ibid.

68 See further L.C. Mugglestone, '"An Historian not a Critic": The Standard of Usage in the *OED*', in Mugglestone, *Lexicography and the OED*, 189–206.

69 MP/10/12/1906. J.A.H. Murray to G.K. Harrison, 10 December 1906.

70 'A New English Dictionary', *The Times*, 26 January 1884: 6.

71 Review of *NED* Part 1: A-Ant, *Athenaeum*, 9 February 1884: 177.

72 OED/MISC/59/1/11. Review of *NED E – Every*, *Manchester Guardian*, 14 July 1891.

73 OED/MISC/59/2/20. Review of *Everybody – Ezod*, *Bradford Observer*, 1 May 1894.

74 Murray, 'General Explanations', x.

75 [A. Smith], unsigned review of '*A Dictionary of the English Language* by Samuel Johnson', in *The Edinburgh Review, Containing an Account of all the Books and Pamphlets Published in Scotland from June 1755* (1755): 62, in J.T. Boulton, ed., *Samuel Johnson: The Critical Heritage* (London: Routledge, 1971), 155.

76 Johnson 'Preface', C2r.

77 Johnson, *Plan*, 32.

78 See Aarsleff, 255.

79 S. Johnson, *The Vanity of Human Wishes* (London: Dodsley, 1749).

80 Johnson, 'Preface', C1v.

81 See L.C. Mugglestone, 'Pioneers in the Untrodden Forest: The *New* English Dictionary', in Mugglestone, *Lexicography and the OED*, 1–21.

82 A. Campbell, *Lexiphanes, a Dialogue* (London: Knox, 1767), p. xxxv.

Chapter 8

Ruskin's Revised Eighteenth Century

Dinah Birch

Harold Bloom's introductory study of Ruskin's literary criticism, first published in 1965, identifies three Romantic figures (Turner, Wordsworth, and Shelley) as Ruskin's 'essential teachers'.[1] Bloom singles out Wordsworth's 'Ode: Intimations of Immortality from Recollections of Earliest Childhood' as 'at one with the central and decisive experiences of Ruskin's life',[2] which he interprets as distinguished by both the intensity of its vision and the desolation of its loss. Bloom's argument places Ruskin squarely within his conception of a 'visionary company', finding his work a product of the 'radical version of Romanticism his entire sensibility incarnated'.[3] Writing on Ruskin again in 1986, Bloom refines his analysis of the critical authority of John Ruskin in the light of his own theory of vexed inheritance. 'In some sense', Bloom remarks, 'all of Ruskin's critics are driven back to origins, Ruskin's and their own, because that may be the largest power of his work, to compel us to the dangerous recognition that origin and aim cannot be separate entities, however much we seek to honour Nietzsche's great injunction that, for the sake of life, we ought to keep them apart.'[4]

Bloom's reading was persuasive. His line of thought, which defined Ruskin's works as the record of an 'aesthetic tragedy', whose performance of 'mingled grandeur and ruin ... only make them still more representative of post-Romantic art, and its central dilemma',[5] placed Ruskin's criticism within the parameters of a more general understanding of Victorian culture as the long result of disruptive Romantic energies. Much of the influential writing on Ruskin over the closing decades of the twentieth century was inclined to explore the densely productive relations between his work and that of his Romantic precursors.[6] This was not a misconceived project. Ruskin, like Matthew Arnold or George Eliot, was among the most powerful of those who reinterpreted Romantic values in later nineteenth-century culture. But it was an approach that did lead to some exclusions, and unbalanced emphases, in our understanding of the winding complexities of Ruskin's 'origin and aim'. It prompted his readers to underestimate the importance of religious belief in his work, for reading Ruskin's critical writing as an extended amplification of the challenge to Christian ideologies expressed in early Wordsworth, Turner, or Shelley could not allow for the extent to which his work is driven by his changing relations with varieties of Christian tradition. It encouraged them to be too eager to pattern the narratives of his life as those of Romantic tragedy, fostering the kind of sensational biographical readings, at once condescending and voyeuristic, that have proved a significant obstacle to a serious understanding of Ruskin's work and its legacies. Even Bloom, commonly hostile to such reductive readings, cannot quite resist them in Ruskin's case ('Ruskin was ruined before his thirteenth birthday').[7] Less evidently, but also damagingly, a theoretical paradigm that saw Ruskin primarily in debate with high Romanticism could find little room for the pervasive consequences of his engagement with earlier writing.

Ruskin's evolving understanding of eighteenth-century literature was formed by the cultural politics of his own generation. Many of his first judgements were hostile, an aspect of the dismissal of an outmoded body of thought that seemed alien to his revisionary Christian aesthetics. Eighteenth-century writing was seen to be trivial because it failed to be sublime, or attempted an irremediably inferior kind of sublimity. Later, Ruskin came to deplore such denigration of eighteenth-century work as one of the orthodoxies which allowed his self-satisfied contemporaries to magnify their own importance. He reversed his earlier views, in a series of readings of eighteenth-century authors and texts which articulated an increasingly aggressive rejection of what was modern. His commendation of eighteenth-century literature helped to sustain the construction of a voice emerging from isolation and angry dissent. This was also a Romantic strategy, defined by ideals of noble solitude, and the authority of imagined origin. But it was a variety of Romanticism that founded its claims to credibility in the weight of eighteenth-century precedent. Ruskin's changing position reminds us that the Romantic and post-Romantic aesthetics that he inherited have a long history. They are tightly bound up with perceptions of eighteenth-century thought which persistently inform Ruskin's shifting critical identity.

The deepest roots of Ruskin's origin lay in the life of his parents. Ruskin was unusually loyal to the family values that defined his emotional and his intellectual direction throughout his long creative life. But as a young writer he needed to discover ways of moving beyond their supportive, constraining world. These divisive pressures shaped his changing ideas about eighteenth-century precedent. Thinking, rather ruefully, about his early education, Ruskin recalled the eighteenth-century writing that he associated with the seminal experiences of his childhood: 'My intense vanity prevented my receiving any education in literature (which otherwise might have been possible), except what I picked up myself; but my father never in any instance read a book to me which was bad in style, his taste being excellent; and having Johnson, Goldsmith, and Richardson read to me constantly, led me in the right way.'[8] Ruskin identified the literature of the eighteenth century with the primary voices of his parents, and especially with the voice of his father. But his parents' literary allegiances were not limited to their eighteenth-century reading. Though the established masters of the eighteenth century were a constant presence in their old-fashioned household, Ruskin's parents reserved their deepest affection for those who came after – notably Byron and Scott, great writers of their own generation. Ruskin's later positive images of eighteenth-century literature were often modified and to some extent constructed through his own readings of Byron and Scott, authors who were also closely associated in his mind with the cultural world of his parents.

The independence of Ruskin's earliest critical voice was asserted in his scepticism of eighteenth-century authority. Though his sophisticated remodelling of concepts of the sublime in natural landscape was in itself a development of an eighteenth-century concept (Edmund Burke's *Philosophical Enquiry into the Origins of our Ideas of the Sublime and Beautiful* was, after all, published in 1757), it was partly framed as an attack on eighteenth-century critical ideologies. The five magisterial volumes of *Modern Painters* (1843–60) established Ruskin's credentials as a critic who could interpret the Romanticism of Wordsworth and Turner for a new generation. His central objection to eighteenth-century writing was addressed to its supposed incomprehension of the moral force of natural beauty. Lecturing in Edinburgh in 1853, at a time when his interest in the aesthetics of the sublime was at its height, he denounced 'the strange deadness to the higher sources of landscape sublimity which is mingled with the morbid pastoralism' (XII, 119) that he discerned in eighteenth-century work:

> And although in the second-rate writers continually, and in the first-rate ones occasionally, you find an affectation of interest in mountains, clouds, and forests, yet whenever they write from their heart, you will find an utter absence of feeling respecting anything beyond gardens and grass. Examine, for instance, the novels of Smollett, Fielding, and Sterne, the comedies of Molière, and the writings of Johnson and Addison, and I do not think you will find a single expression of true delight in sublime nature in any one of them. (XII, 119)

Throughout the 1850s, it was Ruskin's purpose to achieve a resolution between his own understanding of the sublime as it is be observed in landscape and his intensely felt evangelical faith, in order to persuade his readers of the 'indisputable truth that the love of nature is a characteristic of the Christian heart, just as the hunger for healthy food is characteristic of the healthy frame' (XII, 122). It was an ambition that led to disdain for eighteenth-century aesthetic theory.

Ruskin's pivotal chapter on the pathetic fallacy, a term which he invented as part of his revisionary interpretation of landscape in the third volume of *Modern Painters* (1856), focuses the terms of his argument. As Ruskin defines it, the pathetic fallacy, the transference of the poet's own emotions to the phenomena of nature, is never found in the greatest literature. But it was all too common in eighteenth-century writing. Its debilitating influence seemed to him especially well demonstrated in the poetry of Alexander Pope. Seeing Pope's poetry as a product of neo-classical formalism rather than the faithful performance of the moral energy of nature, Ruskin singled out his translations of classical poetry for his most cutting censure. The vehemence of his language in doing so signals a decisive challenge to family principle, for in devaluing Pope Ruskin was defying his father's judgement. Pope's translation of Homer was a longstanding favourite with John James Ruskin, and he had been especially pleased to perceive a resemblance between his son's early poetry and 'the beautiful lines of Pope' (II, 57). The translation represented one of the recognized literary landmarks of Ruskin's childhood, and he was later to remember Pope's Homer as 'reading of my own election' (XXVII, 167). In Ruskin's analysis of the pathetic fallacy, Pope's once-revered translation of Homer has become emblematic of the worst kind of poetry. He takes the moment of Ulysses' greeting of Elpenor in the underworld as an example of what can go wrong when a poet writes without genuine feeling:

> O, say, what angry power Elpenor led,
> To glide in shades, and wander with the dead?
> How could thy soul, by realms and seas disjoined,
> Outfly the nimble sail, and leave the lagging wind?[9]

The metaphors of Pope's translation here are, Ruskin claims, 'painful', because they convey no relation between an intense passion and its location in an imagined landscape. Obedient to convention, Pope has sacrificed the emotional reality of the encounter, which Ruskin describes as animated by 'exactly the spirit of bitter and terrified lightness' which is to be found in Hamlet's meeting with the ghost of his father.[10] As a result, Pope's metaphors 'are not a *pathetic* fallacy at all, for they are put in the mouth of the wrong passion – a passion which never could possibly have spoken them – agonized curiosity. Ulysses wants to know the facts of the matter, and the very last thing his mind could do at the moment would be to pause, or suggest in any wise what was *not* a fact. The delay in the first three lines, and conceit in the last, jar upon us instantly like the most frightful discord in music. No poet of true imaginative power could possibly have written the passage' (V, 207–8). It was not only Pope's translations of Homer that drew Ruskin's scorn. The language of the pastoral poetry seemed to him still more mannered, and he is forthright in his contempt: 'simple falsehood, uttered by hypocrisy; definite absurdity, rooted in affectation, and coldly asserted in the teeth of nature and fact' (V, 217). 'Cold-hearted Pope' (V, 216) has the power to resist the overwhelming emotional force with which love and mortality seize the poetic imagination, but this is a strength that can only reflect the derivative procedures of the classicism that it is Ruskin's business to challenge in his work of the 1850s.

In the final volume of *Modern Painters*, he speaks yet more decisively of the corrosive influence of neo-classicism. It is at this point, however, that he begins to suggest that Pope's writing might embody a kind of value that could be dissociated from the contamination of its models. 'It is not possible that the classical spirit should ever take possession of a mind of the highest order. Pope is, as far as I know, the greatest man who ever fell strongly under its influence; and though it spoiled half his work, he broke through it continually into true enthusiasm and tender thought' (VII, 316). That appeared in 1860, as Ruskin's critical interests began to turn away from the aesthetics of landscape and towards the political and economic issues that preoccupied him throughout the 1860s. The movement in his thought is implied by a retreat from the round condemnation of Pope that he had published just four years before. He qualifies his judgement still further with a note: 'Cold-hearted, I have called him. He was so in writing the Pastorals, of which I then spoke; but in after life his errors were those of his time, his wisdom was his own; it would be well if we also made it ours' (VII, 316–7).

Ruskin changed his mind about many things as he grew older, but few revisions were more dramatic than the transformation in his view of Alexander Pope. In the *Lectures on Art* (1870), his inaugural lectures as Oxford's Slade Professor of Fine Art, we find that Pope has been translated from villain into hero. Ruskin now describes him as being, with Virgil, one of the 'great masters of the absolute art of language' (XX, 76). The status of both Virgil and Pope arises, Ruskin maintains, from 'the moral elements of their minds' (XX, 76). It is no longer simply in terms of the aesthetics of literary history that Ruskin chooses to measure the stature of Pope's writing. In these lectures Pope, like

Virgil before him, stands for the spiritual identity of a nation. He takes his place, with Chaucer and Shakespeare, within the fixed ranks of English greatness. Ruskin wishes his undergraduate audiences to study

> the deep tenderness in Virgil which enabled him to write the stories of Nisus and Lausus; and the serene and just benevolence which placed Pope, in his theology, two centuries in advance of his time, and enabled him to sum the law of noble life in two lines which, so far as I know, are the most complete, the most concise, and the most lofty expression of moral temper existing in English words:–

> > *'Never elated, while one man's oppress'd;*
> > *Never dejected, while another's bless'd.'*

> I wish you also to remember these lines of Pope, and to make yourselves entirely masters of his system of ethics; because, putting Shakespeare aside as rather the world's than ours, I hold Pope to be the most perfect representative we have, since Chaucer, of the true English mind; and I think the *Dunciad* is the most absolutely chiselled and monumental work 'exacted'[11] in our country. You will find, as you study Pope, that he has expressed for you, in the strictest language and within the briefest limits, every law of art, of criticism, of economy, of policy, and, finally, of a benevolence, humble, rational, and resigned, contented with its allotted share of life, and trusting the problem of its salvation to Him in whose hand lies that of the universe. (XX, 77)

In *Fors Clavigera* (1871–84), the major series of public letters to the 'workmen and labourers of Great Britain' that Ruskin published throughout his term of office as Slade Professor, we find him contemplating the possibility of writing a biography of Pope in order to 'rescue' (XXVII, 586) him from what he had then come to see as the injustice and inaccuracy of contemporary assessments of his work. Pope now figures among the small group of writers and painters who constitute, for Ruskin, a timeless measure of greatness.

What lay behind this remarkable *volte-face*? It was partly a matter of the changing focus of interest that meant Ruskin grew less concerned with the function of landscape in art and literature, and more interested in reformulating the moral and political ethics of writing. But it also had to do with a shift in the way in which Ruskin perceived his own identity as a writer. Pope had become a potent model for Ruskin's radical reconstruction of his critical voice. The disaffected satire of *The Dunciad* is an unlikely model for the work of the successful public figure that Ruskin seemed to have become in 1870 – 51 years old, with a prestigious critical reputation which had just earned him an appointment to a pioneering professorship in art at Oxford. In fact, the public achievements that his parents had longed for now meant little to him. Ruskin felt himself to be an outsider, remote from the cultural mainstream, voicing what he saw as unchangeable truths in the face of apathy or greed. The sense of bitter withdrawal that characterizes Pope's later satire was partly founded on the example of Horace, who was acquiring a new significance for Ruskin throughout the 1860s and early 1870s. Ruskin had given Horace short shrift in the mid-1850s. Like Pope, Horace showed no instinct for the sublimity of landscape. In the 'disgusting' *Iter ad Brundisium*, for instance, 'Horace takes exactly as much interest in the scenery he is passing through as Sancho Panza would have done'.[12] Ruskin changed his mind about Horace as radically as he did about Pope, and for comparable reasons. Horace came to figure in Ruskin's writing as 'the great Roman moralist' (XVI, 167). His growing reverence for Horace stood alongside his veneration of Pope as a declaration of his alienation from the contemporary taste which he had attempted to influence in *Modern Painters*: 'It is the fashion, in modern days, to say that Pope was no poet. Probably our schoolboys, also, think Horace none. They have each, nevertheless, built for themselves a monument of enduring wisdom.'[13] It was Horace's poetry that provided Ruskin with the title of the serial *Fors Clavigera*, and it was not an accident that those angry Horatian letters began to appear soon after Ruskin's election to the chair at Oxford.[14] The coldness or misunderstanding that had in Ruskin's view marked classical and neo-classical interpretations of landscape were now outweighed by their foundation of a resilient tradition of English cultural satire, a tradition with which Ruskin increasingly identified himself as he grew older and more isolated. Pope could be numbered among those who had trodden this lonely path before him.

It was not difficult to accommodate Byron and Scott, the two Romantic writers who had figured most positively in Ruskin's earlier sense of a writer's identity, within these changing perspectives. Byron, as both rake and moralist, remained the most eighteenth century of the great Romantic poets. Ruskin read his work constantly as a child, and was dazzled by his ease and panache. The exuberant narrative poems that he wrote copiously throughout his childhood and adolescence were Byronic in both style and feeling, modelled particularly on the comic satire of *Don Juan*. These jaunty emulations of Byron were encouraged by John James Ruskin, whose admiration for the poet ran deep. Byron became essential to Ruskin's sense of a retrospective identity, in ways that became bound up with his increasingly close identification with eighteenth-century values. Praising Byron's judgement of poetry in his autobiography *Praeterita* (1886–89), Ruskin cites his hero's admiration for Pope: 'Your whole generation', Byron had remarked, 'are [*sic*] not worth a canto of *The Rape of the Lock*, or the *Essay on Man*, or the *Dunciad*, or "anything that is his"'(XXXV, 147). Byron, like Horace, and like 'Byron's own master, Pope' (XXXIII, 148), is now numbered among those writers who cannot be understood by the modern mind. 'The modern reader, not to say also, modern scholar, is ... ignorant of the essential qualities of Byron' (XXXV, 145), Ruskin remarks in *Praeterita*. Here, he is writing a final testament in old age, remembering the deepest sources of his life and work. The process which led him to number Byron among the elegiac voices that had formed his mind had begun earlier. In *Fiction, Fair and Foul* (1880–81), a rebarbative series of critical essays which amount to the culmination of years of critical analysis and celebration of the writers who had meant most to him, Ruskin consider the 'Isles of Greece', one of his favourite passages from *Don Juan*. He quotes a stanza in which he claims the 'whole heart' of Byron stands revealed:

> What, – silent yet? and silent *all*?
> Ah no, the voices of the dead
> Sound like a distant torrent's fall,
> And answer, 'Let *one* living head,
> But one, arise – we come – we come:'
> – 'Tis but the living who are dumb.[15]

His choice of text is especially instructive. The 'voices of the dead', sounding 'like a distant torrent's fall', now seem to unite a love of 'the beauty of this world' (XXXIV, 330) with an identification with the territories of sacred memory. As Ruskin has come to read it, Byron's poetry confirms his own condemnation of the pusillanimous world of his own generation, and underwrites his own sense of obligation to speak, and to speak alone – the '*one* living head' who must arise in order to wake these saving voices. This is precisely the duty that Ruskin believed himself to be fulfilling in the letters of *Fors Clavigera*, the series he had just resumed, more belligerently than ever, after a break of two years resulting from his first major mental breakdown of 1878.

Byron's peculiar resonance for Ruskin had much to do with his speaking for the dead; but Byron also, as Ruskin heard him, spoke for Scotland. One of the passages that haunts *Fiction, Fair and Foul* tenderly remembers the Scottish Highlands:

> He who first met the Highlands' swelling blue
> Will love each peak that shows a kindred hue,
> Hail in each crag a friend's familiar face,

And clasp the mountain in his mind's embrace.
...
The infant rapture still survived the boy,
And Loch-na-Gar with Ida look'd o'er Troy.[16]

Byron's wide imagination unites the heroic histories of the classical world with intimate memories of the landscapes of Scotland: 'for Byron, Loch-na-Gar *with Ida*, looks o'er Troy, and the soft murmurs of the Dee and the Bruar change into voices of the dead on distant Marathon' (XXXIV, 331). Ruskin's association of the meaning of the eighteenth century with Byron's poetry has to do with a sense of his own, curiously eighteenth-century Scottish past. Though he was not Scottish, he often spoke and behaved as if he were. He was born and brought up in London, became a student and then a professor in Oxford, wrote about France, Italy, and Switzerland, settled in the Lake District. Much of his critical work was directed towards a redefinition of Englishness, and the national guild that he founded in connection with *Fors Clavigera* was called the Guild of St George. Nevertheless, Ruskin never thought himself to be entirely English. His work was part of the life of England, and he committed himself to a confrontation with its perceived failings; but he felt himself authorized to stand apart from England, seeing it the more clearly because it was not wholly his own. This was because his father, John James Ruskin, was a proud Scot, born (in 1785) and educated in Edinburgh. The culture of the London family home of his childhood, where 'my father fondly and devotedly taught me my Scott, my Pope, and my Byron' (XXXIV, 364), was consciously that of Scotland in exile. The basis of the sense of estrangement that marks Ruskin's career lay in that original Scottishness.

When Ruskin's father recalled his youth, what he recalled most vividly was the vigour and confidence of commercial Edinburgh at the turn of the century, the hard-headed city where he learned the disciplines that made him a wealthy London trader. Ruskin came to see his father's business career as heroic, but it was a heroism cast in the mould of the traditionally paternalistic merchant.[17] John James Ruskin was made by the Edinburgh of Walter Scott. His understanding of eighteenth-century Scottish culture was mediated through the sophisticated historical writing of Scott, as novel after novel patiently constructed and interpreted the history of a nation. To a large extent, this was also true of John James's son. Scott's fiction, with Byron's poetry, were fixed points of reference and worth in Ruskin's mind, and this was because they had, together with Pope, constituted the staple of the literary identity he had inherited from his father. Again, Ruskin draws together a lifetime of complex

thought in the allusive arguments of *Fiction, Fair and Foul*. The innovative
writing practices that made Scott the first modern novelist are here impatiently
rejected: 'his own splendid powers were, even in early life, tainted, and in
his latter years destroyed, by modern conditions of commercial excitement'
(XXXIV, 274). It is when Scott looks backward that he is a great writer, in
Ruskin's view. Ruskin grimly discriminates what he sees as the 'woof of
a Waverley novel from the cobweb of a modern one' (XXXIV, 284) in his
readings of Scott. Like Horace, Pope, and Byron, he is among the writers who
matter to him because they can be seen to refute modernity.

   The Antiquary (1816), in which Scott makes a hero of the curmudgeonly
but right-thinking antiquary Jonathan Oldbuck, is an essential text here. Walter
Scott saw this novel as an interpretation of the transition from the old to the new
in the closing years of the eighteenth century. His sympathies are decisively
with the old. Ruskin inclined to the view that Oldbuck was 'a portrait of Scott
himself'.[18] This was not wholly true, but *The Antiquary* is certainly coloured
by unusually extensive autobiographical reference. Its lively memories of youth
made *The Antiquary* Scott's favourite among his novels. It was also much liked
by the Ruskin family. Suspicious, shrewd, and contemptuous of the modern, the
pugnacious character of Oldbuck was especially highly regarded by John James
Ruskin, who used 'Jonathan Oldbuck' as a pseudonym in correspondence with
the press.[19] Ruskin called *The Antiquary* 'this errorless book' (XXXIV, 307), and
fully shared his parents' affection for its principal character. Writing to his mother
in 1845, while travelling in Italy on his first tour without the company of his
parents, Ruskin approvingly notes Francis Palgrave's review of Gally Knight's
The Ecclesiastical Architecture of Italy in the *Quarterly Review*.[20] Scott had
been one of the founders of the Tory *Quarterly*, which was under the editorship
of Scott's biographer Lockhart from 1826 to 1853. It was a publication that the
Ruskin family read regularly.[21] Palgrave (1788–1861), a passionate antiquary
and devoted medievalist,[22] begins his review with a long consideration of *The
Antiquary*, warmly appreciative of Oldbuck's condemnation of the practice
of restoring or repairing old buildings, obliterating historical evidence in the
process. Ruskin agreed wholeheartedly. 'It describes my antiquarian feelings to
the very letter. I find I am become Jonathan Oldbuck, to all but the shoebuckles,
and what it says about restoring and *destroying* might have come from my
indignant pen itself – not quite viperous enough though, for me.'[23] In 1851,
he wrote to his father of the continuing pleasure he took in the book: 'I have
bought *The Antiquary*, which is all beaten gold, and inexhaustible.'[24]

   In *Fiction, Fair and Foul*, Oldbuck's regard for the material traces of an
honourable past is held up as a model for Ruskin's readers. Ruskin quotes

from an encounter in *The Antiquary* between the antiquarian and the modern and efficient town-clerk in the market-place. Oldbuck is offered some carved 'auld stanes' retrieved from an ancient chapel, in return for allowing a new water-course to cut through his land. The clerk cunningly mentions the use to which the stones would otherwise be put, knowing this will secure Oldbuck's consent to the deal:

> 'Deacon Harlewalls thinks the carved through-stanes might be put with advantage on the front of the new council-house – that is, the twa cross-legged figures that the callants used to ca' Robbin and Bobbin, ane on ilka door-cheek; and the other stane, that they ca'd Ailie Dailie, abune the door. It will be very tastefu', the Deacon says, 'and just in the style of modern Gothic.'
>
> 'Good Lord deliver me from this Gothic generation!' exclaimed the Antiquary, – 'a monument of a knight-templar on each side of a Grecian porch, and a Madonna on top of it!' (XXXIV, 304)

The triumphant clerk congratulates himself on his 'dexterity' in disposing so advantageously of redundant and meaningless stones 'which the council had determined to remove as a nuisance, because they encroached three feet upon the public road' (XXXIV, 304).

This transaction encapsulates much that defines the fraudulence of the nineteenth century, as Ruskin understands it. He leaves his readers in no doubt as to where his allegiance lies. 'In this single page of Scott, will the reader please note the kind of prophetic instinct with which the great men of every age mark and forecast its destinies? The water from the Fairwell is the future Thirlmere carried to Manchester;[25] the "auld stanes" at Donagild's Chapel, removed as a *nuisance*, foretell the necessary view taken by modern cockneyism, Liberalism, and progress, of all things that remind them of the noble dead, of their fathers' fame, or of their own duty; and the public road becomes their idol, instead of the saint's shrine' (XXXIV, 305). Ruskin uses Scott's fictional construction of eighteenth-century virtue to condemn nineteenth-century vice. But it is a certain kind of virtue – alienated, angry and marginalized; consciously identifying itself with the abandoned values of the past. Scott's fiction was one of the ways in which an idealized image of the eighteenth century allowed Ruskin to pass judgement on what seemed to him the crass venalities of his age.

Ruskin's view of Scott was steady in its admiration. But his understanding of eighteenth-century fiction, like his judgement of eighteenth-century poetry, underwent some radical changes. One position that did not change was his regard for the instructive gravity of Samuel Richardson, the 'greatest of our

English moral story-tellers' (XXV, 355). In *Praeterita*, where Ruskin speaks of the 'deep admiration I still feel for Richardson' (XXXV, 542), he approvingly quotes the diary entry in which he had recorded his first encounters with *Sir Charles Grandison* as a young man: 'I never met with anything which affected me so powerfully; at present I feel disposed to place this work above all other works of fiction I know. It is very, very grand; and has, I think, a greater practical effect on me for good than anything I ever read in my life' (XXXV, 308). The high-minded and youthful Evangelicalism that prompted this entry sometimes led to a fastidious revulsion from the ribaldries of other eighteenth-century novels. In 1840, at a time when he was still seriously considering becoming a clergyman, he wrote to a Christ Church contemporary, Edward Clayton, who was soon to be ordained:

> As Winifred Jenkins says, 'I can't pollewt my pen' – though, by-the-bye, you may find every piece of coarseness coined in the United Kingdom in that book.[26] I cannot, for the life of me, understand the feelings of men of magnificent wit and intellect, like Smollett and Fielding, when I see them gloating over and licking their chops over nastiness, like hungry dogs over ordure; founding one half of the laughable matter of their volumes in innuendoes of abomination. Not that I think, as many people do, they are bad books; for I don't think these pieces of open filth are in reality injurious to the mind, or at least, *as* injurious as corrupt sentiment and disguised immorality, such as you get sometimes in Bulwer[27] and men of his school. But I cannot *understand* the taste. I can't imagine why men who have real wit at their command should *perfume* it as they do. (I, 417–8)

Interestingly, Ruskin misattributes his quotation in this letter. It is not Smollett's Winifred Jenkins who declares that she cannot 'pollewt' her pen, but Fanny Squeers, in Dickens's *Nicholas Nickleby* (1839).[28] His sense of the coarse vigour of Smollett's language is here confused with what he was later to describe in *Modern Painters* as Dickens's 'cockney dialect' (VII, 355). He defines his objections to Dickens's manipulations of language in an extended analysis of vulgarity in the final volume of *Modern Painters* (1860):

> Provincial dialect is not vulgar; but cockney dialect, the corruption, by blunted sense, of a finer language continually heard, is so in a deep degree; and again, of this corrupted language, that is the worst which consists, not in the direct or expressive alteration of the form of a word, but in an unmusical destruction of it by dead utterance and bad or swollen formation of lip. There is no vulgarity in

'Blythe, blythe, blythe was she,
  Blythe was she, but and ben,
And weel she liked a Hawick gill,
  And leugh to see a tappit hen;'[29]

but much in Mrs Gamp's inarticulate 'bottle on the chimley-piece, and let me put my lips to it when I am so dispoged.'[30]

Ruskin's argument proceeds, as it characteristically does, on the basis of comparison – fiction, fair and foul; or the wholesome literature of the past juxtaposed with its tainted modern successors. Both of Ruskin's examples in this passage refer to drink. The language of old Scottish drinking is sanctified by its evocation of the world of John James Ruskin, whose fortune was founded on selling wine. It is seen as laudable, while Mrs Gamp's furtive bottle is most emphatically not. Scott's historicism stands as ever as a touchstone of value, refuting the 'pollewted' language of modernity. Scott explains the term 'tappit hen' in a note to his *Guy Mannering* (1815), where he quotes the lines from the song: 'The Tappit hen contained three quarts of claret … It was a pewter measure, the claret being in ancient days served from the tap, and had a figure of a hen upon the lid. In later times the name was given to a glass bottle of the same dimension. These are rare apparitions among degenerate topers of modern days.'[31] Language serves as proof of the lost values of a chivalrous past.

Beneath the terms of Ruskin's comparative arguments here lies a corrosive anxiety about the life of the body. The physicality of the eighteenth-century fiction he knew best unnerved him in a way that Scott, whose natural 'purity' (XXVII, 563) he always insists on, did not. As Ruskin came to define them, Scott's novels belong to a clean world of nature, rather than the sordid doings of humanity. They are as 'fresh as the air of his mountains; firm as their rocks' (XXVII, 563). The fiction of the high eighteenth century could not as easily be seen in such terms. When Ruskin was a young man, this troubled him. In 1845, he wrote in his diary: 'It seems to me that in Smollett, Fielding, and Le Sage, none of the Characters have *souls*. They feel and act exactly as animals would do if they had human intellects. They have the affection, the cunning, the rage, jealousy and all other passions of animals, and that which they appear to want seems to me precisely the part of man which is likely to be immortal.'[32] These novels offended both his Romantic sensibility and his Evangelical values. Ruskin makes the point still more vehemently in *Modern Painters*, remarking there that 'neither Gil Blas nor Roderick Random reaches, morally, anything near the level of dogs' (V, 374). Later, Ruskin was less affronted by the supposed animality of these writers. Other qualities had come to matter more. In the 1870s, Henry Fielding is included among the group of instructive writers who authorize his denial of modernity. In *Fors Clavigera* he praises him as 'a truly moral novelist, and worth any quantity of modern ones since Scott's death, – be they who they may' (XXIX, 220). Again and again, the word 'modern' reappears, always in a sharply negative sense. Ruskin's terms of commendation for Fielding's conception of Parson Adams is characteristic: 'I do not know if, in modern schools of literature, the name of Henry Fielding is ever mentioned, but it was of repute in my early days, and I think it right … to refer my readers to a work of his which gives one of the most beautiful types I know of the character of the English clergyman' (XXVIII, 287–8). The moral heroism of Adams is then contrasted with the crude and slovenly thinking of a typical contemporary clergyman, whose emptily fashionable works of popularized science Ruskin goes on to deride.[33]

Joseph Addison, 'as true as truth itself' (XXVII, 275), also plays a part in the construction of an ideal picture of a lost world of integrity in *Fors Clavigera*. In 'The Four Funerals', the letter of March 1872, Ruskin reprints Addison's reverent and emotionally charged description of the funeral of his fictional ideal of an English squire, Sir Roger de Coverley.[34] Ruskin tells his readers this account is 'the most finished piece which I know of English Prose literature in the eighteenth century' (XXVII, 273). But the 'educational effect' of the passage is more than aesthetic. Addison's narrative represents, as Ruskin sees it, a 'perfect' account of 'the funeral of an English squire who has lived an honourable life in peace' (XXVII, 275). De Coverley's life is nostalgically identified as an ideal, consciously and polemically set before a degraded generation of readers for emulation. Addison can now be included among those who are part of the wholesome purity of the natural world. He is a product of 'old quiet English work; in the midst of our steaming and puffing, it is like calm fresh air' (XXVII, 273). Eighteenth-century writing has come to be assimilated into the irreproachably natural landscapes of literature in which Ruskin also locates Byron and Scott.

This construction of an exemplary image of the eighteenth century is part of a larger imaginative structure, which repeatedly sets a principled past against a defiled present. As Ruskin grew older, and more inclined to identify himself with this projected past, the number of writers of the period who are drawn into the pattern grows. Tobias Smollett was formerly prominent among those that Ruskin disparaged on the grounds of his animal crudeness and his indifference to landscape. Later, Smollett came to be especially favoured – partly because he is Scottish, and partly because he had been relished by Ruskin's parents. In *Praeterita*, Ruskin speaks of the 'hearty, frank, and sometimes even irrepressible, laugh' of his mother as having had a 'very definitely Smollettesque' turn in it, and notes that 'between themselves, she and my father enjoyed their *Humphry Clinker* extremely, long before *I* was able to understand either the jest or gist of it' (XXXV, 144). In the mid-1870s, *Humphry Clinker* was among the books that Ruskin chose to read aloud to guests staying in Brantwood.[35] The example of *Humphry Clinker*'s elderly Matthew Bramble, eccentric but generous, is particularly telling. Bramble is an absurd figure, but he is the moral centre of the book. The anger that possesses him throughout most of the novel's picaresque action presages the estranged voice of Ruskin's later texts. Here is Bramble's appalled response to his first sight of London:

> There is no distinction or subordination left – The different departments of life are jumbled together – The hod-carrier, the low mechanic, the tapster, the publican, the shop-keeper, the pettifogger, the citizen, and courtier, *all tread upon the kibes of one another*: actuated by the demons of profligacy and licentiousness, they are seen every where rambling, riding, rolling, rushing, justling, mixing, bouncing, cracking, and crashing in one vile ferment of stupidity and corruption – All is tumult and hurry; one would imagine they were compelled by some disorder of the brain, that will not suffer them to be at rest.[36]

Bramble's rhetoric of contempt prefigures that of Ruskin, who shares to the full this distaste for the undiscriminating rush of a dishonest capital, and condemns it in comparable terms:

> Hyde Park, in the season, is the great rotatory form of the vast squirrel-cage; round and round it go the idle company, in their reversed streams, urging themselves to their necessary exercise ... this fermenting mass of unhappy human beings, – news-mongers, novel-mongers, picture-mongers, poison-drink-mongers, lust and death-mongers; the whole smoking mass of it one vast dead-marine storeshop, – accumulation of wreck of the Dead Sea, with every activity in it, a form of putrefaction (XXVIII, 136–7).

Chaotically futile activity and the breakdown of what both Bramble and Ruskin see as the necessary hierarchies of social order make the city a nightmare of decay and confusion. The anarchy of contemporary urban life generates a hectic literary language that mimes the disorder it describes. This was a strategy that Ruskin had partly learned from Dickens; but the grounds of its satirical perspectives belong to Smollett.

Matthew Bramble's irascibility is seen to be the manifestation of a dangerously vulnerable temperament. His stolidly conventional nephew Jeremy Melford judges him to be a man born 'with a natural excess of mental sensibility; for I suppose, the mind as well as the body, is in some cases endued with a morbid excess of sensation'.[37] Bramble is, as Melford puts it, 'as tender as a man without a skin'.[38] The diseased hypersensitivity of the cultural critic was a familiar trope in eighteenth-century writing, and had itself been satirized in the excesses of Jonathan Swift's Lemuel Gulliver, who declares that at the end of his voyages he 'could not endure my wife or children in my presence: the very smell of them was intolerable'.[39] On rereading *Gulliver's Travels*, Ruskin remarked that 'putting the delight in dirt, which is a mere disease, aside, Swift is very like me, in most things, in opinions exactly the same' (XVIII, lxi). It was the rage behind the satire of Swift, Pope, or Smollett that reflected Ruskin's own sense of cultural disgust most clearly. More placid and rational didactic models, like those provided by Maria Edgeworth, another writer Ruskin had known and admired since his youth, had come to irritate him: 'Miss Edgeworth made her morality so impertinent that, since her time, it has only been with fear and trembling that any good novelist has ventured to show the slightest bias in favour of the Ten Commandments' (XXVII, 562). Maria Edgeworth could tell her readers 'truly how to do right' (XVIII, 300), but she could not tell them that doing right might not be enough. Ruskin understood the Swiftian anger that drove his own later writing as an expression of pathological compassion. Disease and insanity were now the necessary companions of love. Writing from Venice in *Fors Clavigera*, he patiently explains why he is no longer interested in writing about natural beauty. 'For this green tide that eddies by my threshold is full of floating corpses, and I must leave my dinner to bury them, since I cannot save' (XXVIII, 757). Unbearably pained by what others could look on with indifference, Ruskin finds that his intense fear of the life of the body has turned into an equally profound sense of helpless pity in witnessing its death. 'I feel constantly as if I were living in one great churchyard, with people all round me clinging feebly to the edges of the open graves, and calling for help, as they fall back into them, out of sight' (XVII, 411).

Humphry Clinker is linked with both Margaret and John James Ruskin in Ruskin's memory, as part of the indissoluble bond 'between themselves'. His anger became a product of his parents' remembered sensitivity and affection, a legacy of their nurturing care fused with robust ultra-Toryism into an obsessive and alienating identification with the 'voices of the dead'. The overwhelming power of these echoing voices ended in the silence and madness of his later years. This might seem to make Ruskin part of a closed circle, the product of a retrospective pattern of thinking that led nowhere. In fact, it was to a large extent his increasing inclination to turn away from what he saw as worthless modernity that made him a fertile example to those who came after him.[40] As his fame and status as an acknowledged sage gathered weight, Ruskin grew more resolute in his refusal to identify himself with the complacent values of his own generation. He becomes a writer of memory, loss, and fragmentation. In this sense Bloom is right to locate his critical presence within a post-Romantic and predominantly Wordsworthian landscape. It is, however, a landscape which must be seen to include the more distant horizons of eighteenth-century precedent.

Notes

1 Bloom's essay was reprinted in his later, influential collection of critical work on Ruskin. See 'Introduction', *John Ruskin*, ed. Harold Bloom (New York and New Haven: Chelsea House, 1986), 1–14.
2 Ibid., 2.
3 Ibid., 7.
4 Ibid., vii–viii.
5 Ibid., 14.
6 Elizabeth K. Helsinger's *Ruskin and the Art of the Beholder* (Cambridge, Mass. and London: Harvard University Press, 1982) provided a powerful reading of Ruskin's difficult relations with Wordsworth, while John D. Rosenberg's *The Darkening Glass: A Portrait of Ruskin's Genius* (New York: Columbia University Press, 1961), Jay Fellows's *The Failing Distance: The Autobiographical Impulse in John Ruskin* (Baltimore: Johns Hopkins University Press, 1975) and *Ruskin's Maze* (Princeton: Princeton University Press, 1981), and Robert Hewison's *John Ruskin: The Argument of the Eye* (London: Thames and Hudson, 1976) were among the studies that initiated a new generation of critical work on Ruskin.
7 Bloom, 2.
8 Letter to the Rev. W.L. Brown (formerly Ruskin's tutor at Christ Church, Oxford), 8 November 1853; *The Library Edition of the Works of John Ruskin*, ed. E.T. Cook and Alexander Wedderburn, 39 vols (London: Allen, 1903–12), XXXVI, 153. Subsequent references to this edition are given in the main text as volume: page number.
9 V, 207, quoting Pope's translation of *Odyssey*, xi, 56–7.
10 Ruskin compares Ulysses's response with Hamlet's black joke: 'Well said, old mole! Canst work i' th'earth so fast?', *Hamlet*, I, v, 170; V, 207.
11 The reference is to Horace: 'Exegi monumentum aere perennius' ('I have achieved a more lasting monument'); *Odes*, iii, 30, 1.
12 Ruskin made this observation in 'Turner and his Works', a lecture delivered in 1853 (XII, 103).
13 *Deucalion* (Part I, 1875); XXVI, 114–5. Matthew Arnold famously dismissed Pope's credentials as a poet in 'The Study of Poetry' (1880): 'Though they may write in verse,

though they may in a certain sense be masters of the art of versification, Dryden and Pope are not classics of our poetry, they are classics of our prose.' For more discussion of Matthew Arnold on Pope, see Francis O'Gorman, 76–97 above.

14   See Horace, *Odes*, I, 35, 17–20, where the poet speaks of 'stern Necessity' ('saeva Necessitas') carrying nails, hooks, and molten lead, giving Ruskin his form of words – nail-bearing Fate, or Fors Clavigera. For a full discussion of the labyrinthine meaning of Ruskin's title, see Dinah Birch, 'Ruskin's Multiple Writing: *Fors Clavigera*', in *Ruskin and the Dawn of the Modern*, ed. Dinah Birch (Oxford: Clarendon, 1999), 176–7.

15   34.330: Byron, *Don Juan*, Canto III, 86; italics Ruskin's.

16   Byron, *The Island*, Canto II, xii, 280–83; 290–91. Compare Byron's early 'Lachin y Gair', in *Hours of Idleness*: 'Years have roll'd on, Loch na Garr, since I left you, / Years must elapse ere I tread you again: / Nature of verdure and flow'rs has bereft you, / Yet still are you dearer than Albion's plain', 32–6.

17   See Francis O'Gorman, '"An Entirely Honest Merchant": The Domestic Context of *Unto this Last*', *Late Ruskin: New Contexts* (Aldershot: Ashgate, 2001), 9–31, for an illuminating account of the relation between Ruskin's economic theory and the mercantile example of his father.

18   XXXIV, 303. The character is in fact partly modelled on the publisher George Constable.

19   In a series of letters to the *Morning Post*, written in late 1861. See Tim Hilton, *John Ruskin: The Later Years* (New Haven and London: Yale University Press, 2000), 24–5.

20   Francis Palgrave, review of Henry Gally Knight, *The Ecclesiastical History of Italy*, 2 vols (1842–44), in *The Quarterly Review*, 85 (1845): 334–403.

21   Ruskin occasionally reviewed books on art for the *Quarterly Review* in the late 1840s (XII, 169–248; 251–302).

22   He was the father of the poet and critic Francis Turner Palgrave (1824–97).

23   Letter from John Ruskin to Margaret Ruskin, 25 June 1845, *Ruskin in Italy: Letters to His Parents 1845,* ed. Harold Shapiro (Oxford: Clarendon, 1972), 128.

24   Letter from John Ruskin to John James Ruskin, 29 November 1851, *Ruskin's Letters From Venice, 1851–2*, ed. J.L. Bradley (Westport, Connecticut: Greenwood, 1978), 73.

25   Ruskin was a supporter of the Thirlmere Defence Association, which campaigned unsuccessfully to prevent the waters of Thirlmere in the Lake District, Cumbria, becoming a reservoir for the people of Manchester. The Bill permitting the conversion was passed in 1879.

26   Tobias Smollett's *Humphry Clinker* (1771), where Winifred Jenkins figures as Tabitha Bramble's maid.

27   Though Ruskin did not approve of the fiction of Edward Bulwer Lytton, he enjoyed its 'entangled richness of moving mind' (I, 370).

28   Writing to Ralph Nickleby about Nicholas's attack on her parents and subsequent flight, Miss Squeers refers to 'langwedge which I will not pollewt my pen with describing' (*Nicholas Nickleby*, ch. xv).

29   The reference is to an old Scottish drinking song, 'Andro and his Cutty Gun', printed by Allan Ramsay (1684–1758) in his anthology of English and Scottish ballads *The Tea Table Miscellany*, 3 vols (1724–37). It later became the basis for the Jacobite song 'The Wee German Lairdie'. A 'Hawick gill' and a 'tappit hen' are both traditional measures of drink.

30   VII, 355. See *Martin Chuzzlewit* (1844), ch. xix.

31   *Guy Mannering* (1814), M, n. 7.

32 20 October 1845; *The Diaries of John Ruskin*, ed. Joan Evans and John Howard Whitehouse, 3 vols (Oxford: Clarendon, 1956–59), V, 318–19.
33 Ruskin's target was William Houghton (1829?–97), author of *Country Walks of a Naturalist with his Children* (1869), and *Sea-side Walks of a Naturalist with his Children* (1870).
34 From *The Spectator* (1711–12), no. 517.
35 I, 417–8. Ruskin was perhaps thinking of Smollett's Matthew Bramble in naming the last of the many dogs he owned 'Bramble', thus revoking his earlier view that Smollett was among those writers who could not rise to the moral level of dogs. See James Dearden, *John Ruskin: A Life in Pictures* (Sheffield: Sheffield Academic Press, 1999), 184–5.
36 Tobias Smollett, *The Expedition of Humphry Clinker* (1771), Matthew Bramble to Dr Lewis, 29 May.
37 *Humphry Clinker,* Jeremy Melford to Watkin Phillips, 18 April.
38 *Humphry Clinker*, Jeremy Melford to Watkin Phillips, 30 April.
39 Jonathan Swift, *Gulliver's Travels* (1726), Part 4, ch. xi.
40 See the essays in *Ruskin and the Dawn of the Modern*, ed. Dinah Birch; *Ruskin and Modernism*, ed. Giovanni Cianci and Peter Nicholls (Houndmills: Palgrave, 2001) and *Ruskin and the Twentieth Century: The Modernity of Ruskinism*, ed. Toni Cerutti (Vercelli: Edizione Mercurio, 2000) for recent accounts of Ruskin's decisive influence on self-constructions within modernism and the modern.

Chapter 9

Sincerity in Every Department?
Masks, Masculinity, and Market Forces
in Eighteenth-century *English*
Men of Letters

David Amigoni[1]

In Leslie Stephen's biography of Alexander Pope (1880) for Macmillan's influential late Victorian *English Men of Letters* (*EML*) series, the reader is presented with an image of the eighteenth century as the rule of 'bright, clear common sense'. This enlightened common sense was

> for once having its own way, and tyrannizing over the faculties from which it usually suffers violence. The favoured faculty never doubted its qualification for supremacy in every department. In metaphysics it was triumphing with Hobbes and Locke over the remnants of scholasticism; under Tillotson it was expelling mystery from religion; and in art it was declaring war against the extravagant … [and] the romantic.[2]

Stephen's image of the progress of eighteenth-century reason is, beneath its surface optimism, a troubled one. For enlightenment 'supremacy' can only impose itself on 'the extravagant [and] the romantic' by means of tyrannical symbolic violence.

The figure who would exercise this violent 'supremacy' in the department of eighteenth-century literature was 'the wit', or, as Stephen put it, 'taken personally … the man who represented what we now describe by culture or the spirit of the age' (*Pope*, 28). The manliness of the eighteenth-century wit presented itself as a crucial issue. As an historian of eighteenth-century literature, Stephen was preoccupied with, and troubled about, masculinity as a cultural index of the spirit of two ages: firstly, of the eighteenth century, and secondly of an increasingly embattled late Victorian liberal reason, whose social, economic, and moral order was traceable to the eighteenth century. In this context Stephen found it difficult to believe wholeheartedly in Pope's manliness, given the dandified 'elevation of the bard by high-heeled shoes and a full-bottomed wig' (*Pope*, 74). And as Stephen's 'for once', in this chapter's opening quotation, suggests, his certainty that literary history after Pope had progressed inexorably towards enlightened common sense was less than robust.

In Stephen's own time Aestheticism perhaps presented the most tangible reversal away from the realist, empirical legacy of the enlightenment. Aestheticism celebrated the rebirth of the dandified male wit, but made wit itself the opponent of common sense. In Oscar Wilde's dialogue 'The Decay of Lying', the aesthete Vivian comments on the novelist Meredith as 'a child of realism not on speaking terms with his father', and one 'who is always breaking his shins over his own wit'.[3] In Wilde's Aestheticism, 'wit' had become a performative, anti-empirical, anti-realist stylistic attitude that created problems for those who found themselves practising it, despite the sincere impulses of their best selves. As this chapter will suggest, enough of Wilde's sense of 'wit' was discernible in Pope for Stephen to risk engaging with the poet's masks, or performance of roles. The chapter will argue that late nineteenth-century biographies of poets such as Pope and Thomas Gray are important sources for assessing Victorian critics' responses both to the eighteenth century and their own social and cultural anxieties. It is not simply that biographies delineate a canon of cultural 'heroes' from a given period, though they do precisely this. Rather, the discursive inclusiveness of a biography reveals connections between, and attitudes towards, facets comprising 'the spirit of the age'; including literary production, market place activity, and gender, in both the period being represented, and the period in which the representation took shape. In this chapter, I will argue that late nineteenth-century biographies of eighteenth-century poets are a key focus for recent critical work on Victorian culture and political economy, Aestheticism, and gender politics.

Producing 'Letters' and Divisions of Intellectual Labour

English Men of Letters was the title given to Macmillan's collection of biographical primers by the series editor, John Morley. Morley had written biographical studies of three major eighteenth-century figures – Edmund Burke, Denis Diderot, and Voltaire – and eighteenth-century writers were prominent in the series. *EML* actually consisted of two series, the first of which began in 1879, and saw the publication of 39 titles. *EML* was resumed in the early years of the twentieth century, adding another 26 volumes to its canon of English authors. Launching the first series, the very first volume to be published was Leslie Stephen's biography of Samuel Johnson; this set a trend, for of the 39 volumes, 13 volumes were devoted to high eighteenth-century figures. This figure compares to eleven devoted to authors from the period 1780–1830, five from the Victorian period, only four to seventeenth-century men, and four again to writers from the fourteenth, fifteenth, and sixteenth centuries combined. The second series is indicative of a nineteenth century that, in the throes of termination, sought to assess its own contribution to culture. Only four volumes from this second series were concerned with high eighteenth-century authors, compared to 17 from the period 1780–1830 and the subsequent Victorian period, and only five from the sixteenth and seventeenth centuries. Nonetheless, it is clear from the total of seventeen volumes that, overall, the high eighteenth century was considered an important and crucially formative period for English literature. Literature as 'letters' comprised critical commentary, poetry, and imaginative fiction, forms of writing not only pleasurable, but also offering instructive guidance in matters of manners and reflection during periods of social and cultural change.

For the biographers of *EML*, eighteenth-century men of letters were at their most appealing and instructive in moments of apparently transparent autobiographical expression. Stephen praised Pope's 'Epistle to Dr Arbuthnot' because, 'in its some 400 lines, he has managed to compress more of his feelings and thoughts than would fill an ordinary autobiography' (*Pope*, 186). Similarly, H.D. Traill observed of Lawrence Sterne's private letters to Madame de Madalle in his biography of the author of *Tristram Shandy*, that, although 'pitchforked into the book market', his letters were nonetheless

> highly valuable as pieces of autobiography. They are easy, naïve, and natural, rich in simple self-disclosure in almost every page, and if they have more to tell us about the man than the writer, they are yet not wanting in instructive hints as to Sterne's methods of composition and his theories of art.[4]

For Traill, Sterne's letters are both sources of transparent autobiographical expression, and self-consciously artful. Their framing context is the book market. For the eighteenth century saw the emergence of a literature shaped and conditioned by a market place, a market place that was increasingly concerned with the production, distribution, sale, and consumption of print. This combination of factors was, as we shall see, both important and troubling to Leslie Stephen's assessment of Pope as a man of letters: an office that presupposed a sincere, independent, and thus manly producer of literature.

For late Victorian critics, the province of the man of letters' productivity was also understood to extend substantially beyond literature conceived as epistolarity, poetry, drama, and imaginative prose. Stephen's sense, in *Pope*, of 'every department' of thought being supremely enlightened in the eighteenth century was demonstrated by the catholicity of *EML's* biographical and authorial canon. While most of the eighteenth-century authors in the series were dramatists, novelists, and poets, Johnson was included because of his critical common sense.[5] Gibbon was given a place on account of his historical writing; Hume for his empirical philosophy and contribution to the rigours of scientific scepticism; and Adam Smith – whose biography appeared in the second series – for his articulation of the 'laws' of political economy.

Morley's selection of *EML* biographers often implied a connection between late nineteenth-century divisions of intellectual expertise and the 'departments' of eighteenth-century thought. Perhaps the most striking instance of this is the volume on the philosophical sceptic Hume, written by agnostic *savant* Professor T.H. Huxley. The biography of Adam Smith was commissioned for the first series during the 1880s, but it did not appear until the second series. The volume was 'in preparation' as early as 1882, under the authorship of the Radical liberal MP, and former Chair of Political Economy at University College London, Leonard H. Courtney.[6] Thus, the volume on Smith was originally to have been written by an MP, that is to say a 'statesman' (Courtney was described as such in his *DNB* entry) with an academic interest in the science of political economy. Francis Wrigley Hirst eventually wrote the biography of Smith; he was a younger associate of Morley, and developed a reputation as a 'specialist' writer on economics, being appointed editor of *The Economist* in 1907. Hirst's biography of Smith celebrated *The Wealth of Nations* as 'one of the great books of the world'. This eighteenth-century treatise was an outstanding contribution to letters because it functioned as an instructive narrative through which 'the laws of wealth unfolded themselves like the incidents in a well-laid plot'.[7] We shall see, however, that when Leslie Stephen came to narrate the biography of Alexander Pope, the kinds of wealth that this exemplary life had accumulated had indeed been brought about by 'a well-laid plot', though not a very edifying one. Instead, the plot that Stephen unravelled was one based on subterfuge and insincerity; it had troubling implications for the masculine codes in which 'letters' and classical political economy were commonly grounded. The alternative economies that Stephen uncovered presented systems of exchange, consumption, accumulation, and solidarity that disrupted the narrative of enlightened productivity set out in the classic accounts of Victorian political economy, inherited, as *EML* implied, from eighteenth-century figures such as Adam Smith.

Sincere Self-help: Manliness, Classical Political Economy, the 'Marginal Revolution', and the Economies of Knowledge

> He never lost himself in mere generalities, but was prepared to show in detail and to justify by specific arguments the application of his theories to tangible facts, and was therefore eminently fitted on all occasions to put the doctrine of his political teachers into the dialect of the market place.[8]

Thus Leslie Stephen on his friend, Henry Fawcett, who had died in 1884. Stephen's biography of the Cambridge Professor of Political Economy, Radical MP and Postmaster General, appeared in 1885. The quotation above is taken from chapter 5 of the work, entitled simply 'Political Economy', which comprises a defence of Fawcett's adherence to the tenets of classical political economy in his professional and political life. Stephen's chapter was pointed: classical political economy was under ideological pressure during the 1880s, from socialist political organization on the one hand, and radical policies of land nationalization on the other (*Fawcett*, 163). Moreover, political economy was subject, from the early 1870s, to a conceptual reconfiguration from within the discipline itself. This was the so called 'marginal revolution', led by the work of W.S. Jevons, which modified the tradition of Adam Smith and David Ricardo by arguing for the importance of consumption above production. This quiet revolution in economic theory has recently been reassessed for its broader impact on late Victorian culture, which this chapter examines in relation to discourses of Aestheticism and masculinity in *EML* biographies.[9]

Stephen presents Fawcett as an economic theorist who traded in 'tangible fact'. Because, for Stephen, the theoretical nature of political economy was always in danger of degenerating into 'mystifications' (*Fawcett*, 145), Fawcett was valuable as 'a consistent empiricist' (*Fawcett*, 160). Fawcett embodied for Stephen the continuing tradition of enlightenment's struggle with superstition and mystical speculation. As we saw from his biography of Pope, Stephen traced the spread of reason from the eighteenth century, and Fawcett's economic empiricism should be seen in this light, given its alleged power to liberate social classes from 'isolation and intellectual darkness' (*Fawcett*, 168). Fawcett's views were the embodiment of 'common sense' (*Fawcett*, 178, 179, 181) and such a value was upheld and guarded, to Stephen's mind, by Fawcett's innate masculinity. In the Preface to the biography, Stephen styles Fawcett as 'the simplest and most transparent of men'. Simplicity and transparency of thought and action are radically opposed to 'insincere' (*Fawcett*, 161) forms of thought and action that played to popular prejudice. For Stephen, Fawcett was certain that insincerity 'might be successfully opposed and, like other prejudices gradually dispersed, by manly and outspoken criticism' (*Fawcett*, 172). This would ensure that the independent 'spirit of self help' (*Fawcett*, 161), to which Fawcett 'manfully adhered' (*Fawcett*, 178) was preserved as the vital principle of economic thought and civic life itself. 'Manliness' in this sense – possessing virtues proper to a man, namely courage, independence and frankness – has a remarkably consistent semantic history reaching back to the thirteenth century. But it acquired special resonance from the individualistic presuppositions structuring classical political economy. Consequently, it was no accident that Stephen took to defending classical political economy through the form of a biography, given that the manly 'sincerity' rhetorically rehearsed by biography played such an important role in that defence.

Stephen's Fawcett embodies, on the one hand, masculine simplicity and transparency. And yet, Stephen acknowledges that Fawcett's enlightened political economy is cast in language shaped by wants and desires that exist beyond Fawcett's manly individuality. Recognizing that 'the periodical press now acts like the nervous system of the nation', Fawcett was subject to its stimuli and as capable as anyone of transforming 'the doctrine of his political teachers into the dialect of the market place' (*Fawcett*, 179). In other words, even 'sincere' and 'manly' knowledge of economic productivity and independent self-sufficiency was a marketable 'dialect', a consumable commodity in the culture of print.

This insight can be read symptomatically in the light of W.S. Jevons's reorientation of economic theory towards consumption. Jevons encapsulates the shift in his observation that 'every manufacturer knows and feels how closely he must anticipate the tastes and needs of his customers'. In turn, he makes this observation into an allegory of economic knowledge itself: 'in like manner, the whole theory of Economy depends upon a correct theory of consumption'.[10] Jevons argued for a new approach to consumption premised on a neo-Benthamite theory of marginal utility, utility being defined as the avoidance of pain and the maximizing of pleasure. If primary desires are very quickly satisfied, an economy that theorizes the production of more and more of the same basic commodity (for instance, one type of food) mistakes its object. Because the margin of utility diminishes as satiety is quickly reached, Jevons argued that the central object of economy had to be the satisfaction of an enormously wide and complex range of pleasures. Variety would multiply and maximize the margins of utility. This, in turn, led Jevons to expand the content of the organizing categories of political economy, such as capital:

> What, for instance, shall we say of a theatre? Is it not the product of capital? Can it be erected without capital? Does it not return interest, if successful, like any cotton mill, or steam vessel? If the economist agrees to this, he must allow, on similar grounds, that a very large part of the aggregate capital of the country is invested in theatres, hotels, schools, lecture rooms, and institutions of various kinds which do not belong to the industry of the country, taken in its narrow sense, but which none the less contribute to the wants of its inhabitants, which is the sole object of all industry.
>
> I may add, that even the food, clothes, and many other possessions of extensive classes are often capital because they are bought upon credit, and interest is undoubtedly paid for the capital sunk in them by the dealers.[11]

Jevons recognized institutions of cultural production and consumption as crucial deposits of capital formation and accumulation, responding to particular 'wants'. And yet, Jevons's theory still conceived capital primarily as property 'sunk in' material commodities or institutions. It would take the twentieth-century sociology of Pierre Bourdieu to extend the province of materiality by re-conceiving capital as a way of explaining 'culture', that is, as a form of property 'sunk in' artistic practice and knowledge itself, exchangeable into 'symbolic capital' of increased profit or prestige in multiple fields or 'markets'.[12]

Yet, it can be argued that some sense of multiple 'economies' was increasingly open to recognition in the late nineteenth century. Regenia Gagnier's work traces a relationship between Jevons's 'marginal revolution' and its implications for the concept of 'sincerity' in economies of knowledge reconceived along lines mapped by Bourdieu. Gagnier argues in her study of Oscar Wilde that the concept of 'sincerity' was, by the 1880s, under pressure:

> By the 1880s, 'sincerity' was, as Wilde said of the term 'natural', one of the most debased coins in the currency of the language. The metaphor is appropriate, for the nineteenth century's confusion about sincerity was directly related to a mutable social economy. Aestheticism, the possibility of living one's life with the freedom of art, was possible only in a society with social mobility, economic security, and waning sincerity.
>
> There was more margin in society in the 1890s – for new entrants in society, margin for activity, margin for credit, margin for interpretation.[13]

Gagnier's discussion, couched in the language of economics, here indicates the way in which Jevons's marginal revolution subtly influenced the broader social and cultural economies of mobility characterizing the late Victorian period. One can also build on Gagnier's point to argue that Aestheticism was the most exaggerated and visible paradigm of this 'mutable social economy' and the critique of sincerity that it engendered. Aestheticism offered a model for entry into society based on forms of cultural credit derived from the consumption of cultural capital. Aestheticism posited a relationship between audience and producers in which the cultural capital that was produced and consumed was the fashioning of self through art, an artistic (or artful) self articulated and performed through masks. This debased the currency supporting the idea of 'sincerity', particularly for a gendered sincerity proclaiming itself to be masculine.

If Aestheticism was the most visible manifestation of a late Victorian mutable social economy, Leslie Stephen's biography of Pope for *EML* was one of the surprising places in which the pressure on the concept of 'sincerity' was encountered, albeit in a more muted form. In one sense, this should not be a surprise. *EML* was specifically aimed at assisting new entrants into society. Edmund Gosse, the biographer of the eighteenth-century poet Thomas Gray for *EML* (and Jeremy Taylor in the second series), was himself one of the new entrants. From a (famously) non-conformist background, Gosse was not permitted to acquire a degree from the universities of Oxford or Cambridge. Yet Gosse made himself into an 'expert' on English and European literatures: he worked initially at the Department of Printed Books in the British Museum and from this position raised himself into the Civil Service as official translator at the Board of Trade. This enabled him to pursue his main career as biographer, critic, and 'man of letters'. In 1885 he secured the position of Clark Lecturer in English Literature at the University of Cambridge. The English literary history that Gosse espoused in those lectures, charting changes in taste between the writings of Shakespeare and Pope, was jealously guarded as an emergent form of cultural capital.[14] The acquisition of this capital was viewed primarily as a good in its own right: but it was also being assessed in competitive systems of examination for enhanced employability (for example, entry into the Civil Service) and social position.

The content of this cultural capital was knowledge of an author's self and works. *EML* was an instance of a cultural project that provided ways of articulating the relationship between cultural producers and consumers, and the eighteenth century provided a compelling focus for contemplating relations between writers, readers, and markets at the formative point of writing's commercialization. This relation was worked out through a self-consciously, yet fragile, historicist epistemology, as we shall see in the case of Stephen's biography of Pope. For late Victorian critics and readers were haunted by the spectre, or perhaps mask, of Aestheticism. Aestheticism's trope of the mask had troubling implications for the social and stylistic markets in which masculinity had been inscribed and traded.

'Ah, Tell Them, They are Men': Aesthetic Effeminacy in Gosse's *Gray*

Regenia Gagnier's account of the formation of Victorian middle-class identities focuses on the institution of the public school, and begins with a reading of Thomas Gray's 'Ode on a distant prospect of Eton College'. Gagnier reads Gray's poem to point to the difference between the eighteenth-century public school and the elite institution devoted to the production of Victorian homosocial networks. If, for Gray, Eton represented a boyhood idyll – 'Ah fields belov'd in vain, / Where once my childhood stray'd, / A stranger yet to pain!' (ll.12–14) – then by the late nineteenth century, the public schoolboy 'found all the vicissitudes of afterlife … already in place at school'.[15] There was no longer a need to heed Gray's exhortation, 'Ah, tell them, they are men!' (l.60).[16]

Edmund Gosse's biography of Gray for *EML* (1882) articulates an awareness of this cultural shift. Imagining Gray and his friend Horace Walpole wandering through the playing fields of Eton, 'tending a visionary flock', Gosse remarks that '[t]hey were a pair of weakly little boys, and in these days of brisk athletic training would hardly be allowed to exist'.[17] Gosse acknowledges in the Victorian public school a regime of anti-intellectual athleticism and vigorous competition that, it was assumed, would produce the kind of hardened, self-reliant male who could rule either at home or in the empire. However, Gosse suggests that Gray was a figure of otherness even then; for although 'learning was still preferred to athletics at our public schools' (*Gray*, 6), Gray was nevertheless 'considered effeminate at college' (*Gray*, 14). Gray's scholarly 'effeminacy' is, as we shall see, an important touchstone of attitudes to gender that had implications for late Victorian constructions of the eighteenth-century man of letters in the market place.

Gray's performance as a 'producer' of work was slight. Gosse stresses that Gray's 'temperament and mode of study shut him out from every energetic profession', given that he treated 'the acquisition of knowledge as a narcotic' (*Gray*, 67). This view of knowledge acquisition as sensuously narcotic enables

Gosse to construct Gray as a proto-Romantic figure. Describing Gray's Grand Tour with Walpole, Gosse remarks that Gray's account of the Alps 'shows him to have been the first of the romantic lovers of nature' (*Gray*, 32). Gosse builds on this impression towards the end of the biography when he records Gray's tour of the Cumbrian lakes as evidence of his being 'a pioneer of Wordsworth' (*Gray*, 185).

But another context is needed adequately to interpret Gosse's sense of Gray's sensuous, 'narcotic' relation to knowledge, and this can be explained by Gosse's affiliations in the early 1880s. Gosse moved increasingly in networks associated with Walter Pater and John Addington Symonds, key figures in late nineteenth-century British Aestheticism: after Horatio Brown's death, Gosse was entrusted with the responsibility of handling the late Symonds's controversial papers, and he wrote the entry on Pater for the *DNB*.[18] Thus, if Gosse's Gray was proto-Romantic, the *EML* biographer also presents his subject as the champion of a re-born Hellenism at Cambridge, both as an undergraduate and as a fellow. As an undergraduate, 'Gray himself seems to have been the only person at Cambridge who attempted seriously to write Greek verse' for it was 'before the Greek revival, which Gray did so much to start' (*Gray*, 19). As a Fellow of Peterhouse 'he gave himself up almost exclusively for the first four or five years to a consecutive study of the whole existing literature of ancient Greece' (*Gray*, 72). Certainly, by the late 1870s, 'Greekness' had developed controversial connotations relating to sexuality and gender, evinced in such homophobic pieces as Richard Tyrwhitt's 'The Greek Spirit in Modern Literature', which prompted Pater to withdraw his candidacy from the Oxford Chair of Poetry.[19] It was thus in an increasingly fevered context of gender and sexual politics that Gosse's biography of Gray emphasized the presence of gender 'inversion' in its Hellenistic subject. Writing of 1747, Gosse remarks that this was the year in which Gray sat for the German artist Eckhardt who produced 'the most pleasing, though the most feminine, of his portraits' (*Gray*, 78).

The association between Gray's effeminacy and his status as proto-Romantic aesthete at Cambridge is confirmed elsewhere by Gosse, particularly in his representation of the episode of 1756 that leads Gray to abandon Peterhouse and take up residence at Pembroke. Gosse relates a practical joke, instigated by the 'bull-baiting' fraternity at Peterhouse. The prank played on Gray's fear of being trapped in a burning house, a fear he soothed by sleeping always with a rope ladder at his side. A false fire alarm was raised which caused Gray to exit his bedroom window via his ladder and into a tub of cold water that was waiting to humiliate him. Gosse uses this episode to measure the distance between robust eighteenth-century humour and Victorian sensibilities: 'To our modern ideas this outrage on a harmless middle-aged man of honourable position, who had done nothing whatever to provoke insult or injury, is almost inconceivable. But there was a deep capacity for brutal folly underneath the varnish of the eighteenth century' (*Gray*, 125). And yet, Gosse also in part erodes the distance between past and present by using the codes of Aestheticism to characterize the way in which Gray responded to this 'outrage' through fashioning his new rooms in Pembroke:

> He was the first, and for a long while the only person in the University who made his rooms look pretty. He took care that his windows should always be full of mignonette or some other sweetly-scented plant, and he was famous for a pair of huge Japanese vases, in blue and white china. ... Here for fifteen quiet years, the autumn of his life, Gray lived among his books, his china, his pictures. (*Gray*, 127)

The emphasis on Gray's immersion in a life surrounded by these particular aesthetic objects is significant. In a different, later context, a much older Gosse reminisced that the 1870s saw 'the introduction of Japanese art into Europe'.[20] And floral sensuousness was a key motif of Aestheticism, as well as the means by which it could be satirized (Pater is 'Mr Rose' in Mallock's *New Republic* of 1877). These codes would indeed be strikingly brought together in the famous opening lines of Wilde's *The Picture of Dorian Gray* (1891) with its invocation of a 'rich odour of roses ... heavy scent of the lilac ...[and] momentary Japanese effect'.[21] It is important to clarify the point of this account of the codes of Aestheticism in Gosse's *Gray*. It is unlikely that Gosse was secretly sharing gay discourse with a knowing readership. It may have been, as Ann Thwaite's biography indicates, that 1880 was the moment at which the recently married Gosse experienced same-sex desire for his friend, the sculptor Hamo Thorneycroft. It may also have been that, during this period, Gosse was being quizzed on 'Greek' love by Symonds in correspondence.[22] But Gosse was troubled by and repressed this dimension of his sexuality. It is more likely that Gosse turned to Aestheticism as the most available discourse for articulating Gray's effeminate self-exile from the masculine society of Peterhouse. Thus '[h]e went over to his old friends at Pembroke, who welcomed him with one accord as if he had been "Mary of Valens [the founder, in 1347, of Pembroke] in person." Under the foundation of this sainted lady he remained for the rest of his life' (*Gray*, 126).

In this context, Gosse appears to invoke Aestheticism as a gendered, late Victorian code for expressing a critical sense of alienation from the homogenizing tendencies of the popular literary market place, and its increasingly masculine predilections (such as the imperial romance). Indeed, this was an alienation from the market place that had been expressed in gendered terms even during Gray's lifetime. The practical joke that led to Gray's departure from Peterhouse can be read thus. Linda Zionkowski's essay on Gray begins with an account of the very episode in which Gray was duped into dropping from his bedroom window into the cold tub of water. As Zionkowski argues, the episode was written about satirically by one Archibald Campbell. In Gosse's biography, Campbell is described as 'a wild creature ...who actually ventured to tell the tale during Gray's life-time' (*Gray*, 126). In Zionkowski's account, Campbell's telling of the tale, though it emphasizes Gray's effeminacy (Gray descends the ladder holding 'silver tea tongs'), also has a literary and economic point.[23] For the dialogue in which the episode is related is concerned with the commercialization of authorship.

Eighteenth-century authors, as Zionkowski argues, were increasingly becoming defined by circuits of exchange, and consumed as commodities, for '[l]ike paintings, sculpture, or china vases, writers and their works exist as objects whose exchange should enrich their sellers and adorn the lives of consumers'. The commodification of texts and authors led to a redefinition of the poet's status in English culture 'in terms of a new concept of masculine conduct'.[24] Zionkowski presents an account of eighteenth-century literary culture in which critics and writers, irrespective of their class backgrounds or political allegiances, 'began to associate masculinity and cultural power with commercial success, while characterizing poets' detachment from the market as infantile, or effeminate, dependence upon others'.[25] Gray's indifference toward completing his poems and getting them into print could thus be viewed as a symptom of his effeminacy. The success of Samuel Johnson in the market place, by contrast, led to celebrations of his self-helping sense of masculine independence.[26]

Such discourses clearly resonated for late Victorian literary critics defending liberal political economy and its traditions. They certainly did for Leslie Stephen in his *EML* biography of Johnson, and his subsequent life of Pope. Indeed, Stephen writes Pope's biography as a kind of self-help tract, for 'each successive victory in the field of letters was realized the more keenly from [Pope's] sense of the disadvantage in face of which it had been won' (*Pope*, 9). Those disadvantages were Pope's lower-class origins, religion (Catholicism) and, to Stephen's mind the most powerful, bodily infirmity: 'persecution', Stephen remarks, 'like bodily infirmity, has an ambiguous influence' (*Pope*, 4). It is telling that Stephen should find the effects of his subject's infirmities 'ambiguous', for ambiguities figure significantly in his biography of Pope. However, they are more often displacements of Stephen's discomforting glimpses of economies of gender reproduction. Stephen's Pope was clearly a very different biographical subject from Gosse's effeminate Gray. But in writing Pope's biography, and constructing an account of him as a productive, independent, and thus manly economic subject, Stephen came uncomfortably to recognize Pope's immersion in a culture of manliness that was a construct of a market, a consumable aesthetic mask. Manliness viewed through Pope's literary biography could thus be read as a curious condition of dependency on homosocial networks of power. For Stephen this produces a reading of manliness that figures, ambiguously, as a kind of effeminacy; an ambiguity that Stephen desires to make safe by reading it as a symptom of Pope's bodily infirmity.

Leslie Stephen's *Pope*: of Making, Breaking, Masks, and Mystification

For busy Victorians such as Stephen, the editor whose health was to collapse over the production of the *DNB*, the eighteenth century offered the image of a lost land of repose. Observing that 'Pope could not be always writing', Stephen invokes his subject at leisure, 'pleasant[ly] lounging through old-world country lanes of the quiet century. We think of the road-side life seen by Parson Adams and Humphrey [*sic*] Clinker' (*Pope*, 89). And yet work, literary production, and trade were never far away: Stephen narrates an incident in which Pope, riding the country lanes to Oxford, is 'overtaken by his publisher Lintot'

> who lets him into various secrets of the trade, and proposes that Pope should turn an ode of Horace whilst sitting under the trees to rest. 'Lord, if you pleased, what a clever miscellany might you make at leisure hours!' exclaims the man of business; and though Pope laughed at the advice, we might fancy that he took it to heart. He always had bits of verse on the anvil, ready to be hammered and polished at any moment. (*Pope*, 89)

But in what would this making of polished poetry, graphically realized in Stephen's image of labour, result? As we saw at the beginning of this chapter, Stephen conceived the best of Pope's poetry as participating in a kind of enlightened tyranny, breaking down superstition and mystification in the 'thought department' of art. Yet this interpretation of the eighteenth-century poet as the producer of superstition-shattering enlightenment was debated within the *EML* series itself. W.J. Courthope's biography of Joseph Addison

(1884) posited a different assessment of Addison's value, and in the process launched a critique of Stephen's brand of evolutionary positivism:

> To estimate Addison at his real value we must regard him as the chief architect of Public Opinion in the eighteenth century. But here again we are met by an initial difficulty, because it has become almost a commonplace of contemporary criticism to represent the eighteenth century as a period of sheer destruction. It is tacitly assumed by a school of distinguished philosophical writers that we have arrived at a stage in the world's history in which it is possible to take a positive and scientific view of human affairs … it is natural that the great English writers of this period should be described in one way or another in helping to pull down, or vainly to strengthen, the theological barriers erected by centuries of bigotry against the irresistible tide of enlightened progress.[27]

Against this, Courthope argued that the eighteenth century was a period of political, social, and literary reconstruction. In his view, it had been the task of Addison 'to carry on reconciling the traditions of our literature'.[28] *EML* biographers of eighteenth-century figures thus engaged in a debate about how to assess and access the historical significance of that century specifically, and, more generally of 'pastness' itself. Stephen participated in this debate through his critical discussion of Pope as a 'translator' of Homer, an act of reconciling Hellenic classicism with eighteenth-century discourses of civility and virtue. Yet Stephen's comments on the epistemological difficulties presented by such a task resonate more broadly, and disturbingly, as he comes to deal with the trope of the 'mask':

> We see the Homeric poems in their true perspective through the dim vista of shadowy centuries. We regard them as the growth of a long past stage in the historical evolution; implying a different social order – a different ideal of life, an archaic conception of the world and its forces, only to be reconstructed for the imagination by help of long training and serious study. The multiplicity of the laws imposed on the translator are the consequences of this perception. They amount to saying that that a man must project himself into a distant period, and saturate his mind with corresponding modes of life. If the feat is possible at all, it requires a great and conscious effort, and the attainment of a state of mind which can only be preserved by constant attention. The translator has to wear a mask which is always in danger of being rudely shattered. (*Pope*, 66)

Stephen sketches an idea of the Homeric epic as an archaeological window onto an earlier 'stage' of 'historical evolution'. And yet, Stephen is alert to the act of scholarly 'making' that is required on the part of the translator to access the past: 'The translator has to wear a mask which is always in danger of being rudely shattered.' The danger of Stephen's 'mask' is its realization as an elaborate fiction or illusion. In this sense, Stephen's anxieties about masks constitute the mirror image of Oscar Wilde's slightly later exploration of the trope's paradoxical, aestheticized 'truth'. Although Wilde's 'The Truth of Masks' did not appear under that title until the publication of *Intentions* in 1891, Wilde had published his essay on Shakespearean costume and artifice in 1885.[29] In the later version, Wilde added the famous concluding paragraph in which he articulates a manifesto for Aesthetic criticism by disavowing the sincerity of his speaking position: 'Not that I agree with everything that I have said in this essay. There is much with which I entirely disagree. The essay simply represents an artistic standpoint, and in aesthetic criticism attitude is everything.' It follows from this 'attitude' that for Wilde, archaeology is less a painstakingly fragile means of scholarly access to the past, and more an aesthetic performance, so that 'archaeology is not a pedantic method, but a method of artistic illusion'.[30] If Wilde celebrates the shattering of the mask, Stephen fears it. Aesthetic theories of fiction and the performative are thus glimpsed but simultaneously repressed facets of Stephen's critical orientation. This has consequences for his account of Pope the enlightenment poet, or manly 'wit'. For Stephen, in the first place, cannot avoid the conclusion that Pope's authorial image is dependent on the donning and consumption of masks, or elaborate forms of performance. Secondly, in Stephen's account, Pope's masks undermine his claim to the tenets of innate manly virtue that authorized the image of the productive subject in classical political economy.

Significantly, Stephen styles Pope as 'the acknowledged head of the [eighteenth-century] literary world' (*Pope*, 81–2) who had achieved this position by virtue of his being a 'practised man of business' (*Pope*, 116). Stephen's biography represents Pope as a productive, economically successful poet who was able to achieve economic independence through successful marketing and sales of his works; for instance, Pope made the then massive sum of £3,500 for his translation of Homer's *Odyssey* alone. Consequently we find in Stephen's critical account of Pope's life and works the pervasive presence of the language of business and economics. For instance, in Stephen's narration of Pope's formation of the Scriblerus Club, the biographer quips that if 'joint-stock undertakings were practicable in literature, it would be difficult to collect a more brilliant set of contributors' (*Pope*, 112).

And yet, these discourses of business and economics can also lead Stephen to more troubling insights. In his account of Pope's translation of Homer's *Iliad*, Stephen seeks a comparison with Chapman's Homer, made famous by

Keats's sonnet. Stephen finds Chapman's translation of Homer's sea imagery 'clumsy' but 'unmistakably vivid'. By contrast, Stephen finds in Pope's sea nothing but 'error and vagueness, and one would swear that Pope had never seen the sea' (*Pope*, 72). Thus, the wit who would demystify the world cannot confidently be held to have seen it correctly. In accounting for this problem, Stephen finds a metaphor in coinage: 'when he has to speak of sea or sky or mountain [he] generally draws upon the current coin of poetic phraseology, which has lost all sharpness of impression in its long circulation' (*Pope*, 71–2). The 'coinage' of circulating conventions, in Stephen's metaphor, is not a reliable system of exchange in the 'market' of art and perception. What the consumer purchases and reads may not be equivalent to what is.

This problem arises again in connection with Pope's later translation of the *Odyssey*. Stephen acknowledges that by this point in his career, 'Pope ... was tired of translating and he arranged for assistance'. Pope's collaborators were 'a couple of Cambridge men ... small poets capable of fairly adopting his versification', William Broome and Elijah Fenton. As Stephen points out, though Pope spoke in 'ambiguous terms of two friends who were to render him some undefined assistance', the assistants did half of the work (*Pope*, 77–8). Moreover, as Stephen acknowledges, '[t]he shares of the three colleagues in the *Odyssey* are not to be easily distinguished by internal evidence':

> On trying the experiment by a cursory reading I confess (though a critic does not willingly admit his fallibility) that I took some of Broome's work for Pope's, and, though closer study or an acuter perception might discriminate more accurately, I do not think that the distinction would be easy. This may be taken to confirm the common theory that Pope's versification was a mere mechanical trick. Without admitting this, it must be admitted that the external characteristics of his manner were easily caught. (*Pope*, 80)

Stephen finds himself at a remove from a position of critical authority and in the less exalted position of duped consumer. Moreover, the lack of distinction between 'great' and 'minor' poet at the level of style did not translate equitably into remuneration for intellectual labour. As Stephen notes, Pope made his £3,500 for the *Odyssey* after paying Broome £500 and Fenton £100. This leaves Stephen wishing that Pope had been 'a little more liberal with his share of the plunder' (the language of business notably giving way to the language of barbaric conquest). Nonetheless, Stephen also concludes that

> [t]he rate of pay was as high as the work was worth, and as much as it would fetch in the open market. The large sum was entirely due to Pope's reputation,

though obtained, so far as the true authorship was concealed, upon something like false pretences. (*Pope*, 79)

Given that the translation was financed by subscription, Stephen's notion of an 'open market' is something of an anachronistic construct. But if Stephen's fantasy of an 'open market' decides the return on this translation as a 'product', then as Stephen concedes, the poem itself is not really the commodity that is being purchased. Instead, what is being purchased, valued, and consumed is Pope's 'reputation'. Yet this too was built, as Stephen has to acknowledge, at least in part on 'false pretences'. We have seen that the *EML* biographer of Adam Smith, F.W. Hirst, would, in 1907, commend the narrative structure of *The Wealth of Nations* for demonstrating the way in which 'the laws of wealth unfolded themselves like the incidents in a well-laid plot'. By contrast, Stephen failed to find a transparent narrative of political economy to justify the wealth that Pope accumulated. Instead, Stephen finds Pope producing 'elaborate mystifications', and acknowledges the need to 'disentangle the twisted threads of his complex history' which can be 'scarcely given in chronological order' (*Pope*, 82–3). In short, Stephen has to account for the ways in which Pope set about rigging the market, donning masks to make his reputation as a form of cultural capital.

This is a process that Stephen begins to trace early in Pope's career, and is displayed in Pope's cultivation of a friendship with the elderly critic Henry Cromwell, a 'rake and a wit'. Stephen finds in Pope's letters an 'absurd affectation' when, for example, he performs 'the airs of an experienced rake'. Stephen notes that the correspondence comes to an end in 1711, probably because Pope realized that Cromwell was a man 'not likely to reflect much glory upon his friend'. Stephen adds, significantly, that in terminating the epistolary friendship, Pope sought 'a better market for his wares' (*Pope*, 13). Pope found this by entering into a correspondence with the more aged, but still more luminous, Wycherley. Friendship and the market place are strikingly linked in Stephen's formulation.

As Stephen goes on to narrate, Pope's correspondence with Cromwell was launched into the market place much later (1726) at the piratical instigation of Edmund Curll, who had obtained letters from one of Cromwell's mistresses. Stephen records that '[t]he correspondence was received with some favour, and suggested to Pope a new mode of gratifying his vanity' (*Pope*, 138). Stephen recounts this 'new mode' of gratification in lurid and 'painful to track' detail, 'as a detective unravels the misdeeds of an accomplished swindler' (*Pope*, 137). Stephen, as detective, uncovers three incriminating facts. Pope's 'mystifications' led him, first, publicly to perform the storage of his Wycherley correspondence in the library of Lord Oxford, supposedly for safe-keeping. Second, Stephen catches Pope surreptitiously editing the correspondence to his own advantage, making him appear the sagacious and independent lead in the friendship. Third, Stephen discovers Pope arranging for the edited correspondence to be 'stolen' and passed to Curll so that it can be 'piratically' published, apparently against Pope's wishes. Although Pope was suspected of having a hand in these events, Stephen notes that the ironic effect of publication 'was to fill the nation with praises of the admirable moral qualities revealed in Pope's letters' (*Pope*, 146). The mystification bolstered Pope's reputation and public image. Pope's building of a character and reputation was shaped through homosocial discourse and networks. Pope used these and the book market to transform his character into a consumable commodity.

What lesson does the reader learn from following this eighteenth-century detective story involving Pope's '[e]aborate masks of hypocrisy and mystification' (*Pope*, 188)? Ironically, the lesson depends on identifying sincerity and transparency in the 'rogue' source of Edmund Curll. The piratical bookseller, 'versed in every dirty trick of the Grub-street trade', as Stephen put it, kept records which enabled later researchers to uncover Pope's machinations; in any event, Curll was quite willing to expose Pope during his own lifetime. From his late Victorian perspective, Stephen discovers reputation and character as components of an economic system, calculable in a balance sheet of accumulation and loss. Thus Curll, '[h]aving no character to lose ... could reveal his own practices without a blush, if the revelation injured others' (*Pope*, 138). Stephen is forced to conclude that 'it is better to cheat a respectable man than a rogue; for the respectable tacitly form a society for mutual support of character, whilst the open rogue will only be too glad to show that you are even such an one as himself' (*Pope*, 155).

Beneath the mask of a morally self-reliant character, Pope is enmeshed in networks of 'mutual support'. 'Pathetic', remarks Stephen, 'is Pope's constant eagerness to be supported by some sturdier arm' (*Pope*, 179). Stephen's language concludes that, despite appearances, Pope is as effeminate as Gray, 'anxious to lean on some stronger nature' (*Pope*, 95). But the means by which Stephen makes this discovery are quite different from Gosse's account of Gray as a marginal figure of effeminate otherness, aesthetically alienated from the manly competition and productive drive of the market place. For Pope is nothing if not productive and commercially successful. What Stephen discovers in his narrative of Pope's masks, mystificatory tactics, and self-marketing is a supplementary economy to the industrial and commercial productive economy that was assumed to drive wealth creation and social mobility. This supplementary economy was submerged and distinctively constituted, and yet at the same time reproduced the mechanisms and gender discriminations that that broader economy upheld. In short, Stephen recognizes an economy of homosocial power, or networks of male mutual support and rhetorical exchange, in which fictions of male self and character were marketed, consumed, and accumulated. These images helped to sustain and reproduce images of independent, self-reliant masculinity. Stephen's biography of Pope, the eighteenth-century wit and man of letters, discovers to its discomfort that manliness is not innate to a subject. This is a discovery that has the potential to undermine the point about innate manliness that Stephen's rhetoric strives to make in his account of his friend, the politician and political economist Henry Fawcett. Thus, in Stephen's life of Pope, the biographer glimpses, through the aesthetic rhetoric of the mask, a market in manliness that undermined the authority on which the manly edifice of Victorian letters and political economy had been built.

In order to rescue that edifice, Stephen has to misrecognize his subject as a deviant rather than the typical product of homosocial self-fashioning. Consequently, looking at Pope's 'bodily infirmities', Stephen insisted that these were the sources of Pope's 'morbid propensity for mystification'. Victorian manliness was saved from itself by the alibi of Pope's bodily deviance that made him comfortably and explicably effeminate. Pope's immense literary productivity was achieved despite his body. As the poet was racked with illnesses and deformities that made him 'dependent' and 'morbidly sensitive' (*Pope*, 94), Stephen contended that 'it was after all a gallant spirit which got so much work out of this crazy carcase' (*Pope*, 92). The alibi of the body presented Stephen with 'reason to doubt' Pope's 'proud assertion', expressed in the 'Epistle to Dr Arbuthnot', 'That, if he pleas'd, he pleas'd by manly ways' (*Pope*, 9: l.337). But as this chapter has argued, Stephen's doubts went beyond these anxieties about Pope's 'manly ways'. Put another way, anxieties about masculinity, art, and economics were subtly interwoven with anxieties about the resurgent power of romantic and aesthetic 'tyrannies', anxieties that Stephen's optimistic reading of eighteenth-century progress only partially managed to repress. Thus in providing late Victorian readers with an avowedly positive source for reconnecting themselves to an eighteenth-century inheritance founded on reason, individuality, and the commercialization of writing and society, the *EML* biographers of eighteenth-century figures reconstructed a 'spirit of the age' haunted by anxieties about the progress of their own commercial society and its culture.

Notes

1 Thanks to my colleagues in the Department of English at the University of Keele for a stimulating and profitable discussion of an early draft of this paper, and to Francis O'Gorman and Katherine Turner for later editorial advice. Thanks also to Barbara L. Kelly for her comments.

2 Leslie Stephen, *Pope, English Men of Letters* (London: Macmillan, 1880), 28. All future references will be given as, for example (*Pope*, 28), in the main text. *English Men of Letters* hereafter *EML*.

3 Oscar Wilde, 'The Decay of Lying' (1889), *Complete Works*, 1966 (Glasgow: Harper-Collins, 1994), 1076.

4 H.D. Traill, *Sterne*, *EML* (London: Macmillan, 1882), 33.

5 Other eighteenth-century authors covered were Goldsmith, Sheridan, Defoe, Richardson, Fielding, Swift, Cowper, Thomson. (For more on Johnson in the Victorian period, see Katherine Turner and Lynda Mugglestone, 119–43 and 144–62, above.)

6 *EML* advance publisher's publicity appearing in Traill's *Sterne*, not paginated.

7 F.W. Hirst, *Adam Smith*, *EML* second series (London: Macmillan, 1904), 166.

8 Leslie Stephen, *The Life of Henry Fawcett*, 1885, fourth edition (London: Smith, Elder, 1886), 179. All future references will be given as, for example (*Fawcett*, 179).

9 For an account of the 'marginal revolution' and ways of conceiving its relations to the tradition of political economy and writings about culture, see Regenia Gagnier, 'Culture and Economics', *Victorian Literature and Culture* (1998): 477–84.

10 W.S. Jevons, *Theory of Political Economy* (London: Macmillan, 1871), 47.

11 Ibid., 251.

12 See for instance John B. Thompson's introduction to Bourdieu's *Language and Symbolic Power* (Cambridge: Polity, 1991), 14–15.

13 Regenia Gagnier, *Idylls of the Marketplace: Oscar Wilde and the Victorian Public* (Stanford, CA: Stanford University Press, 1986), 14.

14 Gosse published his lectures as *From Shakespeare to Pope* in 1885, and then found himself uncomfortably embroiled in a controversy about the accuracy of his literary historical scholarship which became known as the 'English Literature and the Universities' debate.

15 Regenia Gagnier, *Subjectivities: A History of Self-Representation in Britain, 1832–1920* (Oxford: Oxford University Press, 1991), 172–3.

16 Austin Lane Poole, ed., *The Poems of Gray and Collins*, 1919, 3rd edn (London: Oxford University Press, 1950), 31–5.

17 Edmund Gosse, *Gray*, *EML* (London: Macmillan, 1882), 4. All future refs. will be given as, for example (*Gray*, 4), in the main text.

18 See Ann Thwaite, *Edmund Gosse: A Literary Landscape* (Oxford: Oxford University Press, 1984), 321. See also Laurel Brake, 'The *DNB* and the "Pater"', in *Subjugated Knowledges: Journalism, Gender and Literature in the Nineteenth Century* (London: Macmillan, 1994), 169–87.

19 See Laurel Brake, *Walter Pater*, *Writers and Their Work* (London: Northcote House, 1994), 39.

20 Edmund Gosse, Preface, *Collected Poems* (London: Heinemann, 1911), vi.

21 Wilde, *Complete Works*, 18.

22 Thwaite, *Edmund Gosse*, 194–5, 181–2.

23   Linda Zionkowski, 'Gray, the Marketplace, and the Masculine Poet', *Criticism*, 35:4 (1993): 589. See also Simon Bainbridge's '"Men are we": Wordsworth's "Manly" Poetic Nation', *Romanticism*, 5:2 (1999): 216–31.
24   Zionokowski, 'Gray, the Marketplace and the Masculine Poet', 591.
25   Ibid., 592.
26   Ibid., 593.
27   W.J. Courthope, *Addison*, *EML* (London: Macmillan, 1884), 4.
28   Ibid., 7.
29   The essay was originally published as 'Shakespeare and Stage Costume', *The Nineteenth Century*, 17 (May 1885): 800–18.
30   Oscar Wilde, 'The Truth of Masks', *Complete Works*, 1173.

Chapter 10

'I am Nothing': A Typology of the Forger from Chatterton to Wilde

Nick Groom

> ... only the circumstances were false, the time and one or two proper
> names ... (Jorge Luis Borges, 'Emma Zunz')[1]

There is a story told of Alexander the Great, that he did not die in Babylon
before the age of 34, but, rather, he was captured and enslaved and spent the
second half of his life as the anonymous servant of an Indian potentate. In
his 60s, having given some 30 years of service, he was one day summoned to
his master and presented with a silver coin that his master did not recognize.
He asked his slave if he knew where it was from. It was Greek, and when
Alexander looked at it, he recognized a familiar leonine head. With tears
streaming down his cheeks, he replied, 'Yes, I know where this is from. It is
from the days when I was Alexander the Great.'

The self, in other and uncanny incarnations, past and future, may haunt its
own self. One may be haunted by a – or rather *the* – iconic past self that, as in
this case, implacably resides in a now utterly lost and alien world, emerging
only enigmatically in the form of a rogue coin. The subtext of this story about
Alexander the Great is fear for the authenticity of the self, fear of one's own
history: might the coin be in fact counterfeit? Might 'Alexander the Great'
simply be a fabulous history, or a dream?

Victorian attitudes to eighteenth-century literary forgery are haunted by
such an anxiety of personal authenticity, by the problems generated when
different versions of the self compete with and contradict each other, by what
constitutes authentic and legible character. Indeed, this concern with the nature
of authentic humanity pervades the fiction of the period to the point of being
one of its central features. This restless attention to authenticity derives at least
in part from the cultural anxieties inspired by literary forgery. Writers of the
Romantic period had advocated originality and authenticity in contradiction
to literary forgers, but had at the same time dematerialized such writers and
heralded them as supernatural agents of inspiration. In the celebrated case of the

poet Thomas Chatterton (1752–70), the skein is further tangled because of his tragically short life, his apparent neglect, suicide, madness – and indisputable genius. Regarding Thomas Griffiths Wainewright (1794–1852), who arrives at the end of a succession of literary forgers from James Macpherson to William Henry Ireland, the case becomes complicated by serial murder, bank fraud, and ultimately transportation. Chatterton and Wainewright and indeed Ossian, three very different figures, nevertheless merged in the nineteenth century into a composite or typological forger that was then deployed in different ways by writers from Charles Dickens to Oscar Wilde.

Ossian was celebrated by the Victorians – Victoria and Albert were keen Ossian enthusiasts and visited Fingal's Cave, and Matthew Arnold admired the work as archetypal of the Celtic twilight. Chatterton was more problematic. Joseph Cottle had conclusively established that Chatterton was the architect of Thomas Rowley (in the Southey-Cottle edition of 1803 and later in *Malvern Hills*, 1829), but Chatterton's meteoric career, stopped dead by suicide, was both irresistible to poets (such as Dante Gabriel Rossetti), painters (Henry Wallis), critics (Robert Browning), and biographers (David Masson) and yet at the same time almost unforgivable. So compelling was the myth, so apparently authenticating was the suicide, that until the mid-twentieth century no-one thought to question whether he really had killed himself or not. Robert Southey convinced himself and the reading public that Chatterton was congenitally mad (hence he poisoned himself), and John Dix, whose life of Thomas Chatterton was published the year in which Victoria was crowned, was so eager to prove that the mythological Romantic trinity of genius, madness, and suicide was made flesh in Chatterton that he eventually fabricated new biographical documentation in the shape of an Inquest Report and a desperate suicide note.[2] Walter Skeat appropriated Chatterton in another way: in 1871 he produced an edition translating Chatterton's Rowley poems (supposedly written in Bristol in the fifteenth century and attributed to the fictitious monk, Thomas Rowley) out of their cod-medieval language and orthography into decorous contemporary English. Skeat exhibited a breathtaking degree of editorial literal-mindedness that revealed his blindness to the poetical effects of weird spelling and language that had captivated generations of readers and helped to inspire Lewis Carroll's nonsense ballad 'Jabberwocky', which appeared in *Through the Looking Glass* the following year.

For readers of Chatterton (as, under different circumstances, those of John Keats), the life validates and even overcomes the work, but the work does remain acknowledged. Wainewright, however, exemplifies the triumph of biographical reinvention at the expense of his writing and painting. He was doggedly fictionalized by nineteenth-century commentators, becoming a stranger to himself. When his works were cursorily collected in 1880, he had more attributed to him than merely his own flamboyant writings – not unlike those bawdy anthologies of the previous century that spuriously claimed to be the works of Rochester or Swift. There is, however, an irony here, for the presentation of selfhood in the work of Chatterton and Wainewright is never stable and monolithic anyway – they both wrote under several contrary pseudonyms, and their work tends to be fluid and multifarious, exemplifying Montaigne's contention that he was different persons at different times, not merely double but multiple.[3] Chatterton famously declared that 'A character is now unnecessary; an author carries his character in his pen'.[4] Like Chatterton, Wainewright's life was sensationally recast to fit moral narratives – but in his case, they were narratives that vilified him into an exemplum of evil, or aesthetic patterns that traced his arch dandyism. Moreover, Wainewright might have been dead to the Western world, but he was still walking in Van Diemen's Land. It was a life that, perhaps like Alexander the Great's 21 centuries earlier, was being assiduously reinvented even as he still lived it.

The scene: Newgate. The party: Charles Dickens, incorrigible criminal voyeur, his old friend and eventual biographer John Forster, his sparky illustrator Hablôt Browne, and the actor William Macready. The year: 1837, the year of Victoria's accession. Dickens was taking his habitual notes on the conditions of the inmates of the Gate, researching. One aristocratic prisoner awaiting transportation seemed curiously familiar. His eyes were more accustomed to poring over brush-strokes and cut jewels than the grimy stones of Newgate's cells; his hands had once stroked the coats of purring tortoiseshell cats. In the words of John Forster:

> We made together a circuit of nearly all the London prisons; and, in coming to the prisoners under remand while going over to Newgate, accompanied by Macready and Mr. Hablôt Browne, were startled by a sudden tragic cry 'My God! There's Wainewright!' In the shabby-genteel creature, with sandy hair and dirty moustache, who had turned quickly round with a defiant stare at our entrance, looking at once mean and fierce, and quite capable of the cowardly murders he had committed, Macready had been horrified to recognize a man familiarly known to him in former years, and at whose table he had dined.[5]

According to this account, Wainewright was pathetically proud and unrepentant of both his supposed murders and of his committal for forgery, despite being on the eve of leaving the country. The chance meeting inspired Dickens to make use of Wainewright as the model for Jonas Chuzzlewit (1843–44), as the villain Rigaud *alias* Blandois *alias* Lagnier in *Little Dorrit* (1855–57), as the poisoner Mr Julius Slinkton in the short story 'Hunted Down' (1859), for elements of Abel Magwitch in *Great Expectations* (1860–61), and for other, more shady figures – Wainewright haunts *Bleak House* (1852–53), as I shall discuss, as well.[6] Dickens also published Walter Thornbury's short biography of the man in *All the Year Round* (1867).

This, then, is a curious ghost story. The living are haunted and hunted by the dead – in these cases their dead selves – and the dead take up pursuit as revenants, or shadows. Just as Chatterton lived beyond his own mortality in a series of myths and ghostly appearances, manifesting himself to writers from Samuel Taylor Coleridge to Francis Thompson, so did the multiple writerly personality Wainewright. But there are crucial differences. Wainewright was not so much daemonized into an inspirational presence as demonized into a monstrous villain. He provided a template for the evil genius, a fiendish inspiration for writers of popular literature and their increasingly frequent conflict with moral responsibility and legal dogma. Wainewright, and the eighteenth-century forger mythologically amalgamated with him, snake through the work of Dickens as a theatrical baddie, as a shorthand for wickedness, although Dickens's contemporaries were perhaps not so morally erect as he. Edward Bulwer Lytton claimed that Wainewright was incorporated straight into the plot of *Lucretia; or, The Children of Night* (1846) as the horribly evil Gabriel Varney, to which end Bulwer Lytton had obtained Wainewright's own papers. Such 'Newgate Novels' were heavily criticized for glamourizing criminals and crimes, and in his afterword to the 1853 edition, Bulwer Lytton was prompted to quote the Neoplatonist Proclus in his defence:

> whatever is tragical, monstrous, and out of the common course of nature in poetical fictions, excites the hearers in all imaginable ways to the investigation of the truth, attracts us to recondite knowledge, and does not suffer us through apparent probability to rest satisfied with superficial conceptions, but compels us to penetrate into the interior parts of fables, to explore the obscure intention of their authors.[7]

There is the shadow of daemonism here – a notion that studying paragons of wickedness may reveal psychological mechanisms.

This fascination with evil becomes more decadent as the century falls away. Oscar Wilde specifically took the amphibian Wainewright as the prototype of the dandy aesthete and the genius of a diabolical and seductive version of 'art for art's sake'; indeed, Wilde's prototype of the amoral artist draws on the whole eighteenth-century dynasty of Macpherson, Chatterton, and Ireland, as well as Wainewright. In other words, the aesthete could trace his pedigree back to the 'house of forgery'.[8] The poet laureate Andrew Motion was unable to resist writing his own pseudo-autobiography of Wainewright as a mendacious first-person confession in *Wainewright the Poisoner* (2000), and Wainewright is even there haunting *The Blue Suit* (1995), the auto-fiction of novelist, book thief, credit fraudster, and burglar, Richard Rayner. In all three writers, the supernatural Romanticism of the daemonic sublime has been replaced by a seductive self-destructiveness in which identity is moulded from the legal puzzles that try to define identity, forgery, and possession – perhaps as masking, lying, and stealing. And such values are the consequence of nineteenth-century moral codes being crudely imposed on figures from the past. In the case of Chatterton, this resulted in the farce of Fripp's statue: erected after a subscription 1838–40 on unconsecrated ground at St Mary Redcliffe, taken down in 1846 and abandoned in the crypt for 11 years, resited in 1857, and after a century of neglect eventually dismantled altogether in 1967 – on account of it celebrating a forger and suicide.[9]

The otherworldly and inspirational quality that literary forgery had for Romantic poets in particular shifts decisively in the nineteenth century to a predominantly legal issue of fraud, dealt with in material and bodily ways of incarceration and transportation. Money becomes the defining object: one of Bulwer Lytton's declared intentions was to depict 'the influences of money upon modern civilization'.[10] Wainewright is the crucial transitional figure here: a writer, a shape-shifter, a forger, a felon, and, with an appropriately over-the-top dash of melodrama, a poisoner to boot. Art, forgery, and crime dovetail in Wainewright. The legal implications of literary composition, criticism, and reception introduced in the 1790s in the debate over William Henry Ireland's forged Shakespeare papers became fixed values in the nineteenth century, locking together literature, authenticity, and authorship. Simply put, Wainewright was clear evidence that literary forgery was culturally illegal and required active policing. Writers could now be charged in the dock for writing the wrong sort of thing, and being polyphonic or multifarious was considered no defence for breaking the law. Wilde was outraged at this example of the shifting – indeed shiftless – character of the artist being pinned down by inflexible legal definitions of identity: 'The permanence of personality is a very subtle metaphysical problem, and certainly the English law solves the question in an extremely rough-and-ready manner.'[11] This of course would be proven to Wilde himself, to his own great disadvantage.

Wainewright was awaiting transportation in Newgate in 1837 for forgeries on the Bank of England that had begun 15 years earlier: he had released his annuities by forging the signatures of his uncle Robert Wainewright, and cousins Edward Foss and Edward Smith, realizing £5,250. In the meantime, Wainewright had spent some years in France. He had gone there to escape an insurance scandal and prepare a Court of Exchequer suit against one of the companies. The insurance, for the colossal sum of £16,000, was the life of his sister-in-law, a hale and hearty young woman who had, like her mother and Wainewright's own uncle, died rather suddenly. The rumour was that Wainewright had poisoned all three and escaped to France under a false passport. The rumour was that he had fallen in love with a married woman in Calais whom he poisoned; whereupon her sister then fell in love with him. The rumour was he was starving in Paris. The rumour was that he was staying in Boulogne with an English family, had insured his host's life for £5,000 just before he died, and seduced the daughter. The rumour was that he had been imprisoned for six months for the possession of strychnine. The rumour was that he had been arrested while secretly in London with a lady, and that he had been in disguise. *The Times* reported his abject state on being taken into custody: 'I am nothing … I am no artist. I belong to no trade or profession … I am not yet steady in my head.'

The unrepentant villain recognized by Macready, 'with a defiant stare at our entrance, looking at once mean and fierce', appears entirely at odds with the intangible and cowed creature reported in the press. Wainewright proliferates into many different characters, dogged by myths and slanders. He was lionized by visitors to the Gate as a celebrity, and revered as a master criminal by fellow felons. Tales of the extent of his forgery grew in size and audacity, and there were still the stories of murder. Indeed, before he left, Wainewright was informally questioned by his insurance agents about the murder of Helen Abercromby. They upbraided him. He allegedly replied,

> Sir … you city men enter on your speculations and take the chances of them. Some of your speculations succeed; some fail. Mine happen to have failed; yours happen to have succeeded; that is the difference, sir, between my visitor and me. But I will tell you one thing in which I have succeeded to the last. I have been determined through life to hold the position of a gentleman. *I have always done so*. I DO SO STILL. It is the custom of this place that each of the inmates of a cell shall take his morning's turn of sweeping it out. I occupy a cell with a bricklayer and a sweep. But, by God, they never offer me the broom![12]

This made a deep impression on Dickens, who rehearsed it in the first chapter of *Little Dorrit* to indicate the character of Rigaud: 'Have I ever done anything here? Ever touched the broom, or spread the mats, or rolled them up, or found the draughts, or collected the dominoes, or put my hand to any kind of work?'[13]

In any case, Wainewright would not admit that he had done Helen in for the money; there appeared to be a better reason for killing her: 'he reflected for a moment, and then returned, with a cool laugh: "Upon my soul I don't know – unless it was that her legs were too thick".'[14] This scandalous remark also spread like wildfire – and seemed to run faster on 'thick ankles' than 'thick legs' – though its provenance is even less sound than the previous anecdote. Indeed, it seems to have arisen from nowhere – a ghost to haunt the living, breathing, dying Wainewright. Disgusted, the insurance officers seized his effects from France, including his diary. Thornbury describes it as written with 'voluptuous cruelty and a loathsome exultation worthy of the diseased vanity of such a masterpiece of evil'; and this gorgeous testament of wickedness went through the hands of Bulwer Lytton before it disappeared.[15] It appears to have been a chilling chronology of the decline and extinction of his sister-in-law Helen Abercromby: a timetable for poisoning.

Wainewright was already being forged as a monster of depravity, combining Gothic terror with social horror: the sadism of the vampire with the suffocating self-absorption of the decadent. There is another Wainewright, however, unearthed by Marc Vaulbert de Chantilly, a Wainewright whom it is worth bearing in mind.[16] This Wainewright wrote in desperation to the Home Office even as he was awaiting imminent deportation on the *Susan*. In return for a pardon, he was prepared to give a full account of the death of Helen and possibly even prepared to implicate his wife as well. Wainewright was a forger, but was treated in Van Diemen's Land with the severity reserved for a murderer: condemned to a chain gang. It was only much later that he won a reprieve, became a hospital orderly, and could practise his portraiture again.

Even there, rumours were rife. Thornbury says (in 1867) that it is 'now well known' that he carried a supply of strychnine about with him, concealed in a hollowed-out Borgia-like signet ring, and a version of this ring is also described by Bulwer Lytton.[17] He attempted murder twice with poison, once with a knife, and once with a sharpened file; he also threatened to return to England to murder his cousin Edward Foss who had testified against him. He made salacious remarks to women sitting for their portraits, and even made one sitter scream by sharpening his pencil so savagely. He was a demon:

There is a terrible story told of his savage malignity towards a fellow-patient in the hospital, a convict, against whom he bore a grudge. The man was in a state of collapse – his extremities were already growing cold. Death had him by the throat. Wainewright's snakish eyes kindled with unearthly fire. He saw at once the fatal sign. He stole softly as a cat to the man's pallet, and hissed in exultation into his dying ear:

'You are a dead man, you – In four-and-twenty hours your soul will be in hell, and my arms will be up to that (touching his elbow) in your body, dissecting you.'[18]

Wainewright eventually died in 1847, an opium addict, his only friend a supercilious cat, and in the words of Barry Cornwall, 'raving mad'.[19] Dead and buried. But again there is another Wainewright, in contrast to this dastard: Wainewright the society painter who still refused to sign his portraits, and whose good conduct record eventually won him some freedoms, and eventually a pardon. It came in the same month he succumbed to a fatal stroke. From the Antipodean perspective, he certainly succeeded in reinventing himself. In the Macmillan *Dictionary of Art*, Andrew Sayers gives Thomas Griffiths Wainewright the following entry:

Australian painter and writer of English birth … drawing of amorous couples in a landscape … reminiscent of Fuseli, whom he described as 'the God of his worship.' … reputed to be a poisoner and embezzler … despite his convict status and poor health, he made an important contribution to the early art of Australia. He was, with Thomas Bock (1790–1855) the most skilful convict portrait draughtsman in Hobart in the mid-19th century … His elegant elongation of his subjects and poised line owed much to the style of English portrait painters such as Thomas Lawrence, who was among the artists he most admired …[20]

Lest we forget, it was for forgery, not murder, or embezzlement for that matter, that Wainewright was transported (neither was it, as Wilde archly remarked, for 'his fatal influence on the prose of modern journalism').[21] Wainewright *sans* murder might perhaps still have been transported, but would he still have been so enthusiastically vilified, and with such a mixture of abhorrence and fascination; would he still have painted his diabolical portraits? It was Wainewright's reputation as a poisoner rather than a forger that so excited Thomas De Quincey, for instance, who had been invited to dinner with the man some years before. De Quincey had not been able to keep the appointment, much to his subsequent dismay, but remembered with ghoulish delight that he had indeed once sat down to dinner at the Lambs with the ogre: 'Amongst all the company, all literary men, sat a murderer.' For De Quincey, this retrospective context becomes deliciously pregnant:

> if I had known this man for the murderer that even then he was, what sudden loss of interest, what sudden growth of another interest, would have changed the face of the scene! Trivial creature, that didst carry thy dreadful eye kindling with perpetual treasons – dreadful creature that didst carry thy trivial eye mantling with eternal levity, – over the sleeping surfaces of confiding household life, – oh, what a revolution for man wouldst thou have founded, had thy deep wickedness prospered![22]

It is as if Wainewright himself is poisonous, or amorally contagious. Barry Cornwall concludes his reminiscence with the warning: 'He was like one of those creatures, seemingly smooth and innocuous, whose natural secretions, when once excited, become fatal to those against whom they are accidentally directed.'[23] Wainewright exemplifies the proposition, already argued by De Quincey, and subsequently by Jean-Paul Sartre, that murder is a fine art, and its corollary, that the arts corrupt. This reverberates through the nineteenth century: in the moral debate around the 'Newgate Novels', in Dickens's pragmatic sentimentality, and in the countercultural decadence of Art for Art's Sake and *fin de siècle* movements, culminating in the row about *The Picture of Dorian Gray* (1890). The arts may prove fatal, for 'The fact of a man being a poisoner is nothing against his prose'.[24]

The Wainewright case also confirms that forgery – writing – is potentially more dangerous than murder. It was impossible to dispute that the actual offence of forgery had occurred. Writing leaves a body of evidence much more legible than the faint traces of strychnine and morphine in a young girl's body. Moreover, W. Carew Hazlitt, the first and so far only editor of Wainewright's works, was clearly troubled by a criminal succession that put forgery ahead of homicide: 'First came Forgery. Then followed Strychnine.' Forgery is the crime that exposes Wainewright; forgery sets off a contagious criminality. Wainewright, who unites a trinity of writing, lying, and killing that challenges the distinction between the aesthetic and the criminal, is hunted down by a forgery he had committed a decade before. And yet in a sense, nothing is adequately explained. W. Carew Hazlitt recognized that there was an excess which was not defined by either forgery or murder: 'Still, when all has been said, does not the man, like all such men, remain a sort of enigma and bewildering contradiction?'[25] Like Chatterton, he wrote under a host of different names; to have too many characters is to have none at all, nemocentric rather than nomocentric.[26]

This anxiety regarding the authenticity of character and experience lies at the heart of *Great Expectations*. Dickens's novel is concerned with different versions of the self and of the past haunting the present; indeed the book is suffused with forgery, and Pip uses counterfeiting as a metaphor when he disingenuously lies to himself: 'That I should innocently take a bad half-crown of somebody else's manufacture, is reasonable enough; but that I should knowingly reckon the spurious coin of my own make, as good money!'[27] Magwitch is in the Hulks for uttering stolen notes, a sly analogy to his putting a false Pip into circulation, and Mrs Joe declares that 'People are put in the Hulks because they murder, and because they rob, and forge, and do all sorts of bad'.[28] Compeyson's business, we learn, was 'swindling, handwriting, forging, stolen bank-note passing, and suchlike', and Orlick falls among forgers who can write with 'fifty hands'.[29] One of the deathmasks in Jaggers's office is of a murderer who forged the wills of his victims, and among his collection of curiosities, Wemmick has 'the pen with which a celebrated forgery was committed'.[30] One of Jaggers's clients is, not unlike Wainewright, an ex-military man who bought his discharge and turned to coining; he is sure to hang. Magwitch brings about the death of Compeyson, returning from transportation to avenge himself on his prosecutor; Wainewright had threatened to do in his betrayer, Edward Foss. But to have returned from life transportation is a capital offence and death stalks Magwitch like an uncanny and interventionist biographer, much as Magwitch stalks Pip – invoking different narrative patterns for his life and expectations.

Wainewright is there too in *Little Dorrit*. Rigaud has a smooth, white, Wainewrightian hand, his fingers are full of rings, he refuses to sweep his cell, he insists on being treated as a gentleman.[31] In his moustache, slouched hat, cloak, and the tricks of his eyes, he bears a striking similarity to Theodore von Holst's rakish portrait of Wainewright, later purchased by Bulwer Lytton and therefore available to Dickens ('Phiz' was in any case numbered among the Dickens party that had discovered Wainewright in Newgate). His use of three aliases – Rigaud, Blandois, Lagnier – means we never learn his real name, and he also manages to obliterate Affery's identity. Like Wainewright, he leaves crucial papers in France, eventually retrieved by representatives of the law. More generally, *Little Dorrit* is a novel of doubles and parentage, problems with wills and codicils, papers and signatures – and most significantly money, or rather the lack of it. The universally admired and respected Mr Merdle turns out to be 'simply the greatest Forger and the greatest Thief that ever cheated the gallows'; he commits suicide, taking laudanum as a painkiller as he opens his jugular with a paper knife. Some of these elements overlap with

William Henry Ireland's career: he lived the last years of his life in the stews of Southwark, and could conceivably have been known to Dickens, who also tramped those streets. In 1835, Ireland was buried in the common ground of St George the Martyr, the closest church to the Marshalsea, where many who died in the prison were buried. Little Dorrit sleeps in St George's when she is locked out, and eventually marries Arthur Clennam there. But as Paul Ellis has argued, 'Mr Merdle was modelled, in part on John Sadleir, the financier, forger and MP who committed suicide (Chatterton-style) on Hampstead Heath in 1856'.[32] Ellis emphasizes that Dickens used criminal rather than literary forgers; with Wainewright, we have a transitional figure who inhabits both camps, and Dickens places him firmly on the side of illegality.

The literary myths of Chatterton and Wainewright are most deliberately blended, however, in *Bleak House*, a novel that invokes literary forgery in its Ossianic opening:

> Fog everywhere. Fog up the river, where it flows among green aits and meadows; fog down the river, where it rolls defiled among the tiers of shipping of a great (and dirty) city. Fog on the Essex marshes, fog on the Kentish heights.[33]

This, as we later learn, is a 'London particular'. Wind, rain, and mist pervade the whole book: for example, in the descriptions of The Ghost's Walk at Chesney Wold and while Guppy and Weevle are waiting to see Krook:

> One disagreeable result of whispering is, that it seems to evoke an atmosphere of silence, haunted by the ghosts of sound – strange cracks and tickings, the rustling of garments that have no substance in them, and the tread of dreadful feet that would leave no mark on the sea-sand or the winter snow.[34]

At a more domestic level, Esther falls asleep with Caddy Jellyby on her lap:

> I began to lose the identity of the sleeper resting on me. Now it was Ada; now, one of my old Reading [reading] friends from whom I could not believe I had so recently parted. Now it was the little mad woman worn out with curtseying and smiling; now, some one in authority at Bleak House. Lastly, it was no one and I was no one.[35]

This reference to nobody alerts us (on a second reading) to the character Nemo, who actually advertises himself in an advert as Nemo, care of Mr Krook, or, to put it another way, *no-one, c/o crook*: a suggestive description of a forger. Miss Flite says of him:

The only other lodger … is a law-writer. The children in the lanes here, say he has sold himself to the devil. I don't know what he can have done with the money. Hush![36]

And Snagsby and Tulkinghorn have the following conversation about the mysterious writer:

'Nemo, sir. Here it is. Forty-two folio. Given out on the Wednesday night, at eight o'clock; brought in on the Thursday morning, at half after nine.'
   'Nemo!' repeats Mr. Tulkinghorn. 'Nemo is Latin for no one.'
   'It must be English for some one, sir, I think,' Mr. Snagsby submits, with his deferential cough. 'That's the person's name.'[37]

Snagsby goes on: 'The advantage of this particular man is, that he never wants sleep. He'll go at it right on end, if you want him to, as long as ever you like.'[38]

Nemo is, then, a machine for writing, effacing his own identity with the copying and reproduction of text. At one level he is a metaphor for the entire novel. As Hillis Miller has put it, '*Bleak House* is a document about the interpretation of documents', and Miller goes on to list letters, wills, parchments, scraps, and the contents of Krook's shop; he describes Miss Flite's papers and Richard Carstone's gradual poisoning by an ever-increasing dosage of debilitating documents, even if he misses the crucial and apparently matrimonial correspondence between Esther and John Jarndyce.[39] Of course, much of the action of *Bleak House* takes place as papers or letters or hinges on documents – and many of them are either misread, or not read at all and simply inferred, such as the symbolic status of Tulkinghorn's files with *Jarndyce and Jarndyce* inscribed on the spines. The pivotal character, Krook, boasts: 'I have so many old parchmentses and papers in my stock. And I have a liking for rust and must and cobwebs',[40] but he is illiterate and can only transcribe letters, devoid of meaning. Elsewhere, Caddy Jellyby's penwomanship becomes entirely a matter of personal hygiene, Esther teaches Charley to read and write but not to express herself grammatically, and the final evacuation of paper from the court is a grotesque sort of vomiting: 'presently great bundles of papers began to be carried out – bundles in bags, bundles too large to be got into any bags, immense masses of papers of all shapes and no shapes, which the bearers staggered under, and threw down for the time being, anyhow, on the Hall pavement, while they went back to bring out more'.[41]

   But if there is very little reading in this novel of reading, there are new kinds of reading proposed. Nemo – 'no one' – is the most literate of characters, not least because he reveals his true self through the forensic comparison of his hand with that of Capt. Hawdon. Yet nearly all we experience directly of Nemo is through his death – and what a death-bed scene he presents to Mr Tulkinghorn:

> He comes to the dark door on the second floor. He knocks, receives no answer, opens it, and accidentally extinguishes his candle in doing so.
>
> The air of the room is almost bad enough to have extinguished it, if he had not. It is a small room, nearly black with soot, and grease, and dirt. In the rusty skeleton of a grate, pinched at the middle as if Poverty had gripped it, a red coke fire burns low. In the corner by the chimney, stand a deal table and a broken desk; a wilderness marked with a rain of ink. In another corner, a ragged old portmanteau on one of the two chairs, serves for cabinet or wardrobe; no larger one is needed, for it collapses like the cheeks of a starved man. The floor is bare; except that one old mat, trodden to shreds of rope yarn, lies perishing upon the hearth. No curtain veils the darkness of the night, but the discoloured shutters are drawn together; and through the two gaunt holes pierced in them, famine might be staring in – the Banshee of the man upon the bed.
>
> For, on a low bed opposite the fire, a confusion of dirty patchwork, lean-ribbed ticking, and coarse sacking, the lawyer, hesitating just within the doorway, sees a man. He lies there, dressed in shirt and trousers, with bare feet. He has a yellow look in the spectral darkness of a candle that has guttered down, until the whole length of its wick (still burning) has doubled over, and left a tower of winding-sheet above it. His hair is ragged, mingling with his whiskers and his beard – the latter, ragged too, and grown, like the scum and mist around him, in neglect. Foul and filthy as the room is, foul and filthy as the air, it is not easy to perceive what fumes those are which most oppress the senses in it; but through the general sickness and faintness, and the odour of stale tobacco, there comes into the lawyer's mouth the bitter, vapid taste of opium.[42]

He's dead, of course, and as Tulkinghorn says, 'Here's poison by the bed'.

This is a recognizable portrait of Thomas Chatterton, who was discovered dead in his Brooke Street garret, poisoned with arsenic and opium. Brooke Street is within the half-mile of London's Inns of Court where much of the action in *Bleak House* takes place. Like Chatterton, it is debatable whether Nemo's death is a suicide or an accident. The surgeon called to Krook's recognizes Nemo: 'he has purchased opium of me for the last year and a half', much as the Brooke Street apothecary admitted selling opium to Chatterton. Both writers have their pathetic possessions inventoried, and coroners' inquests are held at adjacent public houses.[43] Chatterton ended up in a pauper's grave in Shoe Lane burial ground; Nemo's body is deposited in 'a hemmed-in churchyard, pestiferous and obscene …'.[44] Indeed, eighteenth-century representations of Chatterton's death tended to dwell on the poverty of his London existence: like Thomas Otway, he was a byword for the poet starving in a garret. Moreover, Chatterton had trained as a legal scrivener or copier in Bristol, and if Nemo did not, like Chatterton, cover the floor of his room with shredded manuscripts, he does have letters – letters spirited away by Krook – which are, like Chatterton's Rowley forgeries, read with a particularly forensic eye in order to establish who Nemo (like Rowley) really was.[45] Chatterton would also stay up all night writing, and even the twice-repeated rumour that Nemo has sold himself to the Devil has a Chattertonian source.

Dickens's fraught set piece influenced Henry Wallis's seminal painting, *The Death of Chatterton*, first exhibited four years later in 1856. As Holman Hunt said, 'The cruelty of the world towards poor Chatterton, whose only offence was that he asked to be heard as a poet under a feigned name, will never henceforth be remembered without recognition of Henry Wallis the painter, who first so pathetically excited pity for his fate in his picture of the death of the hapless boy'.[46] Dickens greatly admired the painting, and one could be forgiven for imagining that he had forged the archetype in his blending of elements in *Bleak House*.[47] In fact, a startlingly similar image had been published as early as 1794, coincidentally the year in which Wainewright was born, as an engraving by Edward Orme. From this, Wallis took the central figure athwart the bed, and telling minor details such as the empty laudanum bottle lying on its side, and one shoe on, one off – Chatterton limping into another world. Dickens must have seen the Orme engraving too.

Elsewhere in *Bleak House*, Chatterton emerges through more subtle similarities: Chatterton, like Esther and Inspector Bucket, rode through snow storms, and endured the hottest city summer for years. Chatterton was, like Richard Carstone's child, posthumous – and indeed the novel is teeming with orphans and bastards. On the other hand, of course, Nemo, for all his Chattertonian inflections, is an ex-soldier with wild black hair and whiskers, and aged 45. So I am not after a *Bleak House* 'original' here; rather, I am proposing a typology of the forger – or what Dickens's contemporary reviewers called a 'daguerrotype'. So Nemo, a middle-aged bewhiskered ex-soldier who expires in a fog of opium, also owes something to Wainewright the poisoner – an orphan who moves in with his guardian (even if this wicked step-son relationship is slightly rewritten by Dickens), and who has an interest in a Chancery suit, who is diabolical ('I don't know what he can have done with the money'), and who has 'poison by the bed'. Nemo is not Chatterton, and neither is he Wainewright, but he is formed from a composite or hybrid of their respective myths of forgery that lace through the novel.[48]

Indeed, the emphasis on the materiality of writing instruments in *Bleak House* is reminiscent of legal attempts in the eighteenth century to detect forgeries by ink, quill, idiosyncrasies of handwriting, and paper. Chapter X, 'The Law-Writer', opens with Mr Snagsby the stationer among his stock, legal stock for legal cases that could quite easily double as the cabinet of a forger:

> In the shade of Cook's Court, at most times a shady place, Mr. Snagsby has dealt in all sorts of blank forms of legal process; in skins and rolls of parchment; in paper – foolscap, brief, draft, brown, white, whitey-brown, and blotting; in stamps; in office-quills, pens, ink, India-rubber, pounce, pins, pencils, sealing-wax, and wafers; in red tape and green ferret; in pocket-books, almanacks, diaries, and law lists; in string-boxes, rulers, ink-stands – glass and leaden, penknives, scissors, bodkins, and other small office-cutlery.[49]

It is among Krook's crooked stock that the new Will is discovered, though Dickens deliberately refuses to entertain whether the document is authentic and valid. This is because the novel ultimately rejects questions of textual value in emphasizing the totalitarianism and self-sufficiency of legal systems of order and interpretation.

Hence the ultimate victory of the legal over the literary is exemplified by an unfortunate writer whose very christening invoked the forgeries of James Macpherson. His mother wrote to her friends in November 1854 to announce the birth of her son: 'He is to be called Oscar Fingal ... . Is not that grand, misty, and Ossianic?'[50] He lectured on Thomas Chatterton in 1886, wrote an essay on Thomas Griffiths Wainewright and a short story on literary and artistic forgery, and was ultimately imprisoned for his failure to convince the law of the incompatibility of legal and literary methods.

Oscar Wilde's essay 'Pen, Pencil and Poison', originally published in the *Fortnightly Review* for January 1889 and derived from W. Carew Hazlitt's edition of Wainewright's writings, offered Wilde the opportunity to develop his subject into a prototype of the aesthete: 'One can fancy him', said Wilde, 'lying there in the midst of his books and casts and engravings, a true virtuoso, a subtle connoisseur ....'[51] Wilde admired Wainewright's taste for fine art, and also for his appreciation of his contemporaries Keats and Shelley, but he saw in Wainewright an opportunity to 'other' the dandy artist-forger and his cultivation of exotic tastes. Wainewright is made strange and uncanny in Wilde's essay. He epitomizes the artist who knows no limits, whose extension of artistic method into forging and poisoning makes the world into a decadent canvas. From this, Wilde proposes an aesthetics of crime, which is brought to life by the inspired complicity of the critic.

It was a position Wilde had already explored in 'The Decay of Lying', in which Vivian quotes from his fictitious article:

> Lying and poetry are arts – arts, as Plato saw, not unconnected with each other – and they require the most careful study, the most disinterested devotion. Indeed, they have their technique, just as the more material arts of painting and sculpture have their subtle secrets of form and colour, their craft-mysteries, their deliberate artistic methods. As one knows the poet by his fine music, so one can recognise the liar by his rich rhythmic utterance …[52]

Having dissolved the ethical dimension of the literary by admitting that all literature is fiction and lies, Wilde concludes 'Pen, Pencil and Poison' with the observation: 'There is no essential incongruity between crime and culture. We cannot rewrite the whole of history for the purpose of gratifying our moral sense of what should be.'[53] He ends the essay with a statement of Wainewright's true worth as the villain of both Dickens's 'Hunted Down' and Bulwer-Lytton's novel *Lucretia*: 'To be suggestive for fiction is to be of more importance than fact.'[54] As Lawrence Danson describes Wilde's reading, 'Wainewright is not only a forger but, as an artist, he is himself a forgery', and this is essentially the Wildean credo: that the artist necessarily stretches invention far enough to make, to forge, his (or her) self.[55]

This position is developed in Wilde's story 'The Portrait of Mr. W.H.', which begins with a discussion about 'Macpherson, Ireland, and Chatterton'. With regard to Chatterton, the narrator declares

> I insisted that his so-called forgeries were merely the result of an artistic desire for perfect representation; that we had no right to quarrel with an artist for the conditions under which he chooses to present his work; and that all Art being to a certain degree a mode of acting, an attempt to realise one's own personality on some imaginative plane out of reach of the trammelling accidents and limitations of real life, to censure an artist for a forgery was to confuse an ethical with an æsthetical problem.[56]

The story itself concerns the identity of the addressee of Shakespeare's sonnets, Willie Hewes, a young actor or 'shadow', whose existence is deduced from the poems, and then proved by a portrait – though this turns out to be a forgery. Wilde tells us all this in the first couple of pages: the remaining thirty-odd thousand words are devoted to an attempt to convince the reader that Willie

Hewes is indeed the subject of the sonnets, despite the fact that as we already know, a) the clinching evidence has been forged, and b) the story is a piece of fiction. In fact, Wilde manages to make the principle of forgery central to his aesthetic philosophy, through performance, self-invention and reinvention, his insistence on masks and truth and lies, and during his trial by his refusal to allow any reading of his letters, poems, or stories that was not purely aesthetic.

Likewise, Wilde's lecture on Chatterton, a relatively early piece (1886), dismisses the ethical nature of the problem of forgery thus:

> Was he a mere forger with literary powers or a great artist? The latter is the right view. Chatterton may not have had the moral conscience which is truth to fact, but he had the artistic conscience, which is truth to Beauty. He had the artist's yearning to represent and if perfect representation seemed to him to demand forgery, he needs must forge. Still his forgery came from the desire for artistic self-effacement.[57]

But Wilde was forever teasing out the implications of forgery. Despite this lecture's success, it was never published – and it was never published because it was heavily plagiarized.[58] Certainly the problems of originality and plagiarism haunted Wilde and provided his enemies with much ammunition, but plagiarism is also essential to Wilde's citational or 'anthological' style.[59] He welcomes different voices into his writing, internalizes the contradictions of the forger, and like Wainewright's pseudonym 'Janus Weathercock', 'saw that it was quite easy by continued reiteration to make the public interested in his own personality'.[60] For Wilde, this form of continued reiteration was also a cascade of apt quotations that provided a running aesthetic commentary on life. This is the 'revolution for man' De Quincey recognizes: an artistic revolution of the everyday that dissolves the dichotomies of romance and realism, invention and imitation, art and life, and most importantly of character.

*

The case of Thomas Griffiths Wainewright, as it is variously received through the nineteenth century, involves issues of original and engraved works, art and craft, counterfeiting and forgery, dandyism and posing, murder and literature. As with Chatterton, the life and myth of the forger, poisoner, and archetypal aesthete tends to overtake the works, except that the life is now seen as an *œuvre*, a body of works rather than a myth, and therefore every act within it, including murder, can be read as a work of art. *Bleak House* firmly, if covertly, delineates the forger by considering craft and copying, lack of character (Nemo), illegitimacy (Esther), the law, suicide, and so forth – and Dickens thereby *buries* forgery in the law courts, even as he is implicitly attacking the fraudulence of the law, by half-hidden allusions to forgery. When Oscar Wilde tries to revive the art of the liar or the Wainewrightian forger, he himself eventually ends up in the dock – imprisoned for writing the wrong sort of letters. The Wainewright case confirmed that forgery was a legal misdemeanour rather than a literary practice. It insisted on the criminality of forgery, on forgery as the first resort of the murderer – much as posing was the first resort of the *'somdomite'* – and so today our current notions of authenticity are underwritten by the mythology of Wainewright, and the trials of Oscar Wilde.

Within a decade of his death, an anonymous columnist in the *Hobart Town Courier* had predicted that 'a famous novel' would be based on Wainewright's life, and in the following years Wainewright was comprehensively mythologized, taking on the expression of the sadistic and unrepentant gentlemen drawn from annals like the *Newgate Calendar*. But this process through which the Victorians engaged with a mythological figure energized by the forgers of the eighteenth century does not culminate in Wilde's 'Pen, Pencil and Poison'. Tracing the contours of Wainewright's sacrifice so delicately, Wilde suicidally anticipated the catastrophe of his own life by fulfilling his own aesthetic claim that life imitates art. His future suffering followed the contours of the redemptive Wainewrightian pattern: from artistic acclaim and luxury to crime, public humiliation, suffering, and obscure death, before mythologization and eventual restoration.

Notes

1   Jorge Luis Borges, 'Emma Zunz', in Donald A. Yates and James E. Irby, eds, *Labyrinths: Selected Stories and Other Writings* (Harmondsworth: Penguin, 1970), 169. Some of the material in this essay appears in chapter 7 of Nick Groom, *The Forger's Shadow: How Forgery Changed the Course of Literature* (London: Picador, 2002). I am particularly grateful to Marc Vaulbert de Chantilly who read and corrected that chapter.

2   For Southey, see Nick Groom, 'Love and Madness: Southey Editing Chatterton', in Lynda Pratt, ed., *Robert Southey and the Contexts of English Romanticism* (Aldershot: Ashgate, forthcoming 2004); for Dix, see *New Dictionary of National Biography* (Oxford: Oxford University Press, forthcoming).

3   From Frank Kermode, *Not Entitled: A Memoir* (London: HarperCollins, 1996), 30–31.

4   Letter from Chatterton to his mother (6 May 1770) in *Complete Works of Thomas Chatterton*, ed. Donald Taylor, in association with Benjamin Hoover, 2 vols (Oxford: Clarendon, 1971), I, 560–61.

5   John Forster, *Life of Charles Dickens* (London: Palmer, 1928), 80–81.
6   See Harvey Peter Sucksmith, 'The Melodramatic Villain in *Little Dorrit*', *Dickensian*, 71 (1975): 76–83.
7   Edward Bulwer Lytton, *Lucretia; or, The Children of Night* (London: Chapman and Hall, 1853), 308.
8   Horace Walpole, *A Letter to the Editor of the Miscellanies of Thomas Chatterton* (Strawberry Hill, 1779), 24.
9   John Goodridge, 'Rowley's Ghost: A Checklist of Creative Works Inspired by Thomas Chatterton's Life and Writings', in Nick Groom, ed., *Thomas Chatterton and Romantic Culture* (Basingstoke: Macmillan, 1999), 287.
10 *Lucretia*, 322.
11 *Complete Works of Oscar Wilde* (London: Collins, 1980), 1006.
12 Thomas Griffiths Wainewright, *Essays and Criticisms*, ed. W. Carew Hazlitt (London: Reeves and Turner, 1880), lxxi.
13 Charles Dickens, *Little Dorrit*, ed. Stephen Wall and Helen Small (Harmondsworth: Penguin, 1998), 22.
14 Walter Thornbury, 'Thomas Griffiths Wainewright (Janus Weathercock), the Poisoner', *All the Year Round* (5 January 1867): 40.
15 Thornbury, 40.
16 See John Ezard, 'Fact vies with Fiction in Pursuit of the Classic English Poisoner', *The Guardian*, 26 February 2000, 3.
17 Thornbury, 39.
18 Ibid., 41.
19 Bryan Waller Proctor ['Barry Cornwall'], *An Autobiographical Fragment and Biographical Notes* (London: Bell, 1877), 193.
20 He supposedly made engravings of Henry Dowland's *Pickwick Papers*, and collaborated with Marcus Clarke in writing *For the Term of his Natural Life*.
21 *Wilde*, 1005.
22 *The Collected Writings of Thomas De Quincey*, ed. David Masson, 14 vols (London: Black, 1897), V, 248.
23 Proctor, 194.
24 *Wilde*, 1007.
25 Wainewright, *Essays and Criticisms*, lxxx.
26 Wainewright: 'Egomet Bonmot' [since disproved], 'Janus Weathercock', 'Cornelius Van Vinkbooms', 'Bevil Seymour', 'Senex'. Among Chatterton's writing names were 'Astrea Brokage', 'Decimus', 'Probus', 'A Hunter of Oddities', 'Harry Wildfire', as well as the Rowley crew.
27 Joep Leerssen has already indicated the Ossianic nature of the opening of *Great Expectations*, in 'Ossianic Liminality: Between Native Tradition and Preromantic Taste', in *From Gaelic to Romantic: Ossianic Translations*, ed. Howard Gaskill and Fiona Stafford (Amsterdam and Atlanta, GA: Rodopi, 1998), 4–5; Charles Dickens, *Great Expectations*, ed. Charlotte Mitchell (Harmondsworth: Penguin, 1996), 225.
28 *Great Expectations*, 15.
29 Ibid., 348, 427.
30 Ibid., 209.
31 See Charles Swann, 'Wainewright the Poisoner: A Source for Blandois/Rigaud?', *Notes and Queries*, 233 (1988): 321–2.

32   Paul Ellis, 'The Life of Rowley', *Times Literary Supplement*, 26 April 2002, 36. For
     Sadleir, see D. Morier Evans, *Facts, Failures & Frauds: Revelations Financial, Mercantile,
     Criminal* (London: Groombridge, 1859), 226–67.
33   Charles Dickens, *Bleak House*, ed. George Ford and Sylvère Monod (New York and
     London: Norton, 1977), 5.
34   Ibid., 400.
35   Ibid., 45.
36   Ibid., 55; rumour repeated by Krook, 124.
37   Ibid., 121–2.
38   Ibid., 123.
39   Hillis Miller, 'Introduction', to Charles Dickens, *Bleak House*, ed. Norman Page
     (Harmondsworth: Penguin, 1985), 11.
40   *Bleak House*, 50.
41   Miller, 17–18; *Bleak House*, 759.
42   *Bleak House*, 124.
43   Ibid., 126.
44   Ibid., 137; see also 202, 894.
45   Ibid., 338, 363, 398.
46   Holman Hunt, *Pre-Raphaelitism and the Pre-Raphaelite Brotherhood*, 2 vols (London:
     Macmillan, 1905), II, 417.
47   Peter Ackroyd, *Dickens* (London: Sinclair-Stevenson, 1990), 810.
48   John Beer notes that 'The tendency to take a rigid moral position and marginalize anyone
     who did not live up to its standards into the posture of a Dickensian character was typical
     of the period' (*Romantic Influences: Contemporary – Victorian – Modern* (London:
     Macmillan, 1993), 157).
49   *Bleak House*, 115–16.
50   Richard Ellmann, *Oscar Wilde* (1987), 16.
51   *Wilde*, 996.
52   Ibid., 972.
53   Ibid., 1008.
54   Ibid., 1008.
55   Lawrence Danson, *Wilde's Intentions: The Artist in his Criticism* (Oxford: Clarendon,
     1997), 99.
56   *Wilde*, 1150.
57   Quoted by Danson, 91.
58   'To plagiarize the biography of a forger is an amusing conceit': Danson, 90.
59   Ibid., 26.
60   *Wilde*, 1002.

Chapter 11

Regarding the Eighteenth Century: Vernon Lee and Emilia Dilke Construct a Period

Hilary Fraser

The late nineteenth-century art historian, feminist intellectual, and trade unionist Emilia Dilke wrote of the eighteenth century: 'the subject is so vast that to attempt to treat it ... may be likened to the child's effort to "put the sea in yonder hole"'.[1] Her sense of the futility of attempting to encapsulate the period did not prevent her publishing a vast four-volume study of French art in the eighteenth century, which covers painting, sculpture, engraving, drawing, architecture, furniture, and decoration. Published from 1899 to 1902, it was her last book-length study devoted to the history of art. Twenty years earlier, at about the time when Dilke, under the name E.F.S. Pattison, published her first book, *The Renaissance of Art in France* (1879), another woman also produced her own first major historical study. Vernon Lee's *Studies of the Eighteenth Century in Italy*[2] appeared in 1880 when she was just 24, and also marked the beginning of a long and productive writing life as an art historian and aesthetician, in which she too was to write important books on the Renaissance as well as the eighteenth century, only while Dilke's centre of interest was always France, her own was Italy. The approaches of these two women to the eighteenth century are differently inflected, as one might expect. Dilke had famously reviewed Walter Pater's *Studies in the History of the Renaissance* in 1873, just a few years before Lee published her own *Studies*, criticizing the impressionistic aestheticism that the younger woman admired and emulated, and Dilke's own brilliant studies of both the Renaissance and the eighteenth century exemplified the 'scientific method' that Pater and Lee abjured.[3] The encyclopaedic comprehensiveness at which she aimed is part and parcel of such an objectivist methodology. Lee's book, by contrast, although also well researched and scholarly, is consciously subjective and fanciful, and avowedly partial. Her subject is carefully circumscribed, her focus not 'the universal character of the century itself', a character which she finds to be 'far more spontaneous and strongly marked in other countries' than Italy (2), but rather the art forms that were national in their origins and characteristics, and had their roots deep in Italian history and civilization; namely the musical, dramatic, and performing arts of the period. Furthermore, her engagement with her material is highly personal and performative. She was later to write of her 'unaccountable passion', as a child, 'for the people and things of the eighteenth century, and more particularly of the eighteenth century in Italy': 'How it arose would be difficult to explain; perhaps mainly from the delight which I received from the melodies of Mozart and Gluck, picked out with three fingers on the piano. I followed those sounds; I pursued them, and I found myself in the midst of the Italian eighteenth century.' Stressing that she means this 'literally', she adds: 'I really did find my way into that period, and really did live in it.'[4] *Studies of the Eighteenth Century in Italy* is the intriguing product of this Orlando-like excursion, and is fascinating amongst other things for its ficto-historical negotiations of the present and the past, the real and the imaginary.

In this chapter, I wish to look at these two works, Vernon Lee's *Studies of the Eighteenth Century in Italy* and Emilia Dilke's four volumes on French painters, architects and sculptors, furniture and decoration, and engravers and draughtsmen of the eighteenth century, and to reflect on the respective ways in which these late-nineteenth-century women imaginatively entered and conjured a period, and how they communicated their palpable pleasure in and profound knowledge of the previous century. Furthermore, I will ask to what extent the preoccupations and scholarship, the historical imaginary, of these two very distinctive scholars, writing of the same period in different cultures, Italian and French, might be seen as gendered? Theirs is, I will suggest, a feminized and foreign eighteenth century, quite other to the masculinist age of reason with which the period was increasingly identified (for debate about the late nineteenth-century construction of the period as rational, see David Amigoni, 182–202 above). I will consider their respective concerns with ephemeral and popular or domestic art forms, with rescuing the forgotten and writing the obscure into history, and with the role of women in cultural production. Finally, I will address these Englishwomen's sense of their own cultural positionality, their performed foreignness, and think about ways in which wider discourses about gender, hybridity, and difference may be said to have shaped, even enabled, their historiographical practice.

I

As she brings *Studies of the Eighteenth Century in Italy* to a close, Vernon Lee describes the moment of eighteenth-century scholarship at which she writes. It is a pivotal time, she points out, when 'The men and things of the Italian eighteenth century have not yet been exhumed and examined and criticized and classified; they have not yet been arranged, properly furbished and restored, like so many waxwork dolls decked in crumbling silk and lace, like so many pretty, quaint, or preposterous nicknacks in the glass cases of our historical museum'. They remain still, but only for a very short time, just within imaginative reach:

> An old book of cantatas of Porpora, an old volume of plays of Carlo Gozzi, does not affect us in the same manner as a darkened canvas of Titian or a yellowed folio of Shakespeare; these latter have passed through too many hands, been looked at by too many eyes, they retain the personality of none of their owners. But the volume of Gozzi's plays was probably touched last by hands which had clapped applause to Truffaldino-Sacchi or Pantalone-Darbes; the notes in the book of cantatas may last have been glanced over by singers who had learned to sing them from Porpora himself. (293–4)

We have never known the people of the eighteenth century, she says, 'but we have met occasionally men and women who have': the lady 'whose hand, which pressed ours, had pressed the hand of Fanny Burney', and the old musician 'who had sung with boyish voice to Cimarosa and Paisiello those airs which he hummed over for us in faint and husky tones' (294). It is this intense desire for tactile contact with a past world about to move beyond her grasp, for the faintest echo of performances which can never again be heard, before its men and women are 'exhumed, restored, put into glass cases and exhibited mummy-fashion in our historical museums' (295), that defines Lee's approach to the eighteenth century.

Her declared interest in identifying and focusing not on 'the universal character of the century itself', a character which she finds to be 'far more spontaneous and strongly marked in other countries' (2), but rather the art forms that were national in their origins and characteristics, and had their roots deep in Italian history and civilization, shapes her subject – principally the music and dramatic arts of the period – and her methodology. First of all, it determines her historicist approach, whereby she insists on the embeddedness of art in the culture that produces it: she is committed to understanding the connections between writers such as Goldoni, Alfieri, and Metastasio and the times in which they wrote, and convinced that 'these men merely represent, they do not constitute, the intellectual life of the nation; for that we must look in the innumerable academies, networks of molecular life, spreading all over Italy, and connecting all the classes of society which possessed, or were supposed to possess, any knowledge of literature' (7). Her interest in nationally specific art forms leads her to investigate the particular historical conditions that produced them (40–41). For example, she describes in some detail how 'The opera was a necessary product of Italy', how 'it developed by the very pressure of Italian culture' (159); how a writer such as Metastasio was subject to 'the requirements and restrictions' due to 'composers, singers, scene-painters, mechanicians', and how this shaped his art (195); and how Goldoni's new genre of comic realism evolved, because it had to, out of the old *Commedia dell'Arte* (253–9).

But her sense of the importance of recovering what was uniquely Italian about the arts in eighteenth-century Italy also, and more intriguingly, extends to the way she conducts and writes about her research. As scholarly and well-researched, and also as culturally mediated, as Lee's study undoubtedly is, she represents herself not as an antiquarian or a literary historian or a music critic or a critical theorist but as 'an aesthetician' (1), one who knows Italy intimately, and whose understanding of its eighteenth-century art and life is felt on the pulses. She performs aestheticism as she was later, in her collaborative work with Clementina Anstruther-Thomson, to perform, through her co-author, and theorize a corporealized spectatorship of art.[5] We are invited to picture her wandering through the streets and rediscovering an eighteenth century that is more authentic because its traces, fragments of a world that has not quite passed away, may still be found in a kind of metonymics of history; may be found in dusty volumes rummaged from market stalls, like Browning's 'old yellow book' that became the basis of *The Ring and the Book*, or in forgotten little archives; in sudden encounters with faded portraits; in the street theatre and puppet shows which are all that remain of a rich indigenous heritage; and in neglected gardens and ramshackle rooms that were once the venues of august cultural gatherings.

Throughout her life, Vernon Lee was obsessed with the idea of the 'genius loci', the way history is embodied in place, and in this early volume places are invested with the spirit of the past, and made into sites of intensified experience and meaning. Thus, the first chapter on 'The Arcadian Academy' begins with an account of how she first visited the decaying Bosco Parrasio, in Rome, 'once the meeting place of the Arcadians, and now the only remnant of their possessions' (8), and how she 'returned often and often to spend the burning afternoons in the shady garden, or in the cool, dismantled rooms, going home at sunset, carrying away bunches of flowers, ... sketches, ... and above all, vague impressions, quaint and sentimental, of the long-deceased and long-forgotten world of the last century' (10). And again at the end of the chapter, she returns us to the desolate remains of the villa, where 'As we stand once more ... we feel even more powerfully than before how deep a gulf separates us from those times, so near to our own, yet so forgotten, when the Academy of the Arcadi represented the whole literary life of Italy' (64). The following chapter, on 'The Musical Life', is similarly framed by her visit to the home of the old Philharmonic Academy in Bologna. And her description of how she 'stumbled one day' on the Paduan house and garden of the formerly great but now forgotten singer Pacchierotti, becomes the occasion for summoning a fanciful memory 'that we ourselves must once, vaguely and distantly, have heard that weirdly sweet voice, those subtle, pathetic intonations' (121).

Vernon Lee does not focus on the visual arts in this volume; indeed, she sweepingly claims that in the eighteenth century 'The plastic arts were dead everywhere, and had not yet been galvanized by criticism into a spectral semblance of life' (4). Nevertheless, there are many points in the text when she herself galvanizes paintings into 'a spectral semblance of life'. At all of the sacred sites she haunts, she is in turn haunted by the shades of the dead, in the form of their portraits. A 'crowd of *rococo* figures', 'time-stained portraits of long-forgotten men and women', look down from the mildewed walls of the Arcadian Academy like an 'assembly of literary ghosts, their gala dresses and gala looks fading away in oblivion' (10). At the once vibrant centre of Italy's music in Bologna, she finds 'a crowd of dead musicians, members of the once-famous Philharmonic Academy, in purple and lilac, and brocade and powder, who look down upon us from the walls' (67). A dusty portrait of Pacchierotti hangs in the darkened lumber-room of his former home, on the basis of whose faded romantic suggestiveness Lee conjures the spectral traces of a man who 'must have been an intense instance of that highly-wrought sentimental idealism which arose, delicate and diaphanous, in opposition to the hard, materialistic rationalism of the eighteenth century' (122). Her lexicon, here and elsewhere, strikingly echoes Pater's when, as he does in his essay on Winckelmann for example, she seeks to articulate an alternative, feminized vision of the period.

The pictures of which Lee writes do not always have such fantastic and ghostly resonances. Sometimes, as in the case of the self-portrait of the beautiful and talented painter Faustina Maratti that Lee finds in the Arcadian Academy, a painting can enable her to resurrect the individual subject in such a way as to 'make one understand' – in the instance of Faustina, why she was so admired by 'the most eminent men of Italy' (19). A portrait of Metastasio is subject to a reading in which every detail of his anatomy and posture is made suggestive of his character (215); while a 'beautiful bust' and a 'smutty portrait' (56–7) of Corilla Olimpica, which attest, among other things, to the 'squinting eye, which was supposed to make the immediate conquest of anyone upon whom she chose to fix it while in the enthusiasm of improvizing' (57), are mobilized by Lee to bring this extraordinary, talented and scandalous *improvvisatore* to life. Sometimes paintings are made to provide the basis for an imagined scenario, as when the concert pictures of Niccolò Abati and Leonello Spada are invoked to bring to life a scene of players and singers on stage sitting around the harpsichord; Lee recalls one such picture in which 'a musician has left the harpsichord and is pacing the boards, plumed hat in hand, with solemn gesture', and wonders 'Is he reciting, or is he singing? Is this a rudimentary opera or merely a play interlarded with concerts?' (160), thus dramatizing the pivotal moment of the birth of the opera as she has been describing it. Elsewhere a painting naturalizes the interpolation of a story into the larger narrative, as when a picture at the Bosco Parrasio of Perfetti in his many-coloured costume enables an account of how he was awarded the crown worn by Petrarch (30–31). Elsewhere, different styles of portraits and prints depict the singer Farinelli, complicating both his character and broader ideas of historical and painterly representation (112–13).

Lee regularly gives vent to her frustration at being unable to make aural reconstructions of eighteenth-century music. Of Gasparo Pacchierotti she writes, 'we feel an indefinable sense of dissatisfaction, a wistful, dreary sense of envy for what did not fall to our lot, and of pain at the thought that all that feeling, all that imagination, all that careful culture, has left no trace behind it. In turning over the leaves of memoirs and music-books we try, we strain as it were, to obtain an echo of that superbly wasted vocal genius' (120). But her visual imagination never lets her down. She sees the singers and the performances that she cannot hear. And so she writes, 'We may picture to ourselves those musical gatherings in the Bulgarellis' house' (157). And picture them she does, in very great detail, and the figures who attend them, such as the 'energetic yet almost regal' singer, the Romanina: 'Yes, we can see her moving about in her rustling brocade and trailing velvet, going from the great singer lolling about the harpsichord, his fat sentimental face half hid in his curly wig and lace frill, one fat bejewelled hand thrust into his satin doublet, the other playing with his music roll … from him to some obscure fair-haired young man …' (157).

Lee is clearly entranced by the eighteenth century as spectacle, as her many luscious descriptions of carnival and other theatrical pleasures attest. Furthermore, her own representation of the period is highly staged – a piece of theatre, like the extravagant operas and shows she invokes for her readers. In her introduction to a later work, *Althea* (1894), she refers to her 'dramatis personae', and to the need occasionally 'to copy from other showmen's boxes a spiritual puppet for which I had no model'.[6] Lancret's *Le Montreur de Lanterne-Magique*, reproduced in Emilia Dilke's *French Painters of the XVIIIth Century*, serves as a suggestive image for the techniques of conjuration and illusion used by Lee to view the past. Like the illusion-generating optical gadgetry that proliferated in the nineteenth century, Lee's prose deceives the reader, through a series of animating special effects. Like the showman with whom she identifies, she translates the two-dimensional page into a believable three-dimensional living world, then draws attention to the trickery, as she returns us to the solid reality of the book. 'Is it a reality?' she asks. 'Has Menego rowed us over the lagoon? … Have we really witnessed this incident of fishing life on the Adriatic?' 'No', she confesses, 'we have only laid down a little musty volume, at the place marked "Le Baruffe Chizzotte"' (268). The historian of film, Tom Gunning, has written of a formative technology of 'attraction' at work in the development of a modernized mass visual culture. His discussion of the strategies of early film throws light on Lee's tactics for engaging the attention of her audience: 'From comedians smirking at the camera, to the constant bowing and gesturing of conjurers in magic films, this is a cinema that displays its visibility, willing to rupture a self-enclosed fictional world for a chance to solicit the attention of the spectator.'[7] Lee's writing manifests the kinds of devices and theatricalities identified by Gunning. While her principal strategy is to persuade us of the authenticity of the eighteenth century which she presents (by, for example, imaginatively entering the experiences of a historical figure such as Dr Charles Burney, retracing his 1770 musical tour through France and Italy, and embellishing the account in his journal with the kind of small detail that creates a 'reality effect'), she regularly disrupts and destabilizes the effect of the real she has so carefully constructed by exposing its textuality and fictiveness.

Pietro Metastasio, Carlo Goldoni and Carlo Gozzi are Lee's exemplary writers, and she draws on portraits, letters, journals and memoirs as well as their creative works to offer personal and speculative accounts of their lives and careers. She was interested in them, as she was in the painters and musicians of the period, not only as artists, who belonged to 'the unchangeable eternal world of the grand and lovely ideal', but also as men, who belonged to 'the ephemeral world of quaint and ludicrous reality' (95). Hard though it may be to find a copy of Gozzi's plays a hundred years after his death, and to reconstruct their performance, they do survive in a material form, as that ephemeral world does not. Lee was more fascinated still by the Italian art of the eighteenth century that had no material existence, and that was itself fundamentally ephemeral, in particular, that of the extemporary poet and the singer. Although, as she notes, 'Italy appears at all times to have produced extemporary poets; and we meet them, male and female, almost as often during the Renaissance as during the eighteenth century' (27), theirs became an independent profession in the eighteenth century; indeed, 'there was a class of men and of women who would improvise, not a couplet here or there, but whole poems of thirty or forty stanzas on any given subject and before assemblies convened for the express purpose of hearing them' (28). There follows an evocative description of this ephemeral art form:

> the performance of a good *improvvisatore* was a wonderful performance: the rapid outpouring of sonorous verse, the succession of image on image, flashing past the mind in vague splendour, the air of inspiration, and the sensuous eloquence which is more potent than that of the reasoning faculties – all this made the exhibition of a Perfetti or a Corilla something fascinating; but a mere exhibition it was, like that of fireworks or some strange theatre scene .... (28–9)[8]

As for the singer, that most powerful and revered figure in eighteenth-century Italian culture, all trace is gone, and Lee laments 'the genius spent in an extemporised vocal ornament which was never transmitted to paper, in the delivery of a few notes which lasted but a second; the genius squandered in the most evanescent performance, the memory of which died with those who had heard it' (122).

Writing of the French painter of *fêtes galantes*, Antoine Watteau, in her *French Painters of the XVIIIth Century*, Emilia Dilke remarks on the poignancy and 'fugitive beauty' represented by such 'visions of a world peopled only by the sparkling images of pleasure' (74). Watteau frequently found his models among the bands of Italian actors and musicians who performed in France. For Lee, as for Dilke in her appreciation of the sources of Watteau's inspiration and peculiar resonance, the ephemeral and the performative exercised particular fascination. Lee is also interested in popular culture. She insists on demonstrating how writers such as Goldoni and composers such as Paisiello learned from popular tradition (90), and represents music as a non-elitist, democratic form, as 'a national necessity, a necessity as much to the petty artisan, the gondolier, the lazzarone, as to the great lady, the senator, and the prelate', as 'a thing for the whole people' (97). She conjures street theatre and humble performances in local churches with the same attention to detail as she brings to grand opera, and visits small medieval towns as well as the cultural centres of Rome, Venice and Naples. She resurrects small acts of kindness and obscure tragedies that take place in the wings of the theatre of history.

Not least, she includes women among her historical actors. Not only do we hear of the powerful women, who played a significant role in eighteenth-century cultural and political life: of Maria Theresa herself, in the Imperial Palace at Vienna; of the Grand-Duchess Dowager of Tuscany, Violante Beatrice of Bavaria, who in 1725 summoned the *improvvisatore* Perfetti to Rome, where he was awarded the crown of the Capitol; of the famous actress and singer Marianna Bulgarelli, commonly called La Romanina, and the Countess Althann, whose love and patronage were so critical to Metastasio's professional career; of the accomplished Arcadian artist and *salonière* Faustina (18–20) and 'the beautiful young princess d'Arce Orsini, composer, poetess, and general patroness of literati' (47); of the leading aristocratic *salonières*, women like the Countess Castiglione at Milan, the countess Grismondi at Brescia, the Marchesa Silvia Verza at Verona, the Countess Roberti at Bassano, and, above all, of the 'lovely Isabella Teotocchi Albrizzi at Venice', in whose drawing rooms 'the most eminent poets, Parini, Pindemonti, Pompei, Cesarotti, were constantly to be met, together with an occasional classical sculptor or emotional singer like Canova or Pacchierotti' (54–5); of 'the innumerable ladies who, as soon as they have exchanged the convent for their husband's house, become refined, literary, nay learned: poetesses, composers, and presiders over intellectual society, the friends, patronesses, and counsellors of the greatest writers in Italy, yet without aspiring to the position of the Dottoressa Bassi, who lectured on Newton's *Optics* before she was twenty' (33).

It is not just of such eminent women that Vernon Lee tells us, but of 'the young ladies of the highest birth [who] go out on riding parties, dressed in almost masculine fashion, no one taking offence thereat, and the poets telling them that in this garb they look like Paris and Endymion' (35); of 'the ladies wearing portraits of great performers, fainting, like Beckford's Paduan lady, from musical rapture ... showing their love of music in a hundred absurd fashions' (94); of the places where 'women are not left out of the literary bustle' (33), and the places where they are, such as Rome where there was 'an absurd regulation forbidding women to perform on any stage in the Eternal City', and where women's parts in the opera were played by boys (124). She writes of Dr Burney's visits to the famous Venetian music schools for girls, conjuring 'the singular sight of an orchestra entirely composed of women, who played in a masterly manner ... one of the musical wonders of the eighteenth century' (101). Elsewhere she discusses domestic life and marriage customs in relation to eighteenth-century Italian culture (34). And she does not forget the professional performers: neither the unnamed female celebrities in anticipation of whose arrival 'the great theatre is put into order', and 'the whole town is in a tumult of excitement' (35), nor those whose names became famous, such as Maria Maddalena Morelli, who performed her extemporary poetry under the Arcadian name of Corilla Olimpica, and who was to achieve greater fame still in her fictional reincarnation as *Corinne* (56–8).

Vernon Lee's account of the rewriting of Corilla's story reveals an astute understanding of how in their afterlife, historical events and experiences are reinscribed with different meanings. Having described how the *improvvisatore* was mocked and abused in Rome at the very ceremony where she received the crown of the Capitol, because by 1775 'the coronation was regarded as a farce or a profanation, the Arcadians as conceited pedants, Corilla herself as an impudent adventuress', she goes on to explain how she came to be transformed by Madame de Staël into 'a radiant sibyl, a sort of personified genius of Italy', and 'unconsciously gave rise to a masterpiece' in *Corinne* (58–9). Lee's sophisticated appreciation of and interest in the process of history and how it is written, even at this early stage in her career, informs her own writing of the past. She is alert to the fact that things signify differently at different historical moments. The French Revolution, for instance, had changed the way the British viewed the French. When Dr Burney visited Paris in 1770, Lee notes, 'He had looked at this strange people without any of the fears and hatred which they were later destined to inspire. The coming revolution had not yet cast its shadow before it' (70). Romanticism, likewise, changed the way people responded to landscape. Lee observes 'How Dr. Burney got across the Alps he does not tell us. In those days, when Alpine roads were unknown and Alpine scenery unnoticed, a journey of this sort was probably looked back upon as equally horrid and uninteresting, and unworthy, therefore, of being recorded' (79). And he crossed the Apennines 'wholly unconscious of the delightful Radcliffian thrills of horror which Mrs. Jameson and Washington Irving were destined to render so popular; indeed the writers of the eighteenth century are so perversely cool and comfortable about the Apennine passes that you might almost imagine brigands and ghastly inn-keepers to have formed part of the travelling paraphernalia of the romanticists of our century, by whom they were introduced into Italy, together with circulating libraries and English groceries'

(114). Furthermore, she explains, the very name 'Italy' 'did not suggest what it suggests to us; it was not the field for the exercise of those faculties which are exercised there in our own day. There had been no Byron, no Sismondi, no Lady Morgan, no Ruskin; the generation of Goethe, of Madame de Staël, of Beckford, nay, even of Ann Radcliffe, had not as yet appeared' (79–80). Therefore the visitor approached it in quite a different way from the modern tourist, 'not consider[ing] Italy as a thing of the past, a remnant of antiquity, of the Middle Ages or of the Renaissance, but as a country like any other modern one; and its inhabitants neither as degenerate descendants of the Romans nor as weird children of the Renaissance' (81).

The question of the relativity of cultural signification provides the occasion for both lighthearted and rather poignant reflection on the vagaries of reputation. Dr Burney, we are told, was not all that impressed by the boy Mozart when he encountered him (116), while Metastasio's joking words in a mock biography – 'In the eighteenth century there lived a certain Abate Metastasio, a tolerable poet among bad ones' (143) – are exposed as a cruel irony in the light of his future reputation. It also underlies Lee's frequent reflections on her own writing practice, and her frank authorial interventions, which refuse to naturalize the telling of history as anything other than a narrative which she can manipulate at will. At one point, for example, she interjects 'According to a bad but invincible tendency of which the reader may often have to complain, we have taken the opportunity of discussing the church music of the eighteenth century in general, when there was no occasion to speak of any save the trifling performances which Dr. Burney attended; keeping our traveller waiting, standing in some dull little church listening to mediocre music' (85). And later, having digressed once more from her reconstruction of Burney's experience of Italy to talk about eighteenth-century singers, and her own discovery of Gasparo Pacchierotti's house and garden, she recalls herself to the past of which she is meant to be writing: 'Whither have our fancies carried us? The garden at Padua, the harpsichord, the portrait – are none of them present. Pacchierotti, so far from being a mere faint recollection, is as yet a scarcely noticed reality, an obscure youth with undivined talents. Dr. Burney has never yet heard his name' (122). Such disarming self-commentary designedly foregrounds the fact that she is not only reconstructing but constructing a period; that this is not a transparent window onto the past, but a narrative, the chronological handling of which the author is in control, and in which the very idea of what constitutes 'the past' is unstable, inevitably determined by and imbricated in similarly unstable notions of 'the present'.

II

Always striking is the modernity of Vernon Lee's conceptualization of history, her keen awareness of the fact that perceptions of the past are culturally positioned, and that history is a construction, 'only a creation of the present',[9] 'a series of … admirable theatrical views; mere delusion'.[10] Fourteen years after publishing her first book, she was to revisit eighteenth-century Italy in a 'dialogue' set in the context of a modern performance of Gluck's *Orpheus* in Rome. One of her characters is a devotee; another a 'modern' for whom the opera 'is the work of a thoroughly bygone past, of a completely extinct art', who contends that 'produced in utter unconsciousness of what the modern soul would be, it no longer answers to the needs of us moderns'; while the third, formerly passionate about the eighteenth century, now infected by decadence, wonders 'Are we restoring life to a thing that can live, or are we galvanising a corpse?'[11] The moment that Lee grasped in writing her *Studies of the Eighteenth Century in Italy* has already, it seems, passed – although we are shown the power of the voice to transport even those who most vigorously deny Gluck's appeal for a modern audience, and also the potential for his work to be re-made for the *fin de siècle*: '"Ah!" exclaimed Carlo, with suppressed enthusiasm [upon the entry of Orpheus], "that is a figure, all glittering with mystic jewel-lights, for one of your pre-Raphaelite painters, or for Gustave Moreau"' (64).

Emilia Dilke was by this time researching her own history of the eighteenth century, which began to appear in 1899. Her own historical approach is also strikingly modern, but in different ways from Vernon Lee's. As Colin Eisler has observed, Dilke's is 'A positivist orientation, keyed towards an objective perspective, devoid of … maundering and prettification'.[12] Scholarship, rather than impressions or fancy, is foregrounded in both her self-representation and her criticism, and she takes an uncompromisingly academic approach to her subject. She acknowledges but also quibbles with other scholars, such as the Goncourt brothers (*Painters*, 115–16), and draws attention to the meticulousness of her research and how long it has taken her. She is concerned that her work be understood for what it is – an original study rather than a 'mere compilation' of second-hand ideas – and proudly asserts that 'I have described nothing, I have criticised nothing that I have not seen for myself' (*Painters*, vi), accusing others of cutting corners and depending on unverified secondary sources. If Vernon Lee quotes frequently in the language of her Italian sources and appends an impressive bibliography, Dilke's text is still more heavily freighted with footnotes and references to the primary and secondary sources she has used, and the reader who does not have a good knowledge of French will find it hard to follow. In her anxiety to differentiate herself as a serious art historian from the mere popularizers of art (as women writers on art were often thought to be), Dilke opened herself up to the charge of excessively parading her learning.[13] But she was wholly justified in her self-representation as a scholar working in the vanguard of modern art history. Her pioneering work brought Burckhardtian *Kunstgeschichte* into English art history for the first time. The extraordinarily comprehensive ambit of her work on the history of French art from the Renaissance to the eighteenth century was based on her belief in the importance of original primary research, of a knowledge of the social and economic conditions under which art was produced, and of examining all the arts of an epoch, both the fine arts and the so-called minor arts, in order to gain a true understanding of the period style.

Not only did Dilke's academic style of presenting the eighteenth century in France differ from Lee's avowedly 'aesthetic' approach to eighteenth-century Italy, but the nature of their respective subjects was very different. While Lee interested herself in popular, democratic and ephemeral art forms, Dilke, despite her personal commitment to social justice and labour organization, focused on the arts produced under the patronage of the French court, on distinctly aristocratic art forms that had an enduring appeal for the very wealthy. While Lee was fascinated by the regional, Dilkes explored the metropolitan. And where Lee specifically declined to discuss Italian art that was influenced by Paris and London and the pseudo-classical revival, neo-classicism was a central theme for Dilke, who saw herself writing of a place and time when the revivalist style 'received an extraordinary moral consecration which carried it forcibly to extreme conclusions'; when 'Men were cut off from the richest sources of fancy by an inexorably revolutionary logic, and strict conformity to classic precedent stood for a sign of heroic character' (*Painters*, 34).

And yet these rather significant differences of approach may be said to have arisen out of their common concern with the social, economic and political determinants of art: with the cultural history of the eighteenth century. Like Lee, Dilke seeks to evoke the world which produced such artworks, 'to trace the action of those social laws under the pressure of which the arts take shape',[14] as well as to analyse the artefact itself, and her focus on the art of the highly privileged may be said to have gone with the territory in the case of eighteenth-century French art. Dilke opens the first volume of her study, *French Painters of the XVIIIth Century* (1899) with a chapter on the Academy and its demise: the French Revolution had entered Lee's own story of the Arcadian

Academy too, but here its influence on the art establishment is, naturally enough, more prominent. Dilke relates how the Royal Academy's fortunes were fatally associated with those of the aristocracy, 'Their very existence ... bound up with that system of privilege and caste which the nation was rousing itself to overthrow' (7). As the century proceeded, she describes how the Academy made itself increasingly elitist and exclusive, securing a monopoly of exhibitions, and generally 'narrowing down the common freedom of the profession which it represented, whilst enlarging the privileges which gave to itself social dignity and influence', with the result that by mid-century it had 'established that monopoly of the arts for which all along it had fought in the name of the dignity of the Crown', a monopoly which was 'now destined, by the disgust it excited in outsiders, to bring about the destruction of the body by which it was maintained' (12). In the end, 'There was nothing left but to endure the strict application of the principles of liberty and equality which were destined to destroy the close fraternity that had had its origin in common sacrifices for the "bien des Arts"' (21), and the fall of the 'Bastille de la Peinture' was the inevitable consequence (21).

This is the context in which Dilke views the 'charming art' of the eighteenth century in France. For Dilke, it is above all an art conveying 'physical pleasure', one that celebrates the often ephemeral 'joys of the senses' (1). Unlike the art of the previous century, the 'Grand Siècle' of which she wrote in her volume *Art in the Modern State* (1888), which she saw as the product of a 'great centralising system', but like Renaissance art, eighteenth-century art has, for all its artificiality, according to Dilke, a kind of integrity. Truth, she argues, either in the sense of the naturalism of Dutch art or in the sense of fidelity to the 'eternal truths of life', was 'impossible to the artists of the latter half of the eighteenth century' (73). Nevertheless, the great decorative painters in particular, for all their contrived artificiality, 'all reflect with an intimacy to which there is perhaps no parallel, the manners and tone of their day' (70). '[J]ust as there never was a day in which art and life were more conventional, so there never was a time when conventions had a greater influence on character and conduct', and in the art of a great decorative painter such as Fragonard, 'far removed as it is from that of nature and of truth, we are still in a real world for the conventions of which it was made up, were an essential part of the lives of those amongst whom he lived and worked' (73).

Dilke's own formal training as an artist equipped her to write expertly on the technical composition and material condition of the paintings which are the subject of her first volume, while her previous studies of Renaissance and seventeenth-century French art meant that she was knowledgeable about the immediate social, political and cultural world from which the art of the eighteenth century emerged. This professional understanding of artefact and context leads to rewarding discussion of the various schools, and their most representative painters whom she discusses on a chapter-by-chapter basis, beginning with the decorative painters such as Boucher and Fragonard, and the painters of *fêtes galantes* such as Watteau and Pater, and moving through the painters of familiar scenes – Chardin, Baudouin, and Greuze – to portraiture, and finally landscape. She writes, for example, with both a keen eye and a keen historical intelligence about Fragonard's brilliant depictions of 'Eternal youth, perpetual pleasure, and all the wanton graces, their insincere airs masked by a voluptuous charm' (70); of his use of colour, particularly 'the lovely tints of beautiful flesh ... wrought to the perfection of sensual charm', and those 'passages which rival the magic of Rubens, and betray the actual physical delight [he] had in painting them' (71); and of how 1789 brought his charmed career to a close, for, having retreated to his native Grasse, where he continued to paint in the same 'spirit of amorous gaity as had rendered his talent delightful to the Paris of his youth', he returned to Paris 'only to find the reign of Pleasure over and the Loves and Graces fled' (70).

Just as there was no place for Fragonard in a new order exemplified by the stern neo-classicism of David, so, in the field of architecture, in the latter decades of the century 'Classic dwellings alone were, it was felt, worthy to shelter "l'homme libre", who now became the ideal of every painter and every sculptor who had a taste for civic virtue' (*Architects*, 5). But before the 'crippling zeal for "correctness"'(5), which was for Dilke the unfortunate accompaniment of revolutionary politics, stifled all other styles, eighteenth-century France enjoyed a period of great distinction, particularly in the arts associated with the development of the modern house as a place where the wealthy could exercise their every desire for a life of luxury and ease, even if, as she wryly notes, 'the wants of men of little means were left to be satisfied by some future age' (7–8). Dilke's interest in the economic framework within which artists and craftsmen worked is everywhere apparent. For example, she draws on the 'Livre-Journal' or 'day ledger' of the powerful dealer, agent and patron Lazare Duvaux, and analyses his complex role in the creation of mid-eighteenth-century *décors*.[15] Equally, the woman who had been involved with the Women's Trade Union League from its foundation in 1874, and its President from 1886 until her death, investigates the economics of production from the perspective of the artists and craftsmen engaged in making luxury items for the rich. And so she writes of the suffering and distress of the tapestry workers at the Gobelins and the Savonnerie and those engaged in the historic

industries of Aubusson and Felletin, who were forced at mid-century to try
to make their work look as exactly as possible like painting. 'The question of
economy itself was very serious' (*Furniture*, 110), notes Dilke, for 'The wages
of the tapestry workers were not only always in arrears but it was impossible
to establish satisfactory rates of payment, as the piece-work system continued
to prevail' (115).

Dilke is as conscious of the economics of the modern market for eighteenth-
century art as she is of the contemporary economics of production. She observes
that 'At the present time the chronicles of the auction room show that the arts
of the eighteenth century inspire the keenest competition amongst those who
look on the possession of costly furniture as one of the most expressive signs of
wealth' (*Furniture*, 203). But whereas the eighteenth-century French financier
'was one whose tastes had been moulded not only by the pressure of tradition
but by the surroundings in which he had been born' (*Furniture*, 203), the same
could not be said of the modern millionaires who are his successors. To these
she issues a sharp reminder that 'the values of style and construction demand
some sacrifice, they can be recognized only by effort, patient attention, and
cultivated habits of observation' (*Furniture*, vi). Despite her barely concealed
contempt for the shallow vulgarity of the market to which such art appeals, she
devotes her volume on *French Furniture and Decoration in the XVIII Century*
to developing greater discernment of these more esoteric values of style and
construction in the items of domestic luxury of which she writes.

The attention Dilke gave to the decorative arts, to the domestic culture
of eighteenth-century France, as she had previously to that of Renaissance
France, signifies the modernity of her historicist methodology. Although,
as she put it, 'the systematic treatment of the art of the eighteenth century
bristles with difficulties' because of the 'bewildering crowd of conflicting
tendencies' (*Furniture*, 1), her deep conviction of the profound connectedness
of the works of decoration, furniture, painting and architecture of a period
made these critically neglected art forms fundamental to her analysis.
Nevertheless, some reviewers of her work saw her interest in the domestic
arts not as groundbreaking but as signifying her 'womanly' sensibilities. An
anonymous reviewer of her first book in the *Westminster Review*, for example,
finds her 'history of the Renaissance in France ... little better than a history
of furniture', and concludes that 'a Renaissance whose chief results lie in the
department of decorative upholstery cannot, of course, hope to vie with the
splendid names and varied qualities of the Italian new birth'.[16] It was clearly
appropriate for a woman to have written about 'all that skilled handicraft can
do to beautify daily life and make lovely the habitations of man'.[17]

But if we reject the derogatory and dismissive implications of such contemporary views of the female intellectual and her womanly capacities, are there ways in which we might see Dilke's work as gendered? She herself was clearly interested in the gender of art. She criticizes the Goncourts, for example, for giving us 'a too slight, a too feminine Fragonard', praising instead the suggestive play of his pen: 'Not a trick of coquetry in dress or manner can escape it. Lively and exact in the appreciation of every pose and movement, of the intentional coyness of the turn of a head, or the wave of a hand, it is equally cunning in the choice of a meaning breast-knot, and in all those devices of the toilet which are intended to create "a sweet disorder in the dress, kindling in clothes a wantonnesse"' (*Painters*, 71). Her own eye might be said to be as sharply attentive to the suggestive detail of dress as Fragonard's pen, and therefore by her account, in a nice irony, to show 'virility' (a quality which she observes in a number of the artists she discusses) rather than femininity. For example, describing the woman in Lancret's 'L'Attache du Patin', she notes how she 'contrives to show not only the blue lining of her dress, her scarlet petticoat and painfully thin white stockings, but also a white furbelow which, if in keeping with the lady's very low bodice, affords no suggestion of that comfortable warmth which the leafless trees and leaden sky of the background would seem to demand' (*Painters*, 106). She reads the rendition of dress in Chardin's 'Toilette du Matin' (Illustration 11.1) with a Jamesian eye for the meaning of costume:

> No prettier lesson in coquettish dressing was ever given than the one conveyed by these two figures. Top-knots peep out scarlet from beneath the hood of the mother's black tippet, delicately blue above the fair child's forehead, the little muff in her baby hand is blue velvet and white fur, whilst by the mass book on the red stool, over which falls the red drapery which enframes the mirror on the toilet, lies another muff of green velvet and sable, cunningly chosen to give the last touch of elegance to the mother's appearance ... one guesses that costumes so finished can scarcely have been donned only to go to church – mass will certainly be followed by less serious engagements. (*Painters*, 122)

Dilke is alert to the nuanced depiction of female subjects, whether they are humble and anonymous or powerful and grand, their treatment intimate or formal, naturalistic or flattering. Of Rigaud's portrait of his mother, Marie Serre (Illustration 11.2), she bids us observe the differences between this highly personal style of portraiture and the 'magnificent manner' in which he rendered 'the pompous types' of his age (he was famous for his official portraits, such as his *Louis XIV* in the Louvre), and tells of the careful provisions the artist

Illustration 11.1   Chardin, 'Toilette du Matin' from Emilia Dilke's
***French Painters of the XVIIIth Century* (1899), by**
permission of the British Library (2266 aa 8)

Illustration 11.2 Rigaud, 'Portrait of Marie Serre, Mère de Rigaud' from Emilia Dilke's *French Painters of the XVIIIth Century* (1899), by permission of the British Library (2266 aa 8)

made in his will for this portrait that meant so much to him. She is notably interested in the representation of the female body. Thus, writing of Greuze, she notes that 'there is certain to be some corner of his pictures in which the eye can detect the immature charms of one of his favourite types of girlish beauty, indiscreetly revealed with an inappropriate and picturesque elegance, verging on the theatrical' (*Painters*, 132). And of Latour, whose fame rests, she notes 'on his portraits of women, to whom he contrived to give a piquant and sensuous beauty which becomes a common characteristic of the most diverse types', she observes the 'mannerisms' and 'tricks of treatment' he employs to flatter his subjects and bring them 'into harmony with the fashionable type of their day': 'On everyone he confers that dimpled elevation of the corners of the mouth, a gift of which nature is chary and which cannot be acquired by art', she writes, adding 'All seem inspired with the desire and the powers to please' (*Painters*, 163). Like the representations of female faces by Dilke's contemporary, Dante Gabriel Rossetti, they are 'not portraits but fantasy',[18] and signify the gender economy of the society that produced them. She probes the relationship of artist and sitter in a number of instances. Thus she describes how Fragonard, following a quarrel with the celebrated dancer 'la Guimard' whom he had painted as the Goddess of the Dance, avenged himself by disfiguring the picture, transforming her features 'into those of a menacing fury'; adding 'So much bitterness has suggested, as a prelude, a little love', but also reminding us that 'the year 1770, in which Fragonard was working for "la Guimard," was the year following his marriage' and that he was then 'the man of the day' (*Painters* 65). Dilke also, as Kali Israel notes, 'sardonically draws attention to images produced by self-serving men of culturally active women'.[19] We are told in *French Engravers and Draughtsmen of the XVIIIth Century*, for example, of the prodigious amateur engraver Vivant Denon that his 'chief occupation was "la gravure et les femmes"', and that he 'seems to have owed much of his success and even his great position at the beginning of the nineteenth century to this means of popularity with women' (3). Later in the volume Dilke reproduces Flipart's engraving, after Cochon *le fils*, of Mademoiselle Clairon sitting (fully clothed) as a model for a life-drawing class to a group of young male artists.

But beside such images of female objectification, Dilke shows us many examples of female agency. One of the most influential figures in the eighteenth-century art world was Mme de Pompadour, the official mistress of Louis XV, and her powerful presence in these volumes testifies to Dilke's appreciation of Pompadour's multi-faceted contribution to the art of her day. Early in *French Painters*, Dilke writes at some length about the favourite's

Illustration 11.3 **Boucher, 'Mme de Pompadour' from Emilia Dilke's**
***French Painters of the XVIIIth Century* (1899), by**
permission of the British Library (2266 aa 8)

relationship with Boucher, her patronage of whom had begun with her reign (see Illustration 11.3). Thereafter, we are told, 'Indispensable to the favourite in her capacity of patroness of the arts, designing not only her furniture, but her fans; guiding her hand when the caprice of the moment prompted her to try her chance with the etching needle, Boucher assured for himself by this familiarity the support of Marigny and the certainty of Royal commissions of the first importance' (54). Kali Israel sees Dilke's representation of their relationship as a key instance of the way her study 'connects male artistic inferiority, female performativity, and illegitimate and eroticized power', and suggests that, for her, 'Boucher and Pompadour together embody their inferior epoch's "artificial tone and temper"'.[20] Dilke argues that Boucher's 'defects', chief among which was 'la vulgarité elegante' which Goncourt identified as his signature, 'contributed to his enormous success', and she paints a picture of a man whose calculated devotion to the theatrical vanities of the king's mistress paved the way to success. Yet despite her critique, she clearly respects 'the remarkable force of character, which enabled this woman to hold out so long in the difficulties of her extraordinary position', and which she finds conveyed in Boucher's portraits of her. When Dilke comments that 'The influence of Mme. De Pompadour ... survived her death [in 1764]', she is explicitly alluding to the fact that Boucher was made first painter to the king in the following year, but she seems also to be referring to the fact that, in these portraits of her, she appears not as objectified female spectacle so much as a self-fashioned 'femme savante,' an icon of court culture signifying at once sexuality and the life of the mind. She later quotes a secondary source to the effect that the favourite's physiognomy was modelled by will rather than nature (158).

Mme de Pompadour is repeatedly invoked in these volumes as a patron and employer responsible for exercising a powerful influence in matters of taste and directing artistic practice. Dilke judges this influence to have been 'in many respects admirably felicitous', owing to 'the rare quality of her instincts and intelligence' and the fact that 'She undoubtedly possessed a sincere and instinctive love of art, and sought the signs of perfection and distinction in all that was executed for her rather than the satisfaction of mere personal luxury' (*Furniture*, 73). But the king's mistress is only the most prominent of a number of women whom Dilke demonstrates to have played a significant role in the eighteenth-century art world, not the least of whom were amateur and professional artists. One whose work is reproduced in the volume is Mme Vigée le Brun, whose portrait of *La Princesse de Talleyrand* (Illustration 11.4) is described by Dilke as 'very fair and delicate in effect, and charm[ing] the eye by a harmony of pale blue, gray, and pure white' (and

Illustration 11.4   Vigée Le Brun, 'La Princesse de Talleyrand' from Emilia
Dilke's *French Painters of the XVIIIth Century* (1899),
by permission of the British Library (2266 aa 8)

compares favourably with 'her well-known and flattering portraits of herself' – a more direct form of the self-fashioning that may be detected in Mme de Pompadour's portraits). Because of her husband's status as a picture dealer, it was only through the Queen's intervention that Mme Vigée le Brun was elected to the Royal Academy (*Painters* 157), but with royal support she was '*agrée et reçue*' into that august body on the same day as another female artist, Mme Guyard.

Only three pages into her first volume on painters, Dilke, who had studied art at South Kensington, launches into a discussion of the position of female artists in the French Academy. Herself a vigorous campaigner for the rights of women to have access to life-drawing classes, she notes wryly 'the fulfilment by the administration of its often deferred promise to enable the Academy to open their Life School without charge, and the vigorous decision, taken in the same year [1706], not to receive women, in future, as "académiciennes"' (3). Dilke goes on to explain how a few women did manage to gain admittance 'in spite of this fixed determination': Rosalba Carriera, Mlle Reboul (Mme Vien), Mme Therbouche, Anne Vallayer, Mlle Roslin. These two last were admitted to the Academy in the same year but, as Dilke acerbically observes, 'these two incursions of women, rapidly following on one another, were evidently regarded as dangerous, and the Academy took occasion to record that, though they liked to encourage women by admitting a few, yet such admissions, being in some sort foreign to their constitution, ought not to be multiplied, and thenceforth it was resolved never to admit more than four'. Despite the fact that Mme Guyard, in particular, 'fought hard for the rights of women academicians, insisting ... that their numbers and privileges should be increased', this notion that the admission of women was somehow 'foreign' to the Academy's constitution persisted, and was reiterated much later, in 1790, when, in the final stages before the Academy's demise, a group of officials and academicians protested that it was not fitting for 'des femmes viennent s'immiscer dans un travail qui leur est étranger' (17).

III

For all their manifest differences, one of the similarities between Emilia Dilke and Vernon Lee is their preoccupation with the 'foreign'. I do not mean by this merely that they were Englishwomen who wrote about the art of other cultures. Rather, I mean to suggest all that the use of the word 'foreign' metaphorically signifies in Dilke's discussion of the French Academy's designation of women.

Interestingly, both Dilke and Lee identified themselves as 'foreign'. From the beginning of her professional writing life, in Oxford, as the wife of a don (her first husband Mark Pattison), Dilke wrote as a foreigner on the margins of academia and without its sanction, unlike art critics such as Ruskin, the 'Graduate of Oxford' and later Slade Professor, and Pater, the Fellow of Brasenose. Furthermore, Dilke cultivated a distinctively foreign style in her self-presentation which was often commented on. Unhappy in her first marriage, and in poor health, she spent many months of the year away from Oxford living and working in Paris or the South of France where she claimed to feel more at home. As she confided in a friend, in France she could 'renew the ravishing sense of being one with the earth & sky wh [*sic*] never comes to me till I am past Marseilles', adding 'yet I love England I love my people, though English landscape is strange and foreign to me, & here I feel at once at home'.[21] An unconventional women, sexually as well as intellectually, whose authorial and social personae were multiple and highly performative, as Francis Pattison she seemed to find in France, both past and present, liberation from the stifling conventionalities of Oxford, while throughout her life her 'Frenchness' was a significant part of the way she fashioned her cultural identity. Vernon Lee, as an English woman who was born in 1856 in France, led a nomadic existence as a child in various parts of Continental Europe ('my friends … imagine me to have been born and brought up in a gypsy-cart'[22]), spent much of her adult life in Italy, and wrote principally on Italian cultural history, felt a similar sense of exile and displacement. Her biographer notes that 'In England Vernon Lee never found herself completely at home' and felt that her 'sympathies were too international to be acceptable even to the least insular among her English friends'. He quotes her as writing to her companion, Clementina Anstruther-Thomson, 'It's funny, though I feel so much more English than anything else (in fact only English) I cannot feel well in body or mind save on this sufficiently big and sufficiently aired and warmed continent'.[23] The consciousness of her cultural hybridity is a defining feature of Vernon Lee's writing on art, cultural history and place; it intersects with her transgressive authorial and sexual identity, and stands in for other, unspeakable identity positions. For both Vernon Lee and Emilia Dilke, the enactment and experience of 'foreignness', and the prominence of 'the foreign' in their writing, signify their positionality as female intellectuals in the business of defining culture, who speak, as foreigners, from difference, and make a virtue of their estrangement: Lee maintains 'that we all of us are the better, of whatever nationality (and most, perhaps, we rather too-too solid Anglo-Saxons) for some fusion of a foreign element'.[24] Their work on the arts of the eighteenth century in Italy and France participates in wider late nineteenth-century discourses about gender and culture, providing avenues for and legitimizing their exploration and articulation of the foreign. Eighteenth-century Italy and France respectively offered them another cultural repertoire on which to draw, in the past and another country, another language in which to speak, if in sometimes coded ways, to and about their own cultural world.

Notes

1   Emilia Dilke, *French Painters of the XVIIIth Century* (London: Bell, 1899), vi. All further references will appear parenthetically in the text.
2   Vernon Lee, *Studies of the Eighteenth Century in Italy* (London: Satchell, 1880). All further references will appear parenthetically in the text.
3   [Emilia Pattison], unsigned review of W.H. Pater, *Studies in the History of the Renaissance*, in *Westminster Review*, n.s. 43 (April 1873): 639–41.
4   Vernon Lee, *Juvenilia: Being a Second Series of Essays on Sundry Aesthetical Questions*, 2 vols (London: Fisher Unwin, 1887), I, 136–7.
5   For details on aesthetic performance and the role of Anstruther-Thomson, see Diana Maltz, 'Engaging "Delicate Brains": From Working-Class Enculturation to Upper-Class Lesbian Liberation in Vernon Lee and Kit Anstruther-Thomson's Psychological Aesthetics', in Talia Schaffer and Kathy Alexis Psomiades, eds, *Women and British Aesthetics* (Charlottesville and London: University Press of Virginia, 1999), 211–29.
6   Vernon Lee, *Althea: A Second Book of Dialogues on Aspirations and Duties* (London: Osgood, McIlvaine 1894), x.
7   Tom Gunning, 'The Cinema of Attractions: Early Film, its Spectator, and the Avant-Garde', in Thomas Elsaesser, ed., *Early Cinema: Space, Frame, Narrative* (London: B.F.I., 1990), 56–62, 57.
8   Emilia Dilke was later to write about the marvellous firework shows and spectacular illuminations that 'the *soi-disant* Italian decorator Servandoni' organized in France at the mid-century: *French Architects and Sculptors of the XVIIIth Century* (London: Bell, 1900), 16–17. All further references will appear parenthetically in the text.
9   Vernon Lee, *The Spirit of Rome: Leaves from a Diary* (London: Bodley Head, 1906), 142.
10   Ibid., 115–16.
11   Lee, *Althea*, 60, 62.
12   Colin Eisler, 'Lady Dilke (1840–1904): The Six Lives of an Art Historian', in Claire Richter Sherman and Adele M. Holcomb, eds, *Women as Interpreters of the Visual Arts, 1820–1979* (Westport, CN.: Greenwood, 1981), 147–80.
13   Kali Israel, *Names and Stories: Emilia Dilke and Victorian Culture* (Oxford: Oxford University Press, 1999), 255–6.
14   Emilia Dilke, *French Engravers and Draughtsmen of the XVIIIth Century* (London: Bell, 1902), v. All further references will appear parenthetically in the text.
15   Emilia Dilke, *French Furniture and Decoration in the XVIIIth Century* (London: Bell, 1901), 163. All further references will appear parenthetically in the text.

16 *Westminster Review*, 55 (April 1879): 595–6.

17 Ibid. See Elizabeth Mansfield, 'Victorian Identity and the Historical Imaginary: Emilia Dilke's *The Renaissance of Art in France*', *Clio: A Journal of Literature, History and the Philosophy of History*, 26, 2 (1997): 167–88, 186–7, 170; and Eisler, 170.

18 Griselda Pollock, *Vision and Difference: Femininity, Feminism and the Histories of Art* (London: Routledge, 1988), 122.

19 Isracl, *Names and Stories*, 65.

20 Ibid., 187.

21 See ibid., 181.

22 Vernon Lee, *The Sentimental Traveller*. See Peter Gunn, *Vernon Lee: Violet Paget, 1856–1935* (London: Oxford University Press, 1964), 25.

23 See Gunn, *Vernon Lee*, 167–8.

24 Ibid., 28.

Selected Bibliography

The footnotes to each contributor's chapter give full references to all cited works. We have included the following selected bibliography to provide readers with a guide to significant works related to the subject of this book.

Aarsleff, Hans, *The Study of Language in England, 1780–1860* (Princeton: Princeton University Press, 1967).

Abbot, Edwin, with Introduction by Edwin Abbott Abbott, *A Concordance to the Works of Alexander Pope* (London: Chapman and Hall, 1875).

Acroyd, Peter, *Dickens* (London: Sinclair-Stevenson, 1990).

Altick, Richard D., *The English Common Reader: A Social History of the Mass Reading Public 1800–1900* (Chicago: University of Chicago Press, 1957).

Amarasinghe, Upali, *Dryden and Pope in the Early Nineteenth Century: A Study of Changing Literary Taste 1800–1830* (Cambridge: Cambridge University Press, 1962).

Anon., *Goody Two-Shoes: A Facsimile Reproduction of the Edition of 1766*, intro. by Charles Welsh (London: Griffith and Farran, 1881).

Armitage, Robert, *Doctor Johnson: His Religious Life and his Death* (London: Bentley, 1850).

Arnold, Matthew, *The Complete Prose Works of Mathew Arnold*, ed. R.H. Super, 11 vols (Ann Arbor: University of Michigan Press, 1960–77).

——, *The Poems of Matthew Arnold*, ed. Kenneth Allott and Miriam Allott (London: Longman, 1979).

Ashton, John, *Eighteenth Century Waifs* (London: Hurst and Blackett, 1887).

Balfour, Graham, *The Life of Robert Louis Stevenson*, 2 vols (London: Methuen, 1901).

Bann, Stephen, *The Clothing of Clio: A Study of the Representation of History in Nineteenth-century Britain and France* (Cambridge: Cambridge University Press, 1984).

Barfoot, C.C., ed., *Victorian Keats and Romantic Carlyle: The Fusions and Confusions of Literary Periods* (Amsterdam: Rudopi, 2000).

Bate, Walter Jackson, *The Burden of the Past and the English Poet* (Cambridge, MA: Harvard University Press, 1970).

Battesin, Martin C., with Battesin, Ruthe R., *Henry Fielding: A Life* (London: Routledge, 1989).

Beer, Gillian, *Arguing with the Past: Essays in Narrative from Woolf to Sidney* (London: Routledge, 1989).

Beer, John, *Romantic Influences: Contemporary – Victorian – Modern* (London: Macmillan, 1993).

Birch, Dinah, ed., *Ruskin and the Dawn of the Modern* (Oxford: Clarendon, 1999).

Bloom, Harold, *The Anxiety of Influence: A Theory of Poetry*, 2nd edn (Oxford: Oxford University Press, 1997).

——, *A Map of Misreading* (Oxford: Oxford University Press, 1975).

——, ed., *John Ruskin* (New York and New Haven: Chelsea House, 1986).

Boswell, James, *Life of Johnson*, ed. George Birkbeck Hill, 6 vols (Oxford: Clarendon, 1887).

Boulton, J.T., ed., *Samuel Johnson: The Critical Heritage* (London: Routledge, 1971).

Bronson, Bertrand H., 'The Double Tradition of Dr Johnson', *Journal of English Literary History*, 28 (1951): 90–106.

Brontë, Charlotte, *Jane Eyre* (1847), ed. Margaret Smith and Sally Shuttleworth (Oxford: Oxford University Press, 2000).

Brougham, Henry, Lord, 'Johnson', in *Lives of Men of Letters and Science, who Flourished in The Time of George III*, 2 vols (London: Knight, 1845).

Browning, Elizabeth Barrett, *The Letters of Elizabeth Barrett Browning*, ed. Frederic G. Kenyon, 4th edn, 2 vols (London: Smith, Elder 1898).

Browning, Robert, *The Poetical Works of Robert Browning* (Oxford: Clarendon, 1983–).

Browning, Robert, and Browning, Elizabeth Barrett, *The Brownings' Correspondence*, ed. Philip Kelley and Scott Lewis, 14 vols (Kansas: Wedgestone, 1993).

Buchanan, Robert, *The Fleshly School of Poetry and other Phenomena of the Day* (London: Strahan, 1872).

[Bunce, O.], *Don't: A Manual of Mistakes and Improprieties More or Less Prevalent in Conduct and Speech* (London: Griffith and Farran, 1884).

Burnett, Archie, 'Tennyson's "Mariana": Two Parallels', *Notes & Queries*, 225 (1980): 207–8.

Burston, W.H., ed., *James Mill on Education* (Cambridge: Cambridge University Press, 1969).

Butt, John, 'The Composition of *David Copperfield*', *Dickensian*, 46 (1950): 90–94, 128–35, 176–80 and 47 (1951): 33–8.

Carey, John, *Thackeray: Prodigal Genius* (London: Faber 1977).

Carlyle, Thomas, *The Works of Thomas Carlyle*, ed. H.D. Traill, 30 vols (London: Chapman and Hall, 1897–1904).

——, *Historical Sketches*, 3rd edn (Edinburgh: Blackwood, 1875).

——, *History of Frederick II of Prussia, called Frederick the Great*, 6 vols (London: Chapman and Hall, 1886).

——, 'Boswell's Life of Johnson', *English and Other Critical Essays* (London: Dent, 1950).

Cary, Henry Francis, *Lives of English Poets from Johnson to Kirke White: Designed as a Continuation of Johnson's Lives* (London: Bohn, 1843).

Cerutti, Toni, ed., *Ruskin and the Twentieth Century: The Modernity of Ruskinism* (Vercelli: Edizione Mercurio, 2000).

Chatterton, Thomas, *Complete Works of Thomas Chatterton*, ed. Donald Taylor, in association with Benjamin Hoover (Oxford: Clarendon, 1971).

Cianci, Giovanni, and Nicholls, Peter, eds, *Ruskin and Modernism* (Houndmills: Palgrave, 2001).

Clifford, J.L., *Dictionary Johnson: Samuel Johnson's Middle Years* (London: Heinemann, 1979).

Collins, Philip, ed., *Dickens: Interviews and Recollections*, 2 vols (Totowa, NY: Barnes and Noble, 1981).

Comte, Auguste, *Cours de philosphie positive, Œuvres d'Auguste Comte* (Paris: La Société Positiviste, 1894).

Conan Doyle, Sir Arthur, *The Conan Doyle Historical Romances*, 2 vols (London: Murray, 1931–32).

——, *The Annotated Sherlock Holmes*, 2 vols in 1, ed. William S. Baring-Gold (New Jersey: Wings, 1992).

Courthope, William James, *The Liberal Movement in English Literature* (London: Murray, 1885).

Craik, Mrs, *John Halifax, Gentleman* (London: Dent, 1928).

Craig, W.H., *Dr Johnson and the Fair Sex: A Study of Contrasts* (London: Low, 1895).

Cross, Nigel, *The Common Writer: Life in Nineteenth-Century Grub Street* (Cambridge: Cambridge University Press, 1985).

Dallas, E.S., 'Introduction', *Clarissa: A Novel* by Samuel Richardson, 3 vols (London: Tinsley, 1868).

Dames, Nicholas, 'Brushes with Fame: Thackeray and the Work of Celebrity', *Nineteenth-century Literature*, 56 (2001): 23–51.

Danson, Lawrence, *Wilde's Intentions: The Artist in his Criticism* (Oxford: Clarendon, 1997).

Dearden, James S., *John Ruskin: A Life in Pictures* (Sheffield: Sheffield Academic Press, 1999).

Dentith, Simon, *George Eliot* (Brighton: Harvester, 1986).

Derrida, Jacques, *Specters of Marx: The State of the Debt, the Work of Mourning, and the New International*, tr. Peggy Kamuf, intro. by Bernd Magus and Stephen Cullenberg (New York: Routledge, 1994).

Dickens, Charles, *The Letters of Charles Dickens*, ed. Madeleine House, Graham Storey, Kathleen Tillotson et al. (Oxford: Clarendon 1965–).

——, *A Tale of Two Cities* (London and Toronto: Dent 1923).

——, *Bleak House*, ed. George Ford and Sylvère Monod (New York and London: Norton, 1977).

——, *David Copperfield*, intro and notes by Jeremy Tambling (Harmondsworth: Penguin, 1996).

——, *Great Expectations*, ed. Charlotte Mitchell (Harmondsworth: Penguin, 1996).

——, *Little Dorrit*, ed. Stephen Wall and Helen Small (Harmondsworth: Penguin, 1998).

——, *The Posthumous Papers of the Pickwick Club*, ed. Mark Wormald (Harmondsworth: Penguin, 1999).

Dilke, Emilia, *French Painters of the XVIIIth Century* (London: Bell, 1899).

——, *French Architects and Sculptors of the XVIIIth Century* (London: Bell, 1900).

——, *French Furniture and Decoration in the XVIIIth Century* (London: Bell 1901).

——, *French Engravers and Draughtsmen of the XVIIIth Century* (London: Bell, 1902).

Dobson, Austin, *Eighteenth Century Vignettes*, 2nd series, new edn (London: Chatto and Windus, 1907).

Douglas-Fairhurst, Robert, *Victorian Afterlives: The Shaping of Influence in Nineteenth-century Literature* (Oxford: Oxford University Press, 2002).

Dowling, Linda, *Language and Decadence in the Victorian* fin de siècle (Princeton: Princeton University Press, 1986).

Edgeworth, Maria, *Letters for Literary Ladies*, ed. Claire Connolly (London: Everyman, 1993).

——, and Edgeworth, Richard Lovell, *Practical Education* (London: Johnson 1798).

Eisler, Colin, 'Lady Dilke (1840–1904): The Six lives of an Art Historian', in Claire Richter Sherman and Adele M. Holcomb, eds, *Women as Interpreters of the Visual Arts* (Westport, Conn: Greenwood, 1981), 147–80.

Elfenbein, Andrew, *Byron and the Victorians* (Cambridge: Cambridge University Press, 1995).

Eliot, George, *The George Eliot Letters*, ed. Gordon S. Haight, 7 vols (New Haven: Yale University Press, 1954).

——, *The Mill on the Floss*, ed. A.S. Byatt (Harmondsworth: Penguin, 1979).

——, *Daniel Deronda*, ed. Graham Handley (Oxford: Oxford University Press, 1988).

——, *Selected Critical Writings* ed. Rosemary Ashton (Oxford: Oxford University Press, 1992).

Ellmann, Richard, *Oscar Wilde* (Harmondsworth: Penguin, 1987).

Evans, D. Morier, *Facts, Failures and Frauds: Revelations Financial, Mercantile, Criminal* (London: Groombridge, 1859).

Fairer, David, *English Poetry of the Eighteenth Century, 1700–1789* (London and New York: Longman, 2003).

Fellows, Jay, *The Failing Distance: The Autobiographical Impulse in John Ruskin* (Baltimore: Johns Hopkins University Press, 1975).

——, *Ruskin's Maze* (Princeton: Princeton University Press, 1981).

Fielding, Henry, *The Works of Henry Fielding, Esq., with an Essay on His Life and Genius*, ed. Alexander Chalmers, 10 vols (London: Johnson et al., 1806).

——, *The Covent-Garden Journal and A Plan of the Universal Register-Office*, ed. Bertrand A. Goldgar (Oxford: Clarendon, 1988).

——, *The History of Tom Jones, A Foundling*, 2 vols, with an introduction and commentary by Martin C. Battestin, text edited by Fredson Bowers (Oxford: Oxford University Press, 1975).

Fielding, K.J., ed., *The Speeches of Charles Dickens* (Oxford: Clarendon, 1960).

Fitzgerald, Percy, *A Critical Examination of Dr G. Birkbeck Hill's 'Johnsonian' Editions, Issued by the Clarendon Press, Oxford* (London: Bliss, Sands, 1898).

Fleeman, David, and McClaverty, James, *A Bibliography of the Works of Samuel Johnson, Treating his Published Works from the Beginnings to 1984*, 2 vols (Oxford: Clarendon, 2000).

Forster, John, *The Life of Charles Dickens* (1872–74), ed. A.J. Happé, 2 vols (London: Dent, 1966).

Forsyth, William, *The Novels and Novelists of the Eighteenth Century, in Illustration of the Manners and Morals of the Age* [1871] (London: Kennicat, 1970).

Gilbert, Sandra M., and Gubar, Susan, *The Madwoman in the Attic: The Woman Writer and The Nineteenth-Century Literary Imagination* (New Haven and London: Yale University Press, 1979).

Gilbert, W.S., *The Savoy Operas* (London: Macmillan, 1926).

Gill, Stephen, *Wordsworth and the Victorians* (Oxford: Clarendon, 1998).

Girouard, Mark, *Sweetness and Light: The 'Queen Anne' Movement, 1860–1900* (Oxford: Clarendon, 1977).

Goede, C.A., *The Stranger in England; or, Travels in Great Britain* (trans. T. Horne) (London: Barnard, 1807).

Gosse, Edmund, *A History of Eighteenth Century Literature (1660–1780)* (London: Macmillan, 1889).

Grant, F., *Life of Samuel Johnson* (London: Scott, 1887).

Griffith, Philip Mahone, 'Boswell's Johnson and the Stephens (Leslie Stephen and Virginia Woolf)', *The Age of Johnson*, 6 (1994): 151–64.

Groom, Nick, ed., *Thomas Chatterton and Romantic Culture* (London: Macmillan, 1999).

——, *The Forger's Shadow: How Forgery Changed the Course of Literature* (London: Picador, 2002).

——, 'Love and Madness: Southey Editing Chatterton', in Lynda Pratt, ed., *Robert Southey and the Contexts of English Romanticism* (Aldershot: Ashgate, forthcoming 2004).

Grylls, David, 'The Annual Return to Old Grub Street: What Samuel Johnson meant to Gissing', *The Gissing Newsletter*, 20 (1984): 1–27.

Gunn, Peter, *Vernon Lee: Violet Paget, 1856–1935* (London: Oxford University Press, 1964).

Hack, Daniel, 'Literary Paupers and Professional Authors: The Guild of Literature and Art', *Studies in English Literature*, 39/4 (1999): 691–713.

Halsband, Robert, *'The Rape of the Lock' and its Illustrations 1714–1896* (Oxford: Clarendon, 1980).

Hannay, James, *A Course of English Literature* (London: Tinsley, 1866).

Harden, Edgar F., *Thackeray's English Humourists and Four Georges* (Newark: University of Delaware Press/London: Associated University Presses, 1985).

Hart, Kevin, *Samuel Johnson and the Culture of Property* (Cambridge: Cambridge University Press, 1999).

Hay, James, *Johnson: His Characteristics and Aphorisms* (London: Gardner, 1884).

Hayward, Abraham, ed., *Autobiography, Letters and Literary Remains of Mrs Piozzi (Thrale)*, 2 vols (London: Longman, 1861).

Helsinger, Elizabeth K., *Ruskin and the Art of the Beholder* (Cambridge, MA and London: Harvard University Press, 1982).

Hewison, Robert, *John Ruskin: The Argument of the Eye* (London: Thames and Hudson, 1976).

Hill, George Birkbeck, *Wit and Wisdom of Samuel Johnson* (Oxford: Clarendon, 1888).

——, 'Preface' to R. Brimley Johnson, ed., *Eighteenth-Century Letters*, 2 vols (London: Innes, 1898).

——, and Powell, L.F., eds, *Boswell's Life of Johnson*, 6 vols (Oxford: Clarendon, 1934–50).

Hilton, Tim, *John Ruskin: The Later Years* (New Haven and London: Yale University Press, 2000).

Holman Hunt, William, *Pre-Raphaelitism and the Pre-Raphaelite Brotherhood* (London: Macmillan, 1905).

Honan, Park, *Matthew Arnold: A Life* (London: Weidenfeld and Nicolson, 1981).

Hoste, James William, *Johnson and His Circle: With some Notices of Recent Johnsonian Literature* (London: Jarrold, 1900).

[Howard, George William Frederick], *The Viceregal Speeches and Addresses, Lectures and Poems, of the Late Earl of Carlisle, K.G.*, ed. J.J. Gaskin (Dublin: McGlashan and Gill, 1865).

Israel, Kali, *Names and Stories: Emilia Dilke and Victorian Culture* (Oxford: Oxford University Press, 1999).

Jay, Elisabeth, *Mrs Oliphant: 'A Fiction to Herself': A Literary Life* (Oxford: Clarendon, 1995).

Johnson, Edgar, *Charles Dickens: His Tragedy and Triumph*, 2 vols (Boston: Little, Brown, 1952).

Johnson, Samuel, *The Plan of a Dictionary of the English Language* (London: Knapton, 1747).

——, *The Rambler* (London: Jones, 1824).

——, *Lives of the Most Eminent English Poets ... with Notes corrective and explanatory by Peter Cunningham*, 3 vols (London: Murray, 1854).

——, *The Yale Edition of the Works of Samuel Johnson*, 16 vols (Newhaven: Yale University Press, 1958–90).

Kachru, B.B. and Kahane, H., eds, *Cultures, Ideologies, and the Dictionary: Studies in Honour of Ladislav Zgusta* (Tübingen: Niemeyer, 1995).

Lang, Timothy, *The Victorians and the Stuart Heritage: Interpretations of a Discordant Past* (Cambridge: Cambridge University Press, 1995).

Leckie, Barbara, *Culture and Adultery: The Novel, the Newspaper, and the Law, 1857–1914* (Philadelphia: University of Pennsylvania Press, 2000).

Lee, Vernon, *Studies of the Eighteenth Century in Italy* (London: Satchell, 1880).

——, *Juvenilia: Being a Second Series of Essays on Sundry Aesthetical Questions*, 2 vols (London: Fisher Unwin, 1887).

——, *Althea: A Second Book of Dialogues on Aspirations and Duties* (London: Osgood, McIlvaine, 1894).

——, *The Spirit of Rome: Leaves from a Diary* (London: Bodley Head, 1906).

Leerssen, Joep, 'Ossianic Liminality: Between Native Tradition and Preromantic Taste', in Howard Gaskill and Fiona Stafford, eds, *From Gaelic to Romantic: Ossianic Translations* (Amsterdam and Atlanta, GA: Rodopi, 1998).

Levine, Joseph, *The Battle of the Books: History and Literature in the Augustan Age* (Ithaca, NY: Cornell University Press, 1991).

Levine, Philippa, *The Amateur and the Professional: Antiquaries, Historians, and Archeologists in Victorian England, 1836–1886* (Cambridge: Cambridge University Press, 1986).

Lindley, David, 'A Possible Source for Browning's "A Toccata of Galuppi's"', *Browning Society Notes*, 9 (1979), 1–2.

Lucas, John, *The Melancholy Man: A Study of Dickens's Novels* (Brighton: Harvester, 1980).

Lukács, Georg, *The Historical Novel*, trans. Hannah and Stanley Mitchell (London: Merlin, 1962).

Lytton, Lord, *The Dramatic Works by the Right Hon. Lord Lytton*, 2 vols (London: Routledge, 1876).

Macaulay, Thomas Babington, *History of England*, 2 vols (London: Longmans, 1848).

——, *The Miscellaneous Writings of Lord Macaulay*, 2 vols (London: longman, Green, Longman, and Roberts, 1860).

——, *Life of Johnson* (1856), ed. John Downie (London: Blackie, 1918).

——, *The Letters of Thomas Babington Macaulay*, ed. Thomas Pinney, 6 vols (Cambridge: Cambridge University Press, 1981).

Maidment, Brian, ed., *The Poorhouse Fugitives: Self-Taught Poets and Poetry in Victorian Britain* (Manchester: Carcanet, 1987).

Maltz, Diana, 'Engaging "Delicate Brains": From Working-Class Enculturation to Upper-Class Lesbian Liberation in Vernon Lee and Kit Anstruther-Thomson's Psychological Aesthetics', in Talia Schaffer and Kathy Alexis Psomiades, eds, *Women and British Aesthetics* (Charlottesville and London: University Press of Virginia, 1999), 211–29.

Mansfield, Elizabeth, 'Victorian Identity and the Historical Imaginary: Emilia Dilke's *The Renaissance of Art in France*', *Clio: A Journal of Literature, History and the Philosophy of History*, 26, 2 (1997): 167–88.

Maxwell, Catherine, *The Female Sublime from Milton to Swinburne* (Manchester: Manchester University Press, 2001).

Michael, Ian, *The Teaching of English: From the Sixteenth Century to 1870* (Cambridge: Cambridge University Press, 1987).

Mill, J.S., *Collected Works of John Stuart Mill*, ed. J.M. Robson et al., 33 vols (London: Routledge and Kegan Paul, 1965–91).

Miller, Henry Knight, 'The "Whig Interpretation" of Literary History', *Eighteenth-Century Studies*, 6 (1972): 60–84.

Minto, William, *The Literature of the Georgian Era* (Edinburgh: Blackwood, 1894).

Mugglestone, Lynda, *Talking Proper: The Rise of Accent as Social Symbol* (Oxford: Clarendon, 1995: 2nd edn, 2002).

——, ed., *Lexicography and the OED: Pioneers in the Untrodden Forest* (Oxford: Oxford University Press, 2002).

Murphy, Paul Thomas, *Toward a Working-Class Canon: Literary Criticism in British Working-Class Periodicals, 1816–1858* (Columbus, OH: Ohio State University Press, 1994).

Murray, J.A.H., *The Evolution of English Lexicography* (Oxford: Clarendon, 1900).

Murray, K.M.E., *Caught in the Web of Words: James Murray and the* Oxford English Dictionary (New Haven: Yale University Press, 1977).

Myers, William, *The Teaching of George Eliot* (Leicester: Leicester University Press, 1984).

Nayder, Lillian, *Unequal Partners: Charles Dickens, Wilkie Collins, and Victorian Authorship* (Ithaca: Cornell University Press, 2002).

Nietzsche, Friedrich, *Jenseits von Gut und Böse/Zur Genealogie der Moral*, Kritische Studienausgabe Herausgegeben von Giorgio Colli und Mazzino Montinari (Berlin: Deutscher Taschenbuch Verlag de Gruyter, 1999).

——, *On the Genealogy of Morality*, ed. Keith Ansell-Pearson, tr. Carol Diethe (Cambridge: Cambridge University Press, 1994).

Norquaym, Glenda, ed., *R.L. Stevenson on Fiction: An Anthology of Literary and Critical Essays* (Edinburgh: Edinburgh University Press, 1999).

O'Gorman, Francis, *Late Ruskin: New Contexts* (Aldershot: Ashgate, 2001).

——, 'Ruskin, Vernon Lee, and the Cultural Possession of Italy', *Journal of Anglo-Italian Studies*, 7 (2002): 81–107.

Oliphant, Margaret, *Annals of a Publishing House: William Blackwood and his Sons, Their Magazine and Friends*, 2 vols (London and Edinburgh: Blackwood, 1897).

——, *Autobiography and Letters of Mrs Margaret Oliphant*, ed. Mrs Harry Coghill (Edinburgh and London: 1899; reprinted with an introduction by Q.D. Leavis, Leicester: Leicester University Press, 1974).

——, *The Autobiography of Margaret Oliphant: The Complete Text*, ed. Elisabeth Jay (Oxford: Oxford University Press, 1990).

Palgrave, Francis Turner, *The Golden Treasury of the Best Songs and Lyrical Poems in the English Language* (London: Macmillan, 1861).

Perkins, David, *Is Literary History Possible?* (Baltimore and London: John Hopkins University Press, 1992).

Perry, Seamus, 'In Praise of Puny Boundaries', *Wordsworth Circle*, 33 (2002): 119–21.

Peters, Catherine, *Thackeray's Universe: Shifting Worlds of Imagination and Reality* (London: Faber, 1987).

Phillips, Steven R., 'Johnson's *Lives of the English Poets* in the Nineteenth Century', *Research Studies*, 39 (1971): 175–90.

Poovey, Mary, *Uneven Developments: The Ideological Work of Gender in Mid-Victorian England* (Chicago: University of Chicago Press, 1988).

Pope, Alexander, *The Poetical Works of Alexander Pope, with a Life by the Rev. Alexander Dyce*, 3 vols (Boston: Little, Brown, 1863, first published London, 1831).

——, *The Works of Alexander Pope*, collected in part by J.W. Croker, with an introduction and notes by W. Edwin and W.J. Courthope, 10 vols (London: Murray 1871–89).

——, *The Poetical Works of Alexander Pope*, edited, with a critical memoir, by W.M. Rossetti (London: Moxon 1873).

——, *Essay on Man and The Universal Prayer* (London: Whittaker, 1860).

——, *Pope: Essay on Man*, ed. Mark Pattison (Oxford: Clarendon, 1869).

——, *Pope: Epistles and Satires*, ed. Mark Pattison (Oxford: Clarendon, 1872).

——, *Pope's 'Essay on Man'*, ed. John Hunter (London: Longmans, Green, 1879).

——, *The Poetical Works of Alexander Pope (Selected)*, ed. John Hogben (London: Scott, 1887).

——, *Alexander Pope: Selected Poetry*, ed. Pat Rogers (Oxford: Oxford University Press, 1994).

Price, Leah, *The Anthology and the Rise of the Novel* (Cambridge: Cambridge University Press, 2000).

Price, Richard, *British Society 1680–1880: Dynamism, Containment and Change* (Cambridge: Cambridge University Press, 1999).

Proctor, Bryan Waller ['Barry Cornwall'], *An Autobiographical Fragment and Biographical Notes* (London: Bell, 1877).

Raleigh, Walter, *Six Essays on Johnson* (Oxford: Clarendon, 1910).

Ray, Gordon N., *Thackeray: The Age of Wisdom* (London: Oxford University Press, 1958).

Reddick, Allen, *The Making of Johnson's Dictionary 1746–1773* (Cambridge: Cambridge University Press, 1990).

Richardson, Samuel, *Clarissa Harlowe*, ed. Mrs. Harriet Ward (London: Routledge, 1868).

——, *The History of Sir Charles Grandison*, ed. Jocelyn Harris (Oxford: Oxford University Press, 1986).

Robinson, Roger, 'The Influence of Fielding on *Barnaby Rudge*', *AUMLA: Journal of the Australasian Universities Language and Literature Association*, 40 (1973): 183–97.

Rose, Jonathan, *The Intellectual Life of the British Working Classes* (New Haven and London: Yale University Press, 2001).

Rosebery, Lord, *Dr Johnson: An Address delivered at the Johnson Bicentenary Celebration, At Lichfield, September 15, 1909* (London: Humphries, 1909).

Rosenberg, John D., *The Darkening Glass: A Portrait of Ruskin's Genius* (New York: Columbia University Press, 1961).

Rousseau, G.S. and Rogers, Pat, eds, *The Enduring Legacy: Alexander Pope Tercentenary Essays* (Cambridge: Cambridge University Press, 1988).

Rousseau, Jean-Jacques, *Émile*, tr. Barbara Foxley (London: Everyman, 1993).

Royle, Edward, *Victorian Infidels, The Origins of the British Secularist Movement 1791–1866* (Manchester: Manchester University Press/[Totowa, NJ]: Rowman and Littlefield, 1974).

Ruskin, John, *The Complete Work of John Ruskin*, ed. E.T. Cook and Alexander Wedderburn, 39 vols (London: Allen, 1903–12).

——, *The Diaries of John Ruskin*, ed. Joan Evans and John Howard Whitehouse, 3 vols (Oxford: Clarendon, 1956–9).

——, *Ruskin's Letters from Venice, 1851–2*, ed. J.L. Bradley (Westport, Connecticut: Greenwood, 1978), 73.

——, *Ruskin in Italy: Letters to His Parents 1845*, ed. Harold Shapiro (Oxford: Clarendon, 1972).

Sadleir, Michael, *Bulwer: A Panorama* (Boston: Little, Brown, 1931).

Sale, Roger, *Literary Inheritance* (Amherst: University of Massachusetts Press, 1984).

Salmon, Richard, 'Authorship and Celebrity', in Francis O'Gorman, ed., *Concise Companion to Victorian Fiction* (Oxford: Blackwell, 2004).

Sanders, Andrew, *Dickens and the Spirit of the Age* (Oxford: Clarendon, 1999).

Scheinberg, Cynthia, 'Recasting "Sympathy and Judgement": Amy Levy, Women Poets, and The Victorian Dramatic Monologue', *Victorian Poetry*, 35 (1997): 173–92.

Scott, Sir Walter, *Waverley: or, 'Tis Sixty Years Since*, ed. Claire Lamont (Oxford: Oxford University Press, 1986).

Seccombe, Thomas, *The Age of Johnson (1748–1798)* (London: Bell, 1900).

Shortland, Michael, ed., *Hugh Miller and the Controversies of Victorian Science* (Oxford: Clarendon, 1996).

Simmel, Georg, *The Philosophy of Money*, tr. Tom Bottomore and David Frisby from a first draft by Kaethe Mengelberg (Boston: Routledge and Kegan Paul, 1978).

Sitwell, Edith, *Alexander Pope* (London: Faber, 1930).

Small, Helen '"A Pulse of 124": Charles Dickens and a Pathology of the Nineteenth-century Reading Public', in James Raven, Helen Small and Naomi Tadmor, eds,

The Practice and Representation of Reading in England (Cambridge: Cambridge University Press, 1996).

Smith, Joseph H. and Kerrigan, William, eds, *Taking Chances: Derrida, Psychoanalysis, and Literature* (Baltimore: Johns Hopkins University Press, 1984).

Spalding, William, *The History of English Literature; with an Outline of the Origin and Growth of the English Language: Illustrated by Extracts. For the Use of Schools and of Private Students* (1853: Edinburgh, Oliver and Boyd, 11th edn 1870).

Spencer, Herbert, *Essays on Education and Kindred Subjects* (London: Dent, 1911).

Spurgeon, Caroline, *The Works of Dr Samuel Johnson* (London: University College, 1898).

Stedman, Jane W., 'The Victorian After-Image of Samuel Johnson', *Nineteenth-Century Theatre Research*, 11 (1983): 13–27.

Stephen, Leslie, *Samuel Johnson, English Men of Letters* series (London: Macmillan, 1878).

——, *Alexander Pope, English Men of Letters* series (London: Macmillan, 1880).

——, *Hours in a Library*, new edn, 3 vols (London: Smith, Elder, 1892).

——, *English Literature and Society in the Eighteenth Century* (London: Duckworth, 1904).

——, *Leslie, Stephen: Selected Writings in British Intellectual History*, ed. Noel Annan (Chicago: University of Chicago Press, 1979).

Stevenson, Robert Louis, *Treasure Island* (London: Cassell, 1911).

——, *Kidnapped* and *Catriona* (Oxford: Oxford University Press, 1929).

Still, Judith, 'Rousseau in *Daniel Deronda*', *Revue de littérature comparée*, 56 (1982): 62–77.

Strachey, Lytton, *Pope: The Leslie Stephen Lecture for 1925* (Cambridge: Cambridge University Press, 1925).

Sucksmith, Harvey Peter, 'The Melodramatic Villain in *Little Dorrit*', *Dickensian*, 71 (1975): 76–83.

Swann, Charles, 'Wainewright the Poisoner: A Source for Blandois/Rigaud?', *Notes & Queries*, 233 (1988): 321–2.

Tennyson, Alfred, *The Letters of Alfred Lord Tennyson*, ed. Cecil Y. Lang and Edgar F. Shannon, Jr, 3 vols (Oxford: Clarendon, 1982–90).

Thackeray, William M., *Vanity Fair: A Novel without a Hero* (London: Bradbury and Evans, 1848).

——, *The English Humourists of the Eighteenth Century: A Series of Lectures, delivered in England, Scotland, and the United States of America*, 2nd edn (London: Smith, Elder, 1853).

——, *Thackeray's Works*, 26 vols (London: Smith Elder, 1911).

——, *The Memoirs of Barry Lyndon, Esq.*, ed. Andrew Sanders (Oxford: Oxford University Press, 1984).

——, *The History of Henry Esmond, Esq.* (1852), ed. Donald Hawes (Oxford: Oxford University Press, 1991).

Thompson, E.P., *Witness Against the Beast: William Blake and the Moral Law* (Cambridge: Cambridge University Press, 1993).

Trench, Richard Chevenix, *On Some Deficiencies in Our English Dictionaries* (London: Parker, 1860).

Trollope, Anthony, *The Vicar of Bullhampton*, ed. David Skilton (Oxford: Oxford University Press, 1988).

Trott, Nicola, 'Framing Romanticism: Keynote Address', *Wordsworth Circle*, 33 (2002): 90–92.

Tucker, Herbert F., ed. *A Companion to Victorian Literature and Culture* (Oxford: Blackwell, 1999).

Vernon, John, *Money and Fiction: Literary Realism in the Nineteenth and Early Twentieth Centuries* (Ithaca: Cornell University Press, 1984).

Wainewright, Thomas Griffiths, *Essays and Criticisms*, ed. W. Carew Hazlitt (London: Reeves and Turner, 1880).

Waller, J.F., *Boswell and Johnson: Their Companions and Contemporaries* (London: Cassells, 1881).

Ward, Thomas Humphry, *The English Poets: Selections with Critical Introductions by Various Writers and a General Introduction by Matthew Arnold*, 4 vols (London: *Macmillan, 1880)*.

—— and Roberts, W., *Romney: A Biographical and Critical Essay, with a Catalogue Raisonné of his Works* (London: Agnew, 1904).

Whale, John, 'Romantic Attacks: Pope and the Spirit of Language', in David Fairer, ed., *Pope: New Contexts* (Hemel Hempstead: Harvester Wheatsheaf, 1990), 153–68.

Wilde, Oscar, *The Letters of Oscar Wilde*, ed. Rupert Hart-Davis (London: Hart-Davis, 1962).

——, *Complete Works of Oscar Wilde* (London: Collins, 1980).

Williams, Carolyn D., *Pope, Homer, and Manliness: Some Aspects of Eighteenth-Century Classical Learning* (London: Routledge, 1993).

Witemeyer, Hugh, 'George Eliot and Jean-Jacques Rousseau', *Comparative Literature Studies*, 16 (1979): 121–30.

Worden, Blair, 'The Victorians and Oliver Cromwell', in Stefan Collini, Richard Whatmore and Brian Young, eds, *History, Religion, and Culture: British Intellectual History 1750–1950* (Cambridge: Cambridge University Press, 2000), 112–35.

Index

homosexuality 192
Works:
*A History of Eighteenth Century
Literature* 85–6, 87, 137
biography of Gray 189–94
Gray, Thomas xiii
Gosse's biography of 189–94
Greene, Donald 77, 86
Griffin, Robert 1

Halsband, Robert 87
Hannay, James 130, 135, 137
Hart, Kevin 119
Hay, James 121, 132, 136
Hazlitt, W. Carew 211, 217
Hill, Birkbeck 126, 133, 134, 138
Hirst, Francis Wrigley 185, 198
Hogben, John 84, 86
Horace 169
Hoste, James 133
Howard, George (Lord Carlisle) 77
Hume, David 108, 185
Hunter, John 81, 130–31
Huxley, Thomas Henry 148

influence, ideas of literary 14 (*see also*
Bloom, Harold)
Dr Johnson's influence 135
Ireland, William Henry 207, 212–13
Israel, Kali 242, 244

Jevons, W. S. 186–8
'marginal revolution' 187–8
Johnson, Samuel xiii, 119–43, 144–62
and Boswell's *Life* 125–7
and manliness 134–5
and Milton's 'Lycidas' 86
and Victorian editions of his work 121–2
and Victorian interest in his life 125–8
and Victorian literary readers 123–5
and Victorian pedagogy 129–31
and Victorian responses to 8, 119–43
and Victorian temperance 133
Works:
Adventurer 148
Dictionary 8, 121, 123, 131, 144–62
plan 150, 152

'Preface' 150–51
prescriptivism 150–52
relation to *OED* 144–62
Lives of the Poets 119, 121, 123,
131–2
'London' 121, 131
Rambler, The xiv, 64–5, 123–4
Rasselas 121
and *Jane Eyre* 124–5
and Victorian pedagogy 130–31
and Victorian stage versions 125
'Vanity of Human Wishes, The' 121, 131,
158

Lacanian theories of development, 2–3
Larkin, Philip xii
Lee, Vernon 5, 10, 223–35
and an idea of Italy 233
and ephemeral Italian art 229–30
and gender 231–2
and *genius loci* 226–7
and history as cultural construction 234
and the eighteenth century as spectacle
229
and Walter Pater 27
compared to Emilia Dilke 235, 246–8
Works:
Althea 229
*Studies of the Eighteenth Century in
Italy* 224–35
Leeds Library, The
acquisition policy 76, 77
Levine, Philippa 3–4
Lewes, George Henry 17, 146
on Alexander Main's Boswell 128–9
on Dickens's book collection 17
Lewis, C.S. xii
Linton, W. J. 122
Locke, John
Essay on Human Understanding 147
Lukács, Georg 108
Lunar Society 45

Macaulay, Thomas Babington 98, 100, 102,
119, 136
and Dr Johnson 120–21, 125–6, 155–6
Maidment, Brian 83